Cinema's Illusions, Opera's Allure

Barefoot:
Gaslight Melodrama

Bondanella:
Italian Cinema, 3rd Edition

Brooker:
Batman Unmasked: Analysing a Cultural Icon

Brooker:
Using the Force: Creativity, Community, and Star Wars *Fans*

Eleftheriotis:
Popular Cinemas of Europe

Harper:
Women in British Cinema

Jones and Jolliffe:
The Guerilla Film Makers Handbook, 2nd Edition

McMahan:
Alice Guy Blaché: Lost Visionary of the Cinema

Murphy:
British Cinema and the Second World War

Tarr with Rollett:
Cinema and the Second Sex: Women's Filmmaking in France in the 1980s and 1990s

Vincendeau:
Stars and Stardom in French Cinema

CINEMA'S ILLUSIONS, OPERA'S ALLURE

The Operatic Impulse in Film

David Schroeder

continuum
NEW YORK • LONDON

2003

The Continuum International Publishing Group Inc
15 East 26th Street, New York, NY 10010

The Continuum International Publishing Group Ltd
The Tower Building, 11 York Road, London SE1 7NX

www.continuumbooks.com

Printed in the United States of America

Library of Congress Cataloging-in-Publication Data

Schroeder, David P., 1946--
    Cinema's illusions, opera's allure: the operatic impulse in film/
David Schroeder.
        p. cm.
Includes bibliographic references and index.
    ISBN 0-8264-1392-7 (hardbound) 0-8264-1536-9 (paperback)
1. Motion pictures and opera. 2. Opera in motion pictures.
3. Operas--Film and video adaptations. I. Title.
    PN1995.9.O64 S37   2002
    791.43'657--dc21
    2002000575

To Emily, Linda and Daniel

With Love

Contents

List of Illustrations

Preface

During my childhood in the 1950s, curbed by a strict religious upbringing, I did not go to the movies. No edict, though, prevented me from attending opera, and it so happened that I saw Verdi's *Aida*, Mozart's *Don Giovanni*, and Johann Strauss's *Die Fledermaus* before I ever went to a movie. In fact, nothing stopped me from seeing *Carmen*, *Salome* (a solid piece on a biblical subject, one could surmise), *Don Giovanni* and even *Lulu*, but on the other hand *Heidi*, *Bambi* and *Quo vadis?* remained taboo. I grew up with a delightfully distorted view of things, and when I first rebelled and went to see a movie, not finding the waywardness I had been sheltered from disappointed me. In the blockbusters which initiated me to the movies in the late 1950s and early '60s, I discovered something not very different in scope from the operas I already knew so well.

The old principle of prohibition inducing unbridled desire worked in my case in the extreme: deprived in my youth of cinema, I have indulged movie going since my late adolescence with unrestrained passion. Entering a movie house has never lost its attraction because even after being thrown out of the church in my youth, it still seems slightly transgressive. At the same time, my enthusiasm for opera remains undiminished, fueled at one time by an aspiration to be a singer, and then by a life as a writer and lecturer on music. My vocal training did not result in a career in opera, but it opened some alluring possibilities for comparing opera and cinema that would not otherwise have occurred to me.

I am very happy to acknowledge a number of people whose unswerving, or in some cases, indirect assistance, deserve my thanks. Since 1994, I have taught a course on film and music, open to students of all disciplines, and they take this course because of their love for movies. Through lively discussions inside and outside of class, I have learned much from these avid filmgoers. Some of the ideas for this book emerged during the seconds before attempting to answer dismayed questions or sharp comments, as well as during the congenial moments of shared enthusiasm.

While I acknowledge the work of numerous authors throughout the book, one stands out: Ken Wlaschin's encyclopedic *Opera on Screen* (Los Angeles: Beachwood Press, 1997) has proved extremely useful to me with its wealth of information on the numerous ways that opera has touched cinema. I often need exactly the kinds of lists and details that Wlaschin provides, and I am much indebted to him for compiling this type of guide.

My visits to the Film Stills Archive at the Museum of Modern Art in New York were very pleasant, thanks to the assistance of Terry Geesken. In facilitating the reproduction of illustrations, she went well beyond the call of duty, and I am most grateful to her for doing this so graciously.

Special thanks to my editor David Barker. Without his keen interest and steadfast support this book would not have materialized. Thanks also to Helen Song for overseeing the production of the book, and to Corrie Schoenberg for promoting it.

The experiences of cinema and opera should be shared with someone equally addicted to both, and since 1977, my accomplice has been my wife, Linda Schroeder. She frequently sees things that I miss and, being a musician of the highest order, she also has an uncanny ability to hear. I would find it difficult to imagine writing a book without her active interest on the subject, lively discussion, reading and rereading of the drafts. For these I cannot thank her enough.

Introduction

Only twelve years after the death of Richard Wagner, motion pictures first flickered across a Lumière Brothers' screen in 1895. As cinema burst into prominence early in the 20th century, it embraced Wagner with a passion, and continued to do so in remarkable ways. Wagner, one of the most influential cultural forces in the past two centuries, might have turned in his grave had he known that filmmakers would be among his most zealous disciples. Not only had they quoted his music or used plot ideas from the works of this giant of 19th-century opera, but more importantly some have devised visual images that seemed to emerge from a non-verbal Wagnerian essence – a formative, musical urge that could underlie a cinematic idea, defying explanation and remaining purely sensory.

A surprising number of major directors have intuited this possibility or followed the course. They include D. W. Griffith, Cecil B. DeMille, Sergei Eisenstein, Charles Chaplin, Fritz Lang, Orson Welles, Luis Buñuel, Alfred Hitchcock and numerous others. Not only Wagner, but opera in general, has riddled cinema through and through, from the earliest feature-length films in Italy, the United States, France, Germany and elsewhere to the most recent films.

The invention of cinema was ingenious, so much so that initially no one knew what to do with it. In its earliest stages, especially with the advent of the feature film, it needed models, and opera proved to be especially useful. The allure of opera to cinema early in the century held up through the "silent" era, into sound films, through the golden age of movies, and into the most recent trends in cinema.

This book explores the numerous ways – some of them predictable, some unexpected, and even bizarre – that this has happened, without trying to cover all possibilities. In some cases, this can be a very serious matter involving politics or religion, or the results can be lighthearted and frivolous. Opera, of course, has been only one of the

1

various diverse forces driving cinema. Yet it remains more potent than generally recognized.

There may, in fact, be a delightful irony in the attitude of many people to opera since the middle of the 20th century: younger generations since the outburst of popular music in the 1950s have often stumbled through adolescence with a disdain for opera. Yet, those who see their dislike for opera as part of the generation gap will be surprised to discover that whether they like it or not, they have been reared culturally on something very close to opera. Not only art cinema, but the most popular adolescence-oriented blockbusters coming out of Hollywood such as *Star Wars* draw heavily on operatic models. In fact, many kids without knowing it, first met Wagner on Saturday morning cartoons – and, they loved him.

An early director such as the Italian Giovanni Pastrone appeared to recognize with his *Cabiria* (1914) that the model for feature-length cinema lay much less with the theater than it did with opera, and Americans such as DeMille and Griffith quickly picked up on this. Unlike the theater where inflections of the voice convey emotions, silent cinema had to sustain them through a combination of visual images or gestures and an underlying musical score (if one existed). With the fusion of various elements that can include epic, narrative, scenes of grandeur and spectacle, fluid and emotive gestures of the actors, and musical accompaniment, numerous silent films from both sides of the Atlantic stood as nothing short of grand opera for the cinema.

I apply the word "operatic" as a term that can be useful to describe cinema, and in many respects the chapters of this book will, in a variety of ways, attempt to define "operatic" as it relates to cinema. Certain facets of the term apply more aptly than others, both to early cinema and much that has happened since. Spectacle certainly has played a major part as the simplicity of the two-reel comedies and romances could give way to extravagance and grandeur with massive sets, casts of thousands, and stories taken from legend, mythology, history or the Bible. Along with spectacle, the irrational has been central to cinema, with a focus on moving audiences through emotions instead of taking them through cerebral, logical exercises, engaging not only emotions but arousing us through horror, passion (even obsession), sexual appeal, and other inherently sensory means. Opera can be forgiven for many of its extravagances because of the ways it engages the senses – especially through the ear but in no small measure its appeal to the eye. Cinema lives by way of a similar sensory enticement, perhaps reversing the role of eye and ear from opera, but recognizing the crucial importance of both, and the necessity of their interplay not only as a balanced duo but also in a way in which one breathes life into the other.

As one would expect, ideas about connections between opera and cinema have been around for a long time. While these ideas reveal themselves most strikingly in films themselves, starting with some of the earliest films from the beginning of the 20th century, numerous filmmakers and critics have also written or talked about the possibility, sometimes with just a comment or a sentence, or in some cases with articles or entire books. Moving pictures were invented more or less simultaneously in a number of countries, and the American inventor Thomas Edison initially saw the most likely use for his invention as a tool for presenting opera. As early as 1893, he stated in *The New York Times* that he hoped "to have such a happy combination of photography and electricity that a man can sit in his own parlor, see depicted upon a curtain the forms of the players in opera upon a distant stage and hear the voices of the singers."[1] That possibility would not emerge for many years but in 1910, he thought it was just around the corner. Again giving his opinion in *The New York Times*: "We'll be ready for the moving picture shows in a couple of months, but I'm not satisfied with that. I want to give grand opera."[2] His concern probably was with the inclusion of sound to motion pictures but he may also have anticipated the emergence of feature films with an operatic disposition.

If Edison lacked clarity on this point, others would soon be much more direct about it, especially after the advent of sound in films in the late 1920s. By the early 1930s, Hitchcock had already made some very fine films, including *The Lodger*, *Blackmail* (which straddles silent film and sound), *Murder!*, and the first version of *The Man Who Knew Too Much*, but these did not yet anticipate the emergence of one of the great directors of the 20th century. The connection of his fledgling artform with opera would arise strikingly in later films, especially *Vertigo*, but in 1934, he saw cinema's potential noting in an interview with Stephen Watts in Edinburgh's *Cinema Quarterly* that "it may sound far-fetched to compare a dramatic talkie with opera, but there is something in common. In opera quite frequently the music echoes the words that have just been spoken. That is one way music with dialogue can be used."[3] Half a century later, aiming at a very different audience, George Lucas would refer to his *Star Wars* films, in an interview with Leonard Maltin, as space operas. Numerous other filmmakers have spoken about their interest in opera and the ways it intersects with film, often singling out a specific opera composer such as Wagner. Many of these will be cited throughout the book.

Aside from filmmakers, critics and not only those most directly involved with media studies have increasingly become fascinated with this subject. It has entered the discourse of philosophy as well, perhaps no more interestingly than in the writing of Stanley Cavell, whose preoccupation with the place of "voice" in philosophy in his *A Pitch of Philosophy* naturally led him to opera and subsequently to opera and film. He sets up his comments about the combination in the following way:

> Why go to film to raise the question of opera? Why not to opera directly? Well, I have in the past couple of years been experimenting with the idea that what happened to opera as an institution is that it transformed itself into film, that film is, or was, our opera. So while it is not my intention to stay indirect, I am moved to take my bearings by noting the repeated appearance opera has made over the years in my texts about film.[4]

Here he seems to suggest something close to reincarnation, and that idea will resonate throughout this book. Cavell does not develop the idea much further in his study, but in the paragraph following the one just cited, he sets up a fascinating possibility:

> ...the connection I would go on to draw between film and opera was to analogize the camera's powers of transfiguration to those of music, each providing settings of words and persons that unpredictably take them into a new medium with laws of its own – each as different from theater, for example, as air from water. Both film and opera we might add at once, were discovered or invented at datable, placeable moments in Western culture; this at once makes their origins and existences both more knowable and more mysterious than those of the ancient great arts...[5]

With words and persons, he just begins to scratch the surface of how this may actually work, since filmmakers discovered this potential well before the inclusion of spoken words. In fact, it gets at something much more basic about film, the very essence of visual images in cinema and their ability to move viewers; and no one understood this better than D. W. Griffith, one of the great founders of the medium.

By now, a number of books on the opera-cinema connection exist, although these seem especially interested in the phenomenon of productions of actual operas designed for the screen. This is true of Jeremy Tambling's *Opera, Ideology and Film* (1987), although one of his early chapters, "Film aspiring to the condition of opera," looks at the other side – the place of opera in film. Similarly Marcia J. Citron's *Opera on Screen* (2000) explores a number of well-known film productions of operas, only briefly touching on topics related to the broader presence of opera in film. Tambling has also edited a book on the subject, *A Night at the Opera: Media Representations of Opera* (1994), and here, he and 14 other authors discuss both film operas and the role of opera in film. Two of the contributions, "The Composing Machine: Wagner and Popular Culture" by David Huckvale and "Movies as Opera (Behind the Great Divide)" by Peter Franklin, address the general issue of opera's influence on cinema. Another book which goes beyond the study of film operas, Richard Fawkes's *Opera on Film* (2000), in this case as an historical survey, briefly touches on a large number of films that have operatic content. Much of that material had already been covered in encyclopedic form by Ken Wlaschin in his *Opera on Screen* (1997),[6] an extremely useful document on the presence of operatic material in films since the inception of cinema. He will be cited often in this book.

There are, of course, many different ways that opera has infiltrated cinema, and perhaps the most significant ones came already in the second decade of the 20th century at the hands of Griffith and DeMille, who appeared to fulfill Edison's remark about film becoming grand opera.[7] Not only did they wholeheartedly embrace the idea of the feature-length film, bucking the short-film trend of the studios in the case of Griffith, but both of them also recognized what Pastrone had already achieved with *Cabiria* – that cinema could draw on opera as its wellspring. Each in his own way marked the beginning of the feature film in America with a distinctive operatic idea, and these will be discussed in the next two chapters. DeMille at first saw his goal in basic operatic terms, taking an existing opera, *Carmen*, and transforming it into a silent film with a leading opera diva, Geraldine Farrar, in the starring role. In taking the subject matter from opera as well as his star actor, he started two trends that would remain popular until the 1950s. Using a popular diva as the star caught fire again with sound films, although for silent films, it played an extremely important role that would resonate in some of the finest films during the rest of the century. This lay in the possibility of the inaudible voice of the singer being heard in the mind's ear, and the way that could affect visual images, imbuing them with a musical essence that could in turn generate emotions not otherwise possible. Much later in the century, Pasolini would explore the same unsung but implied vocalization with Maria Callas in the title role of his *Medea*. The option of using subjects from opera never died out, as we can see from the numerous reincarnations of Carmen.

Unlike DeMille's fairly raw transformation of opera into film, Griffith discovered a more subtle way of infusing his films with opera, and here he created one of the most enduring, sophisticated and alluring operatic approaches to cinema. His own aspiration to be a singer played a key role in this, and building on his awareness of how emotion can be conveyed in singing, he unlocked the method of transferring this to the silent screen, opening a powerful and effective way of pulling on the emotions through a progressive idea that starts as a musical conception. Here, a transformation takes place from something which begins as an operatic or musical notion, and changes itself into visual images. In the filmmaker's mind, the operatic or musical idea comes first, with its power to move the emotions in a heightened way. This urge underlines what we ultimately see on the screen, not only in the appearance and actions of actors but also in their surroundings and all other visual images. Opera through singing and accompaniment had perfected the modes of moving the emotions, and for filmmakers intent on stirring the audience as Griffith wished to with *Birth of a Nation*, this notion of an underlying musical urge proved an exceptionally powerful means.

With a musical essence predetermining the visual images and giving them an inherent musical quality, a filmmaker would also then want to present the audience with actual musical sounds that would come as close as possible to unlocking the musical essence underlying the cinematography. To achieve that, a director would need to work in close collaboration with a composer, or would select existing music from the repertoire which the director already had in mind, and perhaps had used as a temp track during shooting. Once Griffith discovered these possibilities, he opened a floodgate which numerous directors followed with some, such as Eisenstein, acknowledging their debt to him. In spite of the use of opera as a model, audiences do not necessarily recognize it, and those who would not be caught dead at an opera, can nevertheless enjoy an operatic film experience without suspecting that they are absorbing something operatic. Many of the films discussed in this book will one way or another use this principle.

Despite the critical role that opera, or music in general, played for many directors, these filmmakers were themselves not all sophisticated musicians. Some, such as Welles or Buñuel, may have developed modest performance skills in their youth, but most were unencumbered with the musical knowledge that came with years of study and practice. Griffith seemed to set the tone, wishing he could succeed as a singer but never developing a voice that should be put on public display. While actual musical skill may have been lacking in them, all of these directors appeared to be sophisticated listeners, highly conscious of music's metric and rhythmic properties, and able to transfer these to pacing and montage. From Eisenstein, we get elaborate theories on how this works, and he takes this much further to include tonality and counterpoint as well. One suspects that only a non-musician could come up with the theories that he did in which the terminology applied to montage stood at odds with musical meaning. Here, we need to try to discover the musical essence he had hoped to suggest, the underlying musical urge which all other terminology failed to elucidate. For the directors with these interests who did not use existing music by Wagner or other great composers, some had the good fortune to work with outstanding composers who could intuit their musical notions and transform them into audible music, as Sergei Prokofiev did for Eisenstein or Bernard Herrmann for Welles and Hitchcock.

Music has been of vital importance to cinema from the very earliest stages. It had been a much larger issue and a necessity for most films to have a soundtrack or live accompaniment during the silent era. In many cases, of course, the soundtrack offered nothing more than an accompaniment which was added after a film had been shot and edited to serve a variety of purposes that would help to get the viewer engaged in the film. It can add an emotional underpinning to scenes or to dialogue, something that may in fact be essential in a film industry whose box office success depends on stars, some of whom reveal very little aptitude for acting. Film music has a remarkable capacity for providing emotion where it may otherwise not exist. Aside from signaling emotions, the music can do much more – identifying time and place, anticipating events, determining when we should take things seriously, helping to generate the illusion of grandeur, and a host of other possibilities.[8] In some cases, it can virtually carry the narrative, helping the viewer to sort out dramatic complexities or psychological states, often by working subliminally.

Aside from the complex ways that opera could have been a factor in the cinematic ideas of Griffith or Eisenstein, the more conventional approach to film music is also fundamentally operatic, derived in fact from Wagner. Even before the advent of the soundtrack, directors and composers such as Griffith and Joseph Carl Breil, discovered the usefulness of having recurring musical themes which could relate to a person, an object, an emotion, an idea or an event. With a soundtrack, this practice became even more effective through the possibility of precise coordination. The compositional pioneers of sound cinema such as Max Steiner and Erich Wolfgang Korngold set the standard for the use of these recurring motifs. They took Wagner as their model for this, a composer who built his operas on *leitmotifs* which musically tagged the same sorts of things filmmakers had in mind.

Wagner, of course, treated the music in a much more sophisticated way, with his *leitmotifs* part of a complex unfolding of sustained musical development, but Breil, Steiner and Korngold most certainly had Wagner in mind with their invention of film music which could sustain a narrative, add emotional vitality, and allow anticipation or recall. This approach to music dominated films during Hollywood's golden age in the 1930s and 1940s, and in fact never died out as recent film scores by John Williams, James Horner, and numerous others confirm. Aside from the *leitmotif*, film music borrowed other techniques from opera, including the idea of an overture to introduce the work; in movies, this becomes the opening title background, which alerts the viewer to the type of film which will be shown before any visual images appear.

Few things point to the importance of a phenomenon as strongly as satire or parody. Political satire would not capture our attention without the status and recognizability of the subject. Literary satire or parody pays a backhanded compliment to an original work. Since opera played a significant role in the birth of the feature film, among other things trying to make the movies a highbrow form of entertainment, it should come as no surprise that cinema would turn things around and satirize opera. Opera had already done that to itself, and it was only a matter of time until cinema would deflate the notion of "operatic" as it stands in grand but pompous operas and the world of opera as well – especially the social class in America which keeps opera alive. Cinematic parody or satire of opera indulges in the carnivalesque, especially in laughter at authority – the ruling class which perpetuates opera. Parody may be an unconventional mode of cinema connecting with opera, but no discussion of the subject would be complete without it.

Wagner provided the model for film composers and his influence stretches much more broadly to a wide range of other facets of cinema. The discussion of this from silent films to the present forms the core of the book. This can include a landmark work such as Fritz Lang's *Nibelungen* saga, where Lang intentionally misreads Wagner with stunning political implications. The Nazis saw Lang as a fellow Wagnerian, but a close reading reveals Lang subtly advocated an alternative to fascism and antisemitism. DeMille would also use Wagnerian cinematic spectacle to advance a political agenda in the 1950s, moving toward Griffith's approach in more ways than one.

Wagnerian images persist in cinema, giving the underlying basis for films as in the works of Luis Buñuel, providing plots for others, becoming a battering ram of intimidation, and even suggesting models for the ways sexuality has been treated in cinema. One of the most striking reincarnations of Wagner occurs in the space-opera epic which has recently seen an eruption of fanatical devotion after two decades of relative dormancy. The frenzy associated with *Star Wars* seems comparable to the fanaticism some have felt for Wagner. And, if adolescents can enjoy Wagner (without knowing it of course), so can children (including old ones) in Bugs Bunny cartoons.

The Wagnerian principle extends beyond Wagner to include a wide range of operatic modeling, images, borrowing and quotations in cinema. This may be revealed in the way that opera prompts cinematic illusion, the persistent recurrence of Carmen in cinema, and the presence in film of the stereotype of the gay opera lover – which, in *Philadelphia*, transcends stereotype and gives the film emotional depth. Obsession looms as another facet of operatic irrationality. Opera lovers can become obsessed with singers – especially divas – or with opera itself. Responding to it as one might to a lover, and putting this into cinema can generate a level of blind passion that might not otherwise seem convincing. Werner Herzog explores this brilliantly in *Fitzcarraldo*, where the irrational now extends to the madness of opera in the jungle; *Diva* discovers another side of this, linking obsession with danger. The myth of Orpheus has also taken on an operatic quality since opera came into being using the singing role of Orpheus. Cinema has allowed an entry of this aspect of the operatic, with the recasting of the myth by Jean Cocteau in *Orphée* or Marcel Camus in *Black Orpheus*, the latter a striking instance of a musical ideal generating stunningly beautiful visual images. The Orphic idea has permeated numerous other films in less direct ways, and Hitckcock has been especially susceptible to this.

Opera may have played an important role in the formulation of cinema, but it has now also returned as cinema. The final section discusses the presentation of major operas as cinematic works directed by notable directors, four of whom are included here: Franco Zeffirelli, Joseph Losey, Peter Sellars and Francesco Rosi. The results may be mixed, but the efforts curiously bring full-circle the place of opera in cinema. The book starts with *Carmen* and ends with her as well, although it certainly does not finish her off. She stands as a beacon, guiding us from DeMille's use of her to help launch his idea of cinema, through various other Carmen reincarnations along the way, and finally to Rosi's *Carmen* as a highly successful reinvention of opera as cinema.

PART ONE

APPROPRIATION OF OPERA IN EARLY CINEMA

SILENT OPERA: DEMILLE'S *CARMEN*

After the release of Cecil B. DeMille's *Carmen*, a reviewer for *The New York Times* (1 November 1915) found little to praise in the work:

> It is a curious commentary on the crazy economy of the theatre that a supreme dramatic soprano should give any of her precious time to a form of entertainment, to an art if you will, wherein the chief characteristic is a complete and abysmal silence. But, though the call of the movies is audible enough, there is small reason to fear that, after Miss Farrar's success, there will be a great rush of prima donnas to California, for precious few of them could so meet the exactions of the camera.

While her performance deserves praise, to this reviewer it appears wasted on a pointless endeavor which cannot offer the viewer even an inkling of the sound of Geraldine Farrar's magnificent voice. *The New York Times* in 1915 appealed to the upper echelons of society who would naturally take a dim view of a sordid new mode of entertainment like cinema which attracted workers and immigrants; in contrast, the reviewer for the more populist *New York Dramatic Mirror* (6 November 1915) hit on an idea of great importance to cinema:

> Geraldine Farrar has put her heart and soul and body into this picture, and without the aid of the magic of her voice, has proved herself one of the greatest actresses of all times. Her picture, *Carmen*, will live long after her operatic characterization has died in the limbo of forgotten singers. Her acting in this production is one of the marvels of the stage and screen, so natural, so realistic that it is hard to believe that it is acting.

Each of these reviewers marked off his own ideological ground: one saw opera as the highest of all artforms, achieving its height through singing; the other found opera pretentious, perhaps even a dying art, and a great art certainly did not depend on singing. This line, of course, also drew the divide between the respective audiences; one elite, denying that this crude entertainment, cinema, deserved to be called art, while the other praised the new democratic art form, accessible to all, at the expense of what was meant only for the privileged. These antagonistic positions reflected the contradictions of cinema itself early in the 20th century as filmmakers tried to identify their audience. Unlike opera in North America which determined its audience by the price of its tickets, cinema appealed to that audience as well as those with little money for entertainment. Since the two audiences had little in common, one high-brow and the other decidedly low-brow, cinema emerged early in the century with a delightfully contradictory mixture of approaches, images and appeals.

Before the building of movie houses in America, movies could be shown at any number of venues, from opera houses where ticket prices would be comparable to the opera itself to carnival tents or rented store-fronts where tickets would cost a tiny fraction of those at the more sophisticated halls. The enormous success of the latter led to the rapid spread of the nickelodeons where admission costs would not exclude anyone. At the same time, the industry spawned a construction wave of picture palaces – large, ornate halls which could seat as many as 3,000, complete with orchestra pits or fabulous Wurlitzer organs. In a society intent on protecting the morals of the younger generation, the nickelodeons presented a serious threat. These dingy, smoke-filled halls were readily accessible to anyone located in tenement districts. City fathers tried various strategies to control these iniquitous haunts, including making it illegal for cinemas to open on Sundays – the one day working-class people could attend. As a result of pressures from churches and other institutions concerned about morals, the industry itself in the U.S. complied with these forces, accepting censorship and designing films which could be considered morally edifying.[1] That meant tackling subject matter in narrative films based on biblical stories, classical heroes, historical figures, or anything with sufficient elevation.

In choosing the subject matter and mode of presentation, opera quickly emerged as a suitable source for films.[2] Opera, after all, was the reserve of the ruling element of society who forced their morals on everyone else, as operatic subjects, operatic grandeur, and opera stars were made acceptable for the general public. Aside from the matter of compliance with the taste of those with the power to inflict restrictions on the industry, opera itself enjoyed enormous popularity during the early decades of the 20th century, and emulating opera in cinema proved financially rewarding as well. To make the operatic transformation of cinema complete, opera became an ideal artistic model for cinema, and directors such as DeMille or D. W. Griffith who recognized this led the way in the burgeoning industry.

The popularity of opera in America, considering the restricted size of the audience, may seem a contradiction in itself. This popularity, of course, depended on the stars, and the fascination with divas bore resemblance to the fixation of the public on certain members of royalty – especially those endowed with physical attractiveness, to say nothing of an aura of mystery or perhaps recklessness. The fact that the public seldom saw these people did not diminish their appeal; since the press reported their every move, the public believed it knew them intimately. The love affair of an international public with Maria Callas during the middle of the 20th century stands as a vivid example of the phenomenon, and in death she was magnified from a larger-than-life legend into a goddess. Unlike the princess who has reached her status by birth, the diva arrived at her divine status through hard work. For the lower classes, she seemed all the more spectacular because she may have actually come from the ranks of her admirers, rising not just with luck but with determination. For Americans, if the diva happened to be an American, her place at the pinnacle would seem all the more extraordinary, allowing the public to identify with her.

Early in the century, one diva filled all the conditions for fantastic success and popularity as no one else: Geraldine Farrar. Born in 1882 in Melrose, Massachusetts, the daughter of a baseball player, her early success in local festivals led to her departure for Europe – with a loan from a family friend – to study with Lilli Lehmann. After her debut in Berlin at the age of 19, she rose meteorically, which led to engagements in most of the major operatic centers in Europe, performing many of the standard roles from Marguerite in Gounod's *Faust* to Carmen in Bizet's opera of the same title. American correspondents in Europe recognized her as newsworthy for the readers of papers back home not only because of the achievements of an American girl in an art form made popular in Europe, but also because of an emerging fascination about her life. Rumors circulated that the German crown prince, Friedrich Wilhelm, had become her lover, which her mother answered as "ridiculous gossip and shameful observations ripened into the screaming headlines of scandal and libelous affirmation." Her father defended her "in the old-fashioned American way," coming to blows with an editor who allowed lurid things about her to be printed.[3] Before she ever sang a note in the U.S., she was already a sensation, and if the gossip about her did not make that happen, the reaction of her parents surely pushed it over the edge. This strikingly beautiful American made her debut at the Metropolitan Opera in New York in 1906, returning to her home country not only as a diva but in the minds of an expectant public, glowing with a touch of royalty as well.

With her enormous success and popularity as an opera singer in New York, she seemed a natural for Hollywood. It did not strike anyone as unusual in 1915 that a superstar of opera could also be a star of film, although Geraldine Farrar went far beyond opera star status. While opera itself may have appealed mainly to a somewhat older audience, Farrar had a fanatical following among young people, especially those young women who tried to emulate her looks and fashion – the Gerry flappers. In order to attract this element of the public, one had to be controversial if not dangerous, and Farrar was known to behave in ways that would make the powers of the opera world shudder. Her triumphant journey to Hollywood proved no exception; not only treated like royalty with a private train car to accommodate her entourage, she could demand and receive a private pianist to play themes from Rimsky-Korsakov's *Scheherazade* every day en route to California. The pianist, it turned out, caressed more than the ivories on this trip. When he played something jazzier, she would shock almost everyone by climbing on top of the grand piano, scantily clad, and bump and grind to the rhythm. A brakeman who got on the train in Arizona and had not yet encountered her, muttered to himself: "Is that dame nutty?"[4]

When the train arrived in Los Angeles, a band played themes from *Carmen* at the platform of Santa Fe Station, and adoring and screaming West Coast Gerry flappers mobbed her. Not only studio officials but even the mayor greeted her, escorting Farrar along with her parents, manager and press agents over a red carpet to the waiting limousine.

The studio boss, Samuel Goldwyn, saw to it that she had a mansion with servants, a limo and chauffeur, a bungalow at the studio (of course with a grand piano), and the largest salary ever paid to an actress.[5] While many, including DeMille, feared she would be temperamental, smashing china or throwing tantrums if all did not go her way, she in fact proved not at all difficult to direct.

DeMille and his colleague Jesse L. Lasky originally brought Farrar to Hollywood to play a role she had already made famous in the opera house: *Carmen*. The idea of making a silent film version of an opera may strike one as strange, but for a director like DeMille who understood the operatic nature of early cinema, the notion seemed both natural and logical. In fact, this was by no means the first time cinema had incorporated Carmen, with as many as a dozen excerpts from the opera in films before 1915, going all the way back to Edison's 30-second *Carmencita* of 1894.[6] Following DeMille's *Carmen*, there would be a steady flow of cinematic Carmens, about forty in all up to the three striking versions that appeared in 1983/84 directed by Francesco Rosi, Carlos Saura and Jean-Luc Godard; aside from these, roughly another twenty would include material from Bizet's *Carmen*. Few subjects have occurred as often in cinema, and one needs to explore the reason why this character and her story have been so popular since the emergence of film. DeMille claimed that his *Carmen* followed Prosper Mérimée's novel of 1847 rather than Bizet's opera, but he asserted that this was merely to get around the issue of paying royalty fees to the Bizet estate. While the plot may follow the novel's in some respects, the images impress us as much more operatic than literary; DeMille fully expected that individual theaters would provide a musical accompaniment of excerpts from the opera.

With DeMille's *Carmen*, the opera emerged as a prominent force in defining the direction of both narrative films and feature films in America. Feature films of sixty to ninety minutes had been around for at least about six or eight years before 1915, and once again, one would note opera to be very much in the fray. In 1907, the well-known British conductor/composer Arthur Gilbert (of Gilbert and Sullivan fame) filmed the complete *Faust* by Charles Gounod – the first complete opera to be recorded on film, according to *The Guinness Book of Records*. This 66-minute version includes the music as well, made in the Gaumont Chronophone sound-on-disc system and advertised as the "complete opera with 22 arias."[7] As with *Carmen*, a number of short films using material from the opera preceded this *Faust*, going back to 1898. Of the roughly four dozen films based on *Faust* or using material from Gounod's opera, Edison's came in 1909 and the 1925 *Phantom of the Opera* prominently displayed a number of scenes. Some versions, such as F. W. Murnau's *Faust* of 1926, followed Goethe, Marlowe or German folk tales more closely than the opera, but even here the operatic images cannot be avoided.

In order to understand the role of opera in the process of cinematic inventions in the first two decades of the 20th century, it would be very useful to take a closer look at *Carmen* – both the opera and what DeMille attempted to do with it. To this day, *Carmen* remains the most popular work in the operatic repertoire, and by 1915, the fortieth year since its premiere, it already held that status of popularity. In the world of opera, *Carmen* stands as one of the most enticing contradictions since on the one hand, it appeals to the staid audience which supports opera; but on the other hand, no opera in the entire repertoire so subversively thumbs its nose at authority. Many operas have principal characters who behave badly – Don Giovanni perhaps most notably – but few evoke as strong a reaction as Carmen. Women traditionally do not have the luxury to act as Don Giovanni, and therefore no character can be as bad as a bad woman. Any woman who lives like Carmen should be branded as evil; unlike Violetta (from *La Traviata*) or Manon Lescaut, she is no prostitute with a heart of gold. Carmen takes a nice young boy like Don José and twists him inside out, leaving viewers with the impression that he lacks the power to avoid the spell of her enchantment. For upholders of a traditional masculine view of society, her sins seem grievous beyond comparison and Don José's plight invokes pity and understanding. A character like this and the evil she inflicts on that traditional world must be crushed, like Salome, Lulu (alias Pandora) and others of her ilk, and Don José may be forgiven by some for lashing out and finishing her off.

Carmen's death, though, may be deceptive; not only does it not get rid of her but it turns her into a much more powerful force. It may satisfy some members of the audience, just as Don Giovanni's demise leads most moralists to believe all ends well. Mozart, though, grants his hero the last laugh as his pursuers look like fools at the end, first doing a vaudeville act and then singing their moral message in mock liturgical style. Carmen of course does not laugh, but she holds on to her values of not being possessed by anyone and dies for them; this bestows on her even greater power in death than she had in life. Not only can women in patriarchal cultures identify with her but so can anyone who feels oppressed by traditional authority. To drive it home even more forcefully, Carmen the gypsy works in a cigarette factory, placing her outside the mainstream of society as a *Gastarbeiter* or immigrant and tying her to the working class. She may identify with her oppressors as a ruse, pretending in the opera to be from José's hometown, but she does not subscribe to their culture, wanting only their wealth, which she more than happily gains through illicit means like smuggling.

While the audience for the opera *Carmen* seems intent on her destruction, a largely working class and immigrant audience of the film would be more likely to identify with the character and enjoy her subversiveness. Selecting Geraldine Farrar for the role of this early feature cinematic treatment proved a brilliant stroke of casting. Everyone already knew her success in the operatic role, even if most had not seen or heard her in it, and identified the person from what they knew of her in the press with the character. Without trying very hard, Farrar managed to project that image, beginning with the scandal linking her to Friedrich Wilhelm, following that with the affair that played a contributing role to Toscanini not returning to the Met after an initial contract (her ultimatum to him to choose her or his wife apparently violated his traditional view of the submissive role a mistress should play), and then her need for sexual satisfaction which should be included on the studio's tab, to say nothing of her Habañera-like performances on the lids of grand pianos. In *Carmen*, when she dances on a table, swings her hips, gives someone the eye, or throws herself at an attractive young man, she apparently was simply being herself. If this sort of display could be confined to the opera house, the damage could be contained since an opera audience would know what to make of it; when put into a film, which millions of people from all social strata could see, her actions could be perceived as decidedly dangerous.

From all of this, a fascinating contradiction emerges: on the one hand cinema seemed to aspire to the condition of opera, elevating it to a position of grandeur and spectacle, but at the same time it took operatic subject matter and images and turned them into something

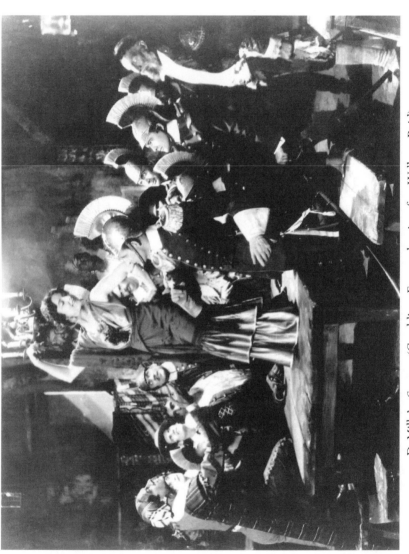

DeMille's *Carmen* (Geraldine Farrar dancing for Wallace Reid)

subversive. While cinema may have aspired to opera, it nevertheless remained a very different art form, and no one understood the similarities and differences as well as DeMille did. The place of Farrar in the transformation of film into something with the grandeur of opera proved decisive, and DeMille delighted in the fact that the "nationwide movie audience would see her in the same role in which opera-goers had thrilled at hearing her at the Metropolitan and practically all other great opera house in the world – *Carmen*."[8] Others recognized what she could do for cinema as well, such as the writer for *The Moving Picture World* who proclaimed that "next to the entry of Belasco into the domain of films... the resolution of this marvelously gifted young woman to employ her talents... in the films is the greatest step in advancing the dignity of the motion picture."[9] Perhaps even people who went to see and hear her in opera would wish to view her on film.

But of course she could not simply do in front of a camera what she did on the stage of an opera house. Most obviously in 1915, she could not sing in motion pictures; but other matters also had to be resolved, such as the fact that opera singers, performing in cavernous opera houses and not accustomed to audiences seeing their faces, used broad and exaggerated physical gestures to help convey emotions. In numerous early silent films actors were expected to use exactly these gestures; but a first-rate director like DeMille would not tolerate that. As for Farrar, not only did DeMille worry about her diva temperament, he also feared they would probably waste large amounts of film before she would drop her operatic gestures and use ones suitable for cinema. Even though she had been lured to Hollywood with a promise of *Carmen* as her first film, DeMille believed the acting transformation would be even more difficult if she started with a role she knew from the opera. Despite fears of her wrath, they proposed shooting another film first, *Maria Rosa*, to give her a chance to adjust to the camera, and like her lack of tantrums, she warmed to the idea, especially with the prospect that *Carmen* would still be released first.

On the differences between acting for opera and the cinema, DeMille had some very specific thoughts:

> There is still no better preparation for acting in films than a sound and thorough training on the stage, but the best stage actor still has

things to learn and unlearn when he comes before a camera; and that, I felt, was particularly true of one coming from grand opera, where the tradition is to over-act and where the glorious music can carry or cover a certain amount of less than glorious acting if necessary. Our cameras were silent. The first step, I told the disturbed executives, was to forget that Miss Farrar had had any connection with opera.

On the stage, an actor is trained to project himself, his character, his actions and thoughts, to an audience the nearest of whom is 30 feet away from him. To be effective, his projection must reach and grip the people sitting in the last row of the top gallery. They must be moved by voice and gesture. They cannot see the actor's eyes. But the camera can, ruthlessly, infallibly. You cannot lie to a camera. That is in part what I mean by the motion picture's ability to photograph thought. Until an actor learns to use his eyes and the slightest flickering change of facial expression to project what is in the mind of the character he is playing, the motion picture audience will not believe him; and they will be, as usual, right.[10]

In the end, DeMille felt he learned more from *Maria Rosa* than Farrar did; he believed that she "had a talent for screen acting as natural, and so as capable of cultivation, as her vocal talent."

Without saying so directly, DeMille seems to have understood an important principle about the parallels and differences between opera and silent cinema. Opera depends first and foremost on *bel canto* singing, an art which when practiced at its highest levels can induce a feeling of something approaching euphoria in the receptive listener. Even though opera occurs on stage, physical gestures have little impact (at least in pre-Callas operatic acting of the early part of the century that was true), and singing can compensate for unfortunate displays of acting. At its best, singing will use some fairly subtle types of gestures, making little progress with vocal histrionics but instead convincing the listener with agility, vocal shadings of tone, the *messa di voce* (crescendo-decrescendo) in the upper register, or the execution of ornaments. While gloriously subtle sounds may come from the mouths of singers, the audience may be just as happy that it cannot see them clearly; use of opera glasses may at times reveal some fairly grotesque sights – of mouths open much wider than they would be in speech and possibly even motion of the tongue or soft palate that most of us would be perfectly happy not to see. In cinematic versions of operas, such as Rosi's *Carmen* of 1983, singers lip-sync to their own studio vocal performances, sparing us the sight of their flapping epiglottises.

In DeMille's *Carmen*, of course, we neither have the sounds of singing nor mouths moving as though they are singing; now the performance of opera depends on something very different, and the subtlety of gesture must replace the subtlety of *bel canto* singing. The camera replaces the larynx, and instead of sound the diva depends entirely on face and body. A new type of soundless opera emerges which must be expressive, touching the emotions, and full of sensuality. In this scheme of things, and here DeMille defined the future of the American film industry, those faces and bodies lighting up the screen must be physically attractive, as was true of Geraldine Farrar, projecting a physical image that the viewer perceives as ideal. Searching for stars thus became the preoccupation of studios, and this primarily meant finding people with the right physical attributes for the screen. These people could be found in bit parts in other films, waiting on tables in Hollywood or New York, or just about anywhere else. DeMille prided himself on discovering Wallace Reid, who played opposite Farrar as Don José, but regretted that he had missed the boat completely on Clark Gable, whom he originally thought "did not have what it takes for a successful career in films."[11]

For all the praise that Farrar garnered for making the transformation from voice to camera, for her use of subtle gesture, for her natural talent, and for (along with DeMille) turning cinema into opera, *Carmen* remained open to satire or parody – to challenges not only from those who could not understand why she would waste her time with film, but from the strongest possible supporters of the new art. With this film Farrar and DeMille walked a tightrope, trying to combine the sophistication and grandeur of opera with a nose-thumbing spirit that would appeal to the masses, but ultimately it could not be entirely achieved. While opera proved useful to the emerging feature film, the solution did not lie in something as overt as cinema modeling itself on actual operas. DeMille's *Carmen* gave us neither the first nor the last of this type, as the forty or so *Carmen* films to follow reveal, but even in the next decade of silent films, including films that star Farrar and others by DeMille, the influence of opera would often reveal itself in much more subtle ways. At the same time, the overt treatment, including specific operas, operatic images, and the opera world itself would continue to permeate cinema. Despite his early temptation to turn cinema into opera, DeMille succeeded eventually in getting that out of his system and moving on to the more subtle treatments of the operatic element in cinema.

D. W. GRIFFITH AS A WAGNERIAN

"**H**e could burst into *Tannhäuser* or any of the arias from opera at any minute. There was tension on the set." With these words, aired in the documentary *D. W. Griffith: Father of Film* (Episode 1),[1] Lillian Gish gave us vital information about David Wark Griffith, not only as the director of *Birth of a Nation*, but also indirectly as a strategist who shaped public opinion. When one appreciates that Griffith admired Richard Wagner, and that he insisted that his closest collaborator on the film should be the composer Joseph Carl Breil, an even more committed Wagnerian, a fascinating new way of looking at this highly controversial film emerges. Wagner had used opera in the 19th century as a vehicle to manipulate the attitudes of Germans toward Jews in general and the consequences of Jewish emancipation in particular; over a period of almost a century, this strategy proved extraordinarily successful. Disapproval of state policy could be combated with anonymous tracts and pamphlets, but the potential of a popular art form using more subtle and insidious means could be staggering. Griffith's love of opera – and Wagner especially – alerted him to the possibility, and as a pioneer in developing a new medium with infinitely more potential than opera for reaching a broad audience, he knew he was on to something good. He also appeared to recognize instinctively that cinema at its most alluring level would achieve its goals through decidedly operatic means.

Griffith inevitably draws comparison with the somewhat younger Cecil B. DeMille; although Griffith had much more directing experience by 1914 with the hundreds of one- and two-reelers made at Biograph studio, he and DeMille came to feature-length films at about the same time. In doing so, they had to buck the conventional wisdom in Hollywood, where studio bosses believed the future prosperity of the industry lay in films no more than thirty minutes in length. The successful tours in the United States of foreign films such as the Italian-made *Cabiria*, the music of which Breil conducted on the American tour, suggested other possibilities, and Griffith found himself in conflict with Biograph when he diverted his energy and that of the cast and crew to the one-hour *Judith of Bethulia* (1914).

With the foray into the realm of the feature-length film, both Griffith and DeMille intuitively turned to opera as a model, and in 1915 Griffith came much closer to realizing how that model would work in the future. Unlike DeMille, who launched into a popular operatic story (*Carmen*) with a diva in the leading role (Geraldine Farrar), Griffith recognized a more subtle connection – one which DeMille would realize with *Joan the Woman* a few years later. Both directors ran into the sound barrier in the late 1920s, at which point Griffith faltered and DeMille flourished. Four years before the advent of *The Jazz Singer*, Griffith articulated the operatic principle which would make the barrier exceedingly difficult to cross: "the very nature of the films forgoes not only the necessity for but the propriety of the spoken voice. Music – fine music – will always be the voice of the silent drama... We do not want now and we never shall want the human voice with our films."[2] That sense of music, both audible and implied, would serve him very well in his silent features, allowing *Birth of a Nation* to become the most popular of all silent films and a recognized cinematic masterpiece. In order to make it, the visionary director had to go cap in hand to friends and the streets of Los Angeles to keep the film rolling.

Good story-tellers usually succeed in leaving ambiguous if not dissimulating impressions of themselves (Fellini would ultimately master this to perfection), and Griffith proved no exception. We know he came from a humble Kentucky background, worked at odd jobs, and became an itinerant and undistinguished actor, but in spite of that he has left the enduring impression of a sophisticated Southern gentleman, somewhat aloof, well-educated and cultured, blessed in youth with a pedigree if not with money. The respect he could command on the set as well as in the boardrooms of financial backers in part depended on this impression. The air of education and culture came from his own assiduous efforts at self-education, and that included familiarity with the operatic repertoire. As with the theater, he did not gain his knowledge of opera as a passive viewer; he pursued an aspiration to be a singer. His brother Jacob became his model, although David perhaps did not muster the same degree of passion. Jacob once told a friend that "if I should ever lose my voice and be unable to sing, I would want to die." David joined his brother in taking lessons from a local teacher, and while she praised his voice, her Protestant convictions censured his wish to use it theatrically. The voice proved not to have career potential, but that did not prevent his belief that he had musical talent.[3] With the visual medium he eventually chose, he discovered that as a director he could make images and characters sing.

The specifics of Griffith's bent for Wagner may not be very easy to document aside from the occasional remark by someone like Miss Gish. With his musical collaborator Breil we have a much clearer sense, and we can only imagine that Breil's Wagnerian inclination had something to do with Griffith's determination to secure the services of the reluctant composer. Before working on the score for *Birth of a Nation* Breil had written an opera, *The Legend*, toured as conductor with *Cabiria*, and provided the music for a number of films. For one of these, *Queen Elizabeth* (1912), a serious drama starring Sarah Bernhardt which required musical dignity and intense emotions, he saw his own approach as similar to Wagner's: "With the limited means of a small orchestra put at my disposal then, I set to work and wrote a dramatic score built very much upon the motif lines set down by Richard Wagner."[4] In a variety of articles on film music, Breil compared his work with that of his competitors who used pre-Wagnerian, non-leitmotivic music; Breil, as Martin Miller Marks notes in *Music and the Silent Film*, believed himself in the vanguard and equated "himself with the 'future Wagners' of film music" (that phrase actually appeared in the subtitle of one of his articles).[5] For Griffith a feature film required not only a musical accompaniment, but the entire film had to be conceived musically or operatically; to pull this off he needed the right musical collaborator, and the Wagnerian Breil was his man.

The saturation of silent film with the spirit of opera worked in a number of ways for Griffith, and the most obvious of these was the necessity of an orchestral accompaniment. Beyond that, now moving to much more subtle and sophisticated levels, Griffith like DeMille saw the possibility of the combination of acting gestures and cinematic images achieving something very similar to *bel canto* singing in opera. Whereas DeMille pursued this with an actual diva in a lead role, allowing Farrar's screen image to be a type of surrogate of her voice, Griffith hit immediately on the possibility that any actor under his direction could sing to the audience, carrying an intensity of emotion which viewers could grasp through their awareness of the persuasive power of song. As a singer himself, he understood what this meant, and his realization of the principle would set the standard for all future cinema. For this to work to the fullest there needed to be a musical backing at specific points in the film, leitmotifs for individual characters, or the emotions they experienced, which could put into audible terms the voice that the actors projected visually. Musical accompaniments then could not be haphazard, banged out at the whim of a theater pianist or organist; they had to be arrived at in a close collaboration between director and composer and synchronized precisely with the images on the screen. The soundtrack, invented in the late 1920s, would make this easy, but for the time being it would require a score to be played or conducted following precise cues. Another feature of Wagnerian opera which Griffith recognized and realized in *Birth* was the effectiveness of putting forward political or ideological positions cloaked in spectacle, emotion and music. In this guise such messages proved exceptionally difficult to resist, and Griffith, like Wagner, could melt an audience, subverting it if he pleased, in ways that politicians or oratorical demagogues could only dream of.

The complexity of the nature of the fusion of music and visual images will not in any way be made more accessible by looking at the collaboration of director and composer; time and legend have obscured this to the point that the two seem to blend into a single force. In fact, legend has it that Griffith may have composed part of the score, or that Breil functioned more as assembler than composer, simply arranging the score Griffith instructed him to compile. There may be some truth in this since Griffith took the music very seriously and knew exactly what he wanted. Views of the extent of Griffith's involvement may also have grown in direct proportion to his incipient sense of what it meant to be an *auteur*. In any event, Griffith never approached his involvement with the music passively, and that even included attempts to conduct the orchestra. At least one musical observer refuted this, the arranger Bernard Brown, who claimed that Griffith "didn't know one note from another,"[6] although this sounds very much like the posturing of a trained musician asserting his musical superiority over an amateur.

From Lillian Gish's report, which we have no reason to believe was tainted — except by a heavy dose of admiration, Griffith certainly could tell one note from another. It struck her particularly that he "had always been singularly conscious of the importance of music in conjunction with a movie... 'Watch a film run in silence,' he would say, 'and then watch it again with eyes and ears. The music sets the mood for what your eye sees; it guides your emotions; it is the emotional framework for visual pictures.'"[7] Something very sophisticated emerges here, more than meets either the eye or the ear, and Miss Gish seemed innately able to understand it even if she could not quite express it. The images received by the eye and ear fuse together, becoming larger than their sum, and the visual images have their own musical quality which the actual music attempts to release. Matching the actual music with the visual images would therefore require extraordinary care, and Miss Gish confirms this happened:

> He [Griffith] often worked for weeks with musicians to find music that would match each character and situation... Each actor had his individual theme. I was called in to hear several pieces of music, and helped choose one for myself that was also Mr. Griffith's choice. It was called "The Sweetest Bunch of Lilacs" and later achieved a different kind of fame as the theme song for the radio team of Amos 'n' Andy. Mr. Griffith had engaged Joseph Carl Breil to do the score for *The Birth*; it was to be based on nineteenth-century music. Mr. Breil would play bits and pieces, and he and Mr. Griffith would then decide on how they were to be used.[8]

She describes something distinctly Wagnerian, not only in the reference to 19th-century music, but especially the conception of the leitmotif, so sensitive to the character or situation that even the actor could have a role in its inception.

In the intensity of the collaborative process, tempers could flare, as Miss Gish continues:

> The two men had many disagreements over the scoring of the film. "If I ever kill anyone," Mr. Griffith once said, "it won't be an actor

but a musician." The greatest dispute was over the Klan call, which was taken from "The Ride of the Valkyries" by Richard Wagner. Mr. Griffith wanted a slight change in the notes. Mr. Breil fought against making it. "You can't tamper with Wagner!" he protested. "It's never been done!" This music wasn't *primarily* music, Mr. Griffith explained. It was music for motion pictures. Even Giulio Gatti-Casazza, General Director of the Metropolitan Opera, agreed that the change was fine. Finally Mr. Breil agreed to it.

Breil, apparently, had no compunctions about tampering with Weber, Beethoven or the pieces of a host of others used for borrowed music; his reverence for Wagner, though, prevented this, and here arranging seemed sacrilegious. Breil had difficulty looking beyond the music itself while Griffith alone saw the larger picture, and that included adapting Wagner in more menacing ways as well.

Film reviewers in 1915 were not ignorant of opera, and a few recognized Griffith's objective for cinema. One reviewer, Grace Kingsley, in the *Los Angeles Times* on 8 February 1915, marveled at what "a tremendous idea that of Mr. Griffith, no less than the adapting of grand-opera methods to motion pictures! Each character playing has a distinct type of music, a distinct theme as in opera. A more difficult matter in pictures than opera, however, inasmuch as any one character seldom holds the screen long at a time."[9] Writing about it some years later, Breil realized the importance of Griffith's operatic conception, and attempted to take the credit for the idea himself: "it finally dawned upon me that the first half of the picture... was a most tragic romance, just such as every opera composer is looking for. And right there I decided that the film would be treated as an opera, without a libretto, of course."[10]

In spite of the difficulties in sorting out the nature of the collaboration, Breil's claim to be the originator of the idea seems as spurious and ill-motivated as Bernard Brown's snub of Griffith's musical ability. One person possessed the vision and ability to pull all the fragmentary parts into a unified whole, and that fell to the actor-singer-writer-cinematographer-director David Wark Griffith. The notion of the *auteur* in cinema would emerge roughly half a century later, and not from the United States where studios made its practice virtually impossible, but already in 1915 Griffith had a vague sense of what it meant. In an interview shortly after the release of *Birth*, probably groping for the right words, he spoke of taking "another man's basic idea [Thomas

Dixon's *The Clansman*], but I must be permitted to develop it according to my own conceptions. This is my art... whatever poetry is in me must be worked out in actual practice; I must write it to my own standards."[11] Richard Schickel takes this in his *D. W. Griffith: An American Life* as writing on the set with a camera, or finding true authorship in cinema through the fusion of the sensory elements of cinema. A number of years later Griffith's idea about this went further, elevating the director to the status of hero, one who becomes the voice of the people: "Your hero is yourself, so the national hero becomes the one who expresses in the highest degree the achievement the people of the nation would like to achieve individually." Could America awaken to an appreciation of art? He saw it poised to do so, with artists emerging as popular heroes: "Perhaps motion pictures will do more to stimulate this interest than any other force."[12]

The idea of the *auteur* may have been a French invention of the mid-20th century, but the basic idea itself existed at least a century before that, in the *Gesamtkunstwerk* (all-embracing artwork) as Wagner explained it in his theoretical writings from the mid 19th century. Developing the idea in his essay *The Artwork of the Future* (1849), Wagner applied the term to his mature operas, in which all the arts, including music, poetry and visual spectacle would come together in a perfect fusion. The idea resides in a single person, and that artist will either create or bring the various elements together in harmony. As opera composer and librettist Wagner could do most of it himself (half a century later Arnold Schoenberg would go ever further as composer, librettist and painter/designer). Griffith surely knew about Wagner's notion of the *Gesamtkunstwerk*, and perhaps even more uncanny is his representation of the artist as one who turns loose the will of the people – the *Volk*, often in defiance of authority or prevailing conventions. This struck to the heart of Wagner's view of the artist's role in society, and put Wagner himself at odds with German authorities, forcing him into exile after the 1848-49 rebellion; later it placed him in virulent opposition to state-sanctioned views of racial tolerance. In this respect, Griffith's course as a shaper of social attitudes ran parallel to Wagner's in striking and disturbing ways. That one did it with opera and the other with a medium modeled on opera appears not to be coincidental.

The spirit of antisemitism ran high in Germany in 1850 since Jews proved a convenient scapegoat in the reactionary aftermath of the

1848–49 revolution, and Wagner's contribution to that with his article *Das Judentum in der Musik* (*Jewishness in Music*) therefore did not seem unusual. When he reprinted it in 1869, with a new preface protesting his own persecution at the hands of Jews, he found himself entirely out of step with society. This reissuing of the pamphlet ran counter to the full emancipation of the Jews, enacted into law in July 1869 in the North German Confederation, a few months after the reappearance of Wagner's article. Even his wife Cosima found the timing unfortunate, and as Barry Millington reminds us in *Wagner*, the reissue "gave notice that in spite of the formal abolition of discrimination, prejudice was still rampant."[13] Pamphlets such as this in a tract-obsessed culture would not necessarily attract much notice, and it could be more or less dismissed as a rush of spleen. If the views expressed in this type of scurrilous document found their way into major artistic works, as they did in *Die Meistersinger* premiered in 1868 or the *Ring* cycle under way at that time and premiered in 1876, very different implications would hold. As part of the fabric of a work with vaulting emotions and enormous persuasive power, these antisemitic views could re-enter the national consciousness, stirring up old malicious attitudes, and eventually resurface in political discourse. All of this happened in Germany, and while Wagner's operas may not have been the only vehicle driving it, they played a potent role for close to a century, with, of course, a profound effect on Hitler and the entire Nazi movement.[14]

Wagner believed that opera could be the voice of the people, appealing to ordinary folk who could be moved to social action, and thus his involvement in the 1848–49 rebellion. The ruling class, as he argued in his *Art and Revolution* (1849), had abandoned its role in genuine culture, and he therefore looked elsewhere for the foundation of the new society he envisaged. Even in the 19th century, opera had little appeal for the class Wagner hoped to arouse, and the process of change moved slowly as his vision could only take hold in a broad social spectrum by getting there through debate instigated by political leaders. As a reincarnation of opera, cinema could build on the effective means of opera to convey emotions, ideas, melodrama and spectacle, and could take these in a new form to the audience Wagner coveted: the *Volk*. Griffith saw not only the possibilities of the medium but the extraordinary potential for conveying a message as well. Like Wagner, in operatic fashion, he reintroduced prejudice to the American consciousness, arguing the same Aryan supremacist position and presenting it in a way that even abolitionists would find hard to resist.

Griffith too ran against the social grain when he unleashed on America his vision of the birth of a united Aryan nation. By 1915 the Ku Klux Klan had all but faded into dormancy, and *Birth* gave it a new infusion of energy, triggering a rapid spread; in John Hope Franklin's words, "*Birth of a Nation* was the midwife in the rebirth of the most vicious terrorist organization in the history of the United States."[15] While the effect on ordinary people was staggering, it also reached the top echelons of politicians and lawmakers very quickly. Thomas Dixon, author of the novel on which Griffith based the film, had a 25% share in whatever the film would gross, and censorship or legislative opposition needed to be overcome. Dixon arranged a private showing for his old schoolmate from Johns Hopkins University, Woodrow Wilson, now president of the country. After viewing it Wilson apparently noted that "it is like writing history with lightning. And my only regret is that it is all so terribly true."[16] Approval gained from further showings for the Supreme Court (the chief justice had been a Klan member) along with members of the Senate and House of Representatives made it virtually impossible for censorship boards, such as the one in New York, to ban it. Opposition may have been vocal, but people saw the film in record numbers; Dixon could assure Wilson that "this play is transforming the entire population of the North and West into sympathetic Southern voters. There will never be an issue of your segregation policy."[17]

In order to make the case, Griffith (and Dixon) used a historical revisionist technique vaguely reminiscent of Wagner's reinterpretation of mythology. If the issue proves difficult in the study of history, it becomes impossible when applied to works of art, which have no inherent responsibility to represent history accurately. If music scholars do not like the depiction of Mozart in *Amadeus*, that is their problem; biographical fidelity has no bearing on the objective of Peter Shaffer and Milos Forman, and gaps in it do not demean the work. In the *Ring* cycle Wagner takes great nordic myths and reinvents them, reworking the legends to make them speak to the 19th century as new Wagnerian myths. Griffith too reinvents the Civil War and the Reconstruction, and while we may deplore this as history, the challenge must be mounted in some other way.

Art and propaganda can walk hand in hand, as Wagner and Griffith so vividly demonstrate, and we remain faced with the problem of admiring the artistic genius which creates the medium while at the same time abhorring the message. That message should not be mistaken for anything other than what it is. In Wagner we have representations of idealized Aryan achievers, such as Walther in *Die Meistersinger* or Siegfried in the *Ring* cycle, and these he sets against foreign, non-Aryans who will try to imitate white Europeans but will fail, who will seek wealth and power, and who will subvert, corrupt and ultimately destroy civilization. These are Beckmesser, Alberich and Mime, all recognizable as Jews through characteristics described in *Jewishness in Music*. In *Die Meistersinger* we have the two rivals in competition for supremacy in an order of singers as well as for the hand of the lovely Eva, daughter of a leading citizen. At no time do we doubt the outcome, but we must witness in excruciating detail the dismantling and defeat of the grotesque Beckmesser.

Griffith gives us a similar rivalry between Ben Cameron, a handsome Southern white, struggling first at war and later against forces of the Reconstruction to preserve a dignified civilization, and Sylas Lynch, a mixed-race leader of the new forces. We know Ben (Henry B. Walthall) from the beginning of the film as an honest, industrious and caring person; the idealized and dignified South he represents overflows with loving families, contented slaves, and visions of the beauty of nature. Lynch, on the other hand (played by George Siegmann in blackface), a "foreigner" from the North, attempts vainly to imitate a white gentleman, but is crude, grotesque, power hungry, corrupt, subverting and destructive. He has ambitions of marriage toward Austin Stoneman's daughter and Ben's fiancée Elsie (Lillian Gish), but complete failure to attract her results in an attempt to force her into marriage. He proves to be a more cunning version of the blacks offensively shown in the new legislature who drink liquor, eat chicken legs, and put bare feet on the desks; he understands power and will go to any lengths to get it.

The struggle for power with the moderate and compassionate Lincoln out of the picture has only two alternatives: rule by blacks, carpetbaggers and scallywags with the likes of Lynch in control, or a new white order of dominance which in restoring the old civilization will not harass blacks who understand their place and will punish those who do not. Blacks cannot aspire to any type of power in this scheme

Birth of a Nation (the KKK riding to the "Ride of the Valkyries")

of things, any more than Jews could in Wagner's vision of Germany. For Griffith only one option stood open, and with civilization on the brink of destruction, it had to be rescued by knights of a holy order. Like Elsa in *Lohengrin* (or her namesake Elsie in the perverse clutches of Lynch), in urgent need of a champion after she has been wronged, who cries for help and is rescued by Lohengrin – a white knight of the holy grail – whose identity must remain concealed, Aryans in the South and North similarly needed a champion, which they get with white knights of the Klan. Lohengrin descends from the heavens on a swan; the Klan amasses members and rides to the rescue with Ben leading the charge. If we have any doubt about the outcome, Breil's arrangement of Wagner's "The Ride of the Valkyries" as the accompaniment to the ride erases that. These are no ordinary forces, but like Brünnhilde and her sisters, the half-goddess daughters of the supreme god Wotan, these semi-deified forces cannot fail. Strong measures were needed, and no one could threaten non-Aryans like the racist Wagner – a principle Francis Ford Coppola would reaffirm many years later with *Apocalypse Now*. With the victory won and blacks disarmed, Griffith returns us to "Dixie" in sound and visual images.

Both Wagner and Griffith take us back to pre-enlightened intolerance, to a nostalgia for an apartheid society which has been virtually impossible to shake in the 20th century. Both made their pitch at times of relative dormancy, reawakening attitudes that never seem to recede very far beneath the surface. Ordinary modes of written or spoken discourse could not achieve these results; it requires a medium seductive in its own right, which opera remains to an ever-faithful audience, and cinema, with its absorption of operatic means and popular appeal, can achieve for most of the population. If opera composers and filmmakers choose propaganda as their goal, many will be unable to resist the message, in part because the spectacle, the emotions, and the sensory appeal of lush visual images and musical ecstasy will allow the message to work in ways unlike normal discourse. It slips in through the back door, seducing like a Don Juan or a siren, making it difficult to resist its ravishing beauty. In the end we can do little but stand in awe of the glorious creation, but at the same time recognize it as a transgressor.

3

STAGE FRIGHT:
PHANTOM OF THE OPERA

In order for opera to live in the grandeur to which it has become accustomed, it must be provided with a suitably palatial home to indulge in its extravagant habits. Since it originated with the *intermedi* at the end of the 16th century as a vehicle for royal families like the Medicis to outshine all other families with their spectacular celebrations of weddings or coronations, it comes as no surprise that the buildings eventually erected to house this form of entertainment would reflect a resplendence that should dazzle the rest of the world. Even after the decline of European monarchies as rulers, new opera houses have continued to be architectural wonders, as monuments to the cities' sense of pride and identity. In more than one great city, the opera house stands as a focal point for the entire city, either located at the hub of the main thoroughfares or placed where it can be the most recognizable fixture which defines the rest of the cityscape.

In Vienna, where the Staatsoper stands at the center of the city — the meeting of the Ringstrasse and Kärntnerstrasse — the famous Ringcorso where anybody who was anybody would strut with all the other fashionable Viennese, attitudes of Habsburg monarchical tradition prevailed when the destroyed opera house had to be rebuilt after World War II. Unlike some cities such as Hamburg, which, when faced with the same situation, opted for an architectural monument to modernism, Vienna accepted its past as its greatest asset, and in a spirit of grandness, tradition and decorum rebuilt the magnificent house as it had been. As for modern cities in the new world, none made as much fuss over its new opera house as Sydney, holding an open competition for a design that would be spectacularly striking, and sparing no expense to erect the house itself. Since the wing-like structure (conceived by Danish architect Jørn Utzon as the sections of an orange) proved to be something of an acoustical nightmare (to say nothing of an engineering impossibility), a fair chunk of that expense went into adapting the building so it would actually stand and opera could be sung in it. Sydney may have gone through some embarrassing times during the years of construction and modification (started in 1950 and finally finished in 1973) as the costs mushroomed out of control to a staggering sum in excess of $100,000,000, but in the end the city has a monument which defines the visual image of Sydney as no other building does.

In city after city, in both the old and new world, the opera house stands as one of the great and defining edifices, regarded with pride and affection by residents and with awe by visitors. Venice's Gran Teatro La Fenice had a devastating fire on 29 January 1996, but there was never a moment of doubt that it would be reconstructed; a great house such as La Scala has few rivals for famous buildings in Milan, and the Royal Opera House (Covent Garden) of London draws attention to itself not unlike the great St. Paul's Cathedral or Westminster Abbey, and probably sees many more people passing through its doors (excluding tourists, of course). In the United States the old Metropolitan Opera symbolized the European cultivation of opera in America, while the new Met, no less opulent, defines a bold new image of New York. Other cities as well, most notably San Francisco, can also boast a major opera house which, in the case of that city, holds its place with other magnificent architectural structures.

As magnificent as the opera houses of the various cities mentioned above may be, or as architecturally defining to the city and strategically placed at the center, none can compare in majesty and centrality to the great Paris Opera House.[1] Italians may have invented opera, but by the end of the 17th century Parisians proved themselves every bit as enthusiastic for it, and as perhaps the greatest city in Europe could cultivate it as no other center could. Unlike London, which also adored opera in the 18th century, Paris could also boast of French composers not only capable of competing with the best in the world but also of defining a distinctly French opera. This began with Jean Baptiste Lully (he may have been born in Italy, but musically he surpassed the French at being French), continued with Jean Philippe Rameau, and extended to the late 18th century with the likes of André Ernest Modeste Grétry, Etienne Nicolas Méhul, François Adrien Boieldieu and Pierre Gaveaux. If non-French opera composers worked in Paris, including those as renowned as Christoph Willibald von Gluck and Luigi Cherubini, they knew perfectly well that they had to write in the French style. Even Mozart when in Paris was badgered by his father to be certain to cultivate the French style. The outstanding French writers of the 17th century, including Jean Racine, Pierre Corneille and Molière, provided ample material for texts, and an army of French librettists adapted their material for opera. The tragedies that evolved from Racine and Corneille shunned artifice, and the French wanted only voices they believed lent sufficient dignity to tragic roles, therefore rejecting the castrati so admired in almost every other country. Some may think that the so-called French Revolution would have dealt a fatal blow to the art form most closely associated with the monarchy, but nothing of the sort happened. Not only that, but if anything opera became even more accepted and spectacular in 19th-century France. Those in power in the new France knew they needed to define the stateliness of their administrations and the decorum of the country itself in the eyes of the rest of a world inclined to think of them as barbarians, and what better way than to maintain a vibrant opera. In one sense this already emerged during the first two decades after the revolution with so-called rescue operas – the direct ancestors of Beethoven's *Fidelio* – which reminded everyone that genuinely noble aristocrats victimized by unscrupulous powerbrokers of the new era remained.

As the conception for the modern capital unfolded, opera stood at the very center of the plan. The *Place de l'Opéra* rises truly as the focal point of Paris, with the seven great thoroughfares of the city radiating from it. This busiest of all squares in Paris has inspired the belief that anyone sitting for more than half an hour at the nearby *Café de la Paix* will sooner or later see a friend or acquaintance – even if from the other side of the world.[2] The Paris Opera may not have the largest seating capacity compared to the other great opera houses of the world, but in every other way it surpasses them, including being the largest theater in the world. No other theater has such a spectacular double horseshoe Grand Staircase, which on gala nights will be lined with members of the *Garde Républicaine* with their white buckskin breeches, helmets and swords. The front vestibule with its mosaic tiles seems more like the entry to an ancient temple; and the top of the grand staircase leads to a gallery and grand foyer decorated with patterns of inlaid marbles prepared by Venetian artisans from the island of Murano. As Peter Haining describes it, one has "the overwhelming feeling of entering a world of timeless grandeur mixed with an air of almost imponderable mystery."[3]

Work began on Charles Garnier's design in 1861 and continued until 1875, interrupted by the Franco-Prussian war and the Commune. At a staggering cost of 47 million francs, its porticoed facade featured statues symbolizing all the arts. A building so large and heavy (covering two and three-quarters acres) needed huge piles extending below the water level to rest on, but to accomplish this the water had to be drained – an operation which took eight months of continuous pumping. With the foundation and flooring in place, engineers allowed the water to return to its natural place, creating an "eerie subterranean lake." The completed house has seventeen floors, countless stairways, corridors (no less than 2,500 doors), ladders and chutes, no easier to navigate than the streets of Paris. Scores of dressing rooms accommodate the performers, while the stars' rooms have anterooms and large closets; other massive rehearsal and dressing rooms serve the chorus and orchestra. The Emperor Napoleon had private facilities exceeding that of royalty in other countries, including salons, cloakrooms and guard rooms, and a stable beneath these large enough for six coaches and fifty horses.[4] The house itself has a traditional horseshoe design with boxes on the upper levels and an orchestra level for common seating, all, of course, ornately decorated.

Every bit as important as the opera and the audience attending it is the opera house accommodating them, appropriate to the spectacular entertainment and the inflated grandeur of the patrons. Just as the opera and its patrons may be vulnerable to attacks of parodists, satirists and burlesquers, the opera house may be similarly open to attack, and in the case of Gaston Leroux and his novel *Phantom of the Opera* (1911), that took the form of horror. Apparently a legend about a ghost haunting the bowels of the Opera already existed, although in reporting this in his Introduction Leroux no doubt manufactured most of the legend in a style he knew well from his journalistic days prior to becoming a novelist. Certainly the maze of passages and stairs behind and below the stage and especially the underground lake lent themselves well to the creation of a horror story, and opera, so often on the verge of horror with devils, evil characters and eerie scenes, offered the ideal setting.

Leroux's novel attracted little attention among the French, perhaps cutting too close to the heart of their beloved capital. It fared better in the United States, a country fascinated by Paris and also well pre-pared for this type of writing by the likes of Edgar Allan Poe. The novel, though, would have quickly faded into total obscurity had it not been for the efforts of Universal Studio to find a suitably menacing role for Lon Chaney after his success in *The Hunchback of Notre Dame* (1923), another story set in Paris, in this case by one of the greatest 19th-century French authors: Victor Hugo. The rights for *Phantom* proved not difficult to secure, and this scenario provided an even better opportunity than *Hunchback* for the make-up artists to work their magic on Chaney. In fact, they succeeded so completely that no images of the phantom could be released in the trailer (except for a fleeting shadow visible through a large gaping mouth), saving the shock of his deformed and eroded face for the famous unmasking scene of the film. In the sound era we have been treated to a steady diet of phantom films, and the story's continued popularity has been guaranteed by Andrew Lloyd Webber's musical.

Phantom of the Opera (1925) turned out to be one of the most suc-cessful American films of the silent era, and while the superb treat-ment of the element of horror had much to do with that, the role of opera may have also helped. Virtually all the actions take place in or under the Paris Opera, and audiences could either identify with going to the opera or they could visualize it if they lacked sufficient means. The set in this case had to approximate the grandeur of the Opera, and it succeeded so ably that the same set was reused for at least one of the later cinematic Phantoms. The possibility of linking opera and horror proved a brilliant stroke on the part of Leroux, and another possible reason for the weak reception of the novel could be that the spectacle of opera does not lend itself well to a medium better suited for the development of character or more intimate types of images. Cinema, with its penchant for grandeur, proved a much more adept medium to achieve that. In this case not only does the opera house provide the set, but the performance of various scenes from Gounod's *Faust* adds a very special dimension.[5]

The Phantom of the Opera (the falling chandelier stops the performance of Gounod's *Faust*)

This film offers much more than the mere appropriation of opera for the purposes of spectacle or emotions; here horror plays the key role, and in this too opera provides a wealth of possible sources. In the standard operatic repertoire from the 19th-Century horror scenes were not uncommon, usually related to demonic or evil forces that had to be overcome. In Beethoven's *Fidelio* the melodrama scene in the dungeon provides the right horrific atmosphere for the scheming of the evil Pizarro; in this case the horror invokes pathos as we see Leonore participating in digging the grave for the husband she desperately hopes to rescue. A few years later the melodrama scene from Weber's *Der Freischütz*, the Wolf's Glen scene, goes even further than Beethoven had in the creation of horror, an eerie surrounding, and the presence not only of evil but of the devil himself. Wagner too employs the forces of horror almost routinely in his operas, especially in the *Ring* cycle, in the domain of the evil Alberich, for example, where the abuse of power results in a horrific setting of enslavement. Wrathful giants, a fierce dragon, or the evil descendents of Alberich also bring in an element of horror.

Horror will always be present where the devil in one of his various guises presides, and 19th-century opera has more than its share of these, usually in his form as Mephistopheles. The most apparent of these, derived from the Faust legend, include, of course, the opera used in the *Phantom*, Gounod's *Faust*, but numerous others can be found, such as Arrigo Boito's *Mefistofele*, Giocomo Meyerbeer's *Robert the Devil*, or even the various appearances of the devil in Jacques Offenbach's *The Tales of Hoffmann*. The *Phantom*, not unlike *Casablanca*, draws on numerous story archetypes, and the Faust archetype presents itself most overtly because of the presence of the actual opera both in the novel and even more vividly in the film. Just as Faust must sell his soul to the devil to achieve his goal of experiencing what his academic life has denied him, Christine Daaé, the Phantom's young protégée, must also make that type of pact in order to become a diva. We must assume that normal voice instruction has not and cannot bring her to that point, and she seems prepared to do anything, including entering into a liaison with a demonic figure she never sees and forfeiting the love of a highly eligible suitor, to reach her otherwise impossible goal. Christine, though, is no Faust, who must surely take full responsibility for his actions and the grief he causes others; her goals appear more reasonable, and her methods, like those of Max in *Der Freischütz*, compacting with the devil for straight-shooting bullets, reflect mostly poor judgement. She perhaps has more in common with the consumptive Antonia in the third act of *The Tales of Hoffmann*, who, led on by Hoffmann's wish and the approving image of her mother conjured by the nefarious Dr. Miracle sings and then dies in the arms of Hoffmann when her lungs collapse. Christine too plays a lethal game, and probably could not sing any better than Susan Alexander in *Citizen Kane* without her Svengali-like Dr. Miracle – the Phantom.

Many archetypes drive the *Phantom* aside from Faust, and the others emerge from a mixture of operatic and mythological sources. A fairly persistent one comes from the Orpheus legend, which played a huge role in the inception of opera with works by Peri, Monteverdi and others at the beginning of the 17th century, and its application to this film will be described in chapter 25. Other operatic archetypes in the *Phantom* come from Wagner, both *Lohengrin* and *The Flying Dutchman*. The Phantom sees himself as a cursed man, condemned by the hatred of humanity to repulsive reclusiveness and acts of venomous revenge, like the Dutchman whose oath in a moment of need condemned him to sail the seas eternally. The Dutchman has only one chance of redemptive release from the grip of endless suffering, and that lies in finding a woman whose love for him will be so profound that she will willingly sacrifice herself for him. The Phantom, known as Erik before his disfigurement, remembers well that he once possessed goodness which only such a woman's purity can reawaken. His salvation depends on her love, which he hopes can be aroused by the remaining good within him: "If I shall be saved, it will be because your love redeems me." But in his Jekyll and Hyde existence, it takes very little to repress the benevolent Erik and trigger the evil Phantom; in the end the monster predominates and he must suffer the final degradation at the hands of those he believes created his fiendish side.

Christine, the Phantom believes, should be grateful for his affection and should return it willingly since her good fortune as a diva depends entirely on him. Her rivalry with the more established diva Carlotta he sees in the same terms as Elsa's struggle against the divisive Ortrud in *Lohengrin*, a scenario in which he plays the role of her champion and rescuer – the knight of the holy grail: Lohengrin. In part Lohengrin's power depends on his mysteriousness, and he places conditions of inscrutability on their relationship in marriage: she must never ask questions about his identity or where he comes from. Christine encounters a very similar condition. When she awakens from her tortured sleep in the bedchamber decorated and stocked by him to fulfill her needs, she discovers a note he has left for her: "You are in no peril as long as you do not touch my mask. You will be free as long as your love for the spirit of Erik overcomes your fear." The mask hides an identity and for her to see what lies behind it would be as fatally destructive as Elsa questioning Lohengrin about himself. Neither woman can resist, and Elsa forfeits her chance of marriage to her white knight; Christine unlocks the pandora's box, releasing not only one of the most hideous sights in the history of horror cinema but all the venom which his ghastly face symbolizes. With that pull of the mask Erik vanishes forever, and he receives his final condemnation to monstrosity.

Other archetypes abound in the *Phantom*, drawn mainly from classical mythology, although these take on a type of operatic dimension, as myths such as that of Orpheus have been a strong stimulus for opera. Most striking of these is the myth of the beautiful young Proserpine and Pluto, the god of the underworld. Pluto saw Proserpine, felt desire, and abducted her, driving his horses mercilessly in their flight. Unable to cross the River Cyane, he struck the bank of the river with his trident, and the earth opened a passage to Tartarus. After a long search her mother learned of her whereabouts, and persuaded Jupiter to send Mercury and Spring to wrest her back from the underworld. They can only accomplish this if she has eaten nothing, and knowing this, Pluto offers her a pomegranate to taste. This prevents her complete release, but as a compromise she can spend half her time in the world of air and sunshine and the other half with Pluto in the underworld (these classical characters have not gone unnoticed in opera, as Mozart's *Don Giovanni* ends with a reference to them, before the final facetious singing of the moral).

The abduction has obvious parallels to Christine's, but so does her release. When Christine begs to be set free and promises to be his forever, he grants her a temporary reprieve: "I shall prove to you the depth of my love. You may return to your world for the present. You may sing in the opera once more. But, remember, you are mine — mine — and you shall not see your lover again! If you do, it is death to you both." After abducting her a second time, he forces her hand by making her choose between blowing up the opera house and accepting him – the price for saving Raoul's life; she opts for the latter. Choices such as this, of course, are the stuff of opera, most notably *Tosca*, in which Tosca agrees to have sex with the villainous Scarpia if he will revoke a death warrant against her lover Mario (both in this case deceive the other, as she makes her promise within reach of a dagger, and he pretends to enact the reprieve but does not).

Despite the Phantom's threat and her promise to the contrary, Christine contacts Raoul immediately after her return from the depths, and they arrange to rendezvous in disguise at the masked ball. As this takes place in the vestibule, foyer and on the grand staircase of the Opera with all attending in extravagant costumes, it offers director Rupert Julian another opportunity to feature the splendor of the house and create more operatic spectacle; even at this point in 1925 a red tint was used to heighten the effect of the ball. This scene appears operatic in more ways than one as it bears some resemblance to the final scene of Verdi's *The Masked Ball*, with its ballroom intrigues, rendezvous and lurking menace. In the film, the entry of the Phantom as Death adds a chilling touch to a scene which should otherwise be mainly merry. Christine and Raoul seek privacy on the roof of the Opera, but the Phantom, always one step ahead of them, hides in the wings of the statue of a muse, overhearing their every word. Like Jupiter who swoops down in the form of an eagle to abduct the hapless Ganymede, the Phantom with flying cape represents a similar menace here high above the *Place de l'Opéra*.

As a film the *Phantom of Opera* stands between two great cinematic traditions, influenced by some of the most outstanding examples of German expressionist cinema – especially *The Cabinet of Dr. Caligari* (1919)[6] – and pointing toward the best efforts in horror films in the U.S. and the U.K. which would follow. The obsession with Lyonel Feininger-like geometric shapes in *Caligari* appears in the *Phantom* in the subterranean stairway and passageway scenes which gain menace through association with their German counterpart. Similarly the extensive use of silhouettes derives from equally sinister portrayals in a film such as Murnau's *Nosferatu*. Numerous scenes became models for future horror films, none more gripping than the unveiling of the Phantom's hideous face, or the mob scenes familiar in Frankenstein films, torture chambers that use heat or water, and a host of other spine-tingling images. Since some of these images derive from opera, and this film relies more strongly than most silent films on operatic ideas, images and presence, opera can be seen to play no small role in the conception and unfolding of the horror film. And, since horror scenes work effectively in an eerie location, what better setting than an accident-prone opera house, especially one already thought to be haunted such as the Paris Opera.

4

A LIFE AT THE OPERA

The extraordinary popularity of *Phantom of the Opera* can be accounted for in a number of ways, not least of which was the attraction of the portrayal of the world of opera. This world held a fascination for ordinary American filmgoers in the 1920s, partly because it seemed so completely alien to their own existence. It resonated with glamor, public attention and eccentricity, yet those at the top, treated like aristocracy, got there not by birth or privilege but through a combination of natural talent and very hard work. Working-class filmgoers could certainly understand the hard work, and the talent part could be grasped as well; almost everyone has been endowed with some sort of voice by nature, and most people like to use their voices too – in church choirs, in glee clubs, in amateur productions, on the factory floor, or, if nothing else, at least in the shower. It staggered the imagination to think that they or someone they knew might have their voice discovered, and after about six years of intensive vocal training could make their debut on the stage, could become wildly famous, and could make unbelievable amounts of money.

As obscure a dream as that may be, it could be fueled by the fact that some had done it, an ordinary girl from New England, for example, like Geraldine Farrar, who returned from Europe having gained nobility in the minds of many. Aside from being probably the most famous woman in the U.S. during the second decade of the 20th century, fame gave this woman from a simple background the freedom to assume whatever identity she happened to like. If she wanted to defy convention and thumb her nose at traditional morality and those who enforced it, or if she wished to give the finger to anyone in authority, she could not only do it but get away with it. DeMille and Jesse L. Lasky saw not only her possibilities as a potential movie star – in an operatic role like *Carmen* or an extension of that in *Joan the Woman* (see chapter 14) – but they also realized that part of the attraction would be to see her in roles that put her in the arena that made her famous. They therefore gave her a role in the same year as *Carmen* in which she plays an opera singer, in *Temptation* of 1915. The assignment of villain here went to the non-musician in a position of authority, an opera impresario, whose resemblance to Giulio Gatti-Casazza of the Metropolitan Opera should not be taken as purely coincidental. As the impresario's nefarious plot unfolds, the sacrifice the singer must make to aid an aspiring composer may remind us of certain aspects of *Tosca*, but it does not end as an operatic tragedy. A few years later she again played an opera singer in DeMille's *The World and Its Women* (1919).

With the advent of sound in the late 1920s, the incentive for displaying the world of opera on screen became even greater since audiences could now hear their favorite singers as well as see them. The mid 1930s saw a burst of films about opera, and many of these proved extremely popular. Aside from the dreams that the operatic life may hold, its portrayal allowed for ready access to high drama at many possible levels, and more often than not the conflict could parallel opera itself. In *Temptation* the plot drew a line between management and musicians, a conflict the working class could relate to vividly as their own struggle between bosses and workers. The tension could extend to include rivalries among the singers themselves, especially between aging divas with bloated egos and big reputations but little left as far as voices go, and young, aspiring singers with boundless talent but little opportunity. We will cheer on these hopefuls, and if management proves nothing but a stone wall, as occasionally occurred in the major opera companies, we may even accept unscrupulous ways of advancement to counter the intransigence of managers. When that happens in *A Night at the Opera*, we will dismiss the inane scheme with applause, and even in *Phantom of the Opera* the Phantom's sinister methods of getting Christine in leading roles may not seem all that unreasonable.

The screen accessibility of singers in both sight and sound also proved to be immensely appealing. People who could not afford the five dollar admission fee to the opera now had a way to see and hear their favorite singers for a mere twenty-five cents. There can be no doubt that an audience existed outside of opera houses, since numerous singers appeared in singing roles in films, and in most cases they made a number of films. In the silent era audiences seemed happy just to see them, and aside from Farrar, other singers on the screen included Bertha Kalich, Lina Cavalieri, Fritzi Scheff, Mary Garden, Anna Case, Marguerita Sylva, Hope Hampton, Marguerite Namara, and even Enrico Caruso. In the sound era the list got much longer, including John Charles Thomas, Pasquale Amato, Andres de Segurola, John McCormack, Lawrence Tibbett, Everett Marshall, Fortunio Bonanova, Nelson Eddy, Jeanette MacDonald, Benjamino Gigli, Kathleen Howard, Felix Knight, Nina Koshetz, George Houston, James Melton, Grace Moore, Ernestine Schumann-Heink, Michael Bartlett, Marion Talley, Marek Windheim, Gladys Swarthout, Jan Kiepura, Helen Jepson, Miliza Korjus, Kirsten Flagstad, Risë Stevens, Lauritz Melchior, Lotte Lehmann, Jan Peerce, Jarmila Novotna, Ezio Pinza, Korothy Kirsten, Robert Merrill, Roberta Peters, Patrice Munsel, Helen Traubel, Salvatore Baccaloni, Claramae Turner, Mary Costa, Walter Slezak and Mario Lanza.[1] The list may seem daunting, but it simply underlines the widespread nature of the phenomenon until the 1950s; some of these singers, as we will see, became enormously popular with cinema audiences.

In comparing films from the 1930s and 1940s with those from the last few decades of the 20th century, one notes that the fascination with certain professions which has gripped recent audiences held little or no interest for earlier ones. Law and medicine now top the list, with business not far behind, probably because of the ways they have been glamorized on television in prime time and soap operas since Dr. Kildare and Perry Mason. Trying to convince audiences before the middle of the century of the attractiveness of these professions would have been a hard sell. Medicine to most people meant the family physician, a typically affable and dull person – part of the tedious existence they hoped to escape at the cinema. Lawyers did very technical things, arguing obscure points of law that simply put one to sleep; besides, much of the population perceived them as sleazy, and it would be a number of decades until that would be enjoyed as entertainment. Lawyers worked for people with money, and if they had anything to do with the working class, as they may have in labor relations, the encounters tended to be unfortunate. Businessmen also seldom received sympathetic depictions in films at that time since they represent the bosses so odious to the working-class audiences; we usually see them as ruthless opportunists who give ordinary people the shaft or as wimpy husbands in tow at entertainments like opera.

If a person's line of work surfaces at all in films from the time, we more often than not find occupations in something out of the mainstream, something adventurous, risky, requiring talent, or even better, something illicit. Therefore we see people in roles as gangsters, smugglers, pirates or cowboys. Soldiers would fit the description, but between the wars and during World War II it remained too painful for many viewers to be bombarded with what they or their families had been through. Only after 1945 did soldier movies become popular as a celebration of the Allied victory (once again after Vietnam, war films would for a time become taboo in the U.S.). Music as a profession proved to be very attractive. Talent, of course, played a crucial part, and risk always lurked not far beneath the surface. The process of watching a great talent develop could be highly engaging as the musician goes through inner struggles with self-doubt, or the conflict could be with an established rival warding off a threat. The portrayal of notable musicians could be equally fascinating, people at the pinnacle of fame and the grand life; their love lives always appear more interesting than other people's, and being in a competitive profession their struggles to remain on top will be engaging. Thus, we will be fascinated by the upward climb of a young Jewish singer in *The Jazz Singer* (1927), the love diversion of a famous violinist with a beautiful young accompanist in *Intermezzo* (1936 and 1939), or we can simply enjoy the great music of Louis Armstrong in his various films. If stories of musicians appealed to audiences in general, nothing worked as effectively as tales of opera singers.

The types of plots involving opera can run a huge range, from horror in *Phantom of the Opera* to biting comedy or satire in *A Night at the Opera*. Between these lie various types of attempts to elevate cinema itself, to present uplifting stories of triumph and achievement unfolding against intrigue, deviousness and backstabbing. Amid the wholesomeness that usually emerges, singers will sooner or later burst into song, sometimes without warning, with arias from grand opera or popular songs of the day (or songs written for the films which the producers hoped would become popular). In fact, many of these films proved to be sappy in the extreme, indulging in an absurd escapism that appealed between the two wars but with a very different effect

on more jaded recent viewers. In some cases these stories are so san-
guine that in the past few decades they cannot be viewed as anything
other than camp.

While one might expect a soprano or a tenor to be responsible
for popularizing films about the opera in the sound era, in fact a lower-
voiced singer achieved this most strikingly, the American baritone
Lawrence Tibbett. Before making films he sang opera in Los Angeles
and at the Met, and critics noticed him because of his acting ability.
He appeared in singing roles in two films in 1931, and in 1935 starred
in a film which deals exclusively with the operatic life: *Metropolitan*. The
title in fact proves to be a negative one, since the film portrays the
Met as a major obstacle to the rise of talented young American singers,
preferring instead aging European singers with big reputations. Here we
have many of the same ingredients as *Phantom*, with a domineering
older diva, a talented young singer making little headway, and managers
who opt for reputation over talent. Instead of using threats and horror
to achieve advancement, the baritone played by Tibbett does it by resign-
ing and hoping for a break somewhere else. Needless to say, that quickly
comes, in this case by way of an over-the-hill diva who starts her own
company with her hen-pecked husband's unlimited resources, and makes
Tibbett the artistic director (she expects much more than singing and
advice from him).

This new company will perform in Philadelphia, not in New York.
In spite of the aging diva's own problems with the Met, she persists
in Met-like behavior when she fires the beautiful young soprano
(Virginia Bruce) Tibbett has fallen in love with because she cannot bear
to be upstaged. The young soprano, it turns out, has a rich father who
salvages the show when her rival pulls the plug on the company. In
spite of the struggles here between young and old or rich and poor,
Metropolitan does not challenge any of the popular assumptions about
opera. The film may bring opera to the masses, with Tibbett singing
not just excerpts but whole arias, but opera still needs money from
the very wealthy to survive – if not the bumbling, stuffed-shirt husband
of the declining diva (a wimp who makes successful businessmen look
like fools), then the unseen father of the young soprano – who hoped
to be taken seriously in spite of her background. Her family may have
indulged her love of singing, but the happy ending belies their probable
reaction to an unpedigreed baritone as son-in-law. Richard Boleslawski's

film may wish to put opera forward as the great class equalizer, but that seems as much an illusion as the plot of an opera.

Tibbett may have been an established opera singer when he made *Metropolitan* but he did not hold opera superstar status, and that allowed him to play the role of the aspiring singer with credibility. Some opera superstars ventured into cinema, with none more prominent than Beniamino Gigli, who also made his first singer-as-opera-star film in 1935. He made *Forget Me Not* simultaneously in three languages (also *Non ti scordar di me* and *Vergiss Mein Nicht*), and his association with Mussolini and fascism did not seem to discourage his English audiences.[2] In fact, films such as this may have been attempts to modify the arrogant and imperious impression that many would have had of this successor to Caruso who refused to return to the Met in 1932 when the Depression required salary cuts.

In *Forget Me Not* (the English version directed by Zoltan Korda) Gigli exudes sweetness and gentility; in spite of being the world's most famous tenor, he wins our affection by playing both father and mother to an adorable little son. He makes an awkward proposal of marriage to a beautiful young fan, who accepts after the disappointments of a recent love affair, and, presumably, because she loves his voice. The title, "Non ti scordar di me," comes from the theme song of the film, which provided the catalyst for her earlier love affair, and awakens the wound when she hears him sing it at concerts. When her former lover reappears in London and tries to persuade her to go to Australia with him, we along with Gigli believe she will go, especially when she realizes his love had been genuine. Gigli returns to his flat dejected, and when his son begs him to sing him to sleep, he does so with such tear-jerking breaks in his voice that he will disarm anyone susceptible to opera. But if we thought his wife would leave him, then we did not have our priorities straight: this film centers on Gigli, not love (in spite of how the film opens), and his wife comes home, entering the bedroom as he finishes singing the tearful lullaby. She, we must believe, prefers the pudgy tenor with the great voice to a dashing young ship's officer.

In the United States opera superstars had an audience for their films, but they could not compete with home-grown American singers, especially with the ones still relatively untainted by the operatic world. Most popular in this respect, in fact, the most successful singing duo ever, were Jeanette MacDonald and Nelson Eddy, known as "America's

Sweethearts," packing people into movie houses as no one else could in the late 1930s. Their *Rose Marie* of 1936, loosely based on the Oscar Hammerstein II operetta, starts with MacDonald in the role of an opera singer, but her later encounter with the Canadian wilderness cures her of that. The film starts with a performance of Gounod's *Romeo and Juliet* in Montreal, with MacDonald in the title role, and considering the popularity of opera in films at this time, it did not concern director W. S. Van Dyke II that these excerpts might put the audience off. In fact, he offers them almost as a hook. MacDonald turns out to be a typical temperamental diva – arrogant, bossy, impetuous, and horrified at the prospect of fresh air from an open window. One wonders how this film played in Quebec at the time, since it seems designed to offend virtually everyone but the Mounties. We not only have an English-speaking premier of the province but one with shades of a British accent (the Quebec premier in 1936 could have been any one of the three francophones Louis Alexandre Taschereau, J. Adélard Godbout or Maurice Duplessis). If French Canadians appear at all, they do so only in the most subservient roles of maids and porters. Even in the north of Quebec French speakers seem nonexistent, and the native people get treatment as bad or worse from Hollywood as African Americans.

Her criminal brother, she learns, has broken out of prison and killed a Mountie, and she leaves with an undependable Métis guide to find him (this guide's accent sound about the same as Chico's of the Marx Brothers). Meeting the singing Mountie in charge of finding her brother, Nelson Eddy, changes her life: now she thrives on the out-doors, rides horses, sleeps in a tent, paddles a canoe, and even enjoys the smell of pipe tobacco (maybe the smoke warded off the blackflies and mosquitoes). Now instead of singing on the opera stage, she croons the "Indian Love Call" with Eddy, and they fall in love singing this legend of native love. Opera, we discover, festers as an unfortunate affliction that turns decent people into monsters, and it takes a good dose of the wilds of the Canadian north to work the cure and human-ize the abusive diva. Real sweethearts must be in tune with nature, and the camp in this case comes directly from camping.

The MacDonald/Eddy duo did not survive the war, but films about opera did, largely because of the popularity of Mario Lanza. Unlike his counterparts from the 1930s, Lanza himself knew little or nothing of the opera world, as he scarcely ever appeared on the opera stage; he made a career as a singing screen actor who popularized opera as no one else did in the 1950s. In his most successful film, the fictional biography *The Great Caruso* (1951), in which the singers Jamila Novotna and Dorothy Kirsten also appear, the old battle between rich and poor continues. The portrayal of Caruso reflects the great tenor's own Italian peasant roots, singing for the enthusiasts in standing room instead of the well-heeled patrons of the golden horseshoe at the Met. One of the Met's most prominent and wealthy patrons takes an immediate dislike to him, and Caruso's marriage proposal to his daughter jars like a declaration of war. Lanza capitalized on the success of this film, with sales of records in the range of 50 million,[3] but he never managed the same level again in a film, and in fact the genre of films about opera more or less died with Lanza in 1959. The type of popularity he achieved would elude most future classical singers, who simply could not compete with the likes of Elvis Presley in the fifties or the Beatles in the sixties. Both the recording industry and Hollywood discovered in the fifties that their most eager market would be the youthful baby boomers whose rebellion included a dislike of opera.

*   *   *

The genre died in the 1950s, but that has not prevented individual films throughout the rest of the 20th century from bringing back the subject of opera. The old formula, though, of placing an opera star in the role of opera singer was doomed to failure, and isolated attempts to bring it back, such as Luciano Pavarotti in *Yes, Giorgio* (1982), celebrating an enlarged ego in hopes that the faithful will rally, have been nothing short of embarrassing. The successful ones do not depend on adulation, and in fact do not star actual opera singers. They may have the voices of notable singers dubbed in for the actor playing a singer, but the basis for success lies in the combination of qualities that make good cinema. North Americans have had a limited appetite for these films, and one of the few to be made in North America, *Under the Piano* (1995) with Teresa Stratas, has not found an audience. Europeans have done much better with these, and one, *Meeting Venus* (1991), produced in Britain but set in Paris and Budapest, will be discussed in chapter 16.

Two others, both from 1994, deserve notice: the Belgian *Farinelli* and the French *Celestial Clockwork*. The latter, by the French based

Venezuelan director Fina Torres, tells a wonderfully engaging story of a bride who bolts from the altar in Caracas and tries her luck as an opera singer in Paris. Surrounded by a delightfully zany assortment of characters that include old friends from Venezuela, a Ukrainian voice teacher who does not consider Italians to be serious about opera, a French psychoanalyst who finds herself attracted to the young singer, a gay Maria Callas fan who marries her to help her beat French immigration law, an African witch doctor, and a frustrated Italian film director mounting a film production of Rossini's *La cenerentola*, she staggers in a Cinderella-like way from one delightful mishap to the next in her quest for the leading role in Rossini's opera. Here the subject deals not with opera on the stage but opera in film, and this visually appealing work gives us a double sense of opera as cinema.

Farinelli attempts something even more experimental, and achieves it with considerable success, finding an audience in North America as well as Europe. Opera this time becomes a subject of historical interest, focusing on one of the superstars of the early 18th century, the castrato Farinelli. The film does not presume to give a historically correct biography, although the screenplay presents various actual details more or less correctly, not unlike the Peter Shaffer/Milos Forman treatment of *Amadeus*. Instead, the plot concerns the fictitious relationship of the singer and his conductor brother, their dealings with the great composer Handel, and the sexual exploits of the two brothers. Fiction also strays into the region of sexual impossibility concerning castrati's virility,[4] a fantasy that Casanova encouraged in the 18th century and Anne Rice, in her 1982 novel *Cry to Heaven*, has indulged much more recently. Since no one really knows what castrati sounded like (the one existing recording of the castrato Alessandro Moreschi from 1902 and 1904 gives a very limited idea), the makers of *Farinelli* digitally fused the voices of countertenor Derek Lee Ragin and soprano Ewa Mallas Godlewska, producing something that sounds fairly gender neutral.[5] The film stands very nicely on its own, but for those interested in the history of opera it provides a valuable service in suggesting that opera singers then resembled pop stars of today and that the world of opera sated itself with sexual energy – with castrati arousing in at least one female listener (a German countess) a "musical orgasm." The power of the singing voice should never be underestimated.

5

SYNESTHESIA:
ALEXANDER NEVSKY AS OPERA

The notion of film director as singer proved to be appealing to directors other than D. W. Griffith. Chapter 2 explored Griffith transferring musical images to the screen, in fact having a distinctly musical sense of particular visual images in order to find the full emotional potential of various gestures, facial expressions, or even larger composite shots and interconnections of shots. Only after conceptualizing the musical/emotional sense, allowing his own passion for singing to come into play, would he then find the appropriate musical accompaniment for the scene, working in collaboration with a composer such as Joseph Carl Breil, designing the musical accompaniment as a surrogate for the inherent music embodied in the visual image. The musical principle at work here was a Wagnerian one, and the resulting union of music and visual images took on an operatic aura based on the Wagnerian principle of *Gesamtkunstwerk*. Griffith became the most influential filmmaker during the early part of the century, and it should not surprise us that this influence would include the way that he conceived of music as an organic part of the process – at least tacitly if not overtly.

Griffith had no admirer more enthusiastic than Sergei Eisenstein, the globetrotting Soviet master of cinema who not only examined Griffith's techniques in detail but also met him on an American sojourn. Not unlike Richard Wagner, who wrote at least as much about music as music itself, Eisenstein could not seem to resist long and detailed pieces on film theory, and one of his substantial essays has the title "Dickens, Griffith, and the Film Today."[1] While Eisenstein appears

57

not to have known the specifics of Griffith's cinematic conception based on music, he indirectly intuited it, as we can tell from the way he describes Griffith's achievements and the association of these elements with music drawn in his other various theoretical essays. Eisenstein may not have been a singer, but he shared Griffith's passion for music, and had a much deeper knowledge and understanding of music than his American idol. Unlike Griffith, who said very little about how music permeates cinema, Eisenstein as theorist went into excruciating detail on it in his essays, and his ideas bear remarkable similarities to Griffith's. Some writers have made a pastime of debunking Eisenstein's theories on musical/visual organicism, especially involving his collaboration with the composer Sergei Prokofiev, but most of these writers have made no attempt to understand the inherent musical conception that precedes the collaboration. The exploration of that conception will bring us back very close to opera, and when put into practice, as in the collaboration of Eisenstein and Prokofiev, we find in a work such as *Alexander Nevsky* the highest achievement of the idea of opera permeating cinema not only in early sound cinema but perhaps in all of cinema.

In his essay on Griffith, Eisenstein gives some very strong hints about his intuitive understanding of Griffith's conception of music. In showing Dickens as a primary influence on Griffith, he notes that "the visual images of Dickens are inseparable from aural images."[2] In transferring this idea to cinema, he notes the place of emotions, emphasizing the formal device of montage as a means of heightening emotions: "Thus the secret of the structure of montage was gradually revealed as a secret of *the structure of emotional speech.* For the very principle of montage, as is the entire individuality of its formation, is the substance of *an exact copy of the language of excited emotional speech.*[3] Montage itself embraces the union of music and picture in what he calls an "audio-visual montage": "For us montage became a means of achieving *a unity of a higher order* – a means *through the montage image of achieving an organic embodiment of a single idea conception, embracing all elements, parts, details of the film-work.*"[4]

In the Griffith article, he takes the musical montage image even further, noting how Griffith as a great master of montage constructions worked with tempo changes and rhythmic variance. For Eisenstein montage was much more than the mere process of film editing; it concerned the means of putting together all cinematic elements, from the smallest details of connection or juxtaposition within a shot to the largest aspects of continuity. At any point treatment of similarity or contrast could come into play, and taking the various aspects of montage as a totality, the working of them allowed the possibility of an organic structure. In his essay "Methods of Montage," he adopts specifically musical metaphors for his breakdown of the various aspects of montage, referring to metric montage, rhythmic montage, tonal montage and overtonal montage. The first two temporal types will not confuse us, as we immediately recognize matters of pace and acceleration as central to cinema. Tonal montage, a term he takes pleasure in using for the first time, will not be as clear, and he explains it as "a stage beyond rhythmic montage." More particularly, while rhythmic montage refers to "movement within the frame that impels the montage movement from frame to frame," in tonal montage "movement is perceived in a wider sense... Here montage is based on the characteristic *emotional sound* of the piece – of its dominant. The general *tone* of the piece."[5] That tone may very well be at odds with the pace, setting up a level of conflict which he also explains musically as counterpoint.

The terms may easily crumble under musical scrutiny, but that sort of analysis misses the point: for Eisenstein the entire process runs parallel to music, and he searched for musical terms to unlock the complexity of this organicism. In fact, he appears to be going even further with this, into the realm of synesthesia – the representation of one type of sensory image by another – a phenomenon he knew and understood well, including his discovery of it in the Kabuki theater's monistic ensemble.[6] Another one of his favorite images underscores this even further, the idea of vertical montage, which he explains with the analogy of a musical score with its several staff lines for individual instruments or instrument groups: "Each part is developed horizontally. But the vertical structure plays no less important a role, interrelating as it does all the elements of the orchestra within each given unit of time." The vertical element defines for him the contrapuntal nature of the work, and "this correspondence, or relationship, could be just as successfully described if, for the image of the orchestral score, we had substituted the montage structure of the silent film."[7]

The orchestral score analogy suggests yet another possibility, one which takes us directly back to Griffith. The term "voice" may be applied to each one of the lines in the score, and the juxtaposing of these voices generates the essence of the work. The separate elements that interact in montage can therefore also be thought of as voices. Here emotions tie in directly, as he noted that "Diderot deduced the theory that compositional *principles* in vocal, and later in instrumental, music derived from the basic intonations of living emotional speech." Still with this idea, he quotes the 19th-century Bach biographer Forkel on Bach's teaching methods: "He considered his voices as if they were persons who conversed together like a select company."[8] Here Eisenstein arrives at the same point that Griffith had, recognizing a principle of vocal definition for characters, one which a singing voice could represent, and one which could imbue a character with emotion.

The process, then, is not one of giving a mostly edited film to a composer and charging that person with the responsibility of coming up with music which could approximate the emotions that the director had in mind. That could not achieve what Eisenstein had in mind, and although most film music comes into being that way, it will not result in what Philip Glass considers to be an organic fusion of music and visual images: that can happen only with the creation of film and music at the same time.[9] In the case of Eisenstein and Griffith before him, the music already had to be present in the cinematic conception, giving the visual images their emotional life, and the music then provided by a composer should be the specific aural realization of this underlying musical force. Griffith had his own ideas what that music should be, and he turned to Breil to help him realize it. Eisenstein too had a deep sense of it, but not being a musician, he could not conceptualize his musical wellspring in actual tones; he required the aid of a composer for that, and to his good fortune he found not only one of the greatest 20th-century composers but one who shared his own primordial musical urges: Sergei Prokofiev.

In the Griffith-Breil collaboration something Wagnerian emerged, both in the approach to leitmotifs in which specific characters or ideas could be identified but also in the process of defining an artwork which extends beyond a single medium or sense. What Griffith began to understand of the Wagnerian principle of *Gesamtkunstwerk* with its fusion into an organic whole of all the disparate elements that make up opera, Eisenstein took it to its highest possible level in cinema. One would expect that in collaboration with a composer of Prokofiev's stature the results would not be strictly of a Wagnerian nature, and while that proved to be the case, with Prokofiev bringing his own high level of musical sophistication, the Wagnerian principle of "organicism" remained central. With Eisenstein's notion of montage as the glue holding every-thing together, it could not be otherwise. Eisenstein's theory of organi-cism went well beyond music and moving images, embracing color as well, and both he and Prokofiev knew the theories and compositions of the turn-of-the-century Russian composer Alexander Scriabin, whose sense of synesthesia worked in the opposite direction – writing music which should project visual images, color, and even smell. In cinema, color and smell could be implied, smell through visual images (such as the rancid meat in *Battleship Potemkin*) and color through both visual and musi-cal means. Eisenstein knew perfectly well that music can suggest colors to many listeners, and he could also exploit this sense of synesthesia.

On various occasions Eisenstein tried to explain the importance of Prokofiev in his organic scheme of things, but here the words generally escaped him as he would lapse into adulation. He could, of course, explain the idea itself, as he does below in moving from silent to sound films, but to place Prokofiev's role in specific terms proved much more difficult:

> Here the "silent" *Potemkin* teaches the sound-film a lesson, emphasiz-ing again and again the position that for an organic work a single law of construction must penetrate it decisively in all its "signifi-cances," and in order to be not "off-stage," but stand as an organic part of the film, the music must also be governed, not only by the same images and themes, but as well by the same basic laws and principles of construction that govern the work as a whole. To a considerable degree I was able to accomplish this in the sound-film proper – in my first sound-film, *Alexander Nevsky*. It was possible to accomplish this, thanks to the collaboration with such a wonderful and brilliant artist as Sergei Prokofiev.[10]

Here we learn what Prokofiev had to contend with, but not what he achieved.

In his essay "P-R-K-F-V," Eisenstein made an attempt to explain what Prokofiev accomplished, although for the usually loquacious the-orist, this stands as one of his shortest essays.[11] Conscious of all Prokofiev's achievements, he sees similarities in aspects of the ballet of *Romeo and Juliet*, the operas *Love for Three Oranges* and *War and Peace*, and the first film the two of them made together, *Alexander Nevsky*. In all of Prokofiev's works, Eisenstein observed a level of understanding comparable to his own definition of montage:

> It is in this particular sense that Prokofiev's music is amazingly plastic. It is never content to remain an illustration, but everywhere, gleaming with triumphant imagery, it wonderfully reveals the inner movement of the phenomenon and its dynamic structure, in which is embodied the emotion and meaning of the event.[12]

This composer could hear the inherent music which lay at the foundation of the creative urge, and could then provide actual music to represent that inner musical conception:

> Having grasped this structural secret of all phenomena, he clothes it in the tonal camera-angles of instrumentation, compelling it to gleam with shifts in timbre, and forces the whole inflexible structure to blossom into the emotional fullness of orchestration.[13]

Here he articulates what Griffith too must have been striving for, but now, with the aid of a musical genius who could think as one with the director, yielding the most satisfying possible collaboration; the two of them reached a level of sophistication that Griffith would have envied.

In describing the nature of the collaboration on *Alexander Nevsky*, Eisenstein emphasized the same facets of Prokofiev's intuitive understanding of the underlying images. No rigid working pattern emerged, as either one could take the lead in conceiving his part first: "There are sequences in which the shots were cut to a previously recorded music-track. There are sequences for which the entire piece of music was written to a final cutting of the picture. There are sequences that contain both approaches."[14] Sometimes Eisenstein had something in mind but could not express it in music and therefore presented the composer with visual images that would suggest his notion:

> One such example occurs in the battle scene where pipes and drums are played for the victorious Russian soldiers. I couldn't find a way to explain to Prokofiev what precise effect should be "seen" in his music for this joyful moment. Seeing that we were getting nowhere, I

ordered some "prop" instruments constructed, shot these being played (without sound) *visually*, and projected the results for Prokofiev – who almost immediately handed me an exact "musical equivalent" to that visual image of pipers and drummers which I had shown him.[15]

Various other examples of this type of interaction occurred, and almost invariably Prokofiev went directly to the heart of Eisenstein's underlying musical image: "Often these fitted so perfectly in the unified 'inner sounding' of the sequence that now they seem 'conceived that way in advance'."[16]

Eisenstein could easily get carried away with his own theoretical rhetoric, and some observers believe he did exactly that in his now famous discussion of the pre-battle twelve-shot montage in *Nevsky*. Here he diagrams the twelve frames with the musical score and moves from these through an illustration of pictorial composition to a graph of movement that shows the audio/visual integration, or in other words the fulfillment of his conception of montage. Hans Eisler and Theodor Adorno object that his diagram accounts not for the music itself but only the written notation, while Roy Prendergast thinks it absurd to expect us to read the shots from left to right since he cannot imagine visual images being grasped in any way other than simultaneously – not in a linear or narrative manner. Others, including Royal S. Brown and David Bordwell, have come to Eisenstein's rescue,[17] although Eisenstein defends himself ably, anticipating the quibbles which might arise. Not only does he anticipate Prendergast's objection, explaining effectively how the eye can move when viewing artworks – and even gives a fine example of it, but he also indirectly answers Eisler/Adorno with his theory of vertical montage in which notation implies something much larger. Still, even the most devoted followers of Eisenstein may wince a little when he says "Hold on there! Isn't it a little far-fetched to match a line of music so exactly to a pictorial representation?" If not at that point, it will be difficult not to at the end of the essay when he quotes Wagner as saying "when you create – you do not explain."[18] After sixty pages of explanation, anyone can be forgiven a glimmer of skepticism.

The quotation of Wagner at this point may be mistimed, but it does remind us that Wagner never stands too far in the background of Eisenstein's organicist view of cinema. Both shortly before and after the making of *Nevsky*, Wagner was very much on Eisenstein's mind, with "A Modern *Götterdämmerung*" – a reworking of the fourth opera of the *Ring* cycle by Ivar Kreuger – as a possible project during 1932, and his engagement to direct *Die Walküre*, also from the *Ring* cycle, at the Bolshoi Opera Theater in Moscow in 1940. Ever the theorist, Eisenstein has given us a detailed account of his thoughts about this latter project, in the article "The Incarnation of Myth" (1940). The pact of non-aggression with Hitler made possible the performance of German works in the USSR, and for Eisenstein directing an opera by Wagner had special significance. Designing the essay (and the performance) for his Soviet audience, he begins by emphasizing Wagner's Marxist qualities – a revulsion toward private property evident in the *Ring* cycle as well as Wagner's involvement in the 1848-49 revolution, and Wagner's view that true art arises from the people (the *Volk*).

Having established his politically correct approach to the production, he gradually steers the discussion to his favorite theme of synthesis or organicism. Fully aware of Wagner's essays such as *Art and Revolution*, *The Artwork of the Future*, and *Opera and Drama* in which Wagner develops his theories of organicism, Eisenstein explores these ideas in Wagner's operas and draws parallels with his own approaches to montage. Inevitably, this gets him to the issue of "inner meaning" in *Die Walküre*, and how his production would capture the sense of the musical wellspring which drives the multi-faceted work: "So here the *mise-en-scène* is purely poetical, or in any case, that is how it should be. And its poetry should be primarily *figurative and musical*, springing from the same ground as the music, the drama in the speeches, the words that are uttered and the eloquence of the phrasing."[19] This embraces the visual elements which should have their own "'plastic leitmotifs,' which intermingle with the leitmotifs of the orchestra."

The origin of the visual elements in opera could work very much as it does in cinema, with the possibility even of "close-ups." The sense of inner meaning, which he sees flowing organically from Wagner's music, brings him directly to the reason for his involvement in the project. "Why did a *film* director *stage* Wagner," he asks, and even more, "what made him actually *leap* at Wagner?" Nothing could be more natural for the filmmaker, who must contend with the same "problem of creating an *internal unity of sound and vision within the spectacle*," and for whom "Wagner's unusually *figurative music* poses with particular acuteness and complexity the question of seeking and finding an appro-priate *visual image*." At the end of the essay, he lays out the answer in no uncertain terms: "there comes a new, beneficial cross-fertilization of film and theatre at the juncture between audio-visual cinema and Wagner's opera, where the independence and difference of both are unchallenged, but where both are used to solve more and more new problems."[20] Eisenstein understood the idea of the *Gesamtkunstwerk* completely, and what he discusses in 1940 about Wagner applies precisely to his work with Prokofiev on *Nevsky* a couple of years earlier.

While the creative conception for *Nevsky* can be seen as adhering to the most deeply held operatic principles of Wagner, the work which resulted can also be described as a piece of cinematic opera. Prokofiev's music plays a major role in defining that operatic essence, but the pos-sibility goes much deeper than that, to the integrated conception which brings together motion, gestures, emotion and music. Some of the most effective scenes are the ones which themselves involve a counterpoint of actions or emotions, where the viewer's response will necessarily be in layers; here Prokofiev works at his best too, building all the layers into his musical counterpoint. Few scenes illustrate this as well as the attack by the German wedge, and Eisenstein took pleasure in describing this scene as a prime example of his conception of montage:

This episode passes through all the shades of an experience of increasing terror, where approaching danger makes the heart contract and the breathing irregular. The structure of the "leaping wedge" in *Alexander Nevsky* is, with variations, exactly modeled on the inner process of such an experience. This dictated all the rhythms of the sequence – cumulative, disjunctive, the speeding up and slowing down of the movement. The boiling pulsing of an excited heart dictated the rhythm of the leaping hoofs: pictorially – the *leap* of the gallop-ing knights; compositionally – the *beat* to the bursting point of an excited heart.[21]

The scene Eisenstein describes begins of course before the attack starts since some of the emotions referred to arise in the anticipation of a battle.

In this pre-battle phase, beginning with the twelve-shot montage just discussed, the menacing advance of the German troops strikes terror into the hearts of even the most seasoned Russian soldiers, and the

Alexander Nevsky (visual counterpoint in the battle scene)

terror increases in the extended anticipation. Eisenstein talks of the inner process on which he modeled this, dictating rhythm and tone, and here, the underlying germination of emotion for the montage has its first stirring as a musical conception. From the visual shots we can sense this, but only with Prokofiev's music do the emotions become absolutely clear. As the Germans advance we hear three separate and simultaneous musical ideas: the first, a chant previously established as the German leitmotif, given by horns and later human voices; the second, a rhythmic ostinato which bends our sense of time, making the wait seem almost endless; and the third, a piercing trumpet figure which laces the anticipation with terror. Before the music stops as the attack begins, we have an excellent example of Prokofiev reading the inner music of the scene and clothing that in actual music, contrapuntal in this case to bring together the components of the complexity of the emotional layering. Other scenes do this admirably as well, such as the massacre at Pskov with the juxtaposition of brutality and pathos accentuated by the alternations of German and Russian leitmotifs.

By the time Prokofiev started collaborating with Eisenstein in 1938, he was already an experienced opera composer, with at least three major operas under his belt: *The Gambler*, *The Love for Three Oranges*, and *The Fiery Angel*. In spite of the difficulties he encountered getting these produced or keeping them in the repertoire, he did not give up on opera, writing *Semyon Kotko* while he worked on *Nevsky* and *War and Peace* shortly thereafter. His operatic experience proved extremely useful in his approach to film scores, and one can see this in the operatic nature of the score to *Nevsky*. Most apparent was his use of the leitmotif which even in his operas took on a more cinematic quality than the way Wagner had conceived the idea. Like other Russian composers Prokofiev claimed to be anti-Wagnerian, but that did not prevent him from using leitmotifs of a melodic nature. In *Nevsky*, Russians and Germans get their own distinctive leitmotifs, suggesting positive nationalistic traits for the Russians and negative religious ones for the Germans — the chant which accompanies the Germans as they pray before battle and when they charge as a wedge into the waiting Russian army.

His use of the human voice also points to his operas, in solo numbers and, especially choruses. Little opportunity exists in a film score for arias, but Prokofiev provides one after the battle as a mezzo soprano offers a lament, achieving through singing a level of pathos to parallel the images of fallen Russian soldiers, and also recognizing valor in requiem-like fashion in a stirring emotional way. Not only the viewer responds to this unseen singer but so do the characters, as the valiant Buslai seems to revive to the sound of her voice. Once again the underlying emotion takes a special musical form, bridging the gap between musical conception and realization by also bridging the divide of the diegetic and nondiegetic (music which can or cannot be identified as arising from a source in the film's narrative). When we hear this lament in purely orchestral form, it remains as moving as in its vocal presentation.

Much of a film score consists of orchestral writing, and here too Prokofiev could draw on his operas. Unlike the more formally self-contained model of the symphony, the orchestral writing in a film comes much closer to the way he had used orchestral excerpts or interludes in his operas – with specific dramatic function. Counterpoint, as in the German wedge scene, could work dramatically instead of in the more formalized manner that counterpoint often appears. The movement back and forth between vocal and instrumental writing, as with the lament, also arises from the exigencies of operatic treatment, and the same applies to his use of the chorus. The chorus plays a prominent role in this film, entering as the first music we hear near the beginning, and sounding at various other strategic points throughout. With the chorus he could not only represent the people but also their sense of national pride and identity and all the emotions associated with these.

In his opera written at the same time, *Semyon Kotko*, one finds a similar use of the chorus, used for a wedding scene in Act 2, musically underpinning the people at a high point in the cycle of life; later he uses the same chorus in the finale to evoke national glorification. Similarly in *War and Peace* a few years later, the apolitical Prokofiev was persuaded to make greater use of the chorus to offer a more politically admissible work and avoid the pitfalls of *The Fiery Angel*, which proved unacceptable to Soviet authorities. The shifting between chorus and orchestra in *Nevsky* played a critical function in Eisenstein's scheme of things too; in his essay on Wagner Eisenstein noted that Wagner "treated the orchestra as an extension of the role played by the chorus of ancient time."[22] With Prokofiev's treatment of chorus and orchestra one could move from ancient times to the present with a sense of national pride. Verdi had set the groundwork for that possibility in the 19th century, using the chorus in his operas such as *Nabucco* and *Macbeth* as the voice of an emerging Italian *Risorgimento* or national awareness.

The treatment of politics and religion in *Alexander Nevsky* may make some viewers in the West uneasy, as it did in the early 1940s. The film came into being to serve the purposes of propaganda, and had to meet with Stalin's strict approval (when Eisenstein inadvertantly omitted a reel in a screening for Stalin, it could not be added later). Anticipating the impending conflict with Germany, Stalin wanted a vehicle to arouse anti-German sentiment, but with the signing of the non-aggression pack with Hitler in 1939, the film had to be mothballed. Viewers from Allied countries could share the anti-German views, but they had much more difficulty putting that in religious terms, as the film appeared to be equating Christianity with belligerent aggression. During the cold war era, the West had problems not only with the religious aspect but the adulation of Soviet society as well. Here perhaps we can learn something from Eisenstein's view of Griffith, in his recognition of Griffith's odious racist ideology:

> Among the most repellent elements in his films (and there are such) we see Griffith as an open apologist for racism, erecting a celluloid monument to the Ku Klux Klan, and joining their attack on Negroes in *The Birth of a Nation*. Nevertheless, nothing can take from Griffith the wreath of one of the genuine masters of the American cinema.[23]

In spite of objectionable aspects of their politics and ideologies, Griffith and Eisenstein stand as two of the great pioneers of cinema, and their accomplishments cannot be ignored. In both cases, an understanding of music – opera in particular – stood at the heart of their achievements.

PART TWO

THE FILM SCORE

$\boxed{6}$

THE LEITMOTIF

In the late 1960s, as an undergraduate with a passion for cinema but in a city with not much of it to offer, I knew some of the film classics – who their directors were – and even the names of a few film composers. My favorite director working in the United States during those years was Alfred Hitchcock, and I knew *The Man Who Knew Too Much*, *Vertigo*, *North by Northwest* and *Psycho* – mainly from late shows on local television. Having seen these films, I had some idea who Bernard Herrmann was, since I had seen his name on the credits of these films as the composer for each one of them. I did not yet know *Citizen Kane*, but it struck me that any composer sought out by Hitchcock for these wonderful films surely must know his craft well. When I saw a poster announcing that Herrmann would be coming to my campus to give a lecture, I eagerly anticipated the event, which certainly fell into that "must attend" category which for me also included the likes of Buckminster Fuller, Allen Ginsberg and Karlheinz Stockhausen. Along with a large and enthusiastic audience I awaited the beginning of this noontime lecture; when an hour passed and he had not yet appeared at the podium, the audience began to thin, and those left behind became increasingly restless. When he did come out at 2:00 p.m., a basically hard-core group of devotees remained; I learned from one of the organizers some time later that, true to form, the irascible Herrmann had managed to get into a squabble with someone, and refused to appear until they resolved the issue to his satisfaction.

This lecture proved something of a watershed for me, although I did not realize that until much later. By performing a very simple experiment on us, Herrmann forced us to consider the role of music in cinema as we had never thought of it before. He played the first three minutes of *Citizen Kane* (a useful choice for me since I did not know the film) twice, once with the soundtrack turned off and then with it on. Before playing either one, he asked us to be aware of how we perceived the film in both cases, in particular, to compare our responses to the two. For the first showing, we watched in silence as the camera gave a series of apparently disjointed images, taking us from beyond the fence of a mansion toward the building, moving inside after the lights go out briefly and eventually to an old-looking Orson Welles who utters the word "Rosebud," expires, and drops a snowy paper-weight which shatters. It seemed a very strange way to open a film, and it made no sense at all.

When we watched it immediately afterwards with the soundtrack, something miraculous happened. Whereas in the first viewing the visual images seemed somewhat tedious in the slowness and disjointedness with which they appeared, with Herrmann's music – strange in the extreme as it starts with bassoons and muted trombones before moving to bass clarinets and contrabassoons[1] – the awareness of pace and frac-tured impression vanished entirely. In fact, one no longer felt conscious of time at all as passing time gave way with the presence of music to *a priori* time – what Igor Stravinsky calls ontological time, a sense of time no longer bound by the limitations of past and future, a type of euphoric capturing of the essence of the present. Similarly, the eye no longer cut the film with the editor as distinct camera shots separating individual images; these breaks in film continuity seemed somehow to disappear, leaving a sense of continuous motion which may not neces-sarily have made sense intellectually but did cinematically. The eye had drastically increased its capacity to comprehend images and put them together in a progression because of the working of the ear, as the camera motion from outside the fence to the mansion with its pecu-liar trappings to the person inhabiting the mansion no longer seemed so strange.

What qualities of the music allowed these various changes in per-ception to occur? Herrmann himself explained little or nothing of this. On the one hand, he had little stomach for exegesis, but on the other, by saying little about it he inadvertently played the best possible role as teacher, allowing those with the inclination to do so the enjoyment of discovering the answers for themselves. Those of us inclined toward music could recognize a motivic quality of the music which, through the techniques of repetition and variation, could bend the viewers' sense of the perception of time. Some viewers even vaguely intuited something else in the music, a thematic quality with one idea distinctive to the first segment which ends when the lights go out, and a second idea accompanying the scene inside the house (in fact, anticipated just before the lights go out). When I finally got to know *Citizen Kane*, I realized, of course, that these two distinct themes at the beginning represent the two most important dramatic forces of the film – the two contradictory sides that make up Kane himself, on the one hand his quest for power and control and on the other the sense of simplicity and humanity he has lost because of that. In fact, if we can remember the second of these themes throughout the film, we would be able, unlike the reporters pursuing their angle on Kane's last uttered word, to place at a fairly early stage in the film the identification of Rosebud.

The technique used by Herrmann here, and by a host of other film composers from the beginning of sound films to the present, is perhaps the most striking appropriation of an operatic device into cinema. When musical themes represent a person, an object, an event, a personal quality, or perhaps even an emotion, they have become leitmotifs, or literally leading motifs, a musical procedure applied by Wagner and defined by his distinctive usage of it. Wagner used musical motifs among other things to represent persons, objects such the sword or gold, and emotions such as desire or longing; fortunately, he never revealed the specific identity of any of these, but left it to others to do this by making the associations. No exact science exists in this procedure, as the music itself does not necessarily have any inherent qualities or associations that would suggest the connection, and different critics may very well disagree on some of the associations. Once an association has been established, Wagner can bring it back in many different ways, including times when the object or person does not appear in the libretto, thereby allowing a type of psychological reminder in the absence of the object or person.

One should also be clear that Wagner's treatment of leitmotif within his distinctive musical language bears little similarity to the way most film composers use it; in Wagner's operas these motifs appear within a highly complex musical language with an intricate sense of structure, and a forward-pressing development of chromaticism – in extended and continuous musical flowings that can last in some cases from half an hour to a full hour, or perhaps even longer. In film music that type of form or continuity does not exist, as ten minutes would be an unusually long segment; most last no more than a few minutes. In that sense film music does something very different from opera, and when I refer at times in these pages to music as operatic, that primary difference should be kept in mind. The comparison here suggests the borrowing of a technique, not the appropriation of a musical language. That borrowing has proved widespread in the extreme; even someone like Herrmann, who claimed not to have much use for it, applied it consistently in his own film scores. Similarly, numerous recent film composers, who seem separated from Wagner or the composers of the golden age of American film who especially championed the Wagnerian leitmotif by what young viewers might perceive as cinematic light years, continue to use the technique.

The use of leitmotifs in cinema operates on a decidedly simpler level than in Wagner's operas, mainly because of the nature of the film score.[2] While Wagner aimed at something of mythic proportions in his use of the leitmotif, using it for much more than the mere representation of persons or emotions in the context of his complex musical language, film composers have generally been satisfied with more modest objectives. In part that modesty has been predetermined by the working conditions in which film composers find themselves, usually allowed no more than about six weeks to compose the score after most of the film editing has been completed. Considering these time limitations, if anything, we can marvel at the quality of some of the scores that emerge. In a few weeks we should not expect musical masterpieces; even the most prolific opera composers need about a year to write a single work, while others like Alban Berg needed something closer to five years. When Arnold Schoenberg discussed writing a film score with MGM vice-president Irving G. Thalberg, his demand for a year to write it and full artistic control struck the industry as laughable.[3] Schoenberg knew well from experience what went into creating an opera, where the composer holds the upper hand in any type of collaboration. In the making of films, the composer holds no such position of centrality.

In the American film industry, with some luck a composer might get to discuss the film with the director, hearing the director's views of what the music should accomplish. In many cases the director would not waste his time on that, simply expecting the composer to go about his job and provide what the studio hired him to produce. In European art films different conditions often prevail, with a genuine collaboration between director and composer, some of the finest examples being those of Eisenstein/Prokofiev or Fellini/Rota. That, of course, can happen in the United States as well, although some of the best examples involve European-born directors such as Otto Preminger, Michael Curtiz or Alfred Hitchcock.

In spite of the often haphazard ways in which films fall together, everyone in the American industry from the top studio bosses through the directors to the actors recognized that music played a crucial role. Especially during the late 1930s and 1940s, when major studios cranked out on average of a picture a week, and many of those on B budgets, the results could be very uneven, often leaving the composer in a position of rescuing the credibility of a film that might have little else to recommend it. In an era when producers hired and fired directors with shooting in progress, or new writers came on to revise scripts already left convoluted by previous writers, it should come as no surprise that rescue often proved essential. The expectation, though, was not to create a musical masterpiece, something that might stand musically in its own right, but to do such things as gloss over incompetent dialogue, provide emotional depth absent from the script or acting, sustain a sense of direction, provide intelligibility where it may not otherwise exist, offer realism where the visual images might otherwise seem absurd, or simply leave something memorable for the viewer. These were tall orders for hapless composers, and remarkably they often turned potential bombs into viable films. Not only could most composers transform films in these ways, but they could also sense the deepest dramatic or emotional potential of a film and enhance that with the score; that enhancement, often not expected and frequently not grasped by studio brass, more often than not involved the use of leitmotif.

No composer distinguished himself more in early sound cinema in this respect than Max Steiner. Born in 1888 in Vienna, he emerged quickly as a musical prodigy, breezing through his music training, studying with Gustav Mahler, and holding his first professional conducting position at the age of 16. He emigrated to the U.S. in 1914; had he stayed (or been able to stay) in Europe, he might have become a leading composer of Viennese musical theater – or perhaps even operetta or opera. In 1929, with the advent of sound in cinema, he sensed an opportunity, and moved to Hollywood. With some early films like *Rio Rita* (1929), *Dixiana* (1930), *Cimarron* (1931), *Symphony of Six Million* and *A Bill of Divorcement* (1932), he discovered this entirely new possible means of existence for a composer. In 1933, he went from journeyman to the leader of the pack of film composers with his score for *King Kong*, directed by Merian C. Cooper. Here, in fact, teetered a classic potential-for-disaster-in-the-box-office film, with Willis O'Brien's beasties, the products of hopelessly primitive design and integration techniques, running the risk of offering little but inadvertent mirth. In a later era, one could imagine Woody Allen picking up the discarded reels, as he did with *What's Up Tiger Lily?* in 1966, and redubbing the film as a joke. In fact, without Steiner's music, the film would have been that without the slightest amount of anarchistic intervention.

Since O'Brien's prehistoric monsters offered nothing that could be mistaken for realism, the producers hoped that Steiner could do something about that with the music. A major problem faced Steiner: he had to generate fear in viewers instead of laughter when a cardboard cut-out-looking dinosaur threatened to squash the humans or overturn their raft. Steiner put himself on the map by actually succeeding. In achieving this, opera came readily to mind to him; in notes to his orchestrator Bernard Kaun he instructs such things as "this should sound like the 'Miserere' in *Trovatore*," or "do this like the dragon" (probably Fafner in *Siegfried*).[4] Instilling fear at the presence of Kong required music of simplicity and effectiveness, and Steiner found exactly the right blend. A simple three-note motive, which could be varied depending on the situation, proved extremely effective; John Williams understood this principle well when he chose a two-note motif for the shark in Steven Spielberg's *Jaws*. Aside from simplicity, it needed to be in a low register, sound chromatic rather than tonal to provide a chilling edge (and allow for easier variation), and use orchestration to reinforce strength, a lumbering quality, and the evocation of sinister forces.

In the extensive musical score, almost continuous from the foggy arrival at Skull Island, Steiner all but tells the story in music. If someone climbs a wall or a tree, the music goes up; if someone falls from a log, scale figures descend rapidly. Another technique, though, proves even more effective than this type of mickey-mousing, taking the viewer beyond these superficial actions into the heart of the drama, and that involves Steiner's use of Wagnerian leitmotif. With the gestural limitations of the beast, the audience could hardly be expected to recognize that Kong developed a crush on his beautiful captive, and we must depend on Steiner to clarify the presence of these emotions. Christopher Palmer gets it right with his description:

> [when] Kong falls to his death from the Empire State Building after depositing Fay Wray in a place of safety – the Kong theme and the Fay Wray theme (which in its pristine state is a pretty waltz melody with more than a suspicion of *fin-de-siècle* Vienna) actually converge and become one, thus usually underlining the explicitly-stated parallel between the story of King Kong and Ann Darrow and the old fairy-tale of Beauty and the Beast.... In these last moments, the music becomes almost operatic in character as it picks up the speech-rhythm of the last line of dialogue: "Beauty killed the Beast".[5]

This compassion of the beast for beauty, fused in a final musical moment, brings us to the heart of the drama, arriving there by way of the use of leitmotif. Without that fusion, *King Kong* would be little but an adventure movie about a large, freakish creature – hardly the classic it has become, imitated by the likes of Spielberg in *The Lost World*.

The instances of similar uses of leitmotif in cinema, where motifs not only identify characters, objects or ideas but actually reveal the essence of the drama, are far too abundant to enumerate, so a few special examples will be singled out. While Max Steiner initially set the standard for Hollywood composers, Erich Wolfgang Korngold, also a child prodigy musician who spent much of his youth in Vienna (although born in Brno, Czechoslovakia), took the use of leitmotif in cinema as far as it could possibly go. We see this in his scores for the swashbuckling films directed by fellow emigré Michael Curtiz, such as *Captain Blood* (1935) and *The Adventures of Robin Hood* (1938), but nowhere more than in *The Sea Hawk* (1940), again directed by Curtiz and starring Errol Flynn. In *The Sea Hawk*, he devises a leitmotif for almost everything one can think of – for the lead characters, the love between Thorpe (Flynn) and Doña Maria (Brenda Marshall), the Spanish ship, the Sea Hawk, and even the monkey Thorpe gives as a gift to Queen Elizabeth.

Few films have ever been given such an overwhelming musical score, as it hits us forcefully during the opening titles, shifts from leitmotif to leitmotif rapidly as the people or things they represent appear on screen, and offers lots of rhythmic or pitch coordination with screen action (such as a descending scale accompanying an object thrown into the water); even Korngold's name appears with unusual prominence in the titles, coming directly before Curtiz's. In one notable scene, beginning with Doña Maria and her attendant Martha picking roses in a royal garden followed by Thorpe's arrival and conversation with Doña Maria, Korngold, in a space of three minutes and forty seconds, alternates among the leitmotifs as many as fourteen times, sometimes holding a particular one for no more than one or two seconds.[6] Instead of playing together they occur sequentially, but the quick alternations provide a musical palate that blends different leitmotifs together almost as one. No film composer approached his art in such an overtly Wagnerian way as Korngold, and for later composers who would return to the technique, such as John Williams in the *Star Wars* trilogy, he provided the ultimate model.

Steiner and Korngold could have built their compositional reputations outside of cinema, and Korngold in part did. One of their contemporaries, Aaron Copland, perhaps the leading composer in the U.S. at the time, scored several films amid his other well-known pieces such as *Appalachian Spring*, *Billy the Kid*, and *Rodeo*. One of these films, *The Heiress* (1949), brought him an Academy Award, although it rankled him that director William Wyler had deleted his score from most of the titles, replacing it with an arrangement of "Plaisir d'amour" (Copland's music strategically returns at the point the composer's name appears in the credits). While this in almost all respects is an excellent film, based on Henry James's *Washington Square* with the leading roles played superbly by Olivia de Havilland (who also won an Academy Award) as the unworldly daughter, Ralph Richardson as her overbearing and morally severe father, and Montgomery Cliff as her ne'er-do-well suitor, it had one or two weak spots which needed to be rescued by the music. In one of these, Catherine plans to elope with her lover and waits with her aunt for the sounds of horse and carriage. On hearing this she proudly bids her aunt farewell and rushes into the street, only to discover a passing carriage. Wyler left this scene unscored, and at a preview the audience laughed.[7] Laughter here would destroy the entire film, so Wyler asked Copland for music; Copland gave him something dissonant and jarring, and every subsequent audience has shared Catherine's distress here.

In this lengthy waiting scene, music plays a crucial role in taking us with Catherine from her highest elation at the prospect of escaping her father to the depths of dejection when her lover fails to come for her. After this grim moment of realization we see her climbing the staircase to her room. In previous scenes she had literally bounced up these stairs, with music associated with her high spirits. Now she can barely drag herself up, and the music used, in a brilliant shift, belongs to her father. We may think of this as a bitterly ironic commentary, confirming her father's rightness in not trusting Morris, but in fact it cuts much deeper. Instead of being entirely crushed, Catherine has undergone a strange metamorphosis as she subsequently goes about her business having developed a cruel streak. She can now stand up to her father, returning his insults with equally sharp invective of her own, and when Morris returns near the conclusion she not only rejects him but wrings out her revenge by getting his hopes up first. Catherine, in fact, becomes her father, assuming the unpleasant aspects of his personality, and Copland's leitmotivic substitution as she climbs the stairs first alerts us to that possibility.

Aside from revealing the deeper level of the drama as in *King Kong* or *The Heiress*, leitmotifs may also be used to help decipher an especially complex set of dramatic relationships, as happens in Roland Joffé's *The Mission*, with music by Ennio Morricone. Sorting out the various levels of conflict in this film can be challenging to some viewers, and when these layers of conflict all converge toward the conclusion, Morricone's leitmotifs make it much easier to bring them together. Aside from the dramatic role of the music, the distinctive character of some of the themes made this a highly attractive and even influential score. The action takes place in central South America in the middle of the 18th century, and involves the self-interests of various European countries, powers and factions, their agents in South America, as well as the native Guarani. Portugal and Spain control the territories, and the Jesuits seek to convert and educate the Guarani. Since the Europeans capture the natives as slaves – the Portuguese openly and the Spanish clandestinely – the Guarani initially extend hostility to all Europeans. That changes when the Jesuit priest Father Gabriel (Jeremy Irons) breaks the ice (enchanting them with his oboe playing), wins their confidence, and establishes a mission which offers them protection.

The tangle of European forces becomes more complicated when the Roman Catholic Church enters the picture, faced with pressure at home to dissolve the Jesuit order or lose its political influence in all the southern European countries. The Vatican will not allow that to happen, and the option of disbanding missions in the new world does not seem too high a price to pay. The Jesuit priests, having established the mission at great personal cost and with a flock that trusts them implicitly, must decide between their vow of obedience to higher church authorities or to stay and defend the people they have rescued from other forms of European brutality. To complicate matters further, one of the novice brothers (played by Robert DeNiro) has only recently been a slave hunter/trader, and he remains fiercely loyal to the Guarani responsible for his own redemption, ready to return to the sword to do so.

Morricone uses a number of motifs to represent different forces in the conflict or alliances among them. When we first see the Guarani's hostility to all Europeans by sending an unfortunate priest over a massive waterfall strapped to a cross, we hear gentle percussion and pan-pipe-like sounds with a distinctly primitive beat. Father Gabriel wins the Guarani over by playing the oboe, and that oboe motif remains associated with the bonding of Jesuits and Guarani and the idea of the mission as a place of protection. Later we hear a choral chant with a distinctive rhythm and meter, not unlike passages from Carl Orff's *Carmina Burana*;[8] while connected to the Guarani, it still suggests an element of fusion, primitive people now living in a westernized mode.

At other times some Guarani sing a motet, an "Ave Maria," now revealing complete subscription to the Western/Christian influences. When put to the test, this group will not respond to violence with violence, but submissively will put their faith in a Christian god. Others, represented by the Orff-like chant, will do whatever proves necessary to defend themselves, including reverting to their primitive modes of warfare. With conflict on the verge of breaking out, trumpet calls or fanfares accompany the advancing European forces. As the battle unfolds, some Jesuits stay loyal to the Vatican (which has sold out to political interests) while others take up weapons against the defenders of the interests of the Vatican, Spain and Portugal, the slave traders and plantation owners who use slaves (all of whom now merge as one force). Some of the Guarani put their hands in the fate of a god whose followers have abandoned them, while others revert to their past ways and fight to the end. In the end, the Europeans slaughter all the Jesuits and Guarani, and only a few naked children survive. They have lost everything, including their primitive traditions, and only a stark, menacing drum beat remains.

With Morricone's leitmotifs interacting during the battle, the complexity of the forces in conflict gives way to an intelligibility that may otherwise be impossible. The use of leitmotifs to identify the forces in battle was of course not new; Sergei Prokofiev had used this brilliantly in *Alexander Nevsky* (1938), William Walton did the same in Lawrence Olivier's *Henry V* (imitating Prokofiev's score), we hear it in the various sea battles in *The Sea Hawk*, and John Williams uses it in virtually all battle scenes from the *Star Wars* trilogy, notably in the ice battle from *The Empire Strikes Back*, itself modeled in some ways on the ice battle from *Nevsky*. All of these owe a debt to Wagner's battle scenes, especially those in the *Ring* cycle, such as Siegmund's fight with Hunding – with Brünnhilde attempting to aid Siegmund and Wotan preventing her in *Die Walküre*, or Siegfried tangling with the dragon (alias the giant Fafner) in *Siegfried*. In each case in the films referred to, the battle scenes in a sense become operatic.

Leitmotifs may be originally composed themes which come to be linked with a person or object purely by association, or they may invoke some previously known association, adding yet another dimension or layer to the associations. In *The Mission*, the "Ave Maria" motet takes on that aspect of the latter, establishing the tie with a well-known Christian-liturgical tradition. A more complex one occurs in *Citizen Kane*, in the first leitmotif heard at the beginning and its numerous subsequent appearances. This stands as the power motif, the unpleasant side of Kane's character which eventually pushes him into isolation from the rest of humanity in his mausoleum-like mansion. Into this motif Herrmann has worked in a brief passage of the *Dies Irae* plainchant, enough of it not to escape notice,[9] the song of the dead in traditional liturgy, quoted at one time or another by most major 19th-century composers, such as Berlioz in Part 5 of the *Symphonie fantastique*. By adding a known death association, Herrmann predetermines an important aspect of the way we will perceive Kane's power.

Even with the absence of established musical associations, composers will generally build some type of musical features into a leitmotif which will in some way be suggestive of the object of representation, especially in the case of emotions. That can be accomplished through other types of musical associations, such as vague resemblances between Darth Vader's theme in *Star Wars* or the love theme for Prince Leia and Han Solo and well-known classical pieces (see chapter 17). Or there may not necessarily be any association, in which case the music will be denotative purely on the basis of how the composer musically conceives an idea and some sort of shared sense of language which will prompt a viewer to respond in a similar way. A number of fairly straightforward factors may come into play here. By using high or low notes, ascending or descending scale patterns, major or minor modes, consonant or dissonant material, fast or slow tempos, rhythms suggestive of dances or other types of movement, and specific instruments or groups of instruments, certain effects can be achieved. Wagner himself operated very much on this basis: in some cases he would borrow his motives from known material, such as the "Dresden Amen," or in others he would simply use the characteristics that emerge from the music itself, such as a rising passage to denote desire at the beginning of *Tristan und Isolde*. In the persistent use of leitmotif in cinematic music, film composers offer us something akin to opera, achieving an operatic effect, without the music actually functioning as it does in opera.

$$\boxed{7}$$

TITLES MUSIC AS OPERATIC OVERTURE

Not all films show the titles and main credits (hereafter simply referred to as titles) at the beginning, and in some rare cases, such as *Alexander Nevsky*, the first few minutes completely lack music. For most films, though, the titles music plays an extremely important role, functioning very much like the overture to an opera in the way it prepares the audience for what will follow. The title itself generally does not tell us if the film will be comic, serious, melodramatic, ironic, a fantasy, a tear jerker, a horror film (here we may know from the title), a film noir, or an adventure. Usually before getting very far into the titles music that question will be answered. The nature of titles music has changed significantly in recent decades, especially in American cinema, and even more particularly for films in the running for Academy Awards. Unlike the scores written by film composers until the late 1960s or early 1970s where the titles music often formed an integrated unit with the rest of the score, more recent filmmakers have been obsessed with the insertion of songs by popular recording musicians during the titles, songs which may themselves win an Academy Award, will sell in their own right, and will certainly help to sell the picture. Occasionally these songs still serve the more traditional function of preparing the audience, but in far too many cases the only connection one can find lies in the accountant's ledger.

The term "overture" may imply a self-contained piece of music which can be detached from an opera and played as a symphonic overture at a symphonic concert. With some that may be possible, but the instrumental music at the beginning of an opera may segue directly into the first vocal number or segment, or may proceed directly without any transition or break, suggesting "prelude" or "introduction" as a more appropriate term. Operas that lack this type of introduction, over the entire history of the genre from the end of the 16th century to the present, are relatively rare. Until late in the 18th century composers usually provided some type of sinfonia as an overture, a fairly detachable piece of orchestral music in a three-part fast-slow-fast format that bore little or no musical resemblance to the rest of the opera, and served the primary function of settling down the audience before the main part of the opera began. The 18th century in fact looked at instrumental music as vastly inferior to vocal music,[1] and one should therefore not be too surprised by this modest purpose for the sinfonia/overture.

That began to change in the last few decades of the 18th century when certain notable composers recognized a more valuable and sophisticated role that instrumental music could play in the dramatic working of opera. Christoph Willibald von Gluck, the finest composer of opera in the 1760s and 1770s, took the lead in this, taking the unprecedented step of integrating the overture music with the rest of the opera in his *Iphigenia in Tauris*. Gluck and some of his better contempories, including Handel before him, also recognized that the overture could do much more than quiet a restless audience, which earlier in the century, especially in Italy, would have kept chattering throughout the entire opera.[2] Perhaps it is no coincidence that many of the great Italian opera composers, librettists and singers finished their careers in Vienna or London where audiences were more inclined actually to listen. Handel, Gluck, and most remarkably Mozart, increasingly treated the overture as an introduction to the opera itself, if not thematically connected at least offering a musical suggestion of the spirit of the opera to follow.

Mozart quickly took this possibility to new heights in his operas, not only in his mature Viennese operas but in earlier ones as well. Two examples can suffice. In *The Marriage of Figaro*, based on Beaumarchais's controversial play of the same name but relatively unknown to Viennese audiences because of Austrian censorship, the overture immediately catches the spirit of what will follow. A light, rapid, pulsating opening invokes the comedy and intrigues of the libretto. But unlike Beaumarchais's play, in which the Countess can forgive her husband's sexual indiscretion in the spirit of comedy, Mozart and his librettist Lorenzo da Ponte do not let him off the hook so easily. We take Mozart's Countess more seriously because of her musical identity, established in "Porgi amor, qualche ristoro" (a cavatina at the beginning of Act 2), our first exposure to her, and at the end of the work her words of forgiveness seem tinged with the same element of musical regret – a recognition that at the next opportunity the count will probably act the same way.[3] Integrated into the middle of the overture Mozart gives a somewhat chromatic passage that temporarily breaks the cheerful mood, pointing to the dark cloud that will emerge. In *Don Giovanni* Mozart goes even further, beginning the overture with the same music used for the Commendatore when his statue makes its menacing appearance late in the opera and oversees Giovanni's descent into hell. But lest we should imagine the work to be a tragedy, Mozart gives a much brighter second section to the overture, preparing us not only for a work laced with comedy but irony as well, in that the last laugh in this work appears to be on the moralists.[4]

With *Don Giovanni* the overture became an art form in its own right, and subsequent composers struggled with the definition of its function. No one did this more than Ludwig van Beethoven, the symphonist *par excellence*, who wrote no less than four overtures for his one opera *Fidelio*.[5] One of these attempts, well known to concert audiences as *Leonore* no. 3, took the principal musical themes from the opera and fused them into a highly dramatic symphonic realization. Even Beethoven realized he had given away too much; in this case the overture virtually told the whole story in orchestral music, and ran the risk of giving away too much of the drama before the opera begins. The overture he ultimately used took a very different tack, giving the audience more of a rousing curtain raiser without letting the cat completely out of the bag. This, however, did not prevent a contemporary, Carl Maria von Weber, from presenting an overture closer to a musical précis in his *Der Freischütz*.

Richard Wagner, as one might suspect, took the issue of the role of the overture very seriously, and carefully considered what Gluck, Mozart, Beethoven and Weber had done before him. Very conscious of the mistake Beethoven had made with *Leonore* no. 3 and Weber's stumbling (or so Wagner thought) into the same trap, Wagner saw *Don Giovanni* as the ideal, combining a limited amount of thematic connection to the remainder of the opera with something that anticipated the drama and sentiment.[6] In *Tannhäuser*, the prelude gives the two main forces in conflict – the religious music of the pilgrims' chorus in contrast to the erotically sensuous outpouring of the love goddess Venus. In later operas the prelude could play a different type of dramatic role by making us aware of certain things necessary to know before the action ensues. That can be accomplished by a type of musical representation in which the nature of the music suggests actions or events, as happens in *Lohengrin*. Here the music of the prelude represents the descent of Lohengrin, a knight of the holy grail, to earth and then his ascent back to his lofty home.

With *Tristan und Isolde*, Wagner demands of the listener something even more complex with the overture, depending in part on our knowledge of the legend itself. The opera begins with Tristan bringing Isolde back to England from Ireland to be the bride of King Mark, but to understand what unfolds we must know something of the prior relationship of Tristan and Isolde. He had slain her fiancé in battle, but having suffered a near fatal wound in the process, went to her for the benefit of her mysterious healing powers. She discovers that he caused her bereavement, and would take the knife to him but for a potent look from him which completely disarms her. That sets up the balance for the ensuing fusion of love and death, and the overture itself offers the essence of these earlier events and the emotions underlying them. The look becomes one of the leitmotifs of the prelude, along with others for sorrow, desire and death.

Opera, like cinema, often takes its material from well-known sources such as novels or plays, and in turning that into something distinctively different than the original author had in mind, it may be left to the overture to ask the audience to wipe the slate clean and adjust to the new approach. Giuseppe Verdi does this in his *Macbeth*, which concerns itself only marginally with the tragedy of Macbeth, focusing instead on the pathos of Lady Macbeth and the presence of the witches.[7] Instead of only three witches, why not a whole chorus? Instead of relegating Lady Macbeth's sleepwalking scene to a small episode in the penultimate act, why not make it the climax of the entire work? To prepare us for these changes, Verdi focuses in his prelude on the witches' music and the music of the sleepwalking scene.

An even more striking revision of this kind occurs in Peter Ilyich Tchaikovsky's *Eugene Onegin*, a work light years removed from the tone of its literary source – Alexander Pushkin's verse novel. The ironic tone of Pushkin's narrator allows us to chuckle near the beginning at the death of an uncle who does not expire soon enough for a bored nephew; at a pompous poet, Lensky, who poetically inclines himself toward German verse and whose premature death may have rescued him from becoming tedious; at an overwrought adolescent girl, Tatyana, who confuses epistolary passion with reality; and at a story which ends unceremoniously at a high point of tension with these disarming lines:

> Whatever in this rough confection
> you sought – tumultuous recollection,
> a rest from toil and all its aches,
> or just grammatical mistakes,
> a vivid brush, a witty rattle –
> God grant that from this little book
> for heart's delight, or fun, you took,
> for dreams, or journalistic battle,
> God grant you took at least a grain.
> On this we'll part; goodbye again![8]

Tchaikovsky's score gives not the slightest shred of irony, as he takes the characters and the story itself seriously; the music of the opera becomes his narrator, and that narration will not allow us to laugh at Tatyana, Lensky or anyone else.[9] It also shows us Tatyana as a much more important character than Onegin. From the opening chords of the prelude, Tchaikovsky makes the nature of his musical narration clear: the rich, warm sounds with extended descending sequential passages with a touch of chromaticism leave no option of irony. He gives us something tender and serious; his musical embodiment of Tatyana, and her aura, unlike in Pushkin, touches and transforms the world around her. The viewer could leave after this short prelude, and know the essential nature of the leading character as well as how events will unfold.

Music served a similar function for cinema from the earliest stages of the medium, although with silent films, with the music provided by orchestras, Wurlitzer organs or pianos, the results could be erratic if the musical decisions fell under the control of local theater musicians.[10] With the invention of the vitaphone, a method for synchronizing recorded sound and film (first used in *Don Juan*, 1926), that changed as music henceforth became an integral part of the film. The future of the vitaphone proved to be short-lived, but the more sophisticated sound system which immediately followed, allowing speech as well as music, continued the musical application which the vitaphone made possible. Already with the score written by William Axt and David Mendoza for *Don Juan* and performed by the New York Philharmonic, one gets a sense of the possibilities of the titles music for setting the tone of the picture. In the next few years, as scoring a film became a more exact science and the music took on a greater role in the emotional support or narrative of films, the titles music soon came to be much more directly involved in preparing the viewer for the film.

Just as Max Steiner and Erich Wolfgang Korngold led the way in introducing operatic music into films by fine-tuning the use of the leit-motif, the same proved true in their presentation of titles music functioning as an operatic overture. John Ford's 1935 film *The Informer*, scored by Steiner, offers a useful example. This low budget film, with cardboard cut-outs of Dublin buildings thrown together in a studio shed, may not have attracted much attention had it not been for Steiner's music, which captured an Academy Award. Set in an embattled pre-revolution Ireland, a large but not too bright lad, Gypo, juggles his loyalty to the cause of Irish independence with his desire to find some money to sail to America and make a better life with his girlfriend. A poster advertising passage to America and another offering a £20 reward for information leading to the arrest of a friend on the lam prove too much for his feeble mind, and he yields to the temptation. Amid a gloomy atmosphere of poverty, rebellion and drink he not only betrays the cause he had been loyal to but squanders the reward money in taverns and brothels. No one doubts that he will have to pay for his sins, in all probability with his life, and Steiner's gloomy – almost morbid – titles music leaves no question at the beginning that this film will not have a happy ending. Gypo has a gimpy leg, and during the titles we see him lumbering along, with music that rhythmically picks up on his limp.[11] Interspersed with the heavy, plodding music associated with Gypo, we occasionally hear some military drums, bringing in the British occupiers to whom Gypo will sell out his friend. This type of musical introduction proved useful to the deluge of film noir presentations that would come just a few years latter; Miklós Rózsa, a Hungarian émigré, would use similar dark, foreboding and plodding music synchronized with the steps of a man in silhouette on crutches in his score for *Double Indemnity* (1944).

By the time Steiner wrote the music for *Casablanca* in 1942 he had years of experience as a film composer, with over thirty scores to his credit. His reworking of Herman Hupfeld's "As Time Goes By" into a centerpiece for the film has, of course, become a cinematic icon. The titles music seems almost designed to put us off the track, unlike his earlier film such as *The Informer*, but in a peculiar way it tells us much about one of the strangest films ever made. After the Warner Brothers logo music, we first hear drums with a Hollywood-African beat, followed by orchestral sounds that pick up on a presumed North African association. One may find that logical enough for a film set in Morocco, except that this film happens to be about the lives of Europeans and Americans. The geographic nature of the music might induce the listener to think of the recently released and popular *Road to Morocco*, and certainly to anticipate some sort of North African adventure film. While there may be adventure here, this is no action thriller. When the *Marseillaise* makes a brash entry, coordinated with the appearance of Steiner's name in the credits, we now think of patriotism, and will probably be confused about the type of film to expect. The confusion increases with the pensive sounds that greet Michael Curtiz's name at the end of the titles.

The film itself, as Umberto Eco has shown with wit, may have gained its cult status at least in part by avoiding a single story archetype, instead throwing in almost every imaginable archetype – over two dozen, in fact, in Eco's own list.[12] The titles music gives us two of these, African adventure and patriotic movie. Very quickly one can add archetypes, as Eco does, to the list: newsreel, odyssey of refugees, international intrigue, magic key to the promised land, the purgatorial test, the Nazi barbarians, the Kasbah, war propaganda movie, the magic horse (airplane), the disenchanted lover, the charming scoundrels, roulette as the game of life and death, the uncontaminated hero and femme fatale, the faithful servant and master (Don Quixote and Sancho Panza), flashback as form, and even more. While the opening music may not give us strong narrative clues about the film, in fact it brilliantly captures the scattered disarray of the multiple archetypes, and in the end, tells us something more important than anything related to the story – which no one, including Curtiz, knew how it would end until writers Julius and Philip Epstein patched it together just before the shooting of the final scenes.

With *Mildred Pierce* (1945), Steiner returned to a more traditional treatment of the titles music. Here he uses what we will soon recognize as Mildred's theme, and the nature of the melody, its harmonization, and the orchestration all let us know that this will be a serious if not melodramatic film. In fact, the somewhat lugubrious tone of this music already seems to undermine Mildred's attempts at gaining independence. Mildred divorces her husband and soon finds startling success in the restaurant business, but in a spirit of misogynistic moralizing, this film tells us she has overstepped her bounds.[13] Not only does the business collapse but she utterly fails as a mother as well, with one daughter dying because of her apparent neglect (her ex-husband must deal with the crisis), and her other daughter so spoiled and depraved that her condition can only reflect in the worst possible way on Mildred's disastrous mothering skills. The narrative implies that only the strong hand of a male authority figure can correct these shortcomings in business and home life, and the sight of Mildred leaving the police station with her ex-husband at the end to triumphant music reinforces a patriarchal vision. In such a scheme of things, with all the political implications of the war years when women kept industry running, the Mildred theme cannot admit any buoyant music, and the titles music therefore already suggests from the beginning that she cannot succeed on her own.

Just as Korngold went the extra step in his operatic approach to the leitmotif, he did the same with his titles music, transforming some of these into genuine operatic overtures both in terms of preparation for the film and even in the treatment of musical form. In *The Sea Hawk* he offers the ideal example of this.[14] The film has two main thrusts, one the adventures of Captain Thorpe along with his merry crew of the Sea Hawk, and the other a love affair between Thorpe and Doña Maria, the beautiful Spanish debutante to the court of Elizabeth. In both cases there will be transitions as events unfold: at first, the adventurers plunder Spanish ships, then endure capture and confinement as galley slaves, and finally escape and return to the good life at sea; Thorpe encounters initial distrust for Doña Maria, but that soon changes to unrestrained love. In neither case does one doubt for a moment that things will end happily. The confirmation for that assurance comes already in the titles music, which Korngold puts in a traditional three-part form. In the opening A section we have a lively fanfare which becomes a leitmotif for the Sea Hawk itself, informing us that

this type of life at sea offers not only adventure, but pleasure, cama-
raderie and excitement. At the appearance of executive producer Hal
B. Wallis's name in the credits, Korngold shifts to the B section, replacing brass instruments with strings and finding a bittersweet quality with
a shift to rich melodic material. Here he gives us the romantic theme
for Thorpe and Maria, introducing the other primary feature of the
film. At Korngold's own name in the credits, the music snaps back
into the fanfare A section, not only blowing the composer's own horn
but clarifying that in the ups and downs of love and battle all will end
well. In this introduction/overture, Korngold bombards the viewer/
listener with a musical deluge unlike anything one normally finds at
the opening of a film; he simply overwhelms us with it, and its formal
structure accurately reflects the film's unfolding and outcome.

Steiner and Korngold achieved brilliant results with their titles
music, but no one treated this music more provocatively than Bernard
Herrmann, as we have already seen in *Citizen Kane*. Some of Alfred
Hitchcock's films of the 1950s and 1960s remain among his most
memorable, and Herrmann's music played no small role in making that
possible. In some cases, the level of visual and aural interest during the
titles may be so high that the viewer has difficulty noticing the titles
themselves, as happens in *Vertigo*. Here the penetrating eye and swirling
graphics command our attention at the beginning, and Herrmann's
musical arabesques, with a pace that eventually doubles, plunge the
viewer over the edge of a vertiginous abyss.

In *Psycho* menace comes early with imprisoning or threatening hor-
izontal and vertical lines which pulverize some of the title names,
including Janet Leigh's and Alfred Hitchcock's. Herrmann's music
intensifies the dread we feel, with a relentlessly driving rhythmic figure
suggesting something primitive; he keeps us on edge with a high degree
of tension which increases toward the end of the titles as the rising pitch
gives a striking shrillness. The persistent rhythmic figure vaguely suggests a well-known musical work from a half century earlier, Stravinsky's
The Rite of Spring, and specifically its final section – the "Sacrificial
Dance." In this primitive enactment through ballet of a piece of Russian
lore, a girl must throw herself into a dance of death, combining erotic
energy, atonement and death. Whether Herrmann had this in mind or
not, the connection works remarkably well. After Hitchcock's name
explodes into fragments and the vertical lines dissipate, the camera gives

an aerial scan of Phoenix, Arizona, and more titles identify the city, the date (Friday, 11 December) and even the time (2:43 p.m.). It appears to be a hot, sultry afternoon, and Herrmann shifts from the grating, driving sounds to something very gentle, a set of descending parallel chords which then ascend and finally descend again as the camera moves in on the window of a sleazy hotel. If the earlier sounds invoked Stravinsky primitivism, these suggest Debussy, perhaps the *Prelude to the Afternoon of a Faun*, which also takes place on a hot afternoon, so hot the faun has difficulty staying awake. In his reveries the faun sees nymphs, and the eroticism of Mallarmé's text comes through in Debussy's sensuous realization. Hitchcock's camera enters the hotel window, to find Marion and her lover partially clad, having just finished lovemaking and still in a sexually playful mood. The music ends with a descending figure when they begin to speak – speech breaking the erotic moment of pleasure and taking them back to an unwelcome reality.

Some operas lack overtures altogether, especially certain 20th-century ones such as Alban Berg's *Wozzeck*, which plunges us into the action with no more than a few chords in advance. In some films the titles appear in total silence, as in *Alexander Nevsky*, which prompted most viewers to believe that Eisenstein had artistic reasons for this silence. In fact, Eisenstein wanted what would have amounted to an operatic overture, but Prokofiev could not see his way clear to compose anything that would do the job; Eisenstein had no choice but to respect Prokofiev's silence.[15] If a film attempts to convey something absurd, fragmented or involving miscommunication, as in the case of French New Wave director Jean-Luc Godard's *Pierrot le fou* (1965), the music can play a strong contributing role. Throughout this film we hear music in fragments, often simply switched on and off, as though Godard played capriciously with the volume control.[16] Godard engaged composer Antoine Duhamel to write four suites for the film, giving him no clues what the film would be about, and then simply applied the music or fragments of it without any assistance from Duhamel. The title music, with a fairly earnest and perhaps even melodramatic sound, completely misleads us about the nature of the film about to unfold. This misdirection, of course, fits perfectly with the incongruous and irrational treatment that ensues.

In more recent films, especially in the U.S., the more traditional titles music has given way to songs, which may or may not have been written by the composer who scores the rest of the film. This trend appeared to start very much by chance, an early example being *Laura* (1944) where David Raksin's theme set Hollywood on its ear; this film left no doubt that a theme could become a song and that a song could have a life of its own, bringing in large revenues by itself and also promoting the film more effectively than any posters or ads possibly could.[17] Raksin's Laura theme, which begins and ends the film and occurs so often elsewhere throughout that it seemed obsessive to Raksin himself, of course has a vital artistic function in Otto Preminger's cinematic vision of Vera Caspary's novel. Films such as this confirmed that songwriters had a new and highly lucrative venue to look forward to. In some cases the exploitation of this has been nothing short of mercenary; at its best, songs have added an exciting artistic dimension to some films.

If a chart-topping song could promote a movie, why not three or four songs to put it over the top? That happened in 1968 with *The Graduate*, in which Simon and Garfunkel's pre-existing hit "The Sound of Silence" covered the titles, and Paul Simon then provided "April," "Scarborough Fair," and "Mrs. Robinson" for other parts of Mike Nichols's view of the generation gap. The enormous success of "The Sound of Silence" gave *The Graduate* a strong boost, but at the same time it proved a brilliant choice in that the content of the text captured the essence of Nichol's disillusioned youth – at least the searching Ben of the early part of the film before he becomes distracted by Mrs. Robinson and her daughter. As often as I have seen this movie, from the first time at its release in 1968, I cannot concentrate on the titles because I am simply enveloped by "The Sound of Silence." While this song may have generational significance, putting college students of the sixties in the right frame of mind, it also succeeded admirably in transforming song into overture. The transformation of songs into accompaniment for the rest of the movie also works well, and surely helped to make Nichols's brilliant film the classic it has become.

Of the numerous movies to follow suit, *Apocalypse Now*, with Jim Morrison's "The End" as overture and an appearance of the Rolling Stones later on, may use its songs in one of the most convincing and successful ways. Simon and Garfunkel and Morrison, to say nothing of the likes of Elton John, Bruce Springsteen or Celine Dion, may seem light years removed from opera and the place of the overture (although perhaps not quite so far when we see Luciano Pavarotti on stage with Bryan Adams or the Spice Girls), yet some of them carry forward the traditional function of the overture, no less than a score composed by the more operatic Steiner or Korngold. If the song introduces us as convincingly to a film as what happens with "The Sound of Silence" or "The End," it carries on a role associated with opera.

PART THREE

CINEMA GIVES OPERA THE FINGER

$$\boxed{8}$$

CASTING OPERA IN OUR TEETH:
CHAPLIN'S *CARMEN*

Carmen, in Cecil B. DeMille's film of that name, seductively approaches Don José with a rose in her mouth as he protects the breach in the town wall, and the love-struck soldier takes the rose from her teeth with his own lips. In Charlie Chaplin's parody of DeMille's *Carmen*, known variously as *Carmen* or *A Burlesque on Carmen*, Edna Purviance as a Farraresque Carmen makes the same approach carrying the flower in her hand; Chaplin as Don José, also protecting the breach in the wall from smugglers, yawns instead of showing the appropriate excitement at her arrival, and she rams the rose into his gaping mouth. With this bit of slapstick humor, Chaplin's film satirizes not only DeMille's version which is vulnerable to this sort of treatment, but opera itself. Unlike DeMille, who took opera as a starting point for cinema, pointing the way to new avenues of grandeur, emotion and (he hoped) dignity, Chaplin, like the Marx Brothers twenty years later, also saw the funny side of opera as the symbol of a bloated establishment, and gleefully lampooned it. If DeMille could try to bring cinema up in the world with a screen version of the opera Carmen, Chaplin could bring it back down very quickly, opening the door to other directors who would satirize, parody or simply rail at opera in their films.

Carmen proved not to be one of Chaplin's more successful works, and in fact he made only about half of what was released; Essanay studio, imagining it could improve on his two-reel film, spliced in enough cut footage and new material to turn it into four reels after Chaplin's departure from the studio. The four-reel version premiered on 22 April 1916, with a new sub-plot involving Ben Turpin as one of the smugglers

Carmen – or, *A Burlesque on Carmen* (Charles Chaplin as an inept Don José)

and his affection for an oversized gypsy girl, material which made the film very different from the parody Chaplin had originally intended. The studio wanted something longer than the piece Chaplin had in mind, but with the splicing it managed to kill much of the film's acidic satire, dragging out certain scenes and adding others which offered nothing but slapstick. After an initial reaction "which prostrated me and sent me to bed for two days," Chaplin sued Essanay, but also realized they had done him a favor: "Although this was a dishonest act, it rendered a service, for thereafter I had it stipulated in every contract that there should be no mutilation, extending or interfering with my finished work."[1]

It should not surprise us to see satire or burlesque happening in cinema as early as 1915, and aside from the possibilities provided by opera, DeMille's *Carmen* proved to be a delightfully satirizable target. While Geraldine Farrar played her part marvelously, she also inadvertently left herself open to lampoons. Her dancing, which comes closer to bumping and grinding, the flower in her mouth, her endless seductions, her virtual invention of women's wrestling, flattening the occasional man in a tavern, her popping out of bushes or through doors with here-I-am flourishes, her smoking of cigars, or her gleeful reaction to combat and gore all may be a bit too much for some.

If she induces the occasional guffaw, her co-star Wallace Reid no doubt proved much more of a satirical inspiration to Chaplin. Wonderfully handsome, we first see him at the breach in the wall looking debonair as he lights up a cigarette, but that image seems entirely incongruous with the shy and innocent impression he emits as Carmen thrusts her body at him. To be sure this proved a difficult role to play as he must respond to the competing forces of sensuality and duty, but he never did manage to get it right. By the end, when he must be out of his mind with jealousy and rage, he still has problems suppressing the little-boy innocence of his first meeting with Carmen; at one point she slaps his face and he recoils in apparent fright. Even as he pulls the knife to stab her, he still looks wimpy; while Farrar plays the death scene with genuine verve, Reid utterly fails to convince us of the menace in the situation. DeMille prided himself on discovering Reid as a star, but here more than with Farrar he created a Hollywood misfit, dragging a good-looking lad with no acting ability out from among the extras, trying to turn him into something he could not be. For Hollywood, though, beautiful looks could always sell more tickets than acting talent, and American cinema remains stuck with the legacy left by DeMille and certain other early directors. Thankfully someone like Chaplin could see it for what it was, and made that a key part of his travesty.

Other aspects of DeMille's *Carmen* may also strike us as more than a little absurd. Carmen seems overly enthusiastic about the fight between Don José and a rival soldier who compares José's holding the key of her jail cell to a fox guarding a chicken coop, but when she joins in the fray, throwing earthen jugs or covering the rival with a mantilla, we have much more difficulty seeing José as a worthy combatant. Again he seems more like a little boy than a virile soldier with passionate anger aroused. Similarly, the morally incorruptible José has the wind let out of his sails when we see Carmen laughing at the idea that he cannot be bought; of course he can be, and with Carmen's taunt the question becomes not if but when. His moral lapse happens just about as soon as it possibly could.

Chaplin takes all of these possibilities and revels in the absurdities they arouse. On the last point, morality, an important one for a film trying to reach a higher level and perhaps even be edifying, Chaplin does not pretend for a moment that his Don José cannot be bribed; when Lillas Pastia, leader of the smugglers, walks away from José after making some nonsensically coded remarks about possible bribery, he discovers that nimble fingers have already picked the money intended for that purpose. Edna Purviance picks up on various of Farrar's excesses and reminds us how laughable they appear. Instead of wrestling she reverts to something even more masculine – boxing, and she likes to smoke cigars (one of the opening intertext screens begins, "Along the shores of sunny Spain, where men do the dishes – and women smoke cigars"). One expects this very attractive woman to have men at her feet; the fascination Frasquita, one of Carmen's cohorts, has for various smugglers and soldiers comes as somewhat less expected, "a lovely little woman" according to an early text, whose ampleness could sink a smugglers' ship. Since Farrar's excessive seductiveness could simply not be matched, the size of the woman offering her favors turned out to be the only thing which could be made more excessive.

DeMille's film may be about Carmen, but Chaplin shifts the attention to Chaplin himself in the role of Don José, and he had a field day making Wallace Reid seem even more ridiculous than he already was. He must, of course, be handsome, or at least he should preen himself excessively. Certainly butterflies under the helmet or tripping over a strategically place rock do not help matters. If Reid seemed like a shy and innocent little boy, Chaplin took that to the extreme, letting his eyes flutter in cartoon-like paroxysms at the first hint of seduction. For the final death scene, Chaplin played it for the most part with real conviction in contrast to Reid's wilting effort, almost duping us for a moment into imagining the unfolding of a tragedy. When Escamillo, the toreador, bursts in on the murder-suicide scene to discover one body draped over the other, Chaplin suddenly revives and gives him a mule kick, sending him flying in a way that no bull could accomplish. With that he and Purviance scramble to their feet, and he shows her the fake knife with retractable blade with which he did (not do) the deed. On this note of indulgent artifice the film ends as in DeMille's, the camera zooming out on the lifeless bodies.

While Chaplin works his burlesque of DeMille in these various ways, his satire cuts deeper, slashing at opera itself and figures of authority. The frontal attack on authority comes very early in the film, with the introduction to the leader of the gypsy smugglers, Lillas Pastia. On an intertext screen shortly after the credits, we read that Lillas Pastia "had spent fifty years of his life learning how to steal – thinking that some day he would be offered a political job." To that can be added the enforcers of authority, the soldiers, who spend most of their time in taverns drinking or in pursuit of women; when put to any sort of test of duty they readily take bribes or can be diverted by a kiss while smugglers get away with their booty. Even the bugler cannot call them to duty since his clogged instrument will not sound. The finest of the soldiers, played by Chaplin, cannot take two steps without tripping over a rock. The corrupting forces here, the smugglers and seducers, seem able to carry on as they like, with no worry of interference from law enforcers since they have them in their pockets.

But just as the Marx Brother did two decades later with *A Night at the Opera*, Chaplin satirizes opera itself with his *Carmen*, and by targeting opera also attacked the ruling class which patronized opera, to say nothing of the attempts of the Hollywood studio executives to elevate motion pictures to a higher form of entertainment. While the Marx Brothers could look at opera as the preserve of those in power and bring them down a few notches with their send-up on the whole world of opera – much to the delight of a working-class or immigrant audience (to be discussed in chapter 9), Chaplin's satire in 1915 took a somewhat different tack because of what DeMille's *Carmen* had tried to accomplish. The presence of the great diva Geraldine Farrar in Hollywood capitalized not only on her Gerry-flapping popularity but the new dignity and respectability that she would bring to a medium perceived to appeal to a lowbrow audience, in spite of the subversive subject matter of *Carmen* and the reputation Farrar had for behavior unbecoming.

Much of that elevation depended on a larger than life impression made by the stars and scenes, such as the chorus scenes in opera, which overwhelm the senses with grandeur and spectacle. As perhaps the most written-about woman in the U.S., Farrar by reputation already stood larger than life, and DeMille felt confident this would carry over to her film presence. He also seemed to believe he could create that type of impression with Wallace Reid, and to some extent it worked although not sufficiently to dispel the characteristics which would leave him open to ridicule. In contrast to the debonair soldier Reid should project, Chaplin of course turns him into a bumbler and a buffoon; he lacks the strength even to hoist Carmen onto the table where she will dance.

The absence of grandeur and spectacle characterizes not only the leading players but some key scenes as well. For example, the bullfighter Escamillo makes a grand entry in a refined carriage into Seville in DeMille's *Carmen* with a resplendent Carmen at his side, thronged by hundreds of adoring fans who give him a hero's welcome. If this scene were to be set in an opera, the crowd would be the chorus, pumping us up with a suitably rousing choral number. In extreme contrast in Chaplin's *Carmen*, Escamillo and Carmen enter an almost deserted Seville, riding in a peasant's wagon pulled by a bedraggled horse. In the earlier *Carmen* we see Don José lurking in the crowd attempting to look sinister; in the burlesque he strolls by them, the only person on the street, now as a gypsy instead of soldier but also with bowler hat and funny walk, invoking the presence of the little tramp. The look on his face instead of menace suggests he has just been kicked in the pants. Before his appearance from around a corner, we see one tipsy peasant waving enthusiastically if spastically, who asks of the wagon, "Is dat one of de new Fords?" before he disappears into a tavern to continue his undisturbed drinking.

Along with the grandeur of operatic images came something that could satisfy the moral views of those at the upper end of society who objected to the poor example set in motion pictures. As appealing as Carmen may be, for some in the late 19th-century operatic audience her demise was necessary – a punishment for loose morals (and no doubt her challenge to patriarchal values). DeMille too keeps the moral element, although, like Bizet, he allows us to enjoy all the bad-girl behavior of Carmen before she meets her fate. Even though DeMille claimed to base his work more on the original novel of Mérimée than the opera by Bizet, in terms of the treatment of gypsies, smugglers and Carmen herself, he follows the spirit of the opera much more closely. DeMille's gypsies, like Bizet's, may be unlike Europeans but they do not lack charm and attractiveness. Similarly the smugglers engage in criminal activity, but not of a very harmful sort; in fact their attempt to foil the soldiers can be seen as a game in which we can simply enjoy their wily outmaneuvering of the authorities.

Mérimée's novel, on the other hand, unfolds from the perspective of an anthropologist who wishes to discover more about gypsies but shares all the common European prejudices about them. We find absolutely nothing endearing about his gypsies and smugglers; his gypsies will cut the throats of innocent Europeans for the tiniest profit, and they use Carmen as willing bait to snare their quarry. We see Carmen through the eyes of Don José, who tells his story to an already biased narrator, and the Carmen who emerges will unlikely evoke erotic fantasies for most men. In contrast to Bizet's Don José, whose fantasies and indulgence with Carmen would be forgiven by a male society whose own sense of morality does not exclude keeping mistresses, the Don José of the novel crosses a line of decency which makes him as much a cutthroat as the thugs he has joined. And Carmen behaves so perversely, even stealing a watch from the unwitting narrator, that it matters little to anyone at the end if she lives or dies.

The moral lapses in Chaplin's *Carmen* extend to the soldiers and especially Don José. In the opera we have some reason to be concerned about the soldiers when they surround the sweet Micaela and toy with her as she asks the whereabouts of Don José, a situation which may have seemed playful to the 19th century but strikes us as more menacing (bordering on a prelude to gang rape, as Francesco Rosi presents it in his film).[2] Also in the opera we know that Don

105

José's past may be slightly checkered, but not enough to alarm us. In the novel we have no Micaela who can play the good angel in contrast to Carmen the bad one, and we also know the seriousness of Don José's transgression which forced him to leave his home. While Chaplin's José and soldiers may in part be what they are in response to DeMille's supposedly incorruptible military men, they may also be unscrupulous and lewd to poke fun at the dignity and morality associated with opera which DeMille hoped to instill in his version. Later in his career Chaplin too, would incorporate elements of opera into his films in a serious way, in, for example *The Great Dictator*, but at this early stage he took much delight in using operatic approaches to film as a punching bag for his wonderfully zany mode of comedy and burlesque. As his later films suggest, this did not arise from disdain; in fact he appeared to have great admiration for opera and its effect on cinema, and paid homage with parody.

ATTACK OF THE ANARCHISTS:
A NIGHT AT THE OPERA

In *A Night at the Opera*, Groucho Marx, as Otis B. Driftwood, looking
for a piece of the lucrative action, pulls up in front of the famous
La Scala opera house in Milan in a horse-drawn carriage, with
sounds of Leoncavallo's *I Pagliacci* in the background, and asks the doorman, "is the opera over yet?" With the answer "almost," he snaps at
the driver, "Hey you, I told you to slow that nag down – on account
of you I nearly heard the opera. Now drive around the park, slowly
– and none of your back talk." A few minutes later he storms into
impresario Herman Gottlieb's box with shouts of bravo and the question, "When does the curtain go up?" Informed that not only the
opera but the whole season has ended, he retorts, "Well, I only missed
it by a few minutes; I can go then, eh?" Does Groucho dislike opera?
He, like much of his American audience in 1935, can't stand it, and
he has difficulty imagining a fate worse than having to sit through three
minutes of an opera, let alone three hours.

Who are these people who subject themselves to this unusual form
of torment, and why do they do it? George Bernard Shaw suggested
part of the answer: "At every one of these concerts, you will find rows
of weary people who are there, not because they really like classical
music, but because they think they ought to like it." Shaw was being
too generous: much of the audience – and certainly the audience portrayed in *A Night at the Opera* – came under duress. At the opera the
social elite congregate, in America the people with money and power,
who come not because they like opera but because this entertainment so
completely turns off the lower classes that they do not have to disbar

them by means that might be interpreted as discriminatory. To enter a shrine to opera, one must pay a sum of money inconsequential to the wealthy but crippling to the working class – as much as a week's wages, and also dress in formal evening wear, as though attending a club with a requisite dress code; these are not the same people who go to baseball games or movies.

As an entertainment for the wealthy, large amounts of money must be raised just to keep the operation going and certainly to attract the finest singers, allowing a city such as New York to claim its opera superior to that of Milan or London. The early plot, if we can call it that, of this film concerns the attempt to persuade the world's greatest tenor, Rudolfo Lassparri, to leave Italy and come to New York. The amount of money required to achieve this invokes Groucho's incredulous response: "You're willing to pay him a thousand dollars a night just for singing? Why, you can buy a phonograph record of Minnie the Moocher for 75 cents. For a buck and a quarter you can get Minnie!" Groucho understands the worth of vaudeville entertainers (his own mother's name was Minnie), but not the extraordinary sums associated with a type of singing so few people will hear. He does, though, recognize a good racket when he sees one, and with his peculiar bent for business, he sees great potential here if he can get a piece of the action. His attempt flounders when he cannot remember the name of the singer long enough to sign up the right one.

The world of opera takes a battering from the Marx Brothers, but of course, the lampooning cuts much deeper than opera itself. In this case we travel from Italy, where opera plays a role in the lives of people of all social strata, to America, where it does not. In America opera stood as a symbol of wealth and power, and an attack on opera must be construed as an attack on its privileged patrons. The working class people who attend movies can identify these patrons as their bosses or other people who make their lives miserable, employers who pay them atrociously and force them to work in squalid conditions, against whom they may periodically go on strike or challenge with other forms of civil disobedience. While the gains in these types of protest may be small, much satisfaction could be achieved by being able to laugh at them – to reduce them to buffoons and turn their exclusive and ordered world upside down, not with paving stones and Molotov cocktails, but with satire, insults and mayhem. No one did this better than the Marx Brothers. Groucho hurls insults at machine-gun pace at Gott-lieb (the director of the New York opera), Lassparri (the great tenor), and Mrs. Claypool, a nouveau-riche widow who sees the funding of opera as her ticket into high society.

Power brokers seal their arrangements with lawyers and contracts, and Groucho and Chico give us their version of this routine, shred-ding a contract by ripping off articles of absurd legalese which Chico, unable in any event to read, certainly disapproves of how they sound; he cannot sign the tiny remaining fragment because he neither reads nor writes, but Groucho one-ups him by offering him a pen with no ink. Before the contract gag, the two of them use Lassparri as an imag-inary bar footrest after Harpo, the tenor's dresser, gets back at his employer's abuse by conking him on the head with a huge hammer (and gets the satisfaction of doing it a second time after reviving him with smelling salts). At the opera itself, Groucho, who always dresses in bad imitation of the upper crust, drops his top hat from the box he occupies after tying up Gottlieb (whose oversized clothes he now wears). He asks a well-heeled patron below to throw his hat back up, and tips him a nickel to buy himself a stogey, insulting the mortified gentleman who would normally be the one to offer a tip.

Throughout the movie, and in Marx Brothers' movies in general, runs a sense of the differences between the old world and the new, the Europe which immigrants have escaped and the vestiges of that class-oriented society surviving in America. The brothers themselves, as the children of immigrants, put into practice survival skills unique to immigrants; the fact that the brothers are Jewish gives these skills an edge they would not otherwise have. While we recognize them as immi-grants by their appearance and accents, in this film we actually witness their voyage across the Atlantic, which they make as stowaways because they cannot afford to pay for tickets. By sheer resourcefulness — and Harpo's handiness with scissors — they avoid deportation back to a Europe which by 1935 not only disadvantaged them but also threatened their safety. America appeared desirable by comparison, but for those already there and trying to build their lives on the Lower East Side of Manhattan, fighting an establishment with strong roots in Holland or Germany, much needed to be accomplished.

While immigrants imported many of their problems from the old world, they also brought many of the assets and tools for coping with them. As one of these imports, opera became a meeting place for the Europeans who made their fortunes in America, providing their entry into polite society. Another import, although almost entirely unnoticed in the United States with the exception of Louisiana, where it has been firmly rooted for centuries, was carnival, also known as Mardi Gras (fat Tuesday) and Fastnacht or Fasching (the eve of lent). A spirit of madness sets in and anything goes as people can behave in any way they like – just so long as it differs from their normal behavior. Class and gender differences vanish, and the downtrodden can take potshots at authority figures without worrying about the consequences. There will be much overindulgence of food, drink, rowdiness and sex, allowing a time of merriment before the severity of lent.

The upside-down mayhem of the Marx Brothers' movies has much in common with carnival, beginning with the way they dress.[1] Chico wears a Tirolian costume but pretends to be Italian, Harpo dresses as a clown (a combination of Harlequin and Pierrot), stuffing his over-sized garb with equipment for his gags (in this film we first see him peeling off various disguises, including the clown and the maiden), and Groucho's tails offer a cross-class imitation. Harpo especially bubbles over with *zanni*, the tricks and gags of carnival, such as snipping beards, neckties, cigars and coattails, or placing his leg in the hand of anyone near him, a familiarity that offends typical male sensibilities. By drooping himself over women he conjures up the image of a satyr, while Groucho's inflated tactics of seduction represent a more traditional carnival variety. When they board the ship to America and Margaret Dumont asks him "are you sure you have everything, Otis," Groucho's reply, "I haven't had any complaints yet," indulges in sexual double meaning which the carnival spirit permits.

The most madcap scene in the entire film, the overstuffing of Groucho's miserably small cabin on the ship with bed makers, cleaners, ship's repairmen, waiters, a manicurist, and someone who simply seems lost – to say nothing of the brothers and the aspiring tenor, gets the biggest laughs. This reminds one of a contest to stuff a telephone booth or a Volkswagen with as many people as possible. When Margaret Dumont (not exactly small herself) heads for the door, we have obvious concerns about how she might fit in. When she opens the door, bodies shoot out as though fired from a cannon. As this two-by-two procession of stuffing the cabin begins with the bed makers, Groucho gives us a bit of mythology as well as opera, saying, "C'mon in girls, and leave all hope behind." Here he verbally flashes the sign that Orpheus encounters before entering the underworld – Orpheus the singer and the model for the invention of opera. While this reference to opera may be unexpected and a little obtuse, others will flow much more freely as the film progresses.

Groucho's rapid-fire use of words, almost as a type of weapon, where non sequiturs become a manner of discourse, also belongs to the improvisational traditions of carnival. Only Chico, with his zany malapropisms ("duplicate" as the five kids up in Canada or "sanity clause"), can slow Groucho down or trip him up. Chico and Harpo exchange huge sausages as gifts, and sausage points to the carnivalesque Hanswurst of southern Germany and Austria (along with its combination of phallic and fecal symbols). The stowaways to America make Groucho order them massive amounts of eggs from a hapless steward, or eat plates piled so high with pasta and other foods that they stagger the digestive imagination. Later, at breakfast in New York, Harpo eats everything in sight, including cigars and neckties, rivaling the gluttony artists of the 18th century who would amaze viewers by eating whole animals, rocks, leather pouches, or other objects too gruesome to mention.[2]

The comparisons with carnival could go on and on, but central to all of them stands the way that authority can be challenged. The convention allows for this challenge without major opposition, and therefore insults do not solicit lawsuits but merely a wince or a frown. Police in this scheme of things prove more a nuisance than menace, and can be tricked into believing they have gone mad. In this film, where opera stands as a symbol of authority, the screwball humor can be directed against opera itself. In order for that to work, the opera in question must be serious, a type of opera suggesting the grandeur of the audience itself. Using comic opera in this case simply would not do, since one can hardly satirize something which already satirizes itself. Mozart's *The Magic Flute*, for example, not only pokes fun at the excesses of serious opera, but it does that with various of the devices of carnival, especially with the role of Papageno. With a serious opera, though, full of inflated emotions and bigger than life characters, the potential for satire or parody seems unlimited. The idea of using serious opera as a punching bag for comedians started, of course, long before the 20th century, already with the comic *intermezzo* late in the 17th century.

When the Marx Brothers get their hands on Verdi's *Il Trovatore*, they turn it every bit as much upside-down as they do the world of opera patrons. The fun begins with Chico and Harpo in the orchestra pit for the overture, Harpo about to stroke a trombone with a violin bow. After making a speech to kick off the new season in New York, full of insults to Mrs. Claypool and everyone else in attendance, Groucho, standing in for the tied-up Gottlieb, calls to the conductor, "play on, Don." The conductor, a typical podium tyrant, slightly resembling "Don" Arturo Toscanini, throws darts with his eyes at Groucho for turning this highly formal form of Italian address into a familiar American "Don." He taps his baton on the podium signaling the orchestra to be ready, but with Harpo out there, he may as well be tickling him under the chin. Harpo, on cue, taps right back, and the tapping war that ensues prompts Groucho to wonder if a flock of woodpeckers has moved in. Waving the baton in a negative gesture accomplishes even less, as Harpo takes this as an invitation to a sword fight.

The unexpected return of Gottlieb forces some fancy footwork from Groucho, who accompanies his escape from the box over the safety rail with an imitation of a Johnny Weissmuller Tarzan call. Weissmuller had made at least two of his jungle films by this time, *Tarzan the Ape Man* (1932) and *Tarzan and His Mate* (1934), and Groucho's yodeling cry took his audience out of the opera house into the low form of entertainment that could not be more antagonistic to opera. The overture finally begins, but with the first page turn the orchestra bursts into "Take me out to the ball game," which the brothers have neatly inserted into the score. With the opera house now transformed into a ballpark, Groucho immediately picks up on this high to low reversal, stepping into the aisles to hawk peanuts – to people who would certainly not eat peanuts from a bag.

When the opera finally begins, Groucho's radio-style running commentary takes us back to the ball park: the eerie looking gypsy Azucena elicits "boogie, boogie, boogie"; to her missing teeth and generally dissipated appearance he asks "how would you like to feel the way she looks?"; a high note from the end of Azucena's canzone brings "was that high C or vitamin D?" Harpo and Chico, trying to evade the police, have joined the gypsy chorus, and needless to say, get right into the thick of the action. During the famous "Anvil chorus" (following Azucena's canzone instead of preceding it), a somewhat brutish gypsy rips the skirt off a gypsy girl; Harpo gets into the spirit of things, stripping off the rest of her small underskirt, and quickly tearing off articles of clothing from everyone in sight. Instead of opera we now have Minsky's burlesque, of which Groucho heartily approves, saying "now we're getting somewhere," to the horror of the polite audience around him.

As the police and management move in on Harpo and Chico, some of them also in gypsy disguise, the culprits take evasive action. Cornered with nowhere to go but up, Harpo goes that direction, scrambling up the set into the flies. Police come at him from every angle, and we return to a Tarzan film as he swings from rope to rope in the fly area. Since these ropes control the positioning of the backdrops, the scene becomes a comedy revue as one absurd set after another descends and in one case hides Lassparri from the audience. The final one of these incongruous drops, a battleship, may very well have given Fellini ideas for his own *E la nave va*. By this point *Il Trovatore* has been turned into complete nonsense, no longer with a shred of seriousness as Harpo has transformed it into pure carnival.

The film viewers probably do not know the plot of *Il Trovatore*, and that does not disadvantage them; in case they are not certain about a battleship in this opera, Gottlieb bristles that it does not belong. If Verdi's plot necessitates suspension of disbelief, the plot of the film requires even more based on what happens next, putting the film itself in good operatic company. The stage lights go out and Lassparri gags on his sustained note; when the lights come back on he has vanished from sight. We know Gottlieb to be something of a cad, but nothing has prepared us for his priorities now; he needs a tenor to finish the opera, and if Lassparri cannot be produced immediately, another tenor will do just as well. The plot here could not be more harebrained, allowing the most famous tenor in the world to be kidnapped to give Ricardo his big break in New York. Not even in opera would one likely find something so improbable; that could only happen in a Marx Brothers' movie which has gone one step beyond opera. Ricardo gets his chance, insists that Rosa, who had been fired earlier, join him on stage, and they become an instant sensation. Lassparri's release proves to be of no interest to anyone, and his attempt at an encore results in jeers from this sophisticated opera audience. It appears that Groucho's influence on them, bringing in an attitude suitable to low forms of entertainment, has had an effect on their taste. When Lassparri complains that the audience pelted him with apples, Groucho logically points out that watermelons are out of season.

How do we account for the opera audience, previously mortified by the smart-alecky insults from Groucho and the shenanigans of his brothers, turning on one of their own and violently expressing their preference for a populist? Of course in a Marx Brothers' film we should not search too hard for logic, but in this case there may actually be a reason. The Lassparri/Ricardo comparison has been pushed since the beginning. Lassparri treats his dresser, Harpo, brutally, and he refuses to sing while boarding the ship if he will not be paid. Fame has placed him among the powerful Europeans who continue to dog ordinary immigrants in the new world. His interest in Rosa strikes us more as harassment than affection, unlike Ricardo's true love for her.

Ricardo will happily sing without gaining from it financially, and on the ship his audience comes from the passengers in steerage. But more to the point, when he does sing for his audience of common folk, he sings popular songs, as in the ship-boarding duet with Rosa or his rendition "Cosi cosa" as a stowaway. Not only that but his voice invokes anything but an operatic tone, leaning much more toward popular crooning as his high notes have a sweet *sotto-voce* quality instead of the *dispositione* of a trained operatic tenor.[3] His success in New York seems to suggest that opera can be fine if it has an American popular sound, and that American audiences should see the light and abandon silly old *bel canto* European singing. Of the various insults to opera in the film, this one may very well be the most stinging; if arias can be sung in the shower, or riding a steamer trunk as Groucho does with *Pagliacci* en route to his closet-sized cabin, that ought to be good enough.

A Night at the Opera proved to be a great box office success, not only because the Marx Brothers had reached the top of their form – and they would not remain there for much longer – but because of the targets of their demolition with which audiences in the 1930s could so readily identify. In *Monkey Business* they had targeted higher education, again a bastion of the privileged, and in *Duck Soup* they painted all politicians with the same ludicrous brush. In some ways, *A Night at the Opera* may have hit a nerve that their other films did not since the focus on opera exposed the ruling class as few other things could. This allowed a glimpse into a private world with its excesses and indulgences, and satirizing it amounted to the same thing as violating an exclusive club where people do peculiar things they may not want others to know about. Not only educators, politicians or some other specific group, but the entire ruling class stood at the wrong end of the satire. Opera in America symbolized their power, but it also seemed to show them at their most absurd, as absurd as the plot of a typical serious opera.

While not just touching the working class or the uneducated, *A Night at the Opera* spoke directly to every immigrant's experience, to say nothing of the ordeals of the children of immigrants. That experience went beyond dealing with a new culture which may be hostile, as it included coping with the very elements people had tried to escape in the old world, whose prejudices and suppression could be much more vicious than anything in the new. Here we find the ultimate counter-attack on these forces, three zany comedians who could not only make us roll in the aisles but could put the oppressors in their place, making them the laughing stock in an upside-down world of theater or cinema where, if we suspend our disbelief enough, we will get doused with reality.

DEFLATED AND FLAT:
OPERA IN *CITIZEN KANE*

Since the mid 1960s, if not earlier, *Citizen Kane* has been hailed with remarkable consistency as the finest of all American films, "the work that influenced the cinema more profoundly than any American film since *Birth of a Nation*," according to Andrew Sarris's evaluation in 1968.[1] As every enthusiast of film classics knows, though, it had a perilous journey to its ultimate release in 1941, with some uncertainty along the way that it ever would be shown. The details of this celebrated episode for Orson Welles and the RKO Studio have generated so much interest that they have recently yielded a feature film about them (*RKO 281*). When William Randolph Hearst finally got wind that the film portrayed him in a most uncomplimentary way and, even worse, turned his mistress Marion Davies into a pathetic drunk, he attempted to intimidate studio bosses into forcing RKO to withdraw the film with threats of public exposure of their unsavoury pastimes or family secrets. The dubious honor fell to Louis B. Mayer to offer RKO $805,000 to burn the reels, but that made little impression on RKO's head George J. Schaefer, who did not bother to take the offer to the board of directors since he assumed they would accept it.[2] Studio lawyers vacillated, fearing Hearst could sue and win, further delaying the release. Welles, already in New York to rehearse *Native Son*, addressed the studio executives with a speech about freedom and the dangers of fascism, a performance which won him little more than polite applause.[3] Hearst, using the poison pen of his Hollywood correspondent Louella Parsons (whose public embarrassment by Welles gave her personal cause to lash out), gradually backed off the assault in his papers, realizing he could not be giving Welles better free publicity. Hearst gave up on legal recourse, but a lawsuit eventually did come, although mostly a minor annoyance over copyright infringement of Ferdinand Lundberg's book *Imperial Hearst*.[4] Still, Welles had to do some nimble stepping to convince the court that any resemblance between Charles Foster Kane and Hearst was purely coincidental.

Flamboyant tycoons whom Welles could claim as prototypes for Kane populated the U.S., although he had difficulties explaining the in-jokes about Hearst and Marion, such as her preoccupation with jigsaw puzzles or "Rosebud" as Hearst's intimate name for Marion's private parts. Welles's co-screenwriter Herman Mankiewicz had been an occasional guest at San Simeon, and of course knew much about Hearst and his entourage. In his defense, Welles, to the surprise of some, claimed that the film dealt "quite as fully with the world of grand opera as with the world of newspaper publishing,"[5] and that Samuel Insull provided the real model for Kane. The roughly 15-20 minutes of operatic content in the film may make that claim something slightly less than preposterous, but the name Samuel Insull does not exactly have the same household ring to it as William Randolph Hearst.

Insull may not have been a newspaper magnate, but he had a great deal to do with opera, in spite of being one of the first electric utilities barons, including building a colossal opera house – in Chicago, the same city where Kane erected his. Welles himself spent his own formative years in Chicago, and since his mother, Beatrice, played the piano ably and was well connected to the musical community, presiding over musical salons at her North Shore apartment, he may actually have encountered Insull on one of these occasions. Along with the career model that Insull may have offered, Welles took the resemblance much further, basing, according to Simon Callow, his own make-up for Kane on photographs of Insull.[6] Having emigrated from England to the U.S. at an early age, Insull found himself in the right place at the right time, for a time working as Edison's secretary, and then possessing the business acumen to know how to market the invention. This self-made man acquired a fortune doing that, creating the utilities system in Chicago; after the stock market crash in 1929 he not only lost everything but faced charges of fraud and embezzlement, had to be dragged back from his hiding place in Greece, and finally was acquitted of all charges. In his native England he developed a taste for opera, prompting him to become a patron of opera in Chicago along with his actress wife Gladys, and he eventually assumed the role of director of the Civic Opera Company – offering it some very healthy years with his fundraising skills among Chicago's Gold Coast set.

By the late 1920s it became clear that no amount of private patronage could clear the debt of the company, especially with Mary Garden's extravagance as artistic director, compounded by the approaching expiry of the lease for the old and very small Auditorium. Drastic steps needed to be taken, and the wily businessman Insull came up with what seemed the foolproof solution: build a new opera house as part of a large commercial structure, and allow the commercial leasers to subsidize the opera. The plan flew, and so did the building, a modern forty-two story structure at 20 North Wacker Drive, quickly recognized as a monument to Insull and dubbed "Insull's Throne" because it looked like one with its high back and armrest-like wings. The opera, at ground level, occupied the seat of the throne. This massive, striking building, remarkably similar to the one depicted in an architect's sketch in the "News on the March" sequence of Kane's Chicago Municipal Opera House, bore no resemblance to any other opera house in the world. In fact, rumor had it that Insull sent the architects around the world to look at all the major houses, to make certain this one would stand out as unique. On opening night, ten days after the stock market crash, extra police and security people had to be hired to protect the bejeweled patrons from petty criminals in this still uncharted territory for wealthy Chicagoans.

While the existence of this house depended on well-to-do patrons, some took a decidedly dim view of the design. Unlike the more aristocratic houses with conspicuous boxes near the stage where some prominent patrons could be as much on display as the opera itself, this one relegated boxes to the back where the beautiful people had to sit in relative darkness and obscurity. And like a slap in the face to the high and mighty, the inexpensive seats were every bit as plush as the surroundings and as ornate as the best boxes or orchestra seats, and they offered as fine a view of the stage. Remembering his own poverty-stricken youthful days in England, when he would forego meals to buy a ticket to the opera,[7] Insull saw to it that these opera enthusiasts could not only get into the house but while there could think of themselves as equal to anyone else. This democratization did not sit

well with some well-heeled patrons, and neither did his views on building the repertoire around the interests of the large German and Italian
immigrant populations of Chicago.[8] To make matter even worse, Insull
designed the schedule intentionally to conflict with the Chicago Symphony,
forcing the more highbrow patrons to opt for the symphony. Insull
even managed to foster an attitude of civic duty about the opera, making
some feel guilty if they did not attend; in the end so much money
went into the opera that some of the other performing arts had difficulty competing. Even the press seemed somehow cowed into upholding
the civic pride, although occasionally a critic might break ranks, such
as the one who complained that "a citizen can't go to the theater if
his wife has him at the end of a chain at the opera two or three
times a week. His cultural cosmos might be widened and made happier
in the theater, but evenings find him asleep in the dark on the arm
of an opera seat."[9] One editorial for the *Tribune* even went so far as
to claim that the Chicago Civic Opera "wasn't civic and it wasn't
grand," and claimed that critics extolled the opera because they dared
not do otherwise.[10]

Much of this sounds like *Citizen Kane*, especially the manipulation
of the public and the press. Kane like Insull championed the working
man, not that he should become a political force himself, but that he
should have a better life and recognize the benevolent source that made
it possible. The public did not know whether to love or hate Kane (at
different times it did both), or whether to accuse him of demagoguery,
communist leanings, fascism, being a robber baron, or to find him a
great American. Both Kane and Insull had dreams and knew how to
make their dreams come true. At least one scene from the film came
directly from an incident involving Mankiewicz as theater critic for *The
New York Times* and Insull's wife. Under her stage name as Gladys Wallis,
she made a return to the stage at the age of sixty-five as Lady Teazle
(a part for an eighteen-year-old) in Sheridan's *School for Scandal*. It
received fine reviews in Chicago, but when it opened in New York,
Mankiewicz "came back to the office drunk, started panning Mrs.
Insull's performance, and then fell asleep over his typewriter."[11] In the
film Kane himself completes the negative review, while the *Times* on 23
October 1925 had to run this humiliating notice: "The *School for
Scandal*, with Mrs. Insull as Lady Teazle, was produced at the Little
Theatre last night. It will be reviewed in tomorrow's *Times*."

Opera plays an unusually large role in *Citizen Kane*, perhaps large enough to force us to think twice about Welles's comment about it. Once again, Welles's own background adds to the possibility. He took enough piano lessons to reach a point of some accomplishment before his mother died. She had aspirations for his musical career but more importantly, she, a patron of opera in Chicago, took him to as many performances as possible, not only at the Auditorium but also the outdoor summer opera festival at Ravinia Park. It has been suggested that Welles himself played non-singing children's roles in some of these productions, including Cho-Cho-San's son in *Madam Butterfly*, although the truth about this remains elusive.[12] The role of Susan Alexander (Dorothy Comingore) as reluctant diva has nothing whatever to do with real women such as Marion Davies or Mrs. Insull (although it may come closer to one of the mistresses of Insull's predecessor as director, Harold McCormick – another possible model for Kane, an untalented Polish soprano by the name of Ganna Walska); instead the focus becomes opera itself and what it represents – primarily in social terms. We see Kane, not unlike Insull, as someone with too many rough edges to be accepted by the most sophisticated element of American society. He may have extraordinary power, courted by world leaders and a kingmaker of politicians, but in the end he remained an upstart to polite society, lacking gentility and family pedigree. One way to penetrate the social barrier may be through marriage, as Kane attempts with his first wife, but a wife from a respected family expects something in return, in short, not to be completely neglected. A wife in this instance can be an ornament, although her luster dims quickly if she uncovers mistresses and scandal. Opera, on the other hand, can be much more than an ornament; it can also be a monument, one which may not necessarily win acceptance from the right element of society but at least will gain tolerance. Here one enters the province of high society, and building an opera house can be a type of peace offering that goes a long way; the other side may still find Kane crude, but at least his heart and his money will be seen to be in the right place.

For his second marriage Kane does not marry a woman – he marries the opera. Of course, he manages this very badly since he presumably could have reached his goal much less painfully if he had selected an established diva. But Kane always bursts in from the outside, and opera proves no exception to that; also, he recognizes in Susan someone he might have been if he had not come into a fortune, and at first, he imagines himself to be the good fairy who grants her wildest dream. Unfortunately, he does not quite get the signals straight, as she did not want a singing career as much as her mother wanted it for her. The result proves disastrous as the grudging Susan drags herself through lessons and onto the stage not out of any desire but because Kane bullies her into it. Very quickly the issue ceases for him to be one of granting a wish as it becomes one more step – and a large one at that – in assuming power. He had been able to achieve power in business, politics and public opinion with relative ease, but being taken seriously by pedigreed wealth presented a very different type of challenge. Here lay his best opportunity to enter that world, and he was not about to allow his new wife's lack of ambition to sabotage that.

The way that Welles and composer Bernard Herrmann present opera here turns it into pure satire, with any chance of success doomed from the beginning. We do not have to be experts in singing to recognize that the pathetic little voice, hopelessly flat on top, crooning Rossini's "Una voce poco fa" (Rosine's cavatina from *The Barber of Seville*), cannot possibly become an adequate operatic voice. Now in unfamiliar territory Kane's judgement errs completely, and even a great expert, the Italian singing teacher Signor Matisti, cannot convince him of the reality. Unlike the persons he aspires to impress or perhaps even be like, who would recognize a bad voice when they heard one – just like the worker high above the stage who holds his nose when the "trained" Susan sings – Kane does not gain culture with the acquisition of an opera house. Not only that, the world of the wealthy opera connoisseurs appears as foolish as the misguided attempt to reach it.

The filmic representation of a great opera house proved simple in the extreme, requiring nothing more than a grandiose architect's sketch. Having Susan perform in an opera presented a much greater problem, especially since no existing opera had exactly those features needed to create the right effect in the film. Mankiewicz, ever conscious of Hearst's life, placed Massenet's opera *Thaïs* in the script, an opera written for one of Hearst's mistresses, diva Sybil Sanderson. Pauline Kael suggests in *The Citizen Kane Book* that Welles abandoned *Thaïs* because the royalties would have been too expensive; that may be partly correct, but other factors proved more influential. Because of Sanderson this opera could have been Mankiewicz's in-joke about Hearst, but attempts to

Citizen Kane (Dorothy Comingore as a reluctant diva)

secure the rights for one scene in the opera, the mirror scene, were unsuccessful.[13] No existing opera suited the film; according to Herrmann, very specific objectives needed to by fulfilled:

> Our problem was to create something that would give the audience the feeling of the quicksand into which this simple little girl, having a charming but small voice, is suddenly thrown. And we had to do it in cinematic terms, not musical ones. It had to be done quickly. We had to have the sound of an enormous orchestra pounding at her while everyone is fussing over her, and then – "Now get going – go!" they throw her into the quicksand.[14]

A telegram to Herrmann from Welles gives us more details:

> Opera sequence is early in shooting, so must have fully orchestrated recorded track before shooting. Susie sings as curtain goes up in first act, and I believe there is no opera of importance where soprano leads with chin like this. Therefore suggest it be original... by you – parody on typical Mary Garden vehicle.... Suggest *Salammbo* which gives us phony production scene of Ancient Rome and Carthage, and Susie can dress like Grand Opera neoclassic courtesan.... Here is chance for you to do something witty and amusing – and is the time for you to do it. I love you dearly. Orson.[15]

Even here, with Mary Garden, Welles brings in the Chicago Civic Opera: in suggesting a parody of Ernest Reyer's *Salammbo*, he invoked a type of opera he knew well from his Chicago youth. Herrmann, then, did compose the "opera," one of the few originally composed operas (or excerpts from it) for any film, setting it in the late 19th-century grand operatic style. Welles needed a dramatic overture, the musical magnitude of which would dwarf the singer who must immediately follow it with a recitative and aria, and since nothing of that nature existed, Herrmann obliged.

> To make the effect all the more striking, Herrmann noted that he wrote this piece in a very high tessitura, so that a girl with a modest little voice would be completely hopeless in it.... We got a very charming singer [a very young Jean Forward] to dub Susan's voice, explaining to her the purpose of the effect. Notice – the reason

Susan is struggling so hard is *not* that she cannot sing, but rather that the demands of the part are purposely greater than she can ever meet.[16]

The deflation in this music complements the irony of the text, which John Houseman, uncredited on the script, said he concocted from Racine's *Athalie* and *Phèdre* for the aria. While appearing in typical operatic style to be "fairly implausible and unintelligible," the text itself, "Oh cruel one! You have to hear me.... It is futile to escape you," leads prophetically to Susan's suicide attempt.[17] When the curtain falls on Susan's debut in Chicago, Kane tries to revive the feeble applause, but while he may be able to influence the masses in his newspapers, he can do nothing of the sort when it comes to high culture. His face shows surprise and embarrassment at the result.

Vocal training does not give Susan much of a singing voice, but it adds extra decibels to her shrillness when she lashes out at Kane after the bad review in his newspaper. In this test of wills, she yells "I'm through singin'," while he insists she will continue; the camera angle, seen from his eyes looking down at her cowering on the floor, leaves little question as to who will win. The opera tour montage turns that around as the light flickers out (a reference to Insull?) while the sound, like a faulty turntable, grinds to a halt. Only after her overdose (when the distorted strains of Rossini still haunt her recovery) does he finally get the hint. She sees the larger picture, recognizing that a whole audience does not want her. He temporarily gets his back up, as he had with his lesson to Matisti on public relations, saying that "That's when you've got to fight them," but he relents: "You won't have to any more." She takes the defeat as personal and cultural; she was out of her depth, knew it, and had to accept the verdict of an audience with ears. For him the defeat cut the last thread with the society he aspired to join, and he has nothing left but a palatial and reclusive retreat. Since no one would accept his monument to culture, society and himself – the Chicago Municipal Opera House – he had to settle for a monument to himself: Xanadu. He could live in such a monument, but since he had married opera rather than a woman, it should hardly be surprising that she has nothing to share with him in this splendid isolation.

When Jedediah returns Kane's declaration of principles with the shredded "severance" cheque after being fired, he exposes the integrity of a newspaper baron for what it is – a sham. The world of grand opera gets a similarly rough ride in this film, with sopranos who sing flat, puffed up singing teachers, meaningless operas that offer nothing but spectacle, and a patron who supports it for no reasons other than a combination of vanity and social climbing. In a film highly critical of the ruling class, what better way to attack the elite than to attack opera itself. The attack appears to come through the performance rather than the opera, although we may be missing something here, especially considering Welles's comment about this as Herrmann's chance "to do something witty and amusing." Singing flat may heighten Susan's pathetic situation, her feeling of standing on quicksand, as Herrmann pointed out, but there may be a poke here at the world of grand opera as well, especially at the most prestigious opera houses which frequently engage singers well past their prime, assuming their reputations will compensate for their inability to hold the pitch. Patrons who want something awe-inspiring tend to want singers with monumental egos as well, and will either forgive their flat high notes or perhaps will not even notice. But even worse than an old diva singing flat is a young one, like Susan Alexander.

While Herrmann had his fun with the performance, he may have enjoyed himself even more with the opera *Salammbo*. A master of irony and wit, Herrmann knew perfectly well that grand opera could be most effectively satirized not by turning it into a joke, with Anna Russell-like spoofs on Wagner or making Bugs Bunny a diva, but by keeping it serious, imitating the actual style as closely as possible. Unlike the theater, where, for example, Biedermeier plays in Vienna ran their course at the beginning of the 19th century, appealing to a peculiar mentality – and thankfully have not been revived – operas of an equivalent type abound in the 20th-century repertoire. These lesser operas may have spoken to their contemporary audiences in some way, but a century later they often offer nothing, although the peculiar mentality that governs operas prefers them to anything new. Perhaps something of that preference relates to their vacuity; if they say nothing to us they cannot be offensive or force us to think about unpleasant things.

Herrmann, in fact, imitated the style so well that fine sopranos such as Eileen Farrell, Kiri Te Kanawa and Rosamund Illing would later perform his *Salammbo* in contexts entirely detached from the film. It should be grand and swollen, but also sufficiently fatuous – "fairly implausible and unintelligible," as Houseman noted of the text, hardly surprising considering it comes from a 17th-century writer, Racine, whose works have proved of little interest in America, and undergoes a transformation to a 19th-century context. To make it even more unintelligible to Americans, the text is not in English, but in French. One recalls Insull's quarrel with Mary Garden over operas in French, which she especially liked, but would make little impression on the predominantly German and Italian immigrants. If one wishes opera to be understood, though, one writes it in the language of the country of the targeted audience; Verdi did not set his operas to German texts, and neither did Wagner to Italian. If Welles and Herrmann had wanted their audience to be able to follow the text, they would have set it in English. In fact, they did not wish it to be understood, any more than 19th-century grand opera should be understood. Opera companies like the Met in New York have recognized the principle, resisting the use of superscripts above the proscenium (or on the backs of seats) for most of the 20th century. Even for viewers of *Citizen Kane* who do understand French, Susan's mangled treatment of the language will effectively prevent anyone from comprehending a word of it.

Opera not intended to be understood seems to stand as a symbol of the inscrutability of the ruling class. They too, with their diamonds, stoles, limos, mansions and office towers should project images of grandeur, but their world should necessarily remain impenetrable. The model for their grandeur remained the 19th-century European aristocracy, and the opera they preferred belonged to that era and social class. For Welles and Herrmann, this could best be satirized by recreating it exactly as it was, since most members of the cinema audience would not only find the opera unappealing but would thoroughly enjoy it being done badly. Whether or not one subscribes to the touting of *Citizen Kane* as the finest American film ever made, characteristics such as the subtlety with which it treats opera underline the fact that, along with its many other extraordinary facets, Welles and his collaborators came up with a work of brilliance.

11

BURSTING OUT INTO OPERA:
FELLINI'S *E LA NAVE VA*

Near the end of Federico Fellini's *E la nave va* (*And the Ship Sails On*), a beautiful girl from an upper-crust family breaks away from the people of her class and joins a poor Serbian student as he and other peasants board a life boat facing an unknown fate, at the hands of their Austro-Hungarian captors on an unforgiving sea. This type of scenario may seem familiar, especially after James Cameron's *Titanic*, and verges on soap opera if not actual opera. Fellini knew the genre well, and does not attempt to deceive us with it: he turns his film into turn-of-the-century grand opera itself,[1] as the cast will periodically burst into arias and Verdi choruses. He makes certain we recognize the artifice;[2] his ships look like wooden bathtub toys, his ocean of plastic sheets could never be mistaken for water, a cardboard cut-out of the setting sun invokes a passenger's comment on its illusory quality, and at the end he shows us the hydraulic workings of the heaving ship in the Cinecittà studio.

Music in Fellini's films, usually provided by Nino Rota, plays an important although not typical role, as it becomes, for example, an image of salvation in works such as *Le notti di Cabiria*, *Il Bidone* or *La Strada*.[3] In these cases, Rota's music has virtually no emotional or narrative function in support of something else but becomes as necessary as a setting, a central object or even a character in both sound and visual terms, a crucial element in reaching the director's goal. In *E la nave va* the music does this by giving us opera, with Fellini manipulating the illusion of cinema into something with a peculiarly operatic twist, with all the artifice, overblown emotion, pomp and ceremony of opera.

Early in the film Fellini takes us through a brief history of cinema; it begins as a silent film in black and white, with appropriately distorted visuals and no sound but the whir of the projector. Gradually sounds emerge, not speaking or music, but the sounds that go with a ship being loaded. When we first encounter the narrator/journalist, his comments appear in subscript, not as in silent film where print occurs on otherwise blank screens which interrupt the visual images, but more in the modern mode of giving the text in translation. Since Freddie Jones, a British actor, plays that role, his words must be presented with subscripts or dubbing, and Fellini does both. Translation proves to be one of the fascinating facets of miscommunication as the film goes on, and Fellini introduces us to the issue early. Eventually color, speech and music emerge, but in the opening few minutes of silent film, Fellini relies on other means for the purposes of communication, and perhaps even here indirectly introduces opera, which had been such a strong model for early silent films such as *Cabiria* (1914), a film whose name Fellini would use half a century later.

Before anyone speaks a word, music makes its entrance, a piano reduction (again the silent film association) of part of Rossini's *Petite messe solennelle* corresponding with the arrival of a hearse carrying the ashes of the great diva Edmea Tudua. This voyage, we learn from the journalist, is a funeral procession, as Edmea's admirers, which include singers, conductors, opera managers, people of means, and members of the nobility, accompany her ashes to the island of Erimo, her birthplace near Greece, where the ashes will be spread. With these people assembled on the dockside, a conductor steps forward, raises his baton, and begins to conduct. To our amazement, they begin to sing operatic material, including choruses and solos, accompanied first by piano and then by full orchestra. The music used proves to be something of a collage, with words suitable to the film prepared by the conductor/arranger Gianfranco Plenezio, and the music largely adapted from Giuseppe Verdi's *La forza del destino* (The Power of Destiny), especially the fate motif first heard in the overture.

Fellini once said "I am a liar, but an honest one." Any artist as fertile and prodigious as Fellini will attract hundreds of interviews, and of course he will see his comments collected in books or other documents which leave a record of his aesthetic views. Chroniclers have dutifully taken down these remarks and writers trying to make sense of the man and his works have believed them, quoting him at length on various subjects, including his views on opera. At the end of *E la nave va*, he gives us a number of options to explain the historic events associated with the sinking of the ships, but none rings true. Fellini does not deal in truth in his films, so why should we imagine that he would in his comments? His films thrust forward a dizzying array of contradictions; even the most autobiographical ones offer mainly equivocation and dissimulation. One can only assume that he took enormous satisfaction in seeing that the confusion has been perpetuated in print, at the hands of earnest truth seekers. On the subject of opera he claimed for years that he disliked it (in fact, music in general, except for Rota's), and remained ignorant of this Italian passion. After *E la nave va* that story changed. Opera, he now professed, had been a part of his youth in his home town, where half the inhabitants regularly attended performances, many getting drunk and serenading under his window while staggering home. "I have always felt like an outsider," he claimed, "carrying a vague sense of guilt because of not wanting to participate in this warm, enveloping, impassioned, collective Italian ritual."[4] Spending a lifetime claiming to prefer the circus to opera required something of a tightrope walk, and at this point he may have temporarily fallen off.

Now it appeared he knew opera very well, especially Italy's beloved Verdi. As one who delighted in spreading confusion, Fellini found opera to be the ideal medium for this purpose, and that cinema could achieve this through operatic means. Detractors of opera like to point out the unintelligibility and even absurdity of operatic plots, a criticism justified in many cases. High emotions may run at a feverish pitch for three hours (or longer), but no one in the opera house has the faintest idea why the characters become upset, ecstatic, angry or passionate. Selecting *La forza del destino* as the musical centerpiece for *E la nave va* appears not to have been coincidental; if Fellini's film seems difficult to understand, it's child's play compared to the incomprehensibility of this opera. Even in a well-known collection of opera synopses, the author calls it "a cumbersome melodrama."[5] No one should try to remember a plot like this: Don Alvaro (tenor), a nobleman from India, loves Leonora (a soprano, not to be confused with the hundreds of other operatic heroines by this name), daughter of the Marquis of Calatrava (bass). Dad does not like the suitor, and intercepts the eloping pair.

Alvaro tells him to get lost (goading Leonora's father to imprison him or take his vengeance), and throws down his pistol which fatally wounds the old man who curses his daughter as he dies.

Here ends the straightforward part: the Marquis has a son too, Don Carlos (not to be confused with the one who has an opera named after him), who swears to avenge his father by killing his sister and her lover. Leonora disguises herself as a man, joins a convent, and lives in a cave without identity – heaping curses in advance on anyone who tries to identify her. Alvaro goes on the lam, joins the Spanish army, and hopes for an early death, believing her to be dead. He saves the life of a wounded man who just happens to be Don Carlos; not only do they become friends but they swear eternal allegiance after Alvaro has been wounded and appears to be dying. He gives Don Carlos a packet of letters and asks him to destroy them, but Carlos discovers a picture of his sister among them. The inevitable challenge follows, but Carlos will not fight; the barely living Alvaro manages to wound Carlos (where but in professional wrestling could that happen?). Thinking he has finished off both father and son, he too heads for a monastery where he becomes Father Raphael. He had not killed Carlos, who finds him and again incites him to fight, which they do in front of the cave in which Leonora hides. Alvaro wins, but cannot perform the last rites because of a curse. Leonora emerges from the cave to recognize her dying brother, and bloodthirsty to the end, Carlos stabs her. Alvaro dives over a precipice and the monks sing a *Miserere*.

Here stood Fellini's kind of story, with excessive emotion, death threats and death itself, but for what: a gun thrown on the ground that went off by mistake. We have no possible reason to care about these people, except that the ingenious composer, Verdi, makes us care by transforming them into music. That is not to say that he makes them seem real; the music of the opera takes cardboard characters in this case and renders them interesting because of a purely artificial medium in which no one talks but instead uses *bel canto* singing, accompanied by rich orchestral tones. Since no one actually communicates that way, not even in Italy, except in opera, no one is deceived; we accept it as pure artifice, and find the appropriate emotional space which only opera can inflate.

Fellini had for many years before 1983 tried to convince his viewers that cinema should not be taken as anything other than illusion and artifice, and now he drove the point home by making his paste-up characters from grand opera burst into song. In fact, only an opera audience would know what to make of this pack of snobs living the good life of the belle epoch, indulging the final moments of decadence, obsession and narcissism before the war in 1914 which pushed their world over the precipice. Orlando, the incompetent, bumbling journalist/narrator, turns to the camera which follows him around for his interviews and identifies these beautiful people: they include the greatest living soprano, Ildebranda Cuffari (Barbara Jefford); an obnoxious tenor, Aureliano Fucilletto (Victor Polette), whose resemblance to Pavarotti appears only partly coincidental; Sir Reginald J. Dongby (Peter Cellier), an English nobleman; his nymphomaniac wife Lady Violet Dongby (Norma West), whom her voyeuristic husband constantly follows about; the pudgy and apparently feeble-minded Grand Duke of Herzog (Fiorenzo Serra); his blind sister the Princess Lherimia (Pina Bausch) who has an on-going affair with the prime minister (Philip Lock); the effeminate Count of Bassano (Pasquale Zito), traveling with his mother and his shrine to Edmea; the mime artist Fred Williams (Sabatino Lepori), also traveling with his mother who must remind him not to be so obvious about staring at sailors with their shirts off; a Russian bass who can hypnotize a chicken with his low notes (and the hapless Orlando as well, who somewhat resembles a chicken — both in looks and brain power); the former secretary of Edmea, who rouses Edmea's spirit during a seance; the elderly former teachers of Edmea, and an assortment of other singers, conductors, and beautiful people.

If we find these characters shallow, distant, one-dimensional, or impossible to identify with, we have missed the point: these characters from Italian grand opera offer us no more or less than such characters would. Lady Violet, a first cousin to a merry wife from Windsor, pursues anyone male and younger than herself; sailors will do nicely, and during a dance scene initiated by the gypsies she becomes ecstatic when swept off her feet by strong young studs who pass her back and forth in a swirling dance. Sir Reginald smiles and laughs nervously as he views her exploits, and seems disappointed to have missed her encounter with a sailor in her cabin. Her name Violet seems no coincidence: her promiscuity rivals that of a prostitute, perhaps a Violetta from *La Traviata* — which the musical score also invokes. Sir Reginald is the classic cuckold of which opera has many, such as Don Alfonzo in

Donizetti's *Lucrezia Borgia*, Reinhart in Verdi's *Un Ballo in Maschera*, or even better, Mr. Ford of Nicolai's *The Merry Wives of Windsor* as well as Verdi's *Falstaff*. He completely lacks power, except to put off Orlando's interview.

Who could be more operatic than a grand duke, a character type found in at least every second grand opera? As Fellini's Grand Duke seems entirely incapable of saying anything intelligent or even beating his blind sister at chess, he becomes purely operatic as a type of stock character. He holds the highest rank of anyone on this ship of fools, and his emotions, such as fear, represent the inflated ones of opera since the person behind them lacks all substance. If opera often says nothing, but says it with great pomp and ceremony, Fellini's Grand Duke goes one step better. Orlando's interview with him proves one of the most delicious scenes of this film/opera; before it begins two bodyguards wrestle Orlando to the floor of the fencing room, thinking him a common intruder, informing us of the greatness of the character about to be interviewed. When released, Orlando states his question in such a garbled way no one has the slightest idea what he wants to know. Rephrasing it, he asks for the Grand Duke's view of the international situation. The reply in German, that "we are sitting on the edge of a volcano," comes through in distorted translation as "we are sitting on the mouth of a mountain." Much arguing ensues not only about the correct word "edge" or "mouth" but about which word the Grand Duke used in German. When they finally get it right, Orlando inquires what that means, and his adolescent-looking interviewee gestures with his arms and says "Poom." Orlando still does not get it, so the Grand Duke amplifies this as "Poom, Poom, Poom," with the instruction to translate that. Orlando now seems to catch on, as the Grand Duke chatters on in an indeterminate German accent, noting, among other things, that "wir sind alle toll" (we are all crazy). The interview ends, and Orlando seems highly satisfied with these words of wisdom, which of course have been completely vacuous. But just when we think the Grand Duke a fop and an idiot, he emerges in full regalia to prevent the Austrian flagship from boarding the Gloria N. and taking the Serbs, who were rescued at sea, as prisoners.

The purpose of this voyage, to take the ashes of the greatest living soprano to her native Greece, of course had a parallel in real life – the funeral cortege of Maria Callas. Real life in this case must be qualified: as the greatest diva of her time and the most famous woman in the world, Callas lived the life of an operatic character – someone much larger than life – whose loves and quarrels became a libretto in the press. Like any prima donna she would have to die before her time, and Callas obliged with this too, elevating her from diva to immortal prima donna. If her fans showed fierce loyalty while she lived, they became positively fanatical after her death, especially among the adoring opera queens of the operatic demimonde. Fellini knew this well, and placed one such fanatic on the voyage, the Count of Bassano, who worships in his shrine to Edmea, caressing the memorabilia, reciting poems he wrote to her, carrying a special flower he sent her daily, and lovingly cranking a projector of film clips of her. Orlando does not believe he really loved her, and trying to find the word to characterize the Count, settles on "ambiguous" – "very ambiguous." The seance offends the young Count, and after bursting out of the room, he returns unnoticed in drag, the shadowy image of his goddess and idol, throwing the participants of the seance for a loop when their invocation yields the ghost of Edmea. The tenor discovers the ruse and congratulates the Count on his disguise; the Count, as though mortally wounded, unleashes a curse on those who would not let her rest in peace. With this curse the opera queen enters the opera himself, protecting his prima donna from her tormentors.

Fellini and Plenizio do not use only operatic music for the film, although even their non-operatic excerpts play a distinctly operatic role. Rossini's *Petite messe solennelle* served well to provide a funereal tone, and rapid motion in the kitchen receives the appropriate orchestral tempo and rhythm. As the camera moves from kitchen to dining room, where waiters must carry themselves with grace and decorum, the music segues into a familiar passage from Tchaikovsky's *Nutcracker*, in fact the "Dance of the Mirlitons" (toy reed pipes). Here Fellini slows down the speed of the film, and the dining room floor becomes a ballet stage, with waiters – trays in hand – gliding gently toward tables with flute-like gracefulness. Attention shifts from the waiters to the beautiful people they serve, and with that the music changes to "The Swan" from Saint-Saëns's *Carnival of the Animals*; a tenor narcissistically preens himself as though looking in a mirror, a swan admiring his own beauty in the reflection of the pond. As the camera pans the diners and Orlando identifies them, the swan gives way to "The Blue Danube" as we see the directors of the Vienna State Opera. When conflict later erupts between the Austro-Hungarian flagship and the Italian vessel carrying Serbians, Viennese waltzes punctuate the strains of Verdi choruses. Since Fellini cannot mount much conflict with his cut-out ships, he gives it to us – if somewhat unmenacingly – with Viennese waltzes and Italian opera choruses. Back at the dining room, the blind princess gives us a demonstration of synesthesia, generating colors in her mind from musical passages or tones of voices; an Austrian general with a grating, guttural voice offers her no color at all – only a void.

A little later the camera returns to the kitchen where the Russian bass will later put a chicken and Orlando into a trance, this time with a table set with champagne glasses and bottles with precisely varying amounts of water, anticipating a performance of the well-known Schubert "Moment musical" in f minor for piano – at, of course, a much reduced tempo. The old singing masters lead this performance rubbing the glasses, and others including the Count join in, tapping a bottle with a spoon, or blowing over the tops of bottles. It ends with an argument about the amount of water in one of the glasses which produced a flat note. This circus-like presentation, like that of the Russian bass, seems to place some of the characters in their real element.

One other musical work, again for piano, receives prominent treatment, always in association with Edmea. After the Count enters his shrine to her and cranks the projector to reveal Edmea mugging for the camera, riding in a river punt, or accepting the applause of her audience after a performance, Debussy's "Clair de lune" from the *Suite bergamasque* accompanies these film-clip images. We hear the same music late in the film, the ship sinking and water at waist level, as the Count remains true to his beloved diva, refusing to abandon his shrine to her, again running film clips to bring her alive as the water engulfs him. At the very end the film returns to the silent era, and after the end credits the screen goes completely dark, remaining this way for a few minutes as "Clair de lune" reaches its own ethereal conclusion. We may know this piece best through this familiar piano version, but even the piano piece is based on a poem by Paul Verlaine, set not only by Debussy as a song, but also Fauré, among other French composers. Since Fellini gives this piece the last word in his film, it may very well be worth noting Verlaine's text:

"Moonlight"
Your soul is a chosen landscape
Where charming masqueraders and dancers are promenading,
Playing the lute and dancing, and almost
Sad beneath their fantastic disguises,
While singing in the minor key
Of triumphant love, and the pleasant life.
They seem not to believe in their happiness,
And their song blends with the moonlight,
The quiet moonlight, sad and lovely,
Which sets the birds in the trees adreaming,
And makes the fountains sob with ecstasy,
The tall slim fountains among the marble statues.[6]

Whether Fellini knew of this poem or not, it very much captures at least part of the tone of the film. Like the characters from an opera, those in *E la nave va* seem charming masqueraders in fantastic disguises, a dying breed grasping for the last remains of the pleasant life, but in the minor key. That of course shows only one side of it as Fellini allows us to laugh at them as well, conscious of their absurdity which induces them to sing operatically as much as speak in normal discourse.

In fact, in turning this film into opera, Fellini may be thumbing his nose at opera and all its trappings. Perhaps like his memories of inebriated people returning from the opera and serenading under his window, his characters here seem intoxicated with themselves, with their belle epoch existence, with fetishes, with the paranormal, and with a world of artifice. Their world may be as dead as Edmea, its ashes to be spread with hers, but that does not prevent them from believing that they still have the power to act decisively in the face of challenge or danger. Their acts of heroism now become the heroic acts of grand opera, separated by the orchestra pit and proscenium from real life, where they in fact are cowards, fumblers and idiots.

While some of the opera scenes may leave some viewers slightly confused, others point with a satirical finger at the excesses and absurdity of opera. No doubt the efforts of the Russian bass to put a chicken into a trance (and by extension Orlando and the operatic audience) fall into that category. Another such delightful scene occurs in the ship's vast boiler room, a purgatorial scene with partially clad Caliban-like creatures stoking the enormous furnaces which drive the deafening engines.

E la nave va (And the Ship Sails On) (the stokers enjoy an operatic display)

On a catwalk high above this squalid floor the sophisticated passengers file in angelically to observe the ship's source of power, soaring here in striking contrast to the wretchedness below. Orlando gets no reply to his question about the length of their shifts, but we can assume they are painfully long when the first mate jests that they get seasick if they come up on deck. A stoker recognizes Signora Cuffari, and makes a request to the captain that she should favor them with a song; the captain contemptuously dismisses the request as preposterous, impossible in any event over the din of the engines, while Signora Cuffari looks on in disbelief. The captain seems not to realize that in Italy opera belongs to the entire population, not just the elite, and he certainly cannot understand their continued shouts of adoration in spite of his refusal.

While the soprano remains mortified, the tenor Fucilletto, himself a much earthier sort, perhaps from the working class, belts out a high note, to the stokers' delight. Another tenor goes one better, singing a whole phrase with an equally high note. Fucilletto, not to be outdone, holds an even higher note for an impossibly long time, to cries of "bravo" from below. An aging soprano joins the fray, to Cuffari's disbelief, but realizing she has been upstaged, Cuffari herself finally joins in. Now Fucilletto cuts her off in mid-phrase, bursting in with the famous misogynistic aria "La donna e mobile" from *Rigoletto*, joined by the other tenor near the end, and even the distressed Cuffari for the final high cadence. This triggers a series of similar cadences, either held longer than the last one or on a note higher than the one Verdi wrote; Fucilletto's tongue flaps in the breeze as he outdoes the previous singer, and Cuffari goes into glass-breaking range with her final coup. They leave to a flurry of "bravos" from the stokers standing near the gaping doors of the flaming furnaces; even the other passengers on the catwalk join in the applause. Opera may have been reduced to its basest form here, a laughable competition among inflated egos, but it also bridged the gulf between the coal-blackened workers and the beautiful people.

While this scene may be pure satire, the operatic scene near the end enters the realm of the exaggerated emotions of grand opera. The Austrians have agreed to leave the ship alone until the completion of Edmea's funeral ceremony, the highlight of which features a recording of Edmea herself singing. Orlando complains that the singing could not move the Austrians, a remark much more loaded than its specific meaning here as they force the Serbians off the Gloria N. Orlando defiantly resists the Austrians, and his shouts of "no" lead into a chorus of defiance. These opera people may be able to imagine defiance as an operatic scene with the appropriate musical emotions, but they remain utterly powerless to do anything about it; the Serbian prisoners depart as they continue to sing. In fact, amid the disembarkation, the chorus shifts to "Va pensiero" from Verdi *Nabucco*, a chorus which in its original opera expresses the grief of a nation (the Israelites) in captivity, wistfully mindful of its precious but lost homeland. They have now succumbed entirely to fate, and the chorus returns to the fate motif from *La forza del destino*. Verdi then gives way to a Viennese waltz as the Austrian domination appears complete.

E la nave va ends in chaos as the 1914 political situation complicates the lives of these opera stars and opera fetishists. The Serbian student/terrorist with whom the pretty English girl leaves tosses a small incendiary device into the Austrian ship, and Orlando gives us various interpretations of what may have happened. None of his explanations seems plausible, and his final one, which he refuses even to mention, leaves us in a complete state of confusion. Yet another operatic chorus scene, this time conducted as near the beginning of the film, brings everyone, including the stokers, together for a dramatic finale. If nothing else has been accomplished, at least under the umbrella of opera there can be some class equality. The explosions of the ships expose the ruse of the set, as we watch hydraulic supports of the Cinacittá ship and the technicians manipulating the set and us. In symmetrical fashion Fellini goes back to black and white and then silent film; the final shot shows Orlando, informing us that most of these people survived, rowing a lifeboat with a rhinoceros as his only passenger. By this point, Fellini has exposed the artifice over and over, not only with opera but also by taking us inside the workings of the set. What, we might wonder, did the survivors survive? Themselves, Fellini's directing, the absurdities of the plot, the voyage in a cardboard ship, the opera fanatics, or opera itself? If Fellini could withstand opera, this most Italian of institutions, so could his cast. As an Italian, thumbing his nose at opera for Fellini meant something very different than it would to someone else – especially a North American. For him insulting opera is a little like mocking a favorite relative – something which can only be done with affection. Just as the film takes us through a mini-history of cinema, it also shows us that cinema and opera have much in common, and in Fellini's realm we miss the boat entirely if we imagine that the images and emotions in either one serve a realistic end.

$$\boxed{12}$$

THE CHARMING OPERA SNOB IN
HANNAH AND HER SISTERS

Woody Allen thoroughly dislikes certain types of snobs. Most objectionable among these stands the overbearing intellectual whose reviling view of the world destroys any chance of enjoyment, whose oppressive logic demolishes any touch of emotion or feeling, or whose relentless criticism of anything but high culture becomes ridiculous in its dogged narrowness. Various persons of this nature populate Allen's films since they are very much a part of the New York he shows us – upper middle class people of whom a good number happen to be academics or artists. Some snobs Allen will portray affectionately, allowing us to enjoy and even identify with their foibles or obsessions, but not the type of snob just described. Such a person must be put in his place, exposed as an ass, and punished in some way, such as losing the woman who once admired his intellectual prowess after she sees through it, or through a public humiliation by being beaten at his own intellectual game.

No one represents this type of character more strongly in Allen's films than Frederick in *Hannah and Her Sisters*, played with obsessive intensity by Max von Sydow; the intellectual strictures of this artist's world are so excruciatingly narrow that he pinches the life out of all who come near him. Allen almost makes it difficult to laugh at him because of his intensity; most viewers will likely just feel revulsion toward him, and wonder how the beautiful Lee (Barbara Hershey) could have fallen for him in the first place. That can be explained by her need for father/mentor figures, but even someone with those needs can take only so much, and she eventually leaves him because of more powerful emotional attractions – and just to lighten up a little. When she leaves, Frederick simply fades into celluloid oblivion, perhaps the most fitting punishment for someone who tried to exert influence in the way that he had.

A slightly – but only slightly – less objectionable cousin to Frederick is the media professor from Columbia University standing directly behind Alvy (Allen) and Annie (Diane Keaton) in a film queue in *Annie Hall*, whose spouting of tedious theories on the arts and culture drives Allen to distraction. One cannot turn around and tell someone like that to shut up, especially if one also tries to make sense of the world. Similarly, arguing with him would not accomplish anything, since he will simply pull rank as he did – noting that in his capacity as a professor he can say whatever he wants by way of interpreting Marshall McLuhan, and one should defer to his position of academic authority. One can only beat that type of intellectual snob by one-upping him, by somehow pulling rank on him in order to dismantle his presumed authority. Allen does it in this case by pulling Marshall McLuhan himself out from behind the ticket booth, who tells the Columbia prof that he has heard everything he said and that this presumptuous academic has failed entirely to understand him. That shuts the very embarrassed snob up, and a satisfied Allen says to the audience, "don't you wish life would always turn out that way."

Another type of snob turns up in *Hannah* who also could be in for a rough ride, but in fact Allen treats him with sympathy and even affection: the opera snob. In many films before Allen's, people who go to the opera are made to look foolish, and the one Allen probably would have been most conscious of was the Marx Brothers' *A Night at the Opera*, considering that Allen uses a scene from *Duck Soup* later in *Hannah* as his epiphany – the stroke of salvational humor which puts an end to Mickey's incompetent attempts at suicide. The Marx Brothers could take an oppressive world and let us laugh at it by deriding its pretensions, and while for them opera and its patrons deserved the very best they could dish out, Allen could not share their position on this point. For Allen the opera enthusiast remains a snob and deserves to be mocked at least a little; we certainly see him as a snob, but a charming and likeable one whose obsession may be indulged.

In *Hannah*, the opera snob first appears in "The Stanislavski Catering Company in Action" segment, with Holly (Diane Wiest) and her friend April (Carrie Fisher), two aspiring actors not making any headway in auditions, on their first catering stint. One of the guests, David (Sam Waterston), bored stiff with the snobs and superficially urbane people at the party, strays into the kitchen and strikes up a conversation with the caterers, first about the delicious food, and then about the women being too attractive to be caterers. In seeking refuge from the tedium of the party, he heads for a radio in the kitchen and turns on a broadcast of *Aida*, hoping this will not disturb them or that he will not get in their way. Both women, very much on the lookout for a handsome and sophisticated man, not only assure him to the contrary but profess their own affection for opera: Holly, racking her brains, stammers out that "we saw, um, Pavarotti, eh, uh, in *Ernani* at the Met, and I cried..."[1] Only another opera buff would recognize the title *Ernani*, an opera by Verdi, or why she would cry. When David readily admits that "I cry at the opera," April picks up on the tone of the conversation, confessing that "Oh, I-I-I go limp in the last scene in *La Traviata*." In American cinema men generally avoid crying, and certainly should not cry at the opera, where presumably most of them go only because of being dragged there by society-conscious wives. Here we have a single man who not only goes willingly to the opera but gets emotional about it: "I have a private box at the Met. I bring my little bottle of wine, I open it, I sit there and I watch and I cry. It's disgusting." Some viewers may agree, but Allen means no malice here; what should we think?

Most of Allen's films of course give us a unique and distinctive backdrop which could only be New York, so much so that New York almost becomes another leading character in each film.[2] And Woody Allen's New York of the 1980s and 1990s bears little resemblance to the one inflicted on us by television police shows or crime films that focus on the city's dark underside, smeared with graffiti, or squalid slums overrun by gun-toting thugs. People in his films do not fear walking on the streets, although certain areas that should be avoided may be omitted from his visual images. These films do not push social consciousness at us, urban decay, political corruption, or psychopathic killers; the nearest he comes to that is his peculiar and distinctive impression of the neurotic New Yorkers or the occasional joke about dazed people with their life possessions in a shopping cart or a paper bag. The side of New York that interests him focuses on the lives of educated people, their love relationships, their interests in reading or the fine arts, and the bearing that New York with all its seductive possibilities has on these people. We do not see the city of *The Pawnbroker*, *Midnight Cowboy*, or *Taxi Driver*.

Allen's films do not necessarily appeal to the young audience that most movies target since that audience will have difficulty identifying with the impression of New York he presents – an elegant and sophisticated New York relatively free of the drug culture. The choice of music in *Hannah* reflects the New York that Allen loves along with the establishments where that music would be performed, including jazz, Broadway tunes, classical music and opera. If rock music turns up, Allen treats it negatively, as he does in *Hannah*, and here he takes a poke at the drug culture as well. In a flashback of an unfortunate date with Holly, she drags Mickey (Allen) to a rock club, the 39 Steps, where "three punkers – a girl with pink hair, a girl with a spiked mohawk, and a guy with Stevie Wonder braids and sunglasses – watch and bop their heads to the sounds of the off-screen rock band." The camera shifts to a sleazy-looking rock band, and then to Mickey (the only person there wearing a suit) and Holly sitting at a crowded and smoky table.

Holly, enjoying herself, asks Mickey why he keeps grimacing. He shouts "I can't hear you. I can't hear anything. I'm, I'm, I'm, I'm gonna lose hearing in my ear!" Holly boasts that he is witnessing genius, but he protests, "I, I, my ears are experiencing a meltdown! I can't hear anything." She revels in the energy, the bombarding vibrations, and opens a vial of cocaine, to which he responds with, "Holly, I'm frightened! I'm – After they sing... they're gonna take hostages!" When she produces a metal straw and starts snorting the cocaine, he pleads with her to stop: "You're gonna burn a hole in your... You're gonna develop a third nostril!" Out on the street she says she loves songs about extraterrestrial life, and he comments he can do without them being sung by extraterrestrials. She accuses him of being a "tightass," while he laments "I can't understand you. Your sisters, both sisters have such good taste in music. I don't know where you went, went wrong." When he meets Holly again, some time after this disastrous date, which she ends with "you don't like rock music, you won't get high... It's like I'm dating Cardinal Cooke," it is in the jazz section of a record store, after which their relationship blossoms into marriage. She reforms, thanks to a little sternness from Hannah too, and Allen can return to his drugless, rock-less New York.

The Metropolitan Opera stands as a central fixture of that vital New York for Allen, one of the great institutions of the city. It may be patronized by an element of society that even Allen has no interest in, but that does not prevent it from offering something very special to the entire psyche of the city – the presentation of works of great beauty which allows for an outpouring of emotion in a world that otherwise shuns emotion. Here, of course, we have something very distinctive to New York, as no other city in the country has such a venerable opera house, in fact famous throughout the country because of the long-running Saturday radio broadcasts, regarded by many non-New Yorkers as that which makes the city great. Yet, one must be in New York to enjoy it fully, not only to hear the sounds but to bask in the full visual glory as well. Those who do so may be snobs, but in a place of sophistication their snobbery proves to be the most acceptable and desirable kind.

When David strays into the kitchen and starts the conversation about opera, Allen sets the stage for his impression. Opera becomes a refuge from mindless superficiality, and in the conversation with the caterers something human happens which could not happen otherwise at this type of party. Within a few sentences these three people discover of each other that they do not fear or shun emotions, and therefore that the basis exists for friendship and perhaps even more. Holly especially would like there to be more, and kicks herself as she sees April outmaneuvering her in snaring David. Some time later, we see Holly and David in his private box at the Met, watching a scene from *Manon Lascaut* and sipping wine. As they look at each other and raise their glasses to a toast, we catch something of the emotion in their eyes. Holly will not end up with David, but he has nevertheless proved himself to be a worthy catch.

As if it is not enough simply to present opera as one of the predominant features of New York, Allen takes that a step further, linking the opera lover with the best possible vision of the city, the architectural tour of some of the great landmarks. David turns out to be an architect, the owner of a Jaguar, an opera lover, and a snob; Holly and April do not hesitate for a moment to get into his Jaguar and take the Manhattan tour – the New Yorkers being shown New York, Woody

Allen indulging us in his own love of a great city. His running commentary borders on the academic jargon that Allen takes such pleasure in satirizing in the likes of Frederick or the McLuhanite in *Annie Hall*, but as this tour now reveals what Allen himself loves profoundly, he spoofs his own inability to express why it affects him so deeply. David, looking from a building he designed to Holly and April, notes that "the design's deliberately noncontextual. But I wanted to... keep the atmosphere of the street, you know, and the proportions." April, the clever university-educated woman, manages "I-i-it has an o-organic quality... It's almost... almost, uhhh, entirely wholly interdependent, if you know what I mean. I-I... can't put it into words. The important thing is-is-is it-it breathes." She sounds absurd, but instead of a McLuhanist rebuff, the architect encourages her: "You know, April, people pass by vital structures in this city all the time, and they never take the time to appreciate them. I get the feeling you tune in to your environment." Holly, having muttered but a series of "uh-huh... oh... uh... right... oh... oh yeah... oh... it's really important," later in the back seat reflects on her defeat: "Naturally I get taken home first. Well, obviously he prefers April. Of course I was so tongue-tied all night. I can't believe I said that about the Guggenheim.... Where did April come up with that stuff about Adolph Loos and terms like 'organic form'? Well, naturally. She went to Brandeis."

After looking at David's buildings they take the tour of his (Allen's) favorite landmarks of the city. These include:

the Dakota, complete with surrounding winter trees, the Graybar building on Lexington Avenue, an incredibly ornate building on Seventh Avenue and Fifty-eighth Street, a red-stone church, an old building with embellished, bulging windows on West Forty-fourth Street, the Art Deco Chrysler Building, a red-brick building, Abigail Adams's old stone house, and the Pomander Walk nestled off Broadway on the Upper West Side. The group can be seen walking down the path between the old-fashioned row houses and shrubbery.

Allen has already established the connection between the physical beauty of New York and the grandeur of opera, but on this tour he takes it even further, accompanying it with a grand musical flourish from opera, in fact, an excerpt from Puccini's *Madam Butterfly*. But Allen did not select just any excerpt from the opera; his choice reveals genuine directorial brilliance. He uses the prelude from the beginning of *Madam Butterfly*, an instrumental passage which denotes excitement and radiance, accompanying, in fact, an architectural tour of sorts in the opera. At the start of the opera, Goro, a Japanese marriage broker and real estate agent, shows the American navy lieutenant Pinkerton the interior of a villa which Pinkerton will rent for his mistress (she believes wife) Cho-Cho-San.

The connection here may be more than enough to make this a most apt selection for the architectural tour of New York, but in fact it goes one very large step further. Contrary to the musical practice of other late 19th or early 20th-Century operas, Puccini designs this prelude as a fugue (technically a fugato, although we need not split hairs about that), perhaps the most architecturally structured of all musical formats. The heyday of the fugue came in the first half of the 18th century, most notably with the music of J. S. Bach, whose *48 Preludes and Fugues* are masterpieces, whose Art of the Fugue takes it to the highest possible level, and whose numerous other fugal movements in various instrumental and vocal works remain unsurpassed. An almost mathematical constructive element in Bach's fugues provides them with a structural principle that dazzles the ear of anyone prepared to try and follow his musical logic. After Bach's death the fugue may have taken a temporary recess, but when Haydn and Mozart discovered Bach's fugues, they eagerly set out to write their own, in keyboard works, string quartets and other types of works where it seemed appropriate. Beethoven embraced the fugue as well, especially in the finales of some of his late piano sonatas and string quartets, shifting the focus of these works to these movements which take on a spiritual quality in part because of the association of fugal writing with liturgical music.

Because of this mathematical or technical element of the fugue, many later 19th-century composers had less interest in it, perhaps fearing that it would constrict the more overtly emotional impact they often wished their music – and opera in particular – to have. Puccini among others proved that to be a groundless concern, as his fugue at the beginning of *Madam Butterfly* not only captures the essence of the tour of the villa but also evokes the appropriate spirit for the feelings of enthusiasm experienced especially by Cho-Cho-San (or Butterfly). As for the constructive features of the fugue, without going into that in too much detail, it would be useful to have some idea as to how it works. Typically, it will have three or four voices; it begins with one voice by itself, adding the others in a fairly prescribed and orderly fashion, showing the constructive principle of starting with one structural unit – the single brick as it were – and then building toward greater complexity and context. That single voice begins the exposition by providing the subject, which a second voice will then imitate or answer, followed by the third and fourth voices doing the same. As each new voice enters, the previous voice shifts to a countersubject role or may simply offer free counterpoint; by the time the last voice enters, the richness of the counterpoint in the other voices gives something highly complex yet tightly integrated.

After all the voices have entered, the fugue can move into an episode, and then proceed with such things as stretto (imitating motives from the subject) or invertible counterpoint (allowing a lower voice to be placed above higher ones). When sufficient contrast or development has taken place, there will be a return to the subject matter of the exposition, rounding the whole thing off in a type of closed form, making the structural design complete. Aside from the technical or constructive elements of the fugue there can be something more specifically communicative as well, following the basic principles of classical rhetoric. In the exposition the composer presents a formal proposition, while the episode may refute that with opposing material. Later the initial proposition will be strengthened, and a forceful conclusion will drive it home.

Since the Puccini excerpt in question uses fugato instead of fugue (fugato being more fugue-like than real fugue), it does not go through all the structural elements just described, but by association with the fugue it will invoke those features. With the somewhat less formal design it can also be freer to explore the emotional side of things, and this Puccini certainly does, making his operatic treatment especially apt for the architectural tour in *Hannah*. Here the sense of beauty of New York, the idea of vital structures being in tune with the city environment, and the sense of three passionate people aware of these things and conscious of their emotions and perhaps future relationships all come together. For Woody Allen opera offers an ideal image for this type of blending, a fusion which in America probably could not be possible anywhere other than in New York.

PART FOUR

WAGNER'S BASTARDS

13

MISREADING WAGNER: THE POLITICS OF FRITZ LANG'S *SIEGFRIED*

We may be astounded by the extent of Richard Wagner's influence not only on film music but on cinema itself; but one suspects that Wagner himself, who did not lack a large ego, would have somehow taken it in stride. If he could be a serious force in new directions in literature, as he was well before he died, having a striking effect on major writers such as Poe, Baudelaire and the whole school of French symbolist poets, then why not Griffith, Eisenstein and the numerous others about to be explored. For pure Wagnerians, who measure his achievements strictly in operatic terms, this apparent Wagnerian turn in the direction of cinema may seem something of a digression – resisting definition as the master's legitimate cultural progeny. But Wagner himself had a vision of all the arts coming together in one massive medium, a fusion that could yield something (so he believed) no individual art form could approach. When he died in 1883, opera ventured to do this with music and literature, but the operatic stage could not reach the visual heights he envisaged. Cinema has brought in the visual element as an equal partner, and one can only imagine that Wagner himself would have been delighted by the possibility. In the Wagnerian scheme of things music lies behind all else, infusing the other arts with their underlying meaning which resists definition with words. The genuine Wagnerians of the 20th century have been filmmakers, perhaps artistic bastards as some may see it, but remarkably keeping alive the legacy of this extraordinary cultural force through a combination of emulation and misunderstanding.

* * *

Traversing the treacherous waters of the Atlantic to its first showing in the United States, Fritz Lang's *Siegfried* received a welcome from Moraunt Hall of *The New York Times* on 24 August 1925 comparable to the arrival of a new masterpiece by Puccini: "In 'Siegfried,' a pictorial version of the Nordic sagas which was presented before a distinguished gathering at the Century Theatre last night, there is, for the first time, more than a mere suggestion of the invasion of the sacred realm of opera." For anyone expecting a cinematic facsimile of Richard Wagner's *Siegfried*, he offers the following warning: "Its characters and the scenes will conflict with the opinions of those who are thoroughly familiar with the trilogy, who may have their own conceptions of heroic figures, gained from years of faithful attendance to opera." By "trilogy" he apparently means "tetrology" minus one (*Das Rhinegold*), since the first work of the *Ring* cycle plays no part in Lang's plot.

Most writers on Lang since 1925 have berated Hall and other American reviewers of the time for imagining Lang's two-part opus *Die Nibelungen* (*Siegfried* and *Kriemhilds Rache* [*Kriemhild's Revenge*]) to be some sort of misguided attempt to adapt Wagner to the screen. Lang, in fact, had no interest in retelling this tale in the same way that Wagner, Friedrich Hebbel or anyone else from the previous century had. Lang recognized that any version of the story must reflect an epic engendering of the great German myth, one that argues a vital position of how German society regards itself, or where it finds its strength.

Lang himself comments on the issue, and while he sets us straight in general terms, his more specific comments simply muddy the waters. In fact, it could be argued that he intentionally misleads us because his underlying objective – the one that emerges from the shadows of the film itself – would be much too difficult to swallow; that message must be subliminally absorbed into the consciousness where its wordless urges can grow and eventually permeate attitudes. Here, he has much in common with Wagner on the methods of achieving such results, recognizing that the visually seducing means of cinema can touch the psyche in much the same way as the musically alluring pull of opera, but as for the message itself Lang's position could not be further removed from Wagner's.

Having been accused of supporting the cause of the Nazis with *Siegfried*, Lang on numerous occasions came to his own defense, putting it in terms of national pride and boosting sagging spirits in the aftermath of World War I. In the last interview he gave, published in the *Village Voice* on 16 August 1976, he was still trying to set the record straight:

> By making the Siegfried legend into a film, I wanted to show that Germany was searching for an ideal in her past, even during the horrible time after the First World War in which the picture was made. To counteract the pessimistic spirit of the time, I wanted to film the great legend of Siegfried so that Germany could draw inspiration from her epic past, and not, as Mr. Kracauer suggests, as a looking-forward to the rise of a political figure like Hitler or something stupid of that sort. I was dealing with Germany's legendary heritage.[1]

That view did not differ significantly from the one expressed at the time he made *Siegfried*, as noted in the program book to the film:

> We are not dealing with just any old filmic adaptation of a work that already exists in some other form. Rather, what we're dealing with here is the spiritual shrine of a nation. Thus our task with the Nibelungen project was necessarily to create a film in a form that would not banalize its sacred-spiritual aspects; [it is] a film that would belong to the *Volk*.[2]

Here he points to the film's fundamental spiritual and national purposes, something that could inspire all Germans.

On Lang's description of the scope and purpose of the project we need not quibble too much, but about his more specific claims we should be wary. In an article appearing just before the release of *Siegfried*, he went on the attack of the way Americans envisage film, claiming to have avoided that approach. Elaborating on the creations of his set designers Otto Hunte and Erich Kettelhut, he noted that they:

> Constructed the German cathedral and the German forest on the studio grounds at Babelsberg. Not in the American style. And yet, I would be so bold as to claim that the spirit that pervades the Nibelungen sets has more of the breath or universality than has ever arisen from the grounds of Los Angeles, since it stems from the original essence of a great nation.[3]

Lang no doubt saw German cinema as superior, but to attempt to reduce the purpose of the film to that type of national rivalry, as some have, is to fall into the trap that Lang sets. The primary enemy for Lang, in spite of the recently ended war, was not the United States and its new cultural invasion in the form of mindlessly spectacular cinema. The enemy lay within Germany itself, and by deflecting the focus in his comments to something external, he could successfully prevent its identification in precise terms, allowing the film itself to work its magic beneath the threshold of consciousness.

Lest critics should recognize that he modeled his cinematic process on Wagner's music, as Norbert Jacques appeared to as early as 2 March 1924 in the *Neue Züricher Zeitung*, he would also need to throw up disclaimers on this. Not only did he emphasize how fundamentally his plot and Wagner's differed, and that he personally would never be caught dead in an opera house, but he derided Wagner along with all classical music, and vigorously objected to the use of music by Wagner to accompany the film.[4] This ploy proved every bit as successful as the deflection of the target since most observers have dutifully dismissed all Wagnerian connections. Yet, a reviewer like Mordaunt Hall, who presumably did not know any of the pieces Lang had written about the film, naively hit upon the essence of the film. He appeared to recognize that even though the stories did not mesh, the film displayed operatic grandeur on a scale only Wagner could conjure up, not only in the larger than life characters and sets, but in the way that cinematic visual images could be surrogates for the musical images of a Wagnerian score. Silent film required musical accompaniment, and this one seemed to need the sounds of Wagner.

The operas of Wagner invariably serve the social and political objectives of their creator. He achieves this in part by the representation of that which is bad, for example, by depicting odious characters seeking wealth and control.[5] Numerous writers have come to the same conclusion about these types of characters, as Theodor Adorno did in the 1930s: "All the rejects of Wagner's works are caricatures of Jews... the gold-grubbing, invisible, anonymous, exploitative Alberich, the shoulder-shrugging, loquacious Mime, overflowing with self-praise and spite, the impotent, intellectual critic Hanslick-Beckmesser."[6] In a number of recent studies on Wagner this view has become much more sharply focused, revealing a political and social view on Wagner's part in which Jews can have no part.[7] Wagner's own writing on Jews, especially his tract *Jewishness in Music*, in which he defines the characteristics of Jews in stereotypical manner (see chapter 15), becomes the model for his representation of Jews in his operas.

Wagner characterizes all Jews as dangerous. He does not need to identify Mime, Alberich and Beckmesser as Jews; he leaves this for the viewer to discern, perhaps subliminally, through musical features such as Beckmesser's hopeless mangling of Walther's song, underscoring his foreignness, or the character portrayals of Mime or Alberich. In contrast to bad representations there will always be good ones, such as Walther's nobility, grace, articulation and pedantry-free art, or Siegfried's courage and straightforwardness, unlike Mime's duplicity or Alberich's treachery. In *Die Meistersinger* Wagner allows the viewer to savor the defeat of the bad, but in the *Ring* cycle he reveals the apocalypse that will result if those in power lack sufficient resolve or become diverted from their proper course. Left to himself, Wotan could have saved the gods, but he made a fatal mistake in taking the advice of his meddling wife Fricka whose jealousy and imposition of conventional morality caused the house of the gods to collapse. Wagner warns not only about Jews but also about women who will bring nothing but destruction if allowed to have power or even influence those in power. Sometimes an evil may be necessary to counteract a greater evil, and only a man will accept the consequences and have the resolve to carry this out. One can easily see why such a view of the world would be so immensely attractive to Hitler.

Lang's *Siegfried* and Wagner's *Ring* share one especially notable feature; at least two of the most despicable characters in the film, Mime and Alberich, also appear to reveal stereotypal Jewish features. Curiously, the most pointed fingering of this comes from words imputed by Lang's official biographer, Lotte Eisner, to Siegfried Kracauer, and not from anything actually stated by Kracauer. In Eisner's words, "Kracauer alleged that Lang's Alberich has markedly Jewish features, and he reads into this a deliberate gesture of anti-semitism."[8] It seems highly unlikely that Kracauer actually thought that, since his own description, involving the assertion of absolute authority and the triumph of the ornamental over the human, makes Alberich look more like a Nazi.[9] Nevertheless, Eisner let the cat out of the bag, and she proceeds to describe the actual Jewish source for the depiction of Alberich by Lang and his make-up artist Otto Genath, "the grotesque character make-up used by the Russo-Jewish Habimah ensemble that was currently visiting Berlin."[10]

As for Mime, Eisner admits that "the shaggy, bow-legged forest inhabitant Mime is contrasted to the blond Siegfried," but she protests that "if anyone at Ufa [studio] enjoyed the emphasis on racial differences, it was certainly not Lang or [producer Erich] Pommer, who simply followed the action of the saga."[11]

Official biographers have an uncanny knack for getting things wrong, misrepresenting facts in ways that suit their subjects. Since everyone knows that Lang did not simply follow the action of the saga, we need to be wary about the rest of the statement too. She does not try to conceal the fact that Lang used a distinctive Jewish model for Alberich, in fact, a "grotesque" one, and Lang surely wished Mime and his shuffling cohorts to make the same impression. Since Kracauer did not label Lang's Alberich or Mime as Jewish, but that identification came from Lang's biographer, who submitted all her material to Lang "for approval and for verification of dates and facts," we must assume that the words put into Kracauer's mouth actually came indirectly from Lang himself.

Before we jump to conclusions about Lang as an antisemite cut from the same cloth as Wagner, a few other matters need to be addressed. Unlike Wagner, who had reasons to question if his own father may have been Jewish, Lang knew of his mother's Jewish origin, although she converted to Catholicism prior to her marriage. By the mid-1920s his Jewish lineage still did not need to be an issue, as he was the child of practicing Christians and presumably had never seen the inside of a synagogue; he seldom mentioned his mother's background, and if he did, he treated the matter in a dissimulating way.[12] Even in 1933, in the famous incident(s) of Lang's summons to Joseph Goebbels's office, where he expected a rebuke about *Das Testament des Dr. Mabuse* but instead received an offer for him to head the new film production agency in the Third Reich, Goebbels met Lang's admission of not being a "pure Aryan" with the assurance that something, such as bestowing the title of *Ehrenarier* (honorary Aryan), could be arranged.[13] Lang claimed he fled Germany immediately after this meeting, but it appears he hesitated and gave the offer serious consideration.

While Wagner branded all Jews as subversive and dangerous, Lang regarded some Jews as troublesome, but clearly not all. He, of course, came from Vienna, a city with an exciting cultural life early in the 20th century, and he spent his first twenty years in this hothouse of literary and artistic brilliance, a disproportionate amount of which came from Jewish intellectuals, writers and artists. As a frequenter of the lively coffeehouse scene before his departure from Vienna in 1910 because of a rift with his father, he came into contact with the best minds of the city, and no one stirred him more than the poet, dramatist, satirical essayist, lecturer and a beacon to every young dissident in Vienna, Karl Kraus. Kraus could see through political sham in a moment, and his satirical attacks on corruption, waste, absurd customs, and abuse of power left his enemies powerless to counterattack. Lang frequently attended Kraus's lectures and avidly collected Kraus's tri-monthly journal *Die Fackel* (*The Torch*) for many years after his departure from Vienna.[14] The attitude of the assimilated Kraus to Judaism bordered on antisemitism, causing a complete separation from his Jewish background. Many others went the same direction, including Peter Altenberg (also much admired by Lang), Otto Weininger, Franz Werfel, Victor Adler, Arthur Schnitzler, Max Brod, Franz Kafka, Arnold Schoenberg, Sigmund Freud, and many more. Some converted to Christianity; others did not bother. These people stood on the leading edge of 20th-century culture and Lang knew it; without them, Vienna would be nothing but a sterile backwater of conservatism, which it became after the Anschluss in 1938.

In the eyes of the young Fritz Lang, the hope for German greatness lay with these people, and not with the powerbrokers who had led Germans into a devastating war, whose unscrupulous motives for doing so had been bitterly attacked by Kraus since the beginning of the war. Change in rearguard Austria may have seemed hopeless, but a more free spirited Germany need not make the same mistake. If people like these could take their rightful place in German culture and politics, there would be reason for hope after the post-war turmoil and deprivation. After late 19th-century liberalization of policies toward Jews, antisemitism again reared its ugly head and that threatened to plunge Germany into chaos even deeper than the one it had just come through. In 1924, Lang believed he knew the answer to the problem, and in *Die Nibelungen* he boldly yet subtly put it forward.

For Lang both good Jews and bad Jews existed. The bad ones could be readily recognized as Jews by their appearance, demeanor and behavior, and in relation to modern German society these could be characterized as "grotesque." These were religious Jews who went to extremes to keep themselves apart from the rest of society; they did not serve the greater national interest and were perceived as avaricious, capable of gaining undue political power through their wealth. Good Jews, on the other hand, opted for assimilation, and for these Jews (who sought to become non-Jews) the other type of Jew stood every bit as dangerous – if not more so – as to Gentiles. Assimilated Jews should be distinguished from other Jews who might deter them.

Wagner had given good models and bad models, Aryan Germans and Jews of foreign origin; Lang would paint a social portrait that would set up opposites as well, now with Jews divided into two camps and home-grown Germans also in two groups: genuine and decent folk (and leaders) who will need help to foster a pluralistic society, and Aryan demagogues who, if left uncurbed, would be the greatest danger of all. All four of these appear prominently in *Die Nibelungen*, and in constructing it in this way, his new myth diverges notably from the original legend or any of its retellings. The different groups or individuals may not always be easy to identify, and even if they can be, such as the fair-haired Siegfried, it may take some reflection to realize that he stands as more of a menace than a heroic hope. In Wagner we see Siegfried as the potential savior whose goal is to thwart the forces of treachery, and since Lang's Siegfried starts out as Wagner's does, the perception of him as dangerous necessarily arises from the portrayal and new understanding of Hagen. Hagen, in fact, turns out to be the central and most crucial character for Lang.

As for the Jews, the good ones may be more difficult to recognize than the nasty dwarfs Mime and Alberich, and that should not surprise us since their assimilation obscures distinguishing characteristics. Yet, Lang leaves a few physical clues. In a talk given at Yale University in 1966, he noted that he "was interested in bringing to life a German saga in a manner different from Wagnerian opera, without beards and so on."[15] In Wagner, we have no reason to notice beards unless we think of them as identifying Jews. In Lang's film, only one character has a beard aside from the dwarfs: Hagen. Further, Hagen frequently wears a headpiece with eagle's wings extending upward; the German word for eagle, *Adler*, can be recognized as a prominent German-Jewish name, especially in Vienna.

In fact, there may be an actual model for the representation of Hagen as Adler. Victor Adler, leader of the Austrian Social Democratic Workers Party, converted to Christianity and became fiercely antisemitic; he and his colleagues demonstrated unshakable loyalty to Emperor Franz

Joseph. Victor's son Friedrich caught the attention of the entire world when he assassinated Prime Minister Count Karl Stürgkh in 1916, who governed Austria for two and a half years without convening the Reichsrat. At his trial he condemned wartime exploitation so convincingly that his execution was postponed.[16] While Kraus used the pen, Adler went further, thrusting with rhetoric and the sword. Postponement of execution, in fact, eventually led to pardon; Emperor Karl appears to have concluded the villain Adler did the nation a service, as Gunther would similarly recognize although not publicly declare of Hagen.

As for Victor Adler, he and his circle searched for an ideology to replace the insensitive and unjust system running the country. They found this, as Steven Beller notes, in the German irrationalists: Schopenhauer, Wagner and Nietzsche. This revealed itself politically in the ideology of the *Volk*, reuniting society on a new Wagnerian model.[17] The *völkisch* movement had not yet been taken over by rabid antisemites, and by becoming German Nationalists, Jews like Adler could prove their credentials by rejecting their Jewish backgrounds and joining the German *Volk*.[18] Here we have Lang's Hagen/Adler exactly, except for not shaving off his beard. In the words of Thea von Harbou, Lang's wife and the screenwriter for *Die Nibelungen*, "The Nibelungen film is intended to serve this very German *Volk* as its singer, its storytelling poet of the self...: a hymn in celebration of unconditional loyalty."[19] Cinema too, works its magic through the irrational, and in spite of Lang's protests to the contrary, achieves that through Wagnerian modes of representation.

Throughout *Die Nibelungen*, Lang casts Hagen as King Gunther's faithful advisor, a task which Hagen performs with fierce loyalty. Since much of his advice focuses negatively on Siegfried we initially perceive him as a villain, and that view remains in place when he literally stabs Siegfried in the back, discovering through apparent treachery Siegfried's one vulnerable spot. Yet, at no point can we see him acting out of self-interest; every piece of advice he gives or action he takes serves the best interests of his sovereign and the state. Only in *Kriemhild's Revenge* do we recognize Siegfried's menacing influence, capable of seducing or inspiring Kriemhild with such fanatical devotion that she will turn into a monster to avenge him.

In the destructive aftermath we can reflect back on Hagen's acumen, that he recognized the danger and took the necessary step of eliminating this wolf in sheep's clothing, a white knight adventurer who rides a white horse, and in fact appears altogether too fair. Not only does he allure Kriemhild but he seduces Gunther, a weak king who would give everything to this interloper, as well. Only the sharp mind of Hagen sees through Siegfried, and only the intellectual skills of Hagen can facilitate the demise of this apparently invulnerable hero. Like a lawyer in the role of prosecutor he gets crucial information from Kriemhild to find the weak spot, and he even manipulates her into marking the spot with a threaded x. Like a lawyer he finds the loophole, and uses the witness for the defendant against the accused. Hagen as assimilated Jewish lawyer/advisor serves his state admirably; what we may mistake as treachery in fact reveals itself as intelligence at the highest level in the service of the state's best interest. He, like Karl Kraus, can see lurking problems that others cannot, and he is not afraid to take unpopular steps to achieve the correct long-term solution.

Two women also play central roles, and Lang engenders his Kriemhild and Brunhild with some distinctively Wagnerian attributes. On the one hand Kriemhild can be seen as a vestige of social vulnerability to a dangerous force, but at the same time she stands as a character similar to Wagner's Senta, pensive, beautiful and submissive, prepared to sacrifice all for a man. The youthful Lang wished to become an artist, and no one more than Gustav Klimt influenced him in that direction. Various commentators have noted the extent to which the physical image of Kriemhild (before revenge consumes her) represents one of Klimt's women. Klimt created a *Frauenkult*, turning his women into fetishes of sensuous beauty and grace with the potential for men to admire if not worship. The power of these women lies in their sensuality which can enfold men, like the spreading circular shapes of the woman's gown in *The Kiss*, humanizing men by imbuing them with feminine characteristics. In this portrayal, supported by the writing on women by Kraus, Altenberg and Weininger, women should not seek to assert power in stereotypically masculine ways. Lang, very conscious of women's movements in the 1920s, appeared to support the views of his Viennese compatriots, as his representation of women here confirms.

In extreme contrast to the fair and initially submissive Kriemhild stands the dark, man-devouring Brunhild, and she too brings one of Klimt's women alive, especially near the end of *Siegfried*. When Gunther returns after the hunt to announce the death of Siegfried (whose death Brunhild has insisted on), Lang gives us a shot of her in which her

Siegfried (Hanna Ralph's likeness to Klimt's *Judith 1*)

resemblance to Klimt's *Judith I* of 1901 cannot be mistaken. In fact, Hanna Ralph may have been chosen for the role because of the likeness of her face to Judith's; her hair was styled in the same way, and the design of Judith's gown was provided. Lang also implies the decapitated head of Holophernes, barely visible as Judith cradles it against her stomach in the bottom right hand corner of Klimt's portrait, since the most vivid parallel to Klimt's Judith occurs after Siegfried has been killed. The gloating Brunhild now reflects on her treachery in achieving this – her lie to Gunther about having been defiled by Siegfried; Lang frames this with shots of Siegfried's body on the bier. Klimt's *Judith I* emphasizes beauty with the ornamental background, her flowing sash, and the soft lines of her body (unlike the sharply delineated *Judith II* of 1909, with distorted, murderous hands), reminding us that her triumph over Holophernes succeeded because of her beauty. Brunhild has other powers as well, but these too can be enacted because of her beauty, which Lang shows in its most striking radiance near the end of the film.

Judith of the Apocrypha overrides the authority of the male magistrates and through cunning deceit and seductive allure can sever the head of the most powerful man in the world. Also, she is Jewish. By association, Brunhild appears also to be Jewish, and if the Judith images do not clinch the point, the helmet she wears while in competition does, with eagle wings stretching outward, making her another member of the Adler family. She lives in seclusion surrounded by a ring of fire, and cannot be successfully wooed unless her suitor can beat her at three track and field events. The weak Gunther proves no match, but aided by the olympian but invisible Siegfried, Gunther wins. The Olympic sports continue in the bedchamber, as she easily wrestles the hapless Gunther into submission, a dishonor which only Hagen witnesses; Hagen then sends Siegfried to Brunhild's bed, transformed by the Tarnhelm (magic helmet) into Gunther, to tame her. This act of sexual dominance proves to be Siegfried's undoing; Kriemhild by chance learns of it, and in a spiteful moment of conflict with Brunhild, boasts that Siegfried vanquished Brunhild, information that Brunhild will use to convince Gunther that they must get rid of Siegfried. What Hagen understands about Siegfried, she intuits from his Nordic fairness and then from her recognition of him as her subduer. The two people with

Gustav Klimt's *Judith I*

no doubts about the necessity of Siegfried's demise are Brunhild and her ally Hagen – the two Adlers.

Sorting out the allegorical significance of Lang's Brunhild proves to be less than straightforward. Typically commentators have taken her as a Wagnerian Brünnhilde run amok, as a man-hating Amazon who takes delight in castrating men and asserting her political authority over them. The young Viennese Jewish medical writer Otto Weininger had warned of this kind of woman in his extraordinarily successful *Geschlecht und Charakter* (Sex and Character), a book which went through an unprecedented twenty-six printings between 1903 and 1924. In his own virulent brand of antisemitism Weininger also equated women and Jews, relegating both to the junk heap of humanity; Lang's Brunhild could be a combination of the two, fusing Jew and woman together into one devastating force which, if left unrestrained, could wreak unimaginable damage. A parallel could be drawn with the exotic, foreign and Jewish wife of Franz von Hervay (a Styrian district administrator), a woman convicted of bigamy (in a case brought to public notice by Karl Kraus in 1904) and branded by the antisemitic press as a "modern vampire" and a "Jew-woman of devilish nature."[20] Since Lang sets things up initially to secure the viewer's sympathy for Siegfried, he seems to turn us against Brunhild with the same stroke. Yet, since we must ultimately accept Siegfried as dangerous and applaud his demise, that forces a reconsideration not only of Hagen but Brunhild as well; in fact, Lang appears to come to her defense, as Kraus does to Frau Hervay.

Despite the rising tide of female emancipation since the turn of the century in Germany and Austria, it seems unlikely that Lang saw Brunhild as a filmic champion of the movement. She may give men a fatally hard time, but her goal does not appear to be greater political empowerment for herself or women in general. Her portrayal continues to be that of *femme fatale*, a beautiful woman modeled on the seductive and deadly Judith, and she will not survive to the end of *Siegfried*. Her sisters are not real feminists such as the Austrian Rosa Mayreder, the Swiss Emilie Kempin or Sweden's Ellen Key, but rather the vamps of painting and literature, certainly like Klimt's Judith, but also Frank Wedekind's Lulu, Émile Zola's Nana, the Salome of Oscar Wilde and Richard Strauss, or Altenberg's Anita. In the distinctions drawn by Kraus and others between "Weib" (the sexually emancipated female) and "Frau" (the social aspect of woman), these writers championed the cause of their peculiar notion of "Weib," the woman who can flaunt her sensuality and has the sexual freedom of a prostitute. Kraus and Altenberg wrote at length about this type of woman and Klimt defined her visual image. Lang apparently did not feel he could reveal her as overtly in cinema as G. W. Pabst had with Lulu (*Pandora's Box*) or Josef von Sternberg with Lola (*The Blue Angel*) only a few years later, but for those able to see the Judith connection, he nevertheless adumbrates her.

When Harbou refers to *The Nibelungen* film as serving the German *Volk* as its singer, she opens a door that Lang himself may have wished to leave closed – that cinema and opera have much in common. Kracauer too finds this type of comparison unavoidable, admitting that "even though *The Nibelungen* film differs entirely from *The Ring of the Nibelungen*, it is rich in events which no one can witness without being haunted by Wagnerian leitmotifs."[21] Here he strikes a stinger chord, cutting through the nonsense espoused by many critics and Lang himself that no connection exists between Wagner and the film; of course, the mythical plots and allegorical goals differ, but the means for achieving them appear remarkably similar. Harbou also argued that literature could no longer unlock the realm of fantasy and imagination. Cinema seemed to have that capacity, but in 1924 filmmakers were still discovering the ways; opera offered an answer.

For cinema to carry the burden of mythic representation, it needed to realize a sense of grandeur through dimensional expansiveness as well as probe the images at deeper psychological and even spiritual levels. The dimensional part could be accomplished with grand sets, such as the massive trees made for *Siegfried* which would dwarf anything that actually grew in Germany, the palatial stairway of the cathedral, and the hundreds of extras to fill these massive spaces. As impressive as Lang could make his sets, the Americans like D. W. Griffith and Cecil B. DeMille could always make theirs larger; the transformation to the mythic level needed to work by other means. Here, Wagner provided the model. Forest trees must not only be huge but they needed to capture the majesty of nature, not dwarfing Siegfried as he rides through them but somehow elevating him with their majesty to the level of mythic hero. They must then function as a visual leitmotif, realizing their majesty and grandeur in the way that Wagner elevates objects such as the sword, heroic persons, or profound emotions through musical leitmotifs of mythic dimensions.

Visual leitmotifs can be generated in various ways and one of the most effective could be the reconstruction of visual images already elevated to mythic dimensions by their association with works of art. Lang had no difficulty coming up with these images and painting them into his film. By no means did Klimt provide his only source; as Eisner and others have noted, Arnold Böcklin's *Great Pan*, also known as *Schweigen im Walde* (*The Silence of the Forest*), inspired the image of Siegfried as he rides through the light-shafted, misty forest. Other Böcklin paintings also appear, including the representation of the meadow and spring where Hagen kills Siegfried; the naked children from *Kriemhild's Revenge* emerge from an etching by Max Klinger.[22] Other associations have been identified as well, including ones with Caspar David Friedrich's *Landscape with Rainbow*, Böcklin's *The Isle of Death*, some of Heinrich Vogeler's *Jugenstil* idylls, and various others by Friedrich Kaulbach, Franz von Stuck, Hans Thoma, Johann Heinrich Füssli, and Julius Schnorr von Carolsfeld.[23]

Other types of visual leitmotifs can also be found, such as the bell (or bells) in the cathedral tower, pealing ominously – transforming visual image directly into implied sound. The zigzag pattern on Burgundian gowns works as a leitmotif as well, providing much more than a decorative design. The appearance of this pattern on Siegfried's clothes binds him to the Burgundians after the oath of brotherhood and a broken version for Brunhild suggests her continuing defiance and disaffection. Hagen, while loyal, nevertheless remains a partial outsider as his blank clothes distance him from full assimilation. Perhaps the most vivid visual leitmotif is Lang's ingenious shot of the linden leaf covering a spot on Siegfried's back as he baths in the dragon's blood, which of course leaves his body vulnerable. The x sewn by Kriemhild to mark the spot for Hagen could be seen as yet another variation on the Burgundian zigzag pattern, distorted in this case with fatal implications.

In his operas, Wagner opts for a very slow musical and dramatic pace, avoiding rapid action which would diminish the sense of epic grandeur. Since the music provides the primary vehicle for this, Wagner replaces the apparent lack of action on stage with a musical unfolding which transforms passing time to an ontological state, effectively removing the listener from notions of temporal normalcy with an elevation to timelessness. The mythic could not be otherwise: a rapid pace would reduce the drama to the ordinary if not comedy or parody. Lang's

Nibelungen film has been mercilessly attacked for its slow pace, but Lang knew it could not be otherwise. This permits grand gestures to be grand, but more importantly allows the visual images, at times as still shots, to permeate the viewer's consciousness with the depth and full mythic stature that the painterly images require. When motion occurs, it un-folds more as a pageant than anything realistic, again reaching to mythic grandeur. With the penetration of the sensory images, Lang also seeks a blend of the spiritual and the sensual so apparent in Wagner's scores, now letting the viewer fathom, for example, the nature and depth of the bond forged in the extended love-at-first-sight look between Sieg-fried and Kriemhild. By connecting Kriemhild to Klimt's fetishist women and Siegfried to Böcklin's Pan, this potent meeting of eyes becomes not only spiritual but charged with eroticism by association.

Appropriation of Wagnerian aesthetic principles had its dangers, and what Lang feared most – that his epic would be linked to Wagner's for all the wrong reasons – in fact happened. Subtlety too can be risky, and if viewers do not catch the cryptic message, they may substitute distorted ones regardless how vociferously one protests the association with Wagner and refuses that composer's music as accompaniment. While it may have been perplexing to Lang that Americans in 1925 should present the film with a Wagnerian musical pastiche, that paled in comparison to what happened in Germany in 1933. The ultimate distressing irony existed for Lang in that the film he conceived as diverting an Aryan supremacist fascism in the end proved a powerful weapon to promote the attitudes he abhorred. *Siegfried* became favorite viewing for Hitler and Goebbels, and after Goebbels' speech praising it in March 1933, the Nazis authorized a re-release of *Siegfried* with a voice-over by Theodor Loos (the actor who played Gunther) and a newly arranged Wagnerian score to accompany it. According to Kracauer, *Siegfried* provided the inspiration for the official Nazi film *Triumph of the Will* of 1934, which achieved its propagandistic purposes with similar doses of grandeur and pageantry. The Nazis equated the medium with the message; they could see in the process of the visual medium the representation of their beloved Wagner's music, and they took the mes-sage to be the same. With the message ironically misunderstood, Lang could do nothing but flee the clutches of those who would have him turn out more mind-shaping pageantry, and protest his innocence on the other side of the Atlantic.

CINEMA AS GRAND OPERA:
POLITICS, RELIGION AND DEMILLE

Religion sells. Cecil B. DeMille never doubted this for a moment, and he was prepared to wager his personal fortune on it when studio executives and financial backers questioned it. Not only does religion sell, but selling is a religion (to say nothing of a political ideology), and for DeMille the two sides of this came together in an extraordinary fusion of ideology and profitability. No one sold the American dream of personal wealth better than DeMille did, and cinema proved to be the ideal medium for propagating his ideology. Profit, though, comes with a price, as every capital venture requires risk, and adversaries must be defeated. In DeMille's scheme of things no greater enemy existed than communists, socialists and trade unions; and he eagerly fingered such people in his own profession well before it became a cause in Washington. In DeMille's view of America not only should the battering ram be taken to enemies who needed to be exposed and attacked but in more subtle ways it needed to be revealed that only some should aspire to the dream that could not possibly be for everyone. Success for some will come at others' expense, and the dream appeared limited to enterprising white males. But since this group would create a prosperous society, those excluded from the prospect of individual wealth and freedom would nevertheless still benefit as spouses or as contented workers.

In 1915, DeMille had also discovered that opera sells; placing a leading operatic diva in the title role of *Carmen* vaulted him ahead as a filmmaker. While this may have put him on the cinematic map, the future did not lie in more filmic adaptations of other specific operas.

DeMille's anticipation of outrageous success appeared to rise from his ability to bring two other successful forces together and fuse them into something extraordinary; the two forces in this case were religion and opera. In the case of opera, he discovered how to present operatic images without his extravaganzas being perceived by moviegoers as opera, thereby opening the doors to the public which might otherwise sneer at opera. Curiously, he achieved very much the same result with religion, taking familiar Bible stories or great historical legends of religious courage and coaxing out of them narratives that served his own political America-defining agenda. By couching the message in religious terms it could reach a vast audience already sympathetic to fundamentalist Christianity. By offering it as implied grand opera, with every device of opera with the exception of *bel canto* singing, he could also reach the audience which may feel somewhat more ambivalent about religious indoctrination, preferring high culture. The result in *Joan the Woman*, *The Ten Commandments* and *Samson and Delilah* was not simply to bring these two groups together, but it gave rise to a unique and unprecedented achievement.

DeMille may have initially seen his *Carmen* as a vehicle to drive cinema into the realm of respectability, but of course, it became much more than that. The opera belongs to high culture, but the woman has loose morals, allowing an element of titillation to remain in a newly respectable medium; in DeMille's *Carmen* titillation grew to lasciviousness as Geraldine Farrar played her seductiveness to the hilt, ensnaring not only a weak-kneed Wallace Reid but most of the male audience as well. Without this appeal to sex the *Carmen* experiment may have gone nowhere, and its success seems to have suggested some future possibilities, including the presence of sexual content in religious drama. The Bible itself does not avoid it, replete with a healthy supply of Delilahs and Salomes; if the biblical narrative in question lacks the suitable female character, script writers could add them and few but the most biblically versed would be any the wiser. For his female viewers he adds a romantic interest to films that would otherwise be too severe, and to his male viewers he sounds a warning about female treachery but not before an erotic indulgence has been thoroughly enjoyed. Heroes will never be strictly confined by normal moral codes, and even worse, they would be bores if they were; the possibility of redemption for a sinner makes a good story, and in the male scheme of things even better if it proves possible to have it both ways and still find redemption.

Opera politic

The new role of politicized spectacle that DeMille assigned to cinema was of course nothing new in the performing arts; theater had done it for centuries, but DeMille's image of it much more specifically resembled the 19th-century operatic type. The foundation of opera at the end of the 16th century probably had more to do with spectacle than singing, and while spectacle has always been part of opera, especially the serious variety, nothing could compare with the lavishness of 19th-century grand opera in Paris. Arising when it did, around 1830, its grandeur reflected attitudes of how the French perceived themselves vis-à-vis the rest of the world. But these works offered much more than an opportunity for the new ruling class of France to preen itself; as improbable as it may seem, the texts of these operas served subtle political ends as well, as the classical, historical or religious subjects drew parallels with the present time. For example, elements of popularity and emphasis on public function replaced focus on specific kings or royal activity.[1] Composers such as Daniel Auber, Hector Berlioz, Giacomo Meyerbeer and Jacques-François Halévy (often using librettos by Eugène Scribe), could broach subjects of a revolutionary nature, not with didacticism or the sort of overt propaganda that would later characterize much opera in the Soviet Union, but cloaked in grandeur and a sense of self-satisfaction reflecting much more subtly the current French regime. The golden age of grand opera had run its course by about 1870, and its late 19th and early 20th-century offspring – French works by the likes of Jules Massenet and Camille Saint-Saëns – kept the spectacle but not the political bite. By then opera had become more market driven, and those who attended wanted entertainment more than political content.

Outside of France political content in opera also thrived, and that includes the two giants of 19th-century opera: Verdi and Wagner. Verdi was born in 1813, when the Italian states fell under the control of Napoleon. Within two years Napoleon had been defeated, and at the Congress of Vienna, Austria gained these states with the mandate to reorganize them as it saw fit. The Habsburgs had no love for notions of self-government, and the firm rule spawned nationalist sentiments previously unknown in the Italian states, a movement known as the *Risorgimento*. While this new force gained attention through novels and other forums, nothing could reach Italians more effectively than their principal art form and entertainment: opera. Verdi, who shared these political sentiments, emerged by the early 1840s as the champion of the cause, and some of his earliest operas, such as *Nabucco* (1842) and *I Lombardi* (1843), gave *Risorgimento* a subtle yet decisive push.[2]

Nabucco has a biblical setting – the captivity of the Israelites in Babylon and their painful endurance of King Nebuchadnezzar's brutality. The strongest voice of suffering comes from the people themselves, through the chorus, and no chorus achieves it more effectively than "Va, pensiero, sull'ali dorate." The text, "Oh, mia patria si bella e perduta! Oh, membranza si cara e fatal!" (Oh, my country so beautiful and lost! Oh, memory so dear and fatal!), set in an opening unison which later bursts into full harmony, could not but be taken by every Italian in the audience as a parallel to their plight under the Austrians. Yet, since the text came from the Bible, Austrian censors could hardly object. When hysterical audiences on the verge of riot demanded encores of such politically volatile numbers and Austrian officials refused, the conductor caught in the middle usually took his chances with the audience.[3] With *I Lombardi*, the Italians identified with the crusaders and cast the Austrians as the Saracen debasers of the Holy Land; once again, a Lombard chorus triggered near-riots. Even in *Macbeth*, the cry of the chorus "O patria oppressa" under the oppression of Macbeth invoked the same type of response.[4] Spectacle in these early works carried over to later ones as well, and none more strikingly than *Aida*. As in France, the turn-of-the-century Italian operas by Puccini, Mascagni and Leoncavallo would retreat from political content into stories of personal pathos and tragedy, and these would form the cornerstone of the early 20th-century operatic repertoire, especially in the United States.

Wagner as well took politics seriously, but his ability to play both sides of the political spectrum left audiences in doubt as to how they should perceive his works. He did not hide his own political sympathies, revealing them by participating in the revolution of Dresden, but he also remained a firm believer in authoritarian rule. Those who searched for the political left or right in his works, as the first Paris audience for *Tannhäuser* did, were likely to be disappointed by not finding either; Wagner's political agenda proved to be a much more complex one, not reducible in any conventionally factional way. While DeMille could draw on grand opera and Verdi in some notable ways, it appears that Wagner provided his most striking model. Both Wagner and De-Mille had little to fear from outside conquering forces, believing the real enemy lay within. Both saw their home countries as superior to all others, as superpowers with distinctive goals and features that needed to be preserved at any cost; any internal forces that might try to subvert them should be quickly quelled. These forces may originate from outside the nation, but the damage they would inflict would come not from military attack but from the attitudes or subversion that would be spread by foreign elements from within. Works of art for both DeMille and Wagner had a primary duty to reveal to ordinary people what made their nation great, not by singling out the contaminating or destructive forces and striking a fatal blow (as D. W. Griffith attempts with his klansmen in *Birth of a Nation*), but with more disingenuous means that could instruct through allegorical focus on positive elements, accessible through mythology, classical history, or the Bible.

For Wagner, German superiority revealed itself in many ways, including through moral attitudes, the dignity and demeanor of the people, the German language (he heartily agreed with the philologist Jacob Grimm that the etymological parallel between "deutsch" [German] and "deutlich" [clear or intelligible] suggested something not possible in other languages[5]), the arts – especially music – and adherence to Christian tenets. Germans needed to be reminded of their preeminence, and society must be transformed to meet that standard. Since the ruling class did not care about such things, revolution would be required to make it happen, and with the new society in place the correct ideology could be nurtured and maintained through great artworks such as Wagner's operas. This accounts for his involvement in the Dresden revolution, although he and the peasants made odd bedfellows with their vastly different objectives. But even more dangerous than an isolated, indifferent or decadent aristocracy stood the force that he believed corrupted all the German values he prized most highly, the Jews: thus his broadside antisemitic attack in his 1850 pamphlet *Jewishness in Music* and his more insidious methods in his works.

His operas do not lack models for German greatness, such as Beckmesser's vocal adversary Walther von Stolzing from *Die Meistersinger* (not only a Franconian knight but of noble descent), and Lohengrin, Tannhäuser, Siegfried and Parsifal with their operas named after them. Not everyone can aspire to this type of greatness; they must be Aryan and they must be male. Women can be extraordinary in various ways, but only according to Wagner if they put their deeds to the service of the men they love. Senta reveals this by her willingness to die for the Dutchman or Isolde by working her healing powers on Tristan. Otherwise, the ideal woman must depend on a male champion, as Elsa does, and then be submissive and content – lacking even the curiosity to know his identity or from whence he comes. If that curiosity rears its ugly head, it becomes a form of treachery, and in any event, real treachery, as with Eve, lies in the hearts of women such as Ortrud from *Lohengrin* or Kundry from *Parsifal*. Heroes may sin or break rules because their "Übermensch" qualities vault them above conventional laws or morality (or they may be so purely naive that they can be oblivious to these laws). For some, this allows indulgence in torrid sex with very high-class women of the night (such as Tannhäuser with Venus), and still have the possibility of redemption. Wagner's men, it appears, can have it both ways, and in fact his music becomes the best representation of the fusion.

German opera may never have quite recovered from Wagner, as his brilliance seemed to cast future operatic endeavors in Germany and Austria into the shadows. This provoked their opera crisis shortly after the turn of the century, and the crisis, as Alban Berg and others defined it, had much to do with being a Wagnerian or an anti-Wagnerian composer. While the Austrians got around it with the fluffy offerings of Johann Strauss or Franz Léhar, serious Wagnerians such as Richard Strauss attempted to follow him musically but dropped any pretense of politics or ideology. Strauss's early operas, *Elektra* and *Salome*, seem to be the proverbial sound and fury that signify nothing, while some of his subsequent operas lapse into a type of rebirth of the domesticated 19th-century Biedermeier spirit. As with efforts in France and Italy, these too aim at more straightforward audience satisfaction, steering the direction of 20th-century opera in general (with exceptions, of course) as an indulgent entertainment. The ground which opera appeared to cede at the end of the 19th century, cinema eagerly took up, and DeMille, like Griffith, can be described as a genuine heir to grand opera and Wagner in the 20th century.

Joan the Woman

With Geraldine Farrar under contract, DeMille knew he had the potential for a string of successes, but how he should transfer her operatic
presence to the screen proved to be at least somewhat troublesome.
The Carmen gambit worked, but it also proved to be something of a
dead end; future success still depended on opera, but in more subtle
ways in which cinema could absorb the essence of opera. For the short
term, Farrar should play a part in the process, and she did this with
her next film after *Carmen* (not counting *Maria Rosa*, which she made
before *Carmen* as a test run, although released after it), *Temptation* (1916).
Here she plays a singer embroiled in the operatic life, and as popular
as that type of film would be in the next few decades (see chapter
4), it too did not hold the key to unlocking the medium.

Later in 1916 DeMille found the key, once again featuring Farrar,
not in a role based on any particular opera but in a characterization
and an approach to cinema that captured the essence of opera. With
Joan the Woman DeMille devised his first epic film, combining historical
and religious elements, and scored great critical acclaim (although the
weaker box office dampened the enjoyment). Here he initiated the type
of film that would later assure his fame, but at this stage it too remained an experiment. Audiences may not yet have been ready for it,
and the subject matter itself proved troublesome since it offended certain religious groups – notably Roman Catholics. He would not attempt
the same type of film again until *The Ten Commandments* in 1923, and
even here only in the first part, as a primer for a story of modern-
day morality. Others would follow, such as *The King of Kings* (1927),
The Sign of the Cross (1932), *Cleopatra* (1934), and *The Crusades* (1935),
but he would not find his full stride until the middle of the century
with *Samson and Delilah* (1949), for which he had an operatic model
with Saint-Saëns's opera of the same name, and *The Ten Commandments*
(1956), the most complete transformation of grand opera into cinema
in the entire film repertory – to such a degree that it has become a
cult classic.

Joan the Woman exudes grand opera in almost every respect, with
the possible exception that the leading role belongs to a woman. Like
the operas of Meyerbeer and Auber the subject matter combines historical and religious elements, and focuses on a grand moment elevated

to mythic proportions in modern consciousness. With that in mind, the story must be cloaked in sufficient grandeur to befit the subject, and that involves a cast of thousands, striking costumes, impressive sets, and gestures of grandiloquence – even from the peasant Joan. Since she has been appointed by God to command the French forces, we should not be distressed, as some critics were at the time ("one of Miss Farrar's eyes reflects Riverside Drive, the other, Fifth Avenue"[6]), that she lacks the demeanor of a peasant: an actual peasant as heroine would have no place in grand opera. Song may not come from her lips, but with the role played by a diva, one can imagine her on the opulent stage of the Paris Opera; even the weight she had put on since *Carmen* made her more of the typical diva from grand opera.

One should not expect the scenario of scriptwriter Jeanie Macpherson to follow the original historical events, and that it does not.[7] A purely religious/patriotic Joan may have struck the 1916 audience as hard to swallow, but a Joan with a love interest – with an enemy leader no less – could be very appealing, even if she must abandon romance for her cause. In part Macpherson and DeMille restructured the story to appeal to the contemporary audience, adding not only romance but framing it in the context of a French soldier in the World War I trenches who will accept a suicide mission to blow up an enemy trench after a dream vision of Joan's valor induced by his discovery of an ancient sword. But further, as will characterize his later epics, DeMille also takes the opportunity to give his audience an illustration of what he believes to be right for America (and presumably France as well, where the film was released in a French version). In this respect too he embraces grand opera, which, as has been noted, would not hesitate to take on political issues.

With *Joan*, DeMille waded into one of the thorniest issues of the time, the struggle for women's suffrage. The issue had been put on hold in the 19th century when supporters of the cause diverted their energy to the emancipation of slavery, but after 1869 under the leadership of Elizabeth Cady Stanton, Susan B. Anthony, Lucy Stone and Julia Ward Howe the movement went into full swing until full victory came in 1919. Wyoming led the way as early as 1869, refusing to enter the Union without the adoption of its position on suffrage. Congress reluctantly granted Wyoming statehood in 1890, and soon after other states began to change their laws on suffrage. DeMille would have been especially aware of the issue in 1916, with California yielding in 1915 and New York (his prior home state) bowing to pressure in 1917. The campaign to persuade Congress to amend the Constitution peaked during these years, and despite the rearguard efforts of misogynist politicians and those in a position to influence opinion, Congress passed the Woman's Suffrage Amendment in June 1919.

There can be little question that *Joan the Woman* (not "Joan of Arc," as it might have been titled), addresses the issue with the touch that would later characterize DeMille's treatment of communism and racism. Unlike Griffith, who, to the strains of the "Ride of the Valkyries," rounds up the Klan cavalry to put down black power run amok, DeMille offers a potentially appealing view of a woman with power. She comes from a simple background, has religion on her side, seems capable of tenderness to a man, in fact an enemy, and she has all the physical qualities of the extraordinary woman playing the role. In short, she represents the all-American woman who finds herself in unfamiliar territory – with sword in hand, in full battle dress, and as a leader of men. Derision by those who doubt her ability to lead and incredulous enemies evaporates when she achieves what timorous men have failed to accomplish.

At the mid-point of the film, we have every reason to believe she has achieved not only equality with men but superiority, yet she will not be able to stand up to the pressures of popular opinion, conveniently provided in this case by institutional religion. She may, it seems, have been deluded by the earlier voices she heard and the illusory image of a sword in the shape of a cross; that image will be replaced in the latter part of the film by the ghostly black horseman, a chilling omen of defeat and the possibility that the earlier voices may have been satanic. The issue for DeMille ceases to be one of religion, self-sacrifice or martyrdom. In the end, the question of gender takes over and Joan must finally be destroyed because she refuses to trade her male, military clothes for a woman's dress. Clothes make the man, and Joan cannot see that her military episode has been an aberration and she should now return to what women's clothes imply: submissiveness, support and reproduction. For DeMille a woman in pants had no place in his America, and even blue stockings should make men wary; the position on the vote had already gone much too far by 1916.

Samson and Delilah

DeMille's late epics may strike one as little more than wholesome entertainment, the simple retelling of familiar biblical stories in spectacular technicolor format, but these films attempt veiled persuasion or political posturing no less than the operas of Wagner. *Samson and Delilah* (1949) offers an especially interesting example of this since it deviates significantly from the operatic version by Saint-Saëns, premiered in 1877, to which it most assuredly owes a debt. The opera belongs to that era of post-grand opera which more or less abandoned political objectives without sacrificing any of the spectacle. The story, of course, demands spectacle, with huge crowd scenes and nation pitted against nation, and stunning opulence as well to complement visually the scenes of steamy seduction. The Bible (*Judges* 13-16) provides the text, but no one in opera or cinema sticks to it faithfully, adapting it to their particular purposes. In the opera Delilah is daughter of the High Priest, while in the film she plays the younger daughter of a well-to-do Philestine whose older daughter Samson desires and marries.

The most striking difference in the film, an addition which very much serves DeMille's agenda, involves the presence of a Hebrew woman, Miriam, a woman so good and self-sacrificing that she completely lacks sexual appeal. With Miriam and Delilah we have the virgin and the whore, one who offers stability and reminds Samson of duty, and the other an enchantress, erotically appealing, exciting, dangerous and deceptive. Not only does this Miriam not exist in the opera but she cannot be found in the Bible either; her invention for the film offers a different type of operatic association. Having made his own *Carmen* in 1915, DeMille knew full well that Bizet had suspended his Don José between two similarly contrasting women, although José's self-destruction takes a very different course from Samson's.

Throughout its history opera has been littered with similar conflicts between erotic love and duty, as the dozens of 18th-century versions of *Armida* attest, but the one which perhaps comes closest to DeMille's conception brings us back to Wagner, whose Tannhäuser seems more akin to Samson than Bizet's Don José. Unlike the naive Don José who inadvertently succumbs to Carmen's seductiveness, both Tannhäuser and Samson actively womanize, Samson not only in the fictionalized versions but even in the Bible where he frequents prostitutes.

Samson and Delilah (Victor Mature and the sensuous Hedy Lamarr)

Men who openly flaunt duty, seeking the seductive bliss offered by celebrated enchantresses (and historically or mythologically, few can compare with Delilah or Venus), will be judged severely by their more
sober peers and presumably by God as well. Wagnerian heroes can have
it both ways, and Tannhäuser (see the description in chapter 16) can
slum for a whole year in the grip of the love goddess Venus and still
find salvation. Musically, Wagner also enacts a fusion, already giving it
in the prelude, where the music of illicit love and sober duty merge
into a wedding of erotic and spiritual rapture.

When DeMille's Samson (Victor Mature) idles with Delilah (Hedy
Lamarr), the only news which can dislodge him, brought by Miriam,
concerns the plight of his mother, and even then he delays, fatally, as
it turns out. Virgin and whore now confront each other, and both
appear to have ulterior motives. The scene of seduction at Delilah's
temple lasts longer than any other scene in the entire film; DeMille
could have made his point in much less time. In fact he dwells on it,
wallowing in the sensuality of the strikingly beautiful Lamarr, Samson's
submersion in a pool, lavish food and drink, and the kisses and embraces. In 1949 only a limited amount could be shown on screen, but
when the scene changes from darkness to light, no one imagines that
Samson slept on a sofa by himself. Samson, like Tannhäuser, experiences eroticism to the fullest, and while he will pay dearly for it, the
return of God's strength at the end suggests that he too finds redemption. And more, unlike Saint-Saëns's opera where Delilah taunts him
before he pulls the pagan temple down, in the film he takes a redeemed
Delilah with him to a glorious death.

While the ending may be Wagnerian, so are aspects of the seduction. As for the virgin and the whore, Miriam the virgin seems virtually sexless both in demeanor and her fixation on duty. Delilah, on the
other hand, exhibits her physical and sensuous assets to the fullest –
a true daughter of Eve. From the beginning we see her as a schemer,
and later only she can tame the lion-killing Samson through seductive
treachery, achieving what a thousand soldiers could not. Here DeMille
delivers another message about women, that their treacherous and
destructive powers exceed those of any man. Men beware: do not mix
business with pleasure, and certainly do not confide your secrets to
women. As if this fundamental misogyny is not enough, he brings in
a nationalist element as well, placing treachery not only in the hands

of a woman but a foreign one at that. To be sure, the story pits Hebrews against Philistines, but the roles of the male Philistines, such as the military leader played by George Sanders, men who fight with honor by the rules of warfare, go to good American lads. Hedy Lamarr, Austrian by birth, in spite of being in Hollywood for over a decade at this point, still spoke with a pronounced German accent, making her otherness stand out. To make matters even worse, she had appeared entirely nude in a ten-minute sequence in Gustav Machaty's 1933 film *Ecstasy*, and the fame of that followed her around, especially when she married shortly thereafter and her wealthy husband attempted unsuccessfully to buy and destroy all existing copies of the film. Geraldine Farrar's naughty reputation came from hearsay; Lamarr's burst out on celluloid for all to see. Not only men beware, but Americans beware: seductive women and beguiling foreigners can be harmful to your health and undermine your national values.

Coming as it did just a few years after the end of World War II, the struggle of the Hebrews against the Philistines in *Samson and Delilah* surely had implications for Americans after the war. One enemy had been defeated and a new one quickly surfaced, not only in foreign countries with political inclinations toward communism but in the United States as well, as the rising power of trade unions seemed to portend an inevitable slide into socialist policies. For believers in a rugged America in which no higher value existed than individual liberty (and DeMille subscribed to this with a passion), a lurking virus threatened to undermine the most fundamental principles of the nation, and this called for a potent antidote. The voice-over at the beginning of *Samson and Delilah* clarifies the nature of the struggle for freedom, and a few years later *The Ten Commandments* (1956) took this even further.

In these films, he used the allegory of the Israelites in captivity to illustrate the same issues he already had taken on in his own industry and in society in general. As early as 1944 he had confronted the American Federation of Radio Artists, which assessed its members one dollar each in its battle against an amendment to ban closed union shops. DeMille refused to pay the dollar, and even abandoned his $98,000-a-year position as master of ceremonies of the "Lux Radio Theatre." He fought the union all the way to the Supreme Court and belligerently crossed the picket lines of unions striking against Paramount. He went on lecture tours comparing the situation at home to ancient Rome afire, and he created the DeMille Foundation for Political Freedom, designed to protect the national values he held dear from communist subversion. His attitude, as Thomas H. Pauly has put it, was that "any constraint on his freedom to work was a betrayal of the principles on which the country had been founded."[8] Intent on flushing Reds out of Hollywood and the rest of the nation, he became one of the first to identify a future member of the Hollywood Ten as a communist infiltrator in California.[9]

The Ten Commandments

With his last film, *The Ten Commandments*, DeMille takes his political principles to the largest possible audience with the grandeur of grand opera, as if to underline the magnitude of the issue. He now summons the resources of those operas which had carried out similar objectives in the 19th century, using the same type of subject matter, a larger than life hero played by a larger than life Hollywood star, use of "deus ex machina," grandeur and spectacle equaled only in Verdi's *Aida*, and modes of persuasion familiar from Wagner. The operatic illusion actually begins before the film proper, as the first visual image gives neither titles nor Egyptian landscapes but a large undrawn theater/opera curtain from which DeMille himself emerges, as the impresario or the manager of the house, to make an important announcement before the curtain rises. Because of the theatrical image we almost expect an announcement about an indisposed singer or the name of a sponsor; instead, he offers a short commentary of the film about to be shown, not unlike some orchestral conductors who believe the audience may be lost without their words of guidance: "Ladies and Gentlemen, young and old, this may seem an unusual procedure – speaking to you before the picture begins, but we have an unusual subject. The story of the birth of freedom. The story of Moses..." "Freedom" of course stands as the keyword in this spiel, and the presence of the director in a modern suit before a curtain reminds us that we must apply what we see in this grand cinema to the great struggle looming in the 1950s.

The formula for grand cinema parallels grand opera exactly with one primary substitution: cinemascope/technicolor for bel canto singing. Opera achieves its transcendent quality through the art of singing, something

The Ten Commandments (Charlton Heston with big hair)

which allows singers – specks on the stage to those in the back rows of the balcony – to fill an immense opera house with a glorious sound, turning that mortal-sized shape on the stage into something much bigger than life, capable of stirring our emotions in an elevated manner. With the size possible with the large screen, in vivid technicolor, the spectacle of opera can be replaced with a visual image too large to grasp, especially with a wide screen that stretches the eye beyond the boundaries of peripheral vision. With these possibilities, grandeur can take on new dimensions; instead of the few hundred chorus members who will fit on the largest stage, the film director can use 20,000 extras for "chorus" scenes – in fact, as many as the budget can afford since no barrier exists to the number the camera can accommodate. Instead of sets limited by the dimensions of the opera house's proscenium, the grand cinema set can be as large as the imagination will allow.

Aside from singing, dimensions and color, similarities in the procedures also hold. A leading character such as Moses (Charlton Heston) will give the illusion of singing arias as he crosses the desert alone or approaches God on mountain sides. Love duets will be necessary, between Moses and Nefretiri (Anne Baxter), or the woman Moses will marry, Sephora (Yvonne De Carlo). Duets may pit adversaries against each other, such as Moses against Ramses (Yul Brynner), or some of the chilling scenes with Ramses and Nefretiri. Chorus scenes of course can be provided by the people, either Hebrew or Egyptian, and these can involve action such as chariot pursuit, or they can have soloists such as Moses, Aaron (John Carradine), Joshua (John Derek) and Dathan (Edward G. Robinson) set in ensembles with the chorus. In fact, DeMille's choruses occasionally do sing, such as the chanting of the Israelites as they trek through the parted Red Sea. More specifically with the leads; Nefretiri will be a soprano, Saphora a mezzo soprano, and Moses's Hebrew and Egyptian mothers as mezzos or perhaps contraltos. Sethi (Sir Cedric Hardwicke), the aging pharaoh, sings bass while the young Ramses sings baritone. The young Moses will be a tenor, but presumably as he ages his voice will move down to baritone and perhaps by the end to bass. The voice of God must be played by a Russian bass since it sounds at such a low pitch that one can almost count the vibrations. When Moses has his first meeting with God at the burning bush, we can safely assume he has been transformed from tenor – young impetuous hero and lover – to baritone, as he becomes a solid older man with a primary sense of duty. We may not hear the transformation but we certainly see it, and so does Saphora, who notices his hair. Not only has it become streaked with gray, but he now has big hair, God apparently having conferred the majesty of his deep voice with a coiffure – which keeps getting bigger the closer he gets to the promised land. Samson's holy power also depended on hair, and Moses's ability to lead a people depends on a pompadour higher than Elvis's.

The singing parts may be imaginary, but the operatic orchestral accompaniment is not, provided by the relatively young Elmer Bernstein. DeMille's favorite composer, Victor Young, died in 1956, and the task of finding a new one proved difficult. He did not like what he heard from most of the then-active Hollywood composers, presumably objecting to the deluge of music from a Korngold or a Steiner, or finding the leanness of Rózsa and Herrmann unsuitable for his vision of grandeur. As a director who treated his films like opera, DeMille knew how crucial the music could be; and he liked to collaborate closely with the composer, deciding together on the nature and amount of the music and specifics about the cues. Preminger had discovered the benefits of working with young composers to achieve his ends, especially if the composer had to be available during shooting, and DeMille now took that route. Bernstein auditioned by scoring one of the scenes and was strung out over the course of the production on a non-contractual basis.

Musically he could provide exactly what DeMille wanted, with the appropriate sense of grandeur and the sense to know when to drop out. The score should have elements of grand opera, providing the necessary bigness, sense of the past, and association with the artistic prototype DeMille had in mind, but at the same time the music should take us to the middle of the 20th century, retaining a popular element that audiences would not find alien. A type of Broadway/Hollywood Wagner resulted, using leitmotifs and Wagnerian flourishes but couched in an accessible musical palate. At times the Wagnerian elements will come to the fore, when for example Moses ascends the mountain to encounter the burning bush, and the score uses not only distinctive Wagnerian rising sequences but orchestration including a brass choir. As Moses approaches the bush a hymn-like texture signifies God's presence, and this continues lightly in the background, accompanying the basso profundo voice of God. As Moses returns, big hair and all, his transfixed state can only be grasped in Wagnerian terms, and again Bernstein obliges, leading to the intermission (in an opera, the end of Act 1) with a grand flourish. Even the horn calls occasionally sounded by Joshua will strike Wagnerians as similar to ones we hear from Siegfried in his opera from the *Ring* cycle.

As with Samson, Moses must choose between love and duty, and we see enough boudoir scenes with Nefretiri to understand why the choice may not be easy. To find duty he must be prodded by God, and lest we should not be clear on the nature of the duty, DeMille clarifies that for us in his pre-curtain talk:

> The theme of this picture is whether men ought to be ruled by God's law or whether they are to be ruled by the whims of a dictator like Ramses. Are men the property of the state or are they free souls under God? This same battle continues throughout the world today. Our intention was not to create a story but to be worthy of the divinely inspired story created three thousand years ago: the five books of Moses.

This time, he puts forward "property" as the keyword. The phrase "property of the state" points a finger directly at communism (and no doubt unionists and socialists as well); freedom (capitalism) holds that individuals should own the property. Since communists are atheists and capitalists are Christians in this scheme of things, it follows that the more property one owns (or the greater one's wealth), the more one has been blessed with Christian abundance.

Should we then see the exodus from Egypt as the struggle of a people to find capitalism? Yes, in no uncertain terms. As the Israelites press toward the promised land (the American dream), nearing the river Jordan, individuals emulate the desires of the chorus with dreams of owning their own property, with shady fig trees in the back yard. Aside from the allegorical treatment of the exodus, it strikes at a distinctly American image as well, well-known from cinema, of wagon trains moving west,[10] people in search of a frontier of rugged individualism, a dream which perhaps no longer seemed possible in the East. Here the movie magnates themselves pointed the way, men whose business opportunities and social standing faced severe limitations in New York, but who could gain unimaginable wealth and become the cream of society in

Los Angeles. Hollywood itself became the clearest manifestation of the dream, where one could be waiting on tables one day and become a star the next, or go from a Lower East Side furrier or junk dealer to a czar in the world's most exciting industry; no greater threat existed to this new world of mansions, palm trees and pools, or the dream of it for those aspiring to it, than unions and government controls.

The political agenda bolstering a view of society which came from the tradition of French grand opera had other devious aspects as well, and some of these owe more to Wagner. The pulling of Moses between morality and temptation has much in common with *Tannhäuser*, with Nefretiri as Venus and Saphro as Elizabeth. But Nefretiri plays no mere seductress; she involves herself vigorously in the affairs of state, and her touch becomes the kiss of death. Ramses may have a mean streak, but he plays by the rules. He may have let the Israelites leave much earlier had it not been for her taunting, and even the decision to pursue them in chariots arises from her goading. Her treachery again sounds the alarm to men, a warning how women will behave if allowed into business or government. By contrast, Sephora offered DeMille's ideal model for women, as she stays out of Moses's affairs and gets on with the task of childbearing. In Alan Nadel's words, DeMille's use of Nefretiri as an agent of evil "reinscribes the Christian myth of Original Sin in the body of the woman."[11] Wagner shared this view, as we see with the likes of Ortrud from *Lohengrin*.

One may be surprised by a narrative with a Christian agenda which uses Jews as the means, and Nadel explains this ably as well. Moses in DeMille's conception moves from the Old Testament to the New, becoming Jesus in disguise, a deliverer of the Jews, and scenes such as the daughters of Jethro washing his feet confirm the image. DeMille could hardly attack Jews, considering his own mother's Jewish heritage (although she converted to Christianity at marriage), but in his scenario good Jews and bad Jews can be found. The studio bosses represented the good, since they embodied the principle of individual freedom (and wealth) he espoused; not only that, they denied their Jewishness with a passion, with some of their children completely lacking knowledge of their Jewish origins. One should be wary though of socialist Jews, a widespread phenomenon in New York; not only did their politics come into question but so did their religion, as they were perceived as being atheists. Nadel, noting that the only role in the film played by a real Jew, Edward G. Robinson (Emmanuel Goldenberg) as Dathan – the one who sells out his people, ruefully states DeMille's position: "The only real Jew is the dead Jew, the Jew who in betraying his Deliverer is not Jew but Judas."[12] In spite of that, DeMille's portrayal seems more generous than that of the antisemitic Wagner with his enormous influence on German culture, who judges Jews not by their potential for conversion but by their origins which make them, he believes, inherently odious.

DeMille framed *The Ten Commandments* at beginning and end with blank screens, visuals deferring to Elmer Bernstein's sounds as the movie's audience enters and leaves the theater. At the beginning the blank screen preempted DeMille's personal lecture, and at the end those words ring in the memory, fortified by the musical score. As the audience leaves, only the music remains, the strongest manifestation of the grand opera tradition, a tradition which not only entertains but persuades, verifies and moralizes.

BOMBARDING THE SENSES:
APOCALYPSE NOW

Should anyone be afraid of Richard Wagner? Most certainly, and Francis Ford Coppola forcefully reminds us why in *Apocalypse Now*. Heading up the D'nang River on his mission to find Colonel Kurtz (Marlon Brando) and "terminate [him] with extreme prejudice," Lieutenant Willard (Martin Sheen) and his rag-tag crew encounter a trigger-happy, air-borne helicopter squadron. After inflicting a day's worth of damage, they celebrate with a barbeque and beer – an entire cow flown in suspended beneath one of the helicopters. Willard encounters Major Killgor (Robert Duvall), the untouchable leader of this unit, explains that he needs an escort up the river, but has difficulty diverting the discussion away from surfing. Finally succeeding, he suggests they take advantage of the early morning breeze; the captain doubts if they can navigate the boat through the shallow waters of the mouth of the river. Killgor, smoking a cigarette in a holder, boasts, "We'll pick up your boat and put it down like a baby, right where you want it. It's the first of the ninth, air Cavs, air mobile." More grunting than singing, one of Killgor's men belts out on the syllable "da" the famous five-note rhythmic figure from "The Ride of the Valkyries."

These few belligerent notes of Wagner set off the ride of the air mobile unit, choppers as flying horses, with crew members sitting on their helmets to keep their private parts intact. As they approach their bombing destination, Killgor, after discussing with an ace surfer in Willard's crew the ideal weight for a surfboard, informs this lad that they will soon "turn on the music – we use Wagner; it will scare the hell out of the slopes – my boys love it." Someone turns on the tape deck, we assume at an extraordinarily high decibel level to be heard not only above the deafening drone of the helicopter engines but the explosions of live ammo as well. On comes the instrumental prelude to Act 3 of *Die Walküre* as the fleet, flying in formation like the warrior goddess Brünnhilde and her eight sisters, moves in for the kill. That prelude of course is the music of "The Ride of the Valkyries," familiar even to those who have never seen an opera.

The camera interrupts this scene with a shot of a village square, and at the instant the camera shifts, the music of Wagner ceases. In this square, opening into a schoolyard, we see school children whose gentle singing of folk songs provides a striking contrast to the blare of Wagner. The camera moves gradually back to the helicopters, and as it does a steady crescendo brings Wagner back in, reaching a decibel apex, now with the solo voice of Brünnhilde as the bombardment begins. The executioners of destruction fire indiscriminately, wasting military personnel and civilians, children, animals – whatever happens to be in the line of fire. Once again Wagner defers to the silence of the village square, but now panic sets in as the attack approaches. Some of the choppers land and, as forces go on ground pursuit, Wagner's sounds, now the full chorus of Valkyries, back them up. One lands in the square to pick up the wounded, and as before this scene triggers cessation of "The Ride of the Valkyries," turned off now for the final time. A Vietnamese girl throws a grenade disguised as a rice paddy worker's hat into the chopper, eliciting a response from Killgor of "fucking savages." With sufficient damage inflicted, the warriors can get on with the serious business of surfing the unusually high six-foot peaks, shells still flying as surfers take their positions. Willard's boat, like the cow to be slaughtered for the barbeque, briefly can be seen suspended in air, flown across the shallow mouth of the river, dangling at the end of a cable connected to a massive chopper.

Popular culture associates the music of "The Ride of the Valkyries" with menace, and Coppola may simply have had that in mind when using it here. For some, though, that menace becomes much more specific when linked to Wagner's own antisemitism or when connected to the opera itself. Everyone knows, of course, that Hitler championed the music and drama of Wagner, believing these to be exemplary of the values of his own Nazi regime. In pursuing his policies of world domination and extermination of Jews, along with his attitudes of

German and Aryan superiority, Hitler could proclaim that "at every stage of my life I come back to Wagner." And further, "I was captivated at once. My youthful enthusiasm for the mast of Bayreuth knew no bounds. Again and again I was drawn to his works."[1] Some might say this indicated nothing more than a matter of personal taste and Hitler would not be the first or the last fanatical Wagnerite. Can Wagner be condemned because the perpetrator of the most heinous crimes of the 20th century, a tyrant born six years after the composer's death, happened to like his music?

This subject, of course, has been very thoroughly explored, and continues to be of fascination as we try to make some sense of the unprecedented barbarism of the century which recently drew to a close.[2] Unlike some antisemites who make no public issue of their views, Wagner did. His open declarations took various forms, but none more striking than his 1850 pamphlet *Jewishness in Music*; a pamphlet like this, in the tradition of the Grub Street hacks of the 18th century, would probably be read by a more tolerant society as being scurrilous if not openly vicious. Such considerations failed to deter him, and he minced no words in describing the stereotypical feature of the Jew as a "repugnant caricature" of German attributes. According to that stereotype, the Jew shuffles and blinks, schemes and argues, and while feigning honesty exemplifies untrustworthiness.[3] These apply to music and language as well, as we discover from Wagner's own words in the pamphlet:

> The Jew speaks the language of the country in which he has lived from generation to generation, but he always speaks it as a foreigner.... the Jew speaks the modern European language in question not as a native but only as something learned, a circumstance which is bound to exclude him from an ability to express himself with character and independence in that language.... In this language and this art the Jew can produce only imitative sounds and counterfeit goods – he cannot write truly eloquent poetry or create works of true art.... A completely unidiomatic use of our national language and an arbitrary distortion of words and phrase constructions give the Jew's locutions the unmistakable character of an intolerably confused babble of sounds.... If the Jew's characteristic way of speaking... makes him altogether incapable of articulating artistically his feelings and intuitions through *speech*, how much more incapable he must be of articulating them through *song*.[4]

Wagner rails at the Jews' use in music of the offensive sounds of the ghetto, and a parrot-like repetition completely lacking in expression and emotion, giving trivial and ridiculous results.

But what of Wagner's drama and music – surely he could have these opinions and indulge in their expression without forcing them on his listening public. Could it not be mere coincidence that the heroes and villains of Wagner's operas resemble the Über- and Untermenschen of Nazi ideology? Is it mere paranoia to imagine that Wagner put forward Alberich and other dwarfs of the *Ring* cycle; these villainous, avaricious, deceitful creatures, as stereotypical Jewish types? For the *Ring* that may be so and this has been debated at length, but for a character such as Beckmesser in *Die Meistersinger*, the connection proves much more difficult to dismiss. His appearance, manner of walking, his theft of the song for the song contest, and his critical hostility toward others as a contest judge, all place him squarely into the stereotypical representation, and allow him to embody the classic role of a scapegoat.[5] When we bring his disastrous performance at the contest of the filched song into the equation, he fulfills entirely those characteristics itemized by Wagner himself: he lacks all originality, he has no sense of the language – its phrases or points of emphasis, his bad imitation results in abject confusion, and his complete lack of genuine expression elicits first shock and then laughter from the onlookers. Wagner does not intend the musical caricature in this case in an especially subtle way.

The type of characterization of Jews by Wagner comes close in many ways to the attitude of xenophobic Westerners to just about any type of non-Westerner, especially those in the role of enemy. In older military slang the enemy becomes "Charlie," but to someone who imagines himself to be superior in every respect, the reviling and dehumanizing labels may include the likes of "slopes" or "gooks," terms Major Killgor uses to demean the Vietnamese. As the Untermenschen they have no right to strike back against supremacist attackers: if they do, they can only, like all those of their inferior race, be "savages." If Jews had reason to hear menace in Wagner, it should surely work on southeast Asians as well. We will also be reminded of another famous use of "The Ride of the Valkyries," discussed in chapter 2, near the end of *Birth of a Nation*, accompanying the frantic ride of klansmen coming to the rescue of the white South. Coppola may very well have had this scene in mind when selecting that music for *Apocalypse Now*.

While Wagner's antisemitism in the 19th century may have been more vitriolic than that of some, his attitude represented typically bourgeois European views. Most Europeans managed to contain their prejudices during the second half of the 19th century, but that period of relatively tolerant calm gave way around the turn of the century to renewed open hostility. Since Jews during Wagner's time did not expect anything other than a festering antisemitism, Wagner's brand of it seemed neither unusual nor overly offensive. In fact, many of Wagner's greatest supporters, including Hermann Levi, who conducted the premiere of *Parsifal*, or Josef Rubenstein, who arranged the same work for piano, were Jewish. In spite of what happened, that has continued up to the present, with James Levine, artistic director of the Metropolitan Opera, as arguably the finest current conductor of Wagner.

Taking Wagner from the realm of cultural normalcy to a menacing force for Jews required a transformation of Wagner's sharp but still somewhat inert antisemitism into something which could put one's life at risk. That emerged during the 1920s and beyond, not only in German-speaking countries but in virtually the entire western world, resulting in countries such as Canada preventing almost all Jews from emigrating to it in the 1930s and 1940s or the United States not allowing ships like the St. Louis to enter any of its ports. These acts, of course, convinced the Nazis that they were on the right track with a policy of extermination. Few could have imagined the horrific implications of antisemitism during the 1930s, and the overt connection between the barbarism which finally ended in 1945 and its Wagner-loving perpetrators profoundly changed the way that the music of Wagner would be regarded in the future. No longer did it simply seem menacing but an inexorable link now existed with the Holocaust.

This linkage ran so deep that when the state of Israel came into being in 1948, with many of its new citizens survivors from Europe, everyone understood and respected an unofficial ban on the performance of any music by Wagner. That ban lasted until October 1981, when Zubin Mehta, as guest conductor of The Israel Philharmonic Orchestra, included excerpts from *Tristan und Isolde* in a Tel Aviv concert. The audience became disruptive, preventing the performance from proceeding, and the public debate over Mehta's recklessness proved no less heated. Officials of Yad Vashem (the country's memorial to the Holocaust), took the position that "Wagner's notes are a reminder of the Nazi days... one must refrain from playing this music, which is permeated with elements whose purpose is to express the superiority of the Aryan race."[6] At least one member of the Knesset recommended withdrawal of funding to the Philharmonic, which responded by giving Mehta a lifetime directorship of the IPO. Music critics as well came to Mehta's defense, arguing that the programing decisions should be made on musical grounds, and this also reflected the position of most orchestra members.

The possibility of stirring up this type of controversy and debate in 1981, as well as two decades later in 2001, attests to the power of symbols and associations to evoke the darkest memories of victims.[7] Coppola made *Apocalypse Now* only a few years before this, and he surely recognized the capacity of that music to trigger a response of horror. He succeeded brilliantly in this, and for some the associations can go even further, drawn from the content of the opera itself. During the years immediately following it, the Vietnam War remained something of a taboo in the American film industry, and *Apocalypse Now* emerged as one of the first to wade into this minefield. Unlike the late 1940s and '50s when films could celebrate the valor of the Allied troops along with the victory for the free world, the American foray into southeast Asia – and the ignominious departure – left, to say the least, some very mixed feelings. Lives were sacrificed, many believed, for something very unlike the protection of the free world, and for some the last straw was Henry Kissinger winning the Nobel Prize for peace; at that point Tom Lear got out of political satire, having no idea how he could top Kissinger.

For Coppola, basing his scenario loosely on Joseph Conrad's *The Heart of Darkness*, the journey upriver for Captain Willard and crew starts at a point where reality already seems stretched to the limit and plunges them into a world that seems increasingly like a bad trip on drugs. Willard's own strange world emerges through Jim Morrison singing "The End" at the beginning, and the Rolling Stones, along with an introduction to the unlikely crew of rock-'n'-rollers, somewhat prepare us for the strangeness of what follows. The further upriver they progress, the more tenuous a grasp on life the inhabitants and occupiers appear to have, and it becomes much more difficult to make sense of anything. Eliminating Kurtz may have made sense in the confines of a general's lodging, but as life cheapens, as surfing takes precedence over military operations, as Kurtz's bizarre independence and return to primitivism (he avidly reads Frazer's *The Golden Bough*) – no matter how horrific – seems preferable to following the orders of the military brass. As ordinary men, who back at home would be factory foremen, cowboys or beach bums, now become gods not only with the power over life and death but with a spirit of capriciousness about it, thus, the reason for doing away with Kurtz seems much less clear.

Most stories emerge from a handful of archetypal narratives, and this one, aside from the connection with Conrad's, resembles in some ways the Wagner opera from which Major Killgor's battle music comes. This emerges most strikingly in the association of the flying machines – an air cavalry, horses cashed in for choppers, according to Killgor – with the Valkyries on their flying horses. Other less overt connections seem possible. In *Die Walküre*, Siegmund stumbles into the abode of Hunding where he meets Sieglinde, his long-lost sister whom he fails to recognize. They fall in love and the cuckolded Hunding challenges Siegmund to mortal combat. Wotan, chief of the gods, observes with interest and commands Brünnhilde, his warrior daughter, to protect Siegmund. The gods, in decline and in danger of extinction, urgently need a hero to preserve them. Siegmund might be that hero, in spite of his now incestuous behavior; Wotan wishes to assure his own survival at all costs. Wotan's wife Fricka, on the other hand, cannot ignore the newly-arisen morality issue, and she harangues Wotan until he comes around to her side. Brünnhilde must now be told to preside over Siegmund's death, which, having observed the ecstasy of the incestuous lovers, she refuses to do. In this tangle of taking life, preserving life, interfering with matters that do not concern oneself, incestuous love, mortal combat, a daughter's defiance of her father, and the twilight of the gods, the music of "The Ride of the Valkyries" bombards from the pit, setting into motion Brünnhilde and her sisters.

Many of these actions and ideas apply to *Apocalypse Now*. For the Americans the nagging moral issue will not go away, and Coppola uses very dark satire, including the mixture of surfing and bombing, comments about the victorious smell of napalm, and the Kurtz mission itself, to accentuate it. The military chiefs, like Wotan, desire an outcome most advantageous to their interests, and will control the lives of their subordinates if image problems arise. Kurtz stands as the moral transgressor, in an entirely improper relationship with his new followers,

Apocalypse Now (bombing to the "Ride of the Valkyries")

and the brass dispatches Willard, like Brünnhilde, to deal with him. Willard, again like Brünnhilde, does not know whether to admire or detest his subject, to fight him or join him (as the previous person with this mission had done), to defy or submit to authority. If he carries out his mission, mortal combat will be unavoidable. Coppola started this film in the mid 1970s, and by then he and others could observe, as an aftermath of the Vietnam War, that the role of the United States as superpower stood in serious jeopardy. The next two decades saw a retreat to military Valhalla, with little more than the flexing of muscles (as in Grenada) on the horizon. Superpowerdom would re-emerge in the 1990s with Iraq as the enemy, but in the 1970s it appeared to be in a twilight state, with no hero in sight to find the way back. In Wagner's opera, Siegmund, Sieglinde, Hunding and Brünnhilde have good reason to fear Wotan, the most powerful yet declining god; in Coppola's film the Americans have no cause to be in Vietnam, and many should fear their presence there.

WAGNERIAN IMAGES OF SOUND
AND SENSUALITY

N umerous films from the earliest silent features to the most recent movies have been accompanied in either large or small doses by the music of Richard Wagner. In his *Opera on Screen*, Ken Wlaschin gives a fairly complete account, itemizing under each of Wagner's operas the films that contain music from these operas, and his lists have a few dozen film titles in them.[1] Wagner, of course, was much more than a clever composer whose music has appealed to audiences and filmmakers; he stands as one of the great cultural phenomena of the 19th century whose ideas not only on music but also literature, politics, religion, psychology and organicism have shaped much more of modern culture than some may like to admit. Cinema has turned out to be the ideal medium for igniting this cultural explosion, and appearances of excerpts from Wagner's scores in specific films represent nothing more than the tip of the iceberg. The influence spreads far beyond music to include facets of the other areas just noted, in cinema covering dimensions of plot, character definition, political ideology, treatment of sexuality, and a staggering range of other possible images. While I give full chapters to most of these, I do not wish to ignore some of the others, and this chapter will range broadly through a number of the possibilities.

Buñuel as Wagnerian

As one may suspect, the inclusion of Wagner's music in a film can suggest a much more pervasive penetration of Wagnerian ideas into that film or perhaps the entire output of a certain filmmaker, and nothing could be truer of the director Luis Buñuel. From his brother Alfonso we learn that Buñuel's love of Wagner began very early in life: "Extremely fond of music, he played the piano and violin from childhood... His favorite composer was Richard Wagner, whom he greatly venerated, especially *Tristan und Isolde*." His sister Conchita tells an even more revealing tale:

> When he was about thirteen he started to study the violin, at his own very strong desire; and he seemed to show an aptitude for it. He used to wait till we had gone to bed, then, with his violin all ready, would come to the room where we, his three sisters, slept. He would begin by telling us the "plot," which as I recall it was a very Wagnerian tale, although he was not aware of it at the time. I don't think his music was so Wagnerian, but it was a gift which enriched the adventures of my childish imagination.[2]

The blending of music and narrative in Conchita's description unveils something fascinating about the working of the young Buñuel's mind, suggesting an inseparability of the two – and a Wagnerian fusion at that. One could argue that as a director he worked in a similar way, giving us films that do not depend so much on scripts as a kind of inner or underlying music that inspires and propels the visual images.

That inner music need not only be Wagner: it could also be Brahms, as in *Las Hurdes*, which, he explained to André Bazin in a 1954 interview, seemed perfectly normal to him. Unlike D. W. Griffith, who almost always wanted his inner music to be represented by actual music, Buñuel took the view that audible music might actually interfere with the underlying music. He attempted to explain this in the same interview with Bazin:

> Personally I don't like film music. It seems to me that it is a false element, a sort of trick, except of course in certain cases. I've been amazed to find in this Festival [Cannes, 1954] feature films without music... [it] proves to me that in all events silence would be preferable.[3]

We should not take him too literally here, since in his own films his "certain cases" can occupy large amounts of space. Yet, his apparent disdain for film music seems legitimate, as he believes more often than not it simply patches over mediocre spots in a film. His certain cases, presumably, should allow a heightened possibility of music and visuals working together, generating an intensity in which the fusion of images takes the viewer to the heart of the inner music at the film's source.

A brief look at three of his films, from the beginning, middle and end of his career, will give some idea of the importance of Wagner's operas to his cinematic urge. His first feature film, *L'Age d'or* (*The Golden Age*, 1930), proved incomprehensible to some and offensive to others, but on both counts Wagner may be the key that helps unlock the enigma. In this work he progresses from a nature film on scorpions to bedraggled revolutionaries, past images of annihilated bishops to imperial Rome, through a view of Roman high society to a final degenerate image of Christ raping a virgin. Conflict abounds, but good and evil remain undefined: in struggles between revolutionaries and the ruling class, the church and enemies of the church, men and women, and oppressors and relief givers, no side emerges as preferable to the other. Like scorpions, each will poison the other. Driving all seems to be something irrational, an inexplicable obsession or desire, and central to the film lies a specifically sexual form of it along with the discomfort and anger it arouses among those who have lost passion or never had it in the first place.

Irrationality and obsessive desire work at the base of the film, and since we cannot hope to understand them through reason, we must experience them through a capacity of the mind to function irrationally, that being through music – not just any music, but Buñuel's beloved Wagner. In fact, not just any Wagner, but Buñuel's favorite Wagner: *Tristan und Isolde*. In *Tristan*, rational thought proves utterly worthless. Here a look of desire mingled with despair or a love potion consumed in the belief that death will result become the driving force. Tristan should not love Isolde: he has killed her fiancé and has been entrusted to bring her to her new fiancé, King Mark. Yet he loves her with a reason-defying passion, an urge so strong it cannot be tamed by any sense of duty or decency, and she loves him with equal abandon, with no fear of the consequences – even death. The narrative will not make such a love comprehensible, but if the listener submits to Wagner's music, something illuminating happens. The music itself can sweep us hopelessly into the passion, allowing the sexuality to be transformed into something spiritual. The experience of this lay at the heart of Buñuel's cinematic urge, and he created films which attempt the same level of irrational desire. Here we have his "certain cases," where inner music and real music could correspond, as passages from Wagner's *Tristan* could induce the appropriate feeling of euphoria, allowing an intense melding of images.

In *L'Age d'or*, the site of the bishop's skeletons receives a visit from a flotilla of boats bringing dignitaries from the church, government, the military and society in general, who conduct a ceremony initiating the Golden Age. A disturbance to the ceremony outrages those in attendance; a man (Gaston Modot) and a young woman (Lya Lys), to use Raymond Durgnat's words, embrace with "cries of ecstasy and joy... in paroxysms of lasciviousness, grappling fully dressed in the mud."[4] As this unimaginable act at such an occasion begins, so does the sound of the prelude to Wagner's *Tristan*, conditioning the viewer to identify with the deviants instead of the onlookers scandalized by their behavior. The offended good citizens pull them apart, and send him back to the city handcuffed between two burly guards.

In the surrealist flow of things, instead of ending up at a prison, Modot arrives at a gala for Roman society at the palatial home of the Marquis of X, father of Lys. The guests take seats in the garden for an outdoor concert to be conducted by the Marquis. Modot and Lys, now together again, continue their lovemaking in a semi-secluded part of the garden, perched awkwardly on garden chairs, and as their sexual frenzy begins, so does the music, with the famous "Liebestod," the conclusion of Wagner's *Tristan*. Their passion now seems to be sanctioned as the music no longer sounds as a background but instead becomes diegetic, an integral part of the scene; her father conducts, and he will later kiss his daughter with ardor that verges on incestuousness. In the "Liebestod," Isolde pours out her ecstatic equation of love and death, taking the listener musically to the highest possible irrational heights. When a servant interrupts Modot with a request to answer a phone call; Lys, in the grip of uninhibited ecstasy, prolongs the state by sucking the toe of a statue which stood over their lovemaking. The process of trying to make sense of this film, as some have attempted with Freudian interpretations, has about as much hope of success as finding logic in the surrealistic stream of events; accepting irrationality, with Wagner as Buñuel's salacious accomplice, proves to be more fruitful. Henry Miller perceptively recognized this in his own essay on *L'Age d'or*:

> There was something which shocked their delicate sensibilities even more and that was the effect of Wagner's *Tristan and Isolde* upon one of the protagonists. Was it possible that the divine music of Wagner could so arouse the sensual appetites of a man and woman as to make them roll in the graveled path and bite and chew one another until the blood came? Was it possible that this music could so take possession of the young woman as to make her suck the toe of a statued foot with perverted lasciviousness? Does music bring on orgasms, does it entrain perverse acts, does it drive people truly mad? Does this great legendary theme which Wagner immortalized have to do with such a plain vulgar physiological fact as sexual love? The film seems to suggest that it does. It seems to suggest more… He has distinguished to us… the entire plexus of forces which unite love and death in life.[5]

The music of *Tristan* appears only at a few key points in *L'Age d'or*, just enough to let us know how to experience the film, and it shares billing with the first movement of Schubert's *Unfinished* Symphony and numerous other familiar pieces. In *Cumbres borrascosas* (*Wuthering Heights*), also known as *Abismos de pasión* (1953), the music of *Tristan* (or adaptations of it by composer Raul Lavista) occupies fifty minutes of the ninety-minute film. Buñuel's comments about this confirm that if we do not take what directors say of their own work with a grain of salt, we should. At one point he confessed that "all the surrealists were great fans of Miss Emily Brontë's. *Wurthering Heights* was a great love story for us. I wanted to do it back in 1930 with lots of Wagner on the sound track. When I finally shot it in Mexico, it came out as an anachronism, a sentimental homage to my own youth."[6] In the interview with Bazin, he took that a little further: "For *Cumbres borrascosas* I put myself into the state of mind of 1930; and since at that time I was a hopeless Wagnerian, I introduced fifty minutes of Wagner."[7] On another occasion he gave a very different version, regreting the fifty minutes:

> It was my own fault. My negligence. I went to Europe, to Cannes, and left the composer to add the musical accompaniment; and he put music throughout the film. A real disaster. I intended to use

L'Age d'or (lovemaking to Wagner's "Liebestod")

Wagner just at the end, in order to give the film a romantic aura, precisely the characteristic sick imagination of Wagner. Still, I think that my version reflects the spirit of the novel much better than the one made by Hollywood.[8]

Which Buñuel should we believe, the hopeless Wagnerian, or the one who abandons all control of the music (a director who regards music as "a parasitic element") to the hired composer? Of course, he wanted the fifty minutes, and as a measure of its quality, it proved not only effective but influential; Bernard Herrmann, if he had been pressed on the matter, may have had some difficulties explaining some of the similarities with his own Tristanesque score for *Vertigo*.

We may or may not agree with Buñuel's proclamation about capturing the spirit of *Wuthering Heights*, but most assuredly his telling of the tale embodies all the irrational passions of a Wagnerian opera. Catalina retains an obsessive love for Alejandro after she marries Eduardo, and Alejandro seems unlimited in his capacity for passion, revenge and cruelty. Isabel cannot quell her desire for Alejandro, and her brother Eduardo musters intense hatred for his wife's former lover or anyone who takes this intruder's side after his return. Catalina's brother Riccardo seems capable of boundless cruelty, toward his own son among others, and Riccardo's father indulges a fanaticism for religion. Buñuel had misgivings about the quality of the acting and may in the end have felt that fifty minutes of *Tristan* proved necessary to overcome "scenes with no other cinematographic interest" – his usual criticism for the use of film music. If the actors could not find the inner music – the Wagnerian irrationality – but instead would turn obsessiveness into sentimentality, then Wagner would have to overcome the deficiency. As with *L'Age d'or*, he uses both the prelude of *Tristan* and the "Liebestod," the prelude providing the overture to accompany his own opening titles, and then offering the musical substance in adaptation for most of the film. He shifts to the "Liebestod" three-quarters of the way through, when Alejandro returns to see the dying Catalina. Unlike the Wagner opera, she dies before him; but in an inspired scene at her grave, Alejandro has a vision of her coming toward him, when in fact the advancing figure is Riccardo with rifle pointed. The irrational love ends in death, and Wagner's "Liebestod" sounds throughout this final scene.

In *L'Age d'or* and *Cumbres*, the music of *Tristan* not only underlined irrational desire but it also pointed to similarities between the events of the opera and plot aspects of the films. In Buñuel's last work, *Cet obscur objet du désir* (*That Obscure Object of Desire*, 1977), the reason for the appearance of an excerpt from Wagner's *Die Walküre* at the end of the film seems much more obscure. The aging Buñuel, now seventy-seven, harboring doubts that he would complete the film, probably saw this as his last work, and the Wagnerian conclusion may reflect as much on his career as the film in question. The premise of the work – an aging man (Fernando Rey) with an uncontrollable passion for a sultry adolescent (played alternately by Carole Bouquet and Angela Molina) – invokes themes of past films, including Christian morality, misogyny, and male-female conflict, but other forces in the end supersede them. First among these stands the obsessive desire of an older man for a woman one third his age; the fact that he meets her in the role as his servant places the situation in the context of a long theatrical tradition which includes the *commedia dell'arte* and other 17th- and 18th-Century comedies. Almost invariably in these comedies, the lusty old man learns his lesson at the end as his youthful prey ends up with a suitor her own age.

Comedy can easily get out of hand if one probes beneath the surface of the characters, and Buñuel does that here. The girl proves to be exceptionally complex, virgin and whore rolled into one, leading her pursuer on but never giving in to him. The more she manipulates him, the more obsessive he becomes, submitting to the ultimate degradation of watching her make love to a young man from outside a locked gate in the house he bought for her. A theme of terrorism runs through the film, paralleling his pursuit of her and her resistance of him; terrorist bombs finally catch up with them as one blows them up in a modern shopping complex. Shortly before this fatal explosion, at the very moment she once again becomes resistant, a musical bomb hits; the unexpected blast of an excerpt from *Die Walküre*. Buñuel makes his own exit with Wagner, ending his last film with it as he claimed he intended to do in *Cumbres*, concluding his filmmaking career as he began it with the music of Wagner in *Un chien Andalou* and *L'Age d'or*. The curious if not unintelligible placement here rounds out a career of fascination with inexplicable desire, sexual ecstasy and irrationality, a fascination he shared overwhelmingly with Wagner.

Chaplin's *Lohengrin*

Buñuel by no means stood alone as a filmmaker bringing the music of Wagner into his films, or the development of themes in a film which emerge from the quoted opera by Wagner. This happens, for example, in one of the most prominent films from the early 1940s, Charles Chaplin's *The Great Dictator*. Here the music of Wagner plays a potentially ambivalent role, since the dictator of course is Hitler, and Hitler adored Wagner and used his music as a rallying cry for the Nazi offensive. But Chaplin plays two roles in this film, the dictator of the Double Cross and the Jewish barber; the latter may have some buffoonish qualities, but he represents highly cultured people who, in spite of Wagner's antisemitism, can make their own claim to this part of high German culture. Just as Chaplin embodies the conflict between the oppressed and the oppressor, and allows for the final triumph of good through a case of mistaken identity, he also explores both sides of the culture issue: does the music of Wagner belong to the cause of evil or is it the uplifting possession of all humanity?

For this dual purpose Chaplin uses the prelude to *Lohengrin*, a striking piece of music with a unique function at the beginning of the opera. Lohengrin, a knight of the holy grail, will descend from Mount Monsalvat to come to the aid of the wronged Elsa, and, at the end, he will return to the knights who have pledged their aid to the oppressed. The prelude represents the grail itself approaching the earth, carried, as Wagner himself described it, by a host of angels, "ravishing the senses of the beholder." After pouring out its light on those who witness the grail like a benediction, consecrating them to its service, "the flames gradually die away, and the angel-host soars up again to the ethereal heights in tender joy, having made pure once more the hearts of men by the sacred blessing of the Grail."[9] The music begins quietly in a high register, descends in pitch as the orchestration fills out, climaxes dynamically with full orchestra, and then returns to the gentle heights from which it came. By way of orchestral color and dynamics Wagner represents Lohengrin's descent and ascent, preparing the listener through musical, spiritual and ecstatic means for the knight's entry into an imperfect, tainted world.

When Chaplin first introduces this music, it belongs to the dictator who, relishing the prospect of ruling the entire earth, dismisses his advisor and in solitude plays with a beachball-like globe, bouncing it with his hands, his feet, and even his derrière. The dictator here becomes a greedy child, and in spite of Hitler's predilection for Wagner, the treatment at this point, considering the significance of this music, can only be ironic. The music ends abruptly when the earthly balloon pops. We will hear this music elsewhere, most notably at the end of film, and here Chaplin wrestles it away from the dictator, giving it back to the worthy. The Jewish barber, having escaped from prison and wearing a military uniform, is mistaken for the dictator and must address the throng waiting for him. Like Lohengrin coming down from the mountain, the barber descends early in the film in an upside-down airplane, attempting to aid a disabled pilot during World War I. A crash landing leaves him with amnesia, but eventually he recovers and returns to the ghetto to help his people – especially Hanna, whom he transforms from cleaning woman to a striking beauty.

Before he makes his speech at the end, he ascends the stairs to the podium, accompanied by rising music of the *Lohengrin* prelude and in his speech he becomes the genuine knight of the grail, proclaiming the need for kindness, goodness and unity. After the main speech, he addresses Hanna directly, with the prelude music again backing him up. He tells her to look up (that becomes a leitmotif), that the clouds are lifting, that men will rise above their hate and greed; "the soul of man has been given wings, and at last he is beginning to fly – go into the light of hope." On this final note of ascent, Chaplin completes the reappropriation of Wagner; the forces of good have reclaimed this music and its message of hope for all, and the Jewish barber, having touched down to aid the oppressed, now soars with the voice of the gods.

Love and duty

While Wagner's music may suggest a motif for a film, it can do much more than that, as happens in *Meeting Venus* (1991) in which all events revolve around rehearsals and a performance of *Tannhäuser*. The early part of the rehearsal bears some striking resemblances to Fellini's *Prova d'orchestra* (*Orchestra Rehearsal*, 1979), but as it proceeds, it becomes clear that scriptwriter and director István Szabó wishes to take us through *Tannhäuser* itself with a classic struggle between illicit love and duty. We hear virtually no music throughout the film except for that of *Tannhäuser*, so much so that the titles give credit to Wagner as the composer. Since the film focuses on an opera, Szabó presents only the music with its source recognizable on stage, but at times the music can be heard as nondiegetic background music, allowing Wagner to infiltrate the actions of characters. The film has numerous delightful touches, including the casting of Victor Poletti in the role of Wolfram in the opera, the Italian actor who played the role of the aggressive tenor in Fellini's *E la nave va*.

In the opera, Tannhäuser, a 13th-century minstrel knight, takes refuge from his defeat in a singing competition at the Venusberg, home of Venus, the goddess of love and seducer of men. He succumbs to her enticements, but after a year grows weary of endless lovemaking, and returns to his old world. There he reunites with Elizabeth, who still loves him, but he offends his fellow knights by singing wildly in a singing contest of the sensual love he enjoyed with Venus. A wish for penitence and the hope of regaining Elizabeth drives him to join pilgrims en route to Rome, but the Pope declares his chance of pardon no better than the possibility of leaves growing from his walking staff. Venus beckons him to return to her, and Wolfram reminds him of the pure and devout Elizabeth. Both Tannhäuser and Elizabeth die of unknown causes amid news of a miracle from Rome: fresh leaves have sprouted from the staff he left behind.

In *Meeting Venus*, a Hungarian conductor (Niels Arestrup) arrives in Paris to direct the performance of *Tannhäuser*, and Paris, the city of plenty, quickly becomes his Venusberg. Beautiful young women throw themselves at him, including a young soprano who takes him to her apartment for private rehearsals, the union representative from the orchestra (an old flame from Budapest), and at least one other attractive member of the orchestra. But all of these pale in comparison to the international diva Karin Anderson (Glenn Close), who at first gives him an icy reception but warms quickly after he quells national rivalries with a comic routine at the piano on intolerance. She plays the role of Elizabeth in the opera, but in the film she clearly represents Venus, taking control not only of the stage but the maestro as well. His wife back in Budapest, Edith (along with their daughter), represents his Elizabeth, and Budapest becomes the austere place of duty. During rehearsals he explains the conflict of love and duty in the opera, and after taking his wife and daughter to a recital given by the diva in Budapest, he personally struggles with the conflict. A rowdy attempt on his part to get into his lover's hotel room in Budapest results in an arrest, not unlike Tannhäuser's run-in with the knights. A last-minute strike by backstage workers threatens to cancel the performance in Paris, but the diva's suggestion to play it in front of the safety curtain saves the day. At the end of the magnificent performance, after all their ups and downs, he and the diva look at each other with passion; Elizabeth and Venus have come together in her, and his unlikely salvation materializes as leaves grow from his baton.

Numerous other films use music by Wagner for strategic purposes, including Jean Negulesco's *Humoresque* (1946), Fritz Lang's *The Blue Gardenia* (1953), Fellini's *The Clowns*, Ken Russell's *Mahler*, John Boorman's *Hope and Glory* (1987), and Barbet Schroeder's *Reversal of Fortune* (1990). Wagner, of course, has permeated cinema by means other than his music, playing a shaping role in plot, characters, themes and images, and these films arouse every bit as much fascination as the ones which use his music. In some, the Wagnerian influence may be a little more difficult to pin down when features other than music come into question. The influence of the multi-faceted Wagner spread to various fields, politics being one that has already been considered in earlier chapters. Literature too followed in his footsteps, and nowhere more vigorously than in France, led by Baudelaire and subsequently followed by the symbolist poets. Cinema's indebtedness to Wagner has taken many forms, and aside from the underlying shaping possibilities recognized by Griffith or Eisenstein, that can also be seen in the ideas that give rise to certain individual films. Some may even acknowledge it in the title, such as *Pandora and the Flying Dutchman* (1951), in which James Mason plays a modern flying Dutchman who can only be released from his curse of eternal life by a woman whose love for him includes sacrificing her life for him. The woman in this case, played by Ava Gardner, lacks the passive submissiveness of Wagner's Senta in *Der fliegende Holländer* (*The Flying Dutchman*), but adds some spice by bringing in the destructiveness of the mythical Pandora. Some may argue that a film such as this sidesteps Wagner by going directly to the myth, but Albert Lewin's cinematic approach surely gives it a bigger than life Wagnerian dimension; aside from plot and characters, the visual images of the sea and cliffs, the feats of daring, and the aura of grandeur all emerge as cinematic transferences of Wagner's opera.

Nosferatu

The Dutchman myth pervades other films as well, and one of the most interesting comes from the genre of German expressionist cinema. Jo Leslie Collier has argued that virtually all of F. W. Murnau's films derive their essential imagery from Wagner, and none more vividly than *Nosferatu* (1922).[10] Starting with the broad theme apparent in both Wagner and Murnau, the redemption of the male by the loving sacrifice of the female, Collier moves on to specific connections between *Nosferatu* and *The Flying Dutchman*.[11] Nosferatu the vampire (Max Schreck) carries the same curse of eternal existence as the Dutchman, but like Pandora he brings evil and destruction to all who encounter him. The Bremen real estate agent Harker barely survives a sojourn to the count's castle in Transylvania, and Nosferatu, catching sight of a portrait of Harker's wife Nina, cannot resist moving to Bremen. Nosferatu's coffins are loaded aboard a ship which sails to the North Sea, and as the captain and all the crew die from the plague of his need for human blood, Nosferatu becomes an invisible Dutchman, mysteriously guiding the ship into port at Bremen. Nina, who has experienced many bad omens since her husband went to Transylvania, realizes the source of Harker's malaise and the widespread death in Bremen, and she reads in a book on vampires how it can be stopped: "Only a woman can break the frightful spell – a woman pure in heart – who will offer her blood freely to Nosferatu and will keep the vampire by her side until after the cock has crowed." Nina like Senta can break the curse and save a man, although unlike Wagner's work, the man who needs to be saved is not the one under the curse. She must resolve to let this hideously deformed and evil creature come to her – she must submit to his every wish – and take her chances of not surviving the ordeal, with either her life or her morals intact. The spirit of self-sacrifice overcomes all, Nosferatu dissolves into dust at dawn, and she survives to continue loving Harker.

Since the original *Nosferatu*, numerous vampires have crawled out of the cinematic woodwork, but few have followed the 1922 version with any sense of being a genuine sequel: Werner Herzog's *Nosferatu the Vampyre* (1979) is the exception. Like *Fitzcarraldo* (to be discussed in chapter 23), it stars Klaus Kinski, and like that film Herzog emphasizes

Nosferatu the Vampyre (the sacrifice)

obsession – of Nosferatu for blood and for Harker's beautifully pale wife. In the thumb-cutting scene, for example, Kinski's little moan before he slurps Harker's blood turns the scene into something akin to sexual obsession. If there were any doubts about Wagnerian connections in Murnau's version, Herzog completely erases these in his, adjusting the story to make it more Wagnerian, and adding Wagner's music at two critical points.

To strengthen the tie with *The Flying Dutchman*, Herzog gives us much more of the ship than Murnau had – a dark, mysterious vessel with black sails. The changes near the end though offer a very different twist. When Harker's wife discovers how to release her home town from its misery, she consecrates her home (leaving Harker in an unconsecrated spot) and waits in bed for Nosferatu. He comes, and she leaves no question of the sexual nature of the submission, pulling up her nightgown to her waist. He goes for her neck, where he appears to get both sustenance and pleasure; unlike her 1922 counterpart, she puts her arms around his neck to keep him until the cock crows, and he happily sucks until then. Her actions suggest her interest has shifted from her husband to Nosferatu, and as in Wagner's opera, she dies with the one she has released from the curse. Harker, now on his own, rises from his slumber as a vampire.

The Flying Dutchman may drive certain aspects of the plot, but other Wagner operas come into play as well. Even in Murnau's version, as Collier notes, the overly innocent Harker has much in common with Siegfried and Parsifal. Herzog brings in another possibility, by playing excerpts from the prelude to *Das Rhinegold* just before Harker first meets Nosferatu, and again, when we first see the count in his new home, carrying his coffins to the house Harker has arranged for him. *Das Rhinegold* shows us the underwater world of the Rhinemaidens immediately after the prelude, a strange, unearthly world with objects of desire – women and gold. Alberich disrupts the playful swimming of the Rhinemaidens, and Alberich is surely the most ugly, deformed and evil creature in the *Ring* cycle; his evil spreads like a plague through his hateful power to all who encounter him. Herzog not only uses this music to evoke an Alberich-like character, but he also introduces with it the otherworldly, eerie existence of his vampire. This world of darkness vaguely resembles the murky depths of the Rhine, and on more than one occasion we see a bat flying through the night sky which seems more like water. If there had been any doubt about a Wagnerian connection with *Nosferatu*, Herzog dispels it with his choice of audible images, joining a sizable group of directors who similarly insisted on these sounds.

WAGNER'S *RING* FOR
ADOLESCENTS: *STAR WARS*

In the middle of *The Empire Strikes Back*, Luke Skywalker (Mark Hamill) lands his small spacecraft in a swampy bog on the planet of Dagobah, where he encounters a puppet-like dwarf who, after playing the fool, turns out to be his mentor. This pint-sized guru, Yoda (Frank Oz), tells the fearless Luke that fright will come, and he sends him into the adjoining forest/jungle to discover the terrors of the dark side. An undaunted Luke emerges unscathed, having used the light sword given to him by Ben "Obi-Wan" Kenobi (Alec Guinness), one of Yoda's earlier disciples. As the training continues, Luke proves to be a fairly inept apprentice, but no one doubts he will achieve grand feats, especially Obi (Ben), whose apparition reminds Yoda that "this boy is our last hope." Where does George Lucas get this stuff, we might well ask, the various threads for this bizarre epic that has beguiled an entire youthful generation, adding a whole new set of delirious fans with the remakes two decades later and a new episode in 1999? The rite of passage tale may be familiar enough in various myths and legends, but what about the details – the sword, the dwarf, the lack of fear, the bungled apprenticeship, or the hope for the future?

Opera buffs know it well, although having other sensibilities and being from the wrong generation they stayed away from these fantasy films in droves: this comes straight from *Siegfried*, the third opera in Wagner's colossal *Ring of the Nibelungen*. While there may be connections with other literary epics, including Tolkien's, C. S. Lewis's and others, George Lucas gives us an entertainment that can only be compared in scope to opera. Lucas himself, in an interview with Leonard

Maltin, called this cycle his "space opera" (a term also used by a number of reviewers), and the intended hyperbolic grandeur, supported throughout by John Williams's leitmotivic musical score, can only be described as Wagnerian. Wagner had numerous disciples in the latter half of the 19th century and well into the 20th century, artists who followed him to his shrine of high art and spectacle with extraordinary fervor and devotion. He surely could not have anticipated the *Star Wars* films, and might very well have regarded this as some sort of misbegotten progeny, with very serious genetic flaws. Yet, in some ways this has proved to be the most Wagnerian among the Wagnerians.

The adolescent male audience that *Star Wars* targeted in 1977 imbibed its cultural nourishment from Saturday morning television cartoons, and Lucas could safely bet that they had little exposure to the classic films from which he borrows so freely, or knew anything about opera at all – with the exception of Bugs Bunny in *The Rabbit of Seville* or *What's Opera, Doc?* Even if they did know classic films, as many of his post-adolescent fans would, they could simply enjoy the piling up of these derivative visual images, making a game of identifying them. Some of the images leap right off the screen and have been mentioned by various reviewers, especially *The Wizard of Oz* with C-3PO as the Tin Man, Chewbacca as the Lion, Ben as the Wizard, the Munchkin-like Yawas, and perhaps even R2-D2 (shaped like the typical public washroom paper towel disposal receptacle) as Toto. But the list goes on and on, including Tarzan movies with numerous vine swingers, swashbuckling as in *Captain Blood* (to name one of an entire genre), the hooded Emperor as the evil Teutonic organist from *Alexander Nevsky* (or Death in *The Seventh Seal*, as Pauline Kael prefers[1]), Han Solo (Harrison Ford) as a glib James Bond, the enemy helmets reminiscent of those worn by storm troopers from various World War II films that feature Nazis, the torture chambers from literally hundreds of "B" horror films, and a variety of other associations with *Planet of the Apes*, *King Kong*, *2001: A Space Odyssey*, *Flash Gordon*, and even an ice battle from *Alexander Nevsky*. The Muppet guru Yoda probably would have been a familiar type to the faithful. This list only begins to scratch the surface.

The connections with Wagner would probably escape the hardcore *Star Wars* junkies altogether, but certainly not the reviewers – especially Roger Angell, who jested about "a flick *Götterdämmerung*;"[2] three years later Pauline Kael actually expressed admiration for Irvin Kershner, director of *The Empire Strikes Back*, who "brought the material a pop-Wagnerian amplitude."[3] Pop-Wagnerian, or how about pop-up Wagner – Siegfried as the cat-in-the-hat. In fact, some may find Wagner's *Ring* cycle better suited for children in general, with giants and dwarfs, horses that fly, a helmet that allows its wearer to change into an animal or vanish altogether, rainbows to paradise, magic swords, little birds that tell secrets, or a princess who awakens with a kiss. Few children at the end of the last quarter of the 20th century will have been exposed to this type of saga in the opera house or even on television when it appears as the Met's *Ring* cycle did in 1980. Given the choice of watching this for fifteen hours or cartoons for the same amount of time, most children will have little difficulty choosing. But if the two can be combined, presenting a Wagnerian epic with an assortment of cartoon-like beasties, nasty villains, video arcade shoot-outs, rousing music and heroes who talk like the Smurfs, the prospect becomes decidedly more appealing. Many found Lucas's plan crazy; Wagner got the same treatment a hundred years earlier, and turned to the eccentric Ludwig II of Bavaria to build him his paramount, universal, colossal Bayreuth studio.

For someone the age of ten, power to control the world (or the universe) can be very serious business. This can even be true for older people, and from time to time one of them, perhaps in a position to squander massive amounts of money on it, as what happens in the White House from time to time, may try to do something about it. The forces of good and evil lock in a struggle to the end, and over the years these battles have been played out on Saturday afternoon radio, the matinee movies, Saturday television, and in the 1980s (as well as the beginning of the 21st century) the White House – with dire warnings of the lurking evil empire.[4] How does one gain power over the entire universe? One builds magical laser machines that can zap anything, fry them out of existence in an instant and, if the Defense Department can not do it, those clever props guys over at the studios surely can. In *Star Wars* those with the "Force" could be in control; for Wagner the possessor of the ring held all power; and the ring had been fashioned from the gold of the Rhine. The power of the ring could be used for good or evil, just like the "Force," depending who held it (Alberich or Hagen for evil or Siegfried for good).

Let us run Luke Skywalker through his Siegfried paces. Both have been orphaned and have a strong urge to know their lineage. Siegfried grows up naively under the protection and guidance of the dwarf Mime; Luke lives with an uncle and aunt on a remote farm and later comes under the guidance of the muppet/dwarf Yoda. Siegfried inherits the magical sword which came to him by way of his grandfather Wotan and father Siegmund; Luke receives his light saber in similar fashion, passed on to him from Obi-Wan Kenobi. Neither Siegfried nor Luke understand the concept of fear, and both receive warnings from their midget mentors that they will discover its full force; in fact, both are sent into the forest to encounter it. For Siegfried, the ultimate embodiment of fear stands in the form of a fierce, drooling, tentacled, fire-breathing dragon (actually the giant Fafner who turned himself into a dragon to protect the gold), and he runs the monster through with his sword without learning fear. Luke's test in the forest has more to do with self-control, as he fights an apparition of Darth Vader, but he too meets his dragon, most notably at the court of Jabba in *Return of the Jedi*, when he finds himself having fallen through a trap door into Jabba's pet dragon's lair. Lacking his trusty saber, Luke chucks a projectile at the gate control, and squashes the brute under the weight of the iron grate. Even while Luke takes his tests, Solo and company make a narrow escape from the esophagus of a mammoth astroid dragon.

Like the Wälsungs in the *Ring* cycle, the Jedi stand as a race apart, knights of valor with special powers, entrusted with the sacred task of protecting the earth/universe from evil forces. Their numbers have diminished, and Siegfried and Luke remain the last hope for their respective orders, watched closely by observers (Wotan and Ben) who have a vested interest in their survival and prosperity. Wotan's visit to Mime disguised as the Wanderer resembles Ben's appearance to Yoda as he instructs Luke. Both youths prove to be poor apprentices to their mentors, Siegfried at the forge and Luke in getting control of the "Force," but that does not prevent them from achieving extraordinary results by relying on their own naive instincts. Mime the master smith cannot forge the sword from its broken pieces, but Siegfried does it by breaking all the rules, falling back on dumb instinct that baffles the master, and moving on to a succession of extraordinary feats. Luke may not have completed the apprenticeship, leaving to rescue his friends before he finished the course, but that did not impede him from matching sabers equally with Vader and even eventually converting Vader away from the dark side.

Both of these idiot-savant heroes embody such naive goodness that they have difficulty recognizing temptation – Siegfried in the spiked drink offered by Hagen and Luke in his susceptibility to anger. For Siegfried the lapse proved fatal; Luke for the moment triumphs, but one suspects that in some subsequent installment when Lucas finally grows weary of the whole thing we will reach the twilight of the Jedi.

With a bit of mixing and matching, some other parallels emerge. Princess Leia (Carrie Fisher), in the clutches of the enemy, turns out to be Luke's sister, although he does not discover this until much later. Siegfried's father met Sieglinde under similar circumstances, in her case sleeping with the Wälsung enemy Hunding, although in this case their illicit (incestuous) erotic desire went much further, resulting in the birth of little Sigi (but then Wagner's *Ring* cycle gets an "R" rating compared to "GP" for the *Stars Wars* movies). Princess Leia herself seems to be a combination of Brünnhilde and Sieglinde, without being especially sexy; when we see her scantily clad in the possession of the grotesque Jabba, we likely think more of her bare vulnerability. Here she may very well be Sieglinde in the grip of the miserable Hunding. Or, as a sacrificial prize for services rendered, she resembles Freia, dragged off and held by Fasolt and Fafner until Wotan can pay for her release. As a rebel space warrior, usually flying high and very much in control, she has more in common with Brünnhilde. Leia's rescue from the Empire, while a classic fairytale princess rescue, resembles the release of Brünn-hilde from her fiery slumber by the fearless Siegfried. That Leia and Luke have the same father bears similarity to Siegfried and Brünnhilde in that one is the child and the other the grandchild of Wotan.

Aside from the squat Yoda who can levitate a spaceship with his force, Lucas populates the entire trilogy with waves of dwarf-like crea-tures, from the nasty little Jawas – faceless except for burning coals in place of eyes – of *Star Wars* to the Teddy-bear Ewoks of *Return* who fight on the one hand like Robin Hood's men from Errol Flynn films and on the other hand can be soothed by bedtime stories about the adventures of Luke and company. The fearsome little Jawas appear to inhabit the lowest rung on the social ladder, not unlike the under-worldly dwarfs of the Nibelungen, the slaves of the bloody-minded Alberich – who captures the gold from the Rhinemaidens because of his capacity to renounce love. After Wotan's ruse to separate him from the gold (including the ring and helmet), he spends the rest of his

existence trying to recover the gold – always in waiting – using treachery, cunning or horse-trading tactics, as he attempts with Fafner as
dragon just before Siegfried emerges as dragon slayer. The implications
in Wagner's Ring cycle are not subtle; these avaricious, cunning, bar-
gaining, short people are the antisemitic Wagner's stereotypical Jews,
just as surely as the linguistic and musical incompetence of Beckmesser
in *Die Meistersinger* represents those dimensions of Wagner's antisemitism
noted in chapter 15. The parallel with the Jawas has not gone unnoticed; Jonathan Rosenbaum, comparing them with the lack of embarrassment about the "yellow peril" in the 1936 *Flash Gordon* serial, points
out that "the styling of the Jawas as stingy Jewish merchants –
'Munchkin Shylocks,' in Richard Corliss' apt phrase – is much more
oblique and subtle; one might even have to see the relationship of
'Jawa' to the Hebrew 'Yahweh' in order to catch the clue."[5]

An epic struggle between good and evil needs a colossal villain, and
Lucas obliges with Darth Vader – part bionic man, part Schwarzenegger-
like terminator, part Nazi conqueror, part warlord of the James Bond
film variety with one hand on the detonator switch and the other holding
a saber, part fallen-angel-Satan from *Paradise Lost*, part heavy-breathing
telephone pervert, and part phantom of the opera whose mask covers
a gouged-out, misshapen face symbolic of the evil within. Unlike the
Phantom, especially Lon Chaney's of 1925, whose face evokes genuine
terror, one wonders, after Luke removes it near the end of *Return*, why
Vader had been wearing a mask, considering that most of the face
remains intact except for some unfortunate bridgework. It appears that
he has renounced his humanity, in the form of his mechanical disguise,
to gain ultimate power. Vader's counterpart in Wagner's *Ring* cycle is
Hagen, bastard son of Alberich – and half brother of Gunther; his ille-
gitimate credentials cement his kinship to Don John in *Much Ado About
Nothing*, or more menacingly, to Edmund from *King Lear*. Bastard status,
though, proves curious in the extreme in Wagner's *Ring* cycle, since
the good people Siegmund and Sieglinde also have it, and their child
Siegfried – the designated savior of the gods – results from the incestuous union of two bastards. Breaking the rules appears to be fine
among the gods. Hagen represents the worst in human qualities, showing himself capable of treachery, manipulation, deceit, cunning, avarice
and back-stabbing. For him the ultimate prize, as it is for Vader, looms
huge, nothing short of the control of the universe.

Aside from the characters, Wagnerism creeps into other aspects of the story. If one has the "Force," it becomes possible to read the mind of someone else or to engage in other forms of telepathy in the manner of music hall magicians. At various times, Luke can summon the spirit of Ben to commune with him, or at the end of *Empire*, Leia can sense the presence of Luke and know exactly where to go to rescue him. Vader too, like the giant in *Jack and the Beanstalk*, smells the blood of close relatives or intimate Jedi enemies. Not to be outdone, Siegfried also has the force, which allows him to converse with the birds or to hear every treacherous thought of Mime, who intends to slip Siegfried a poisoned drink after he skewers the dragon. Siegfried uses the horn he always carries to chat with the birds and this horn signal becomes his musical calling card, announcing his arrival in his future encounters. Similar horn calls, now suggestive of Wagner's music, can be heard in the forest scenes of *Return of the Jedi*.

This epic tale, occurring both a long time ago and sometime off in the distant future, with its manufactured mythical universe, needs to be presented with a grandeur befitting its subject matter. In this case that may not be such an easy feat considering the ragtag collection of characters, with the exception of the impressive Vader – both visually and in speech through the voice of James Earl Jones. Here we have a recycled Tin Man with the attitude of a butler and a Lion who cannot stop whimpering, a garbage canister that shuffles along and bleeps, a smart-alec Han Solo whose lines sound like a second-grader struggling with a comic book, a princess with all the charm of a frustrated one-room school teacher and a young peach-fuzzy hero who would rather be at a strawberry social. Putting them on the big screen helps, but as characters, their smallness, not unlike the members of their star-dazed audience, requires something more to transform them into the defenders of the universe. Perhaps Lucas intended the stilted delivery of lines as an attempt at that since normal modes of speech or even dramatic acting would simply keep them in a diminished state. They needed something else to make all of this bigger than life, to give the characters grandeur, to make their exaggerated emotions seem deep, to convince the viewer that something important is going on here, to make the cinematic tricks and computer imaging appear impressive, and perhaps even to imply that one should experience these films at some sort of spiritual level.

Enter John Williams, composer extraordinaire, alias Erich Wolfgang Korngold, alias Richard Wagner; with his musical score he more or less made all of these things happen. Try watching these films without the sound and see what sort of an impression they make. Very little. Of course we would still be amazed by the technological wizardry, but without the score that would be little but a bag of technical tricks. Some have complained that Williams used 19th-century musical models here instead of the more recent avant-garde musical styles of perhaps Edgar Varèse or John Cage – something that might actually suggest the future.[6] These complainers appear to have missed the heading to each one of the films: "A long time ago in a galaxy far, far away." If this is the future, it is a future nostalgic in the extreme for the past. Creatures may buzz about in spiffy little spacecrafts that can travel at the speed of light, but in serious warfare they use huge lumbering four-legged camel-like tanks (or are they dinosaurs?). Laser beams make little impression against this foe (adversaries of "evil empires" take note); to get them down a harpoon line to trip up the legs proves much more effective. Even the best spacecrafts have grown old and rusty; there's nothing like pounding the dashboard to get things working.

To evoke the appropriate ostentatious tone the music had to be from the past; Lucas himself knew this perfectly well and originally wanted to use well-known pieces of 19th-century classical music. Three years later when Irvin Kershner directed *Empire*, he too thought in terms of a temp track during filming, using classical recordings to back up the action, but unlike Stanley Kubrick who kept the temp track for *2001: A Space Odyssey*, which included Richard Strauss's *Also sprach Zarathustra* – even after hearing Alex North's music, Kershner looked forward to Williams's original score. If these films should be Wagner for children, as the plot suggests, then the music should complete the Wagnerian atmosphere, propelling the viewer into a mode of existence of Wagnerian dimensions. That could not happen with popular music, show tunes, hit songs, jazz or anything else that characterized Hollywood scores in the late 1960s and 1970s. Only a 19th-century classical sound would do, with rich, expansive, leitmotivic Wagnerian proportions at that.[7] Unlike most films from the seventies, the score should also be almost continuous, providing a plush wall-to-wall musical underpinning to prevent any lapses in hyperbole.

Models for this type of film score, of course, already existed, most notably in those provided by Korngold, and Williams demonstrated his indebtedness to Korngold not only by adapting his style but by incorporating material from a theme in *The Sea Hawk*, heard when Thorpe and his men escape from the Spanish galley, into his main *Star Wars* theme.[8] Following the Wagnerian scheme, there needed to be musical leitmotifs associated with specific persons, emotions, objects or events, and this Williams provides, even carrying some of them over from one film to the next. He gives us the distinctive *Star Wars* theme already mentioned, as a leitmotif for the rebel forces in general and Luke in particular, a new and more impressive leitmotif for Vader in *Empire*, and one for the emerging love interest between Solo and Leia, a theme which sounds curiously reminiscent of the opening to Tchaikovsky's Violin Concerto. Just before Solo's deep-freezing, which leaves him as a slab of dry ice, Leia says "I love you" with about as much ardor as the ice itself (he replies "I know" with equal frigidity). The Tchaikovsky-like theme underlying the moment, with the warmth it generates on its own along with the passion it implies from its source, not only rescues the avowal but actually makes us believe it. The almost continuous Williams score elevates scenes time after time, and in fact transforms them into impressions of monumental dimensions.

A five-minute fragment very useful for an examination of leitmotifs begins slightly over three-quarters of the way through *Empire*, just before the enemy forces freeze-dry Solo. Here all three primary leitmotifs of *Empire* appear in rapid alternation, supporting the characters or action on the screen: these include the Star Wars' theme (1), familiar from the first episode, adapted from a source where it represented success of a small band of righteous fighters over a daunting enemy force; the Solo/Leia theme (2), with its romantic Tchaikovsky association; and the Vader theme (3), a dirge-like passage with a rhythmic pattern reminiscent of Chopin's famous funeral march from the Sonata in B flat minor. The five minutes in question progress as follows:

0	(2) Solo consoled by Leia after torture
.10	(connective, percussion) Vader speaks
.46	(1) Luke flying toward Lando's base
1:05	(3) Solo led to freezer

1:30   (1) Chewbacca fights back
2:00   (3) Vader looms threateningly
2:20   (2) Leia: "I love you"; Solo: "I know"
3:00   (3) Freezing happens
3:40   (2) Leia looks with concern at Solo as frozen slab
4:10   (connective)
4:30   (3) Vader's temporary triumph

In this short sequence we hear the Vader theme four times, the Leia/ Solo theme three times, and the Star Wars theme twice. With each statement the music reinforces the presence of the characters, their emotions which we should share, or the menace that Vader represents. A scene such as this can aspire to grandiloquence with Williams's music; without it the scene falls flat, or worse, we might even laugh at Solo as ice pack.

In Lucas's space opera we find the Jedi elevated to the status of nobility via a theme adapted from Korngold (himself a great Wagnerian), puppy love assumes passion through the intervention of a Tchaikovsky warhorse, and evil gains a fatal dimension aided by a hint of Chopin's funeral march; taken together, the themes along with their characters operate like a Wagnerian *Gesamtkunstwerk* (the all-embracing artwork), giving us grand spectacle, inflated emotions, and, apparently for some, a new religious experience. The main characters fall readily into standard operatic voice categories: Leia as mezzo-soprano, Solo as baritone, Vader as bass-baritone, C-3PO as spoken role, Chewbacca as mute, and Luke as counter-tenor (or perhaps castrato). Luke may never make it to the level of a Heldentenor, such as Siegfried, Tannhäuser or Lohengrin, but after all, Lucas gives us spaced-out opera for a star-struck audience.

18

WHAT'S OPERA, DOC?

Some people, it seems, were not told that they are not supposed to like opera – and the younger their age, the better they like it. In *Apocalypse Now*, Richard Wagner stands right beside the likes of Jim Morrison and Mick Jagger, and he rouses every bit as much excitement in adolescent viewers as the leading rockers of the late 20th century. Bring the age bar down a few notches for the *Star Wars* trilogy plus one, and we have two generations of early adolescents completely hooked on Wagnerian/Lucasian space opera. And what of pre-schoolers, who are even more receptive? Since the 1950s, with a little help from director Chuck Jones and composer Carl Stalling, they have all been introduced to Wagner in North America, and they all love him dearly (even though they may not know the name).

But before we get too carried away with adulation of Wagner, we should admit that there may be some problems, especially for people with limited amounts of time and especially for those with limited attention spans. Putting all four parts of the *Ring* cycle together adds up to a conglomeration of about fifteen hours, and while Wagner himself may have thought it entirely appropriate to listen to all four parts in succession, few listeners have been prepared to make that sort of sacrifice. Different opera companies will deal with that in various ways, opting in some cases to run them on successive nights. But even then, how many people other than those who have made a pilgrimage to the Wagnerian Mecca – Bayreuth – will spend four evenings in a row doing nothing but having their senses bombarded by Wagner? Back in the early 1970s, the Canadian Opera Company understood the problem and gave us the *Ring* cycle in successive years. It seemed a good idea, spacing

223

them so the audience would not feel entirely overwhelmed, but that created an even more troublesome problem – trying to remember the plot of *Das Rhinegold* or its connection with *Die Walküre* and *Siegfried* when attending *Die Götterdämmerung* three years later.

The only solution left, sacrilegious as it may seem, may be to abridge the *Ring* cycle. Once one takes the first unforgivable step of abridgement, desecrating the holy Wagner, one may as well indulge fully in the iniquitous act and really pare it down. Perhaps it could be squeezed into one evening, not like the five-hour *Parsifal*, which actually makes up two evenings in disguise, but a comfortable three hours (with at least three intermissions for drinks to sustain the four acts). Or perhaps it could conform to the standard cinematic two-hour length, or maybe become a one-act opera like *Salome*, which, barely more than an hour, never shares the evening with another short opera. Since all guilt ceases after trimming the first minute, it matters little if it lasts fourteen hours and fifty-nine minutes, three hours, one hour, or for that matter six minutes. At six minutes, it could hit us between the ears and let us get on with something else; it could not, though, be done in an opera house, with full salaries for singers, the orchestra, and everyone else for only six minutes.

Chuck Jones came up with the perfect solution: turn it into a cartoon and show it on television. He would be neither the first nor the last director to butcher an opera; Richard Strauss had done it in 1926 with his own *Rosenkavalier* to fit it into Robert Wiene's film version, cutting the original opera more or less in half. Many years later Franco Zeffirelli would pull Verdi's *Otello* inside out, distorting it mercilessly (see chapter 26), leaving opera lovers wishing it would end after six minutes. Zeffirelli needed a musical arranger who would collaborate in this mischief and he found a leading conductor, Loren Maazel, prepared to axe numbers like the "Willow Song" so we can wallow in the murder without being disturbed by Desdemona's pathos. But, some may argue, this is still opera since it stars the likes of Placido Domingo, Katia Riccarelli and Justino Diaz; surely it cannot be opera if it stars Bugs Bunny and Elmer Fudd, who neither resemble real people nor have *bel canto* voices.

At the most serious and realistic of times in opera we must still suspend our disbelief, and that includes the matter that in normal discourse people usually speak instead of sing. Considering what one sees on the opera stage, it probably makes little difference if we see divas and leading men or cartoon characters. In fact, going back to the 18th century, opera often presented itself as an entertainment in a comparable way to 20th-century cartoons, using marionettes on their own miniature stage, backed up with the voices of real singers. Joseph Haydn's patron Nicolaus Eszterházy especially liked this type of opera, and Haydn wrote more than his share of marionette operas; anyone who has been to Salzburg recently will know that the practice still flourishes.

Who, we may very well ask, are cartoons like *What's Opera, Doc?* for? Toddlers may enjoy them, but they can hardly appreciate the effort that went into them. Whereas most six-minute cartoons normally have about sixty backgrounds in them, this one has 104, making it almost twice as complex as the usual fare. What's more, Jones and his animators wanted to get the ballet part of it absolutely right, so they studied films of Titania Riavachinska and David Lichine of the Ballet Russe – Sergei Diaghilev's company which earlier in the century starred Vaslaw Nijinsky and premiered the great ballets of Igor Stravinsky, including *The Firebird*, *Petrushka* and even *The Rite of Spring*. When children first watch these special cartoons, which also include *The Rabbit of Seville* and portions from *One Froggy Evening*, they may enjoy them as they would any cartoon, but, it appears, they leave a lasting impression. Legend has it that when a Northwestern University music history professor announced to his class that he would examine the *Ring* cycle, all forty students spontaneously broke into "a massive Valkyrie-esque rendition of 'Kill the wabbit!'"[1] For the generation that grew up on this Saturday morning fare, many passionate fans can be found, some even considering Carl Stalling their favorite composer. The care that went into these cartoon, though, had little to do with the audience; Jones himself made it clear that "these cartoons were never made for children. Nor were they made for adults. They were made for *me*."[2]

Without too much difficulty we may be able to get our minds around the idea of opera cartoons based on Rossini and, in fact, most of them come from Rossini's comedy *The Barber of Seville*. Not only does the subject matter work nicely, but Rossini's music adapts ideally to "mickey-mousing" – the exact coordination of musical rhythm and the rhythm of the action. Even Haydn in his marionette operas did not venture beyond comedy. And one of Rossini's predecessors, Giovanni Paisiello, who set Beaumarchais's *Barber* a few decades before Rossini did, brought in a style of slapstick which already anticipated cartoons in the late 18th century. In one of the trios, Dr. Bartolo attempts to extract information from two servants who have been drugged by Figaro and he gets only yawns from one and sneezes from the other. The musical setting of yawns and sneezes in ensemble is the sort of thing that Carl Stalling would come up with almost two centuries later. Rossini as cartoon makes sense, but what about Wagner – and not just any Wagner, but the massive opera-profunda *Ring* cycle? Chuck Jones has not been the only opera lover to believe Wagner needed to lighten up a little; the comedienne Anna Russell and others have also tried to do something about that. Anything as serious and pompous as a Wagner opera, of course, leaves itself vulnerable to a comic broadside, although these cartoons stir up something other than simple parody or satire. The final product may be reduced, but it shows true respect for the grandeur of the original source.

Bugs Bunny and Elmer Fudd with the nasal twang of Mel Blanc and the stuttering befuddlement of Arthur Q. Bryan take the characters down more than a few notches from the level of the Heldentenor, but grandeur remains a key component. A cartoon version of opera could not do otherwise, but the means of finding spectacle cannot be transferred directly from opera: it must find its model in animation. The perfect model, of course, already existed, and Jones happily took it, even using the music associated with it so that no one could mistake it. At the beginning of *What's Opera, Doc?* we see Elmer in a horned helmet atop a menacing looking mountain – a dark, craggy formation that comes to a peak. Elmer makes ominous gestures which cast gigantic shadows below him and his hairless head which the helmet covers suggests a bald mountain. If we still miss the connection, the music gives it away, since we do not hear Wagner at the opening but Musorgsky's *Night on Bald Mountain*; the music and images come directly from the most frightening part of Walt Disney's *Fantasia*, with the "Chernabog" devil that gave thousands of children nightmares in the 1940s.[3] The scene may start by evoking all the terror of this fiend in *Fantasia* (and a little bit of the tyrannical Leopold Stokowski as well, whose gesture before the animation begins segues neatly into the devilish figure on the mountain), but a diabolical Elmer Fudd – give us a break, please! "Kill de wabbit" is not exactly an infernal threat and even children can put this one down to the nasty habit of an animated menace who likes hunting innocent forest creatures and who usually gets the wrong end of the stick.

If the miniaturized version of Wagner's *Ring* cycle must begin with Musorgsky, then we need not be too concerned about the authenticity of the musical adaptation. Aside from Musorgsky, it will take some original Stalling recitatives to get through the dialogue and some other Wagner passages prove useful as well, such as the pilgrims' chorus from *Tannhäuser*. In fact, we hear little from the *Ring* itself aside from the famous "Ride of the Valkyries." Musorgsky, Wagner's *Ring*, *Tannhäuser* – who can tell the difference anyway; it's all 19th-century bombast, conjuring images against which Bugs and Elmer can look perfectly ridiculous.

If Stalling's music refuses to be authentic to Wagner, we should not expect any more of Milt Franklin's characters. Bugs Bunny soon assumes a not unfamiliar role, in drag, as a docile Brünnhilde (singing "Return, my love" to the tune of the *Tannhäuser* pilgrims' chorus). Elmer wears chest plate and horned helmet, but those belong to Brünnhilde, don't they? And "Kill de wabbit" becomes the text of the "Ride of the Valkyries," music associated explicitly with Brünnhilde as well. Visually Bugs may be the one in drag, but musically that distinction goes to Elmer. Perhaps the two of them make up the dual warrior/lover sides of Brünnhilde. When Elmer pursues the lovely Bugs we assume a connection with Siegfried but when Bugs's helmet falls off and reveals long ears, Elmer quickly reverts back to the "Chernabog" devil role. He also has a magic helmet which he can use for destructive purposes, and then he becomes the villainous Alberich, or later Fafner, who uses the helmet to turn himself into a monster. Lest we should take these roles too seriously, at least one commentator tells us to pay more attention to the horse that Bugs has difficulty riding: "it's huge, like Wagnerian divas."[4]

A Wagnerian plot calls for a Wagnerian conclusion, and generally in Wagner's opera the body count at the end is high. At times, in fact, death may be very desirable, not only for the listener who will not have to endure a certain character for another three hours, but for the characters themselves. The Dutchman, for example, wants to die, and Senta dies so that he can finally get it over with. Throughout the *Ring* cycle they fall like flies: one giant kills the other, and Siegfried skewers the one still alive; Hunding kills Siegmund and Wotan finishes off Hunding; Siegfried does in Mime and Hagan puts an end to Siegfried.

By the end of *Twilight of the Gods* few survive to mourn the departed. In *Tristan und Isolde* we literally have a pile of corpses at the end. Kurwenal kills Melot and Melot's soldiers kill Kurwenal; Tristan expires from the wound he received from Melot, and Isolde, after the "Liebestod" dies of no apparent physical cause – we can only assume that her death happens vicariously and we do not feel compelled to question it on medical grounds – her body collapsing atop Tristan's.

While serious opera may virtually wipe the stage clean by the end of the work, that holds especially true for heroines, who have only a small chance of surviving to the end. Some writers, such as Catherine Clément in *Opera, Or the Undoing of Women*, take this to be a peculiar form of operatic misogyny, especially if these heroines have shown any personal initiative, which a repressive, masculine operatic world must stifle. In *What's Opera, Doc?* we have some gender twouble[5] too, since Bugs Bunny expires in drag. At the end, a not quite dead Bugs Bunny perks up long enough to inform his viewers not familiar with serious opera of the convention: "Well, what did you expect in an opera – a happy ending?"

PART FIVE

CINEMA AS OPERA

$\boxed{19}$

DIZZYING ILLUSION: *VERTIGO*

The magnetism of Wagner may be one of the most persistent allures of cinema toward opera, but the attraction goes far beyond Wagner to include a much larger operatic force field. Alfred Hitchcock's *Vertigo* continues the direction of the previous section in that it gains its inspiration from Wagner, but it takes this to a new and striking level, the operatic idea so completely permeating the film that, in this case, one can genuinely describe cinema as opera. The entry of the filmmaker into an operatic state of being results in a stunning appeal to the senses, the visual gaining essence from the musical, and of course it need not only be Wagner who steers directors down this path, as many other operas, composers or even vague operatic notions can accomplish it. These operatic forces attracting Hitchcock and others can cover a breadth of human experience, including the seductiveness of Carmen, the power of Medea, the persuasiveness of Orpheus and the lunacy of the opera-struck. They can arouse passion, obsession, sincerity and point to artifice, awakening in the viewer an immediate and acute reaction triggered by the musical urge that underlies the intense emotion or state of being. If prepared to follow where Hitchcock, Jean-Luc Godard, Pier Paolo Pasolini, Jean Cocteau, Marcel Camus and numerous other directors lead, perhaps from Wagner as the root force but also from a much broader range of possibilities, we will be lured into the sensuous world of cinema as opera.

* * *

Watching the restored *Vertigo* at a repertory theater a few years ago offered a reality check to someone who has known the film for many years. Most members of this particular audience were in their twenties, and when Scottie (James Stewart) in the act of recreating Madeleine accosts Judy (Kim Novak) with "please, it can't matter to you," the audience laughed. A man attempting to take such complete control of a woman no longer struck them as offensive, this generation which genuinely believes in sexual equality and for whom feminism stands immovable; for them the absurdity of it deserved nothing more than a laugh. In 1958, the year *Vertigo* appeared, this was no laughing matter, although for the post-war generation some may have felt uneasy about Scottie's obsession with transforming Judy into another person – one she clearly did not want to be. In many ways, Alfred Hitchcock's film does not belong to the 20th century at all, but takes us, through the mysterious Carlotta Valdez whose identity Madeleine assumes, into a much earlier time – the 19th century – not only the good old San Francisco that Gavin Elster recalls wistfully, but something distant and foreign as well, suggested by the Spanish mission at San Juan Bautista and also the Spanish name Valdez ("foreign but sweet," according to the McKittrick Hotel attendant).

In *Vertigo*, Hitchcock gives us grand illusion – Madeleine, a woman who does not exist, created for the benefit of one man who should be fascinated by her for the plot to work, but not obsessed since that obsession can only bring his own destruction. Despite that possibility of things flying apart, the plot itself challenges us to suspend our disbelief and even Hitchcock was troubled by certain aspects of its improbability – especially the assumption in the murder scheme that Scottie will not make it to the top of the tower and find the murderer. Not only improbable, the plot of the film has a remarkably structured form, reaching its center point with Madeleine plunging to her death from the mission tower, with events following a very symmetrical – almost palindromic – pattern around that central axis.

Various myths lurk not far beneath the surface, of Orpheus and Euridice, Pygmalion, Persephone and even Faust, with quests for truth and redemption, reaching for transcendence, and these balanced by descent, collapse, abjection and death. Hitchcock had no ordinary film on his hands here and he knew it well; he may have attempted to introduce his audience to this mysterious and fantastical world through the eyes of everyday people like the skeptical Scottie and down-to-earth Midge (Barbara Bel Geddes), but the audience seemed reluctant either to walk through the box office gates or, if accomplishing that, to enter Scottie's strange world. Financially the film flopped, but as a cinematic achievement it stands with a very rarified group. The late James Stewart played one of the most unusual and striking roles in *Vertigo* – quite possibly the darkest – of his long and celebrated career.

In a 1996 review of *Vertigo* and its restoration by Robert A. Harris and James C. Katz, Geoffrey O'Brien speaks of some earlier Hitchcock films and especially *Under Capricorn* as showing "where he really wanted to go – into a rigorous yet operatic playing out of emotional roles – only to discover that audiences had little desire to follow him there." O'Brien suggests that the director wants grand opera, his settings providing "a suitably remote and spacious frame for virtual arias of camera movement," but "the audience prefers crossword puzzles." Here O'Brien links Hitchcock's films with opera through the extremes in emotional roles played by the characters, immoderations as they pass through "stages of self-destructive remorse, hopeless infatuation, jealous rage, and liberating confession."[1] He hits the mark dead center with his operatic images, and others have tried to be even more specific about operatic associations in *Vertigo*. Donald Spoto for one notes parallels with the treatment of love and death in the legend of Tristam and Isoude, and takes the additional step toward Wagner's operatic realization: "Bernard Herrmann's lush, symphonic score for the film – arguably one of the finest musical contributions to the medium – more than once recalls the 'Liebestod' from Wagner's *Tristan und Isolde*."[2] Not everyone would think of Herrmann's score as lush, or refer to the "Liebestod" when, in fact, the music draws mainly on the Prelude to the opera, but he is nevertheless entirely on the right track here.

One can look at *Vertigo* as opera in a number of ways and it appears to be no mere coincidence that Scottie's first view of Madeleine comes at Ernie's restaurant, where Madeleine and Elster dine before going to the opera. Scottie, in this restaurant scene seems already to be at the opera, for the woman he sees defies description as an ordinary mortal. She stands much bigger than life, burning into his mind with her beauty, archaic (spiral) hair arrangement, and poise, like an untouchable dream of a woman on a stage, a diva that one can admire from afar but not come near and touch. Like a diva, her eyes do not meet his, while the mere sight of her transfixes him, changing his life forever. She need only glide across the floor/stage without saying a

Vertigo (at Ernie's restaurant before the opera)

word, looking the elegant character from grand opera he cannot resist. To make it a real opera, Herrmann provides the score, offering melodrama in the truest sense as his Madeleine leitmotif tells us – along with the expression on his face – everything we need to know about Scottie's innermost thoughts and desires.

In the stereotypical scheme of things in America the opera tends to be associated with a social elite, the audience made up of patrons who do not wince at the price of tickets and somehow find the grandeur of their own status reflected in the content of the medium. Hitchcock accepts the grandeur, as Madeleine belongs to a world quite apart from the everyday one, but his audience, which must see through Scottie's eyes, comes very much from that everyday world. Scottie seems down to earth in the extreme: by profession he is a cop, someone much more likely to go to a baseball game than the opera, and he will not be baited by fantastical stories of assumed new identities; his close companion, Midge, has her feet planted firmly on the ground. When the two of them wish to share an entertainment, unlike Elster and Madeleine, they choose the movies – and probably nothing too urbane. But after his first glimpse of Madeleine, Scottie begins to lose touch with his familiar existence; a new world of dreams, beauty and mystery opens up to him, and he turns into a fanatical follower. He discovers, as it were, that he can get into the opera by queuing all afternoon for a five-dollar standing-room place, and then he happily stands through the entire four-hour opera. After his first taste he develops a passion so consuming that he returns day after day, queuing for the ticket and then becoming rapt in the opera, losing track of the normal life he had before – completely oblivious to the cramps in his legs. The diva, or opera itself, now becomes accessible to everyone, as the larger-than-life woman gains essence through the eyes of the ordinary guy, a guy who knows rationally that he should not be taken in by illusion.

If audiences in the fifties preferred good old Hollywood movies to standing room at the opera, posterity has taken a different view, as this film has become a classic – even with its representation of women which youthful audiences of the present find objectionable or simply laughable. Madeleine obviously is no girl next door; she neither looks nor talks like American women, and it does not take long to discover that her transformation to the 19th-century Carlotta Valdes will probably result in tragedy. As she slips into the past, she takes Scottie inadvertently and inexorably with her. He may wish to protect her and help her out of her own painful dreams, but in fact she stands as the much stronger force, a magnet drawing him to the murky depths of San Francisco Bay or the dizzying and terrifying heights of the San Juan Bautiste mission tower. A here-and-now Madeleine – a Judy Barton – proves to be of no interest to him, and his obsession with the illusory Madeleine forces him beyond the bounds of decency as he attempts to recreate the Madeleine of the past.

Both the mysterious Madeleine and manipulated Judy are familiar characters in opera, and like their operatic counterparts, as Catherine Clément ruefully notes in her *Opera, or the Undoing of Women*, in all probability will end up dead. While the operatic women in question often first took form in novels or plays, the spectacle of the deaths in the film – a dramatic ascent of a tower and a religiously subverting fall to a chapel roof – has much more in common with opera than a literary medium which prefers character development or depends on dialogue. Who are these Madeleines of opera? Tatiana, Isolde, Sieglinde, Senta, Lucia di Lammermoor, Norma and Mélisande, to name a few. And Judy Barton? Mimi, Marguerite, Martha, Manon, Violetta, and perhaps even Carmen. Some will die spectacularly, others dramatically or with pathos, some will go mad, some will remain mysterious, and some will die because they could not become what the *uomo primo* wanted them to be.

The life expectancy for female characters in opera is exceptionally low, and for the female lead of *Vertigo*, in effect to die twice can only be described as operatic. In the opera house we have become accustomed to this rate of fatality, and those who do not like it probably in general prefer a medium which requires less suspension of disbelief. Along with the death rate, the men who treat women unkindly if not brutally, who would not hesitate themselves to assume "it can't matter to you," such as Faust, Don Giovanni, Scarpio and Don José, also seem to come with the operatic territory. In the hyperbolic emotions of opera we can detest them as vehemently as we like, and feel acute pity for their victims. In some case, these men actually get what they deserve.

By its nature, opera requires suspension of disbelief; anyone who enters the opera house in search of reality has come to the wrong place. Quite aside from the plot and situations of any given opera, the medium itself suspends reality. In real life, our actions are not accompanied by grand music, and as a rule we do not sing instead of talk. In the face of great opera, we do not question why the music is there or why the characters sing instead of using normal discourse. We need not go into all the dramatic conventions such as the action taking place in a mere 24-hour period or the formal devices which may determine the flow of the action. As for plots themselves, these usually stretch our sense of reality beyond all reasonable limits. Of course, Don Giovanni could not have the number of conquests that Leporello claims, and many operas carry on strictly in the realm of fantasy.

In *Vertigo*, suspension of disbelief becomes cumulative beginning with the suspension of Scottie from an eaves trough far above the streets of San Francisco. The cop who tries to rescue him and falls to his own death has no chance of supporting himself on a 70 degree roof when he entreats Scottie to take his hand. His attempt may have been one of bravery, but it was also unbelievable foolhardiness. The camera leaves Scottie hanging, as it does other times throughout the film; who gets him down from this precarious spot, the thief he had been chasing? Even Hitchcock himself had concerns about the believability of certain aspect of *Vertigo*, as we know from his confession to François Truffaut: "One of the things that bothers me is a flaw in the story. The husband was planning to throw his wife down from the top of the tower. But how could he know that James Stewart would not make it up those stairs? Because he became dizzy? How could he be sure of that!"[3] This so-called flaw did not trouble Truffaut: "That's true, but I saw it as one of those assumptions you felt people would accept."[4] "One of those assumptions" invokes the operatic convention of the suspension of disbelief, a convention the European Truffaut felt much more comfortable with than Hitchcock did in response to his more pragmatic, no-nonsense American audience.

While *Vertigo* appears to have various general associations with the conventions of opera, it also, as Spoto correctly anticipated, seems to have a much more specific operatic model in none other than Wagner's *Tristan und Isolde*. Bernard Herrmann's virtual quotation of this Wagner work in his musical score for *Vertigo* strikes one as something not entirely coincidental. The parallels begin in the basic premise of the plot: the wealthy Gavin Elster as King Mark engages Scottie (Tristan) to transport (in this case mentally) his wife Madeleine (Isolde) back to him from the distant mindscape she now inhabits. As Elster's agent,

Scottie should not become personally involved with Madeleine, but after tasting the love potion he falls hopelessly in love with her, falling into an illicit relationship with the wife of his friend and client. For their transgression both Scottie and Madeleine/Judy will have to pay dearly, she with her life – twice – and he with his life indirectly as he loses his mental stability and will to live.

As in *Tristan und Isolde*, *Vertigo* equates love and death. When Tristan and Isolde drink the love potion, they think it is a death potion; the burning passion which ensues can only result in death, and Wagner culminates this with the famous "Liebestod" at the conclusion of the opera. Scottie begins his assignment with relative disinterest, but Madeleine leads him in a descending vortex down steep San Francisco streets, through a graveyard, and down to the dark waters of the bay, where she attempts, so he believes, to end her life. She prepares the water by throwing in flowers from her spiral nosegay, as if to sweeten the taste, and without a moment's hesitation plunges in. Scottie reacts instinctively, leaping in after her; what starts as a death potion in fact becomes their love potion, with the Golden Gate Bridge above them reaching to the promised paradise, an image possibly inspired by Willy Schlobach's 1890 painting *The Dead Woman*.[5] The real passion, anticipated as Scottie lifts her into the car, will still take a little while to arrive, but it does, as they fall into their first rapturous embrace standing at the edge of the Pacific Ocean – he rushing to her side thinking she may once again end up in the water. With this kiss, backed by surging breakers and operatic music bordering on camp, they are transported to ecstasy and depart the real world forever; such an exaggerated or otherworldly embracing of love can only find its fulfillment in death – the final transcendence to the other world they now desire.

Scottie's new love becomes his new religion, and like Paul on the road to Damascus, he turns into a zealot, embracing it with a red-hot fervor as he allows himself to be consumed by ecstasy. Ordinary and placid religion of prayer books and hymns must now give way to a new one which makes the soul drunk, the intensity of which can only be grasped in terms of a euphoric erotic encounter. How does one achieve that in a 1958 film for a general American audience? Hitchcock does it in the scene in Scottie's apartment following the bay rescue. Madeleine lies in Scottie's bed, not yet conscious after her trauma, with every article of her clothing hanging in one place or another to

Vertigo (James Stewart rescues Kim Novak under the Golden Gate Bridge)

dry. The viewer knows perfectly well that Scottie has undressed her, has seen her naked body, and then covered her between his own sheets. To him, she is no longer just a woman of beauty and mystery but she has become a goddess whose gloriously sculpted form he now knows in intimate detail. When she revives, and realizes what he has seen and touched, she remains far from distressed, emerging to talk with him clad in nothing but his bathrobe. He offers her a drink, hoping to prolong the effect of the potion; as he offers her more coffee, his hand touches hers.

As she assumes goddess status he becomes a passionate worshipper. But the old religion lurks menacingly in the background as he follows her through the chapel of the Mission Dolores into the graveyard, to the McKittrick Hotel kitty-corner from a prominent San Francisco church, and finally to the mission at San Juan Bautiste. The church takes its revenge, claiming Madeleine whose shattered body lies in spiral formation on the roof of the chapel, and even more directly Judy, whose fall to the same roof is prompted by the dark figure of a nun unexpectedly arriving at the top of the tower. This conflict between religion and ecstasy permeates Wagner's operas, perhaps none more than *Tannhäuser*, where Tannhäuser himself can indulge in erotic escapades and still receive miraculous dispensation. In Wagner's scheme of things ordinary Christians are decidedly inadequate; room must be made for those who break the rules – even moral law – exceptional beings who rise above the mundane and arrive at ecstasy. For Wagner the highest form of religion requires sensuality, a fusion which he achieves most effectively in the music itself.

Hitchcock's own description of eroticism in *Vertigo* veers much more sharply to the prosaic, but nevertheless confirms the importance of it in his vision of the film. In his classic mode of understatement, Hitchcock summarizes the Wagnerian concept of love and death with, "to put it plainly, the man wants to go to bed with a woman who's dead."[6] While most viewers, including Truffaut, do not see the transformation of Judy into Madeleine as something erotic, Hitchcock apparently did:

> Cinematically, all of Stewart's efforts to re-create the dead woman are shown in such a way that he seems to be trying to undress her, instead of the other way around. What I liked best is when the girl came back after having had her hair dyed blond. James Stewart is disap-

pointed because she hasn't put her hair up in a bun. What this really means is that the girl has almost stripped, but she still won't take her knickers off. When he insists, she says, "All right!" and goes into the bathroom while he waits outside. What Stewart is really waiting for is for the woman to emerge totally naked this time, and ready for love.[7]

As unlikely as this may seem ("that didn't occur to me," quipped Truffaut), Hitchcock was determined to link the recreation of Madeleine with the earlier nude scene in the apartment which so ignited Scottie's passion.

Despite the crude description, he seems to suggest that the eroticism underlying the first half of the film holds equal importance for the second half, and that it is arrived at almost palindromically as eroticism lies behind the completion of the transformation. The temporarily "dead" Scottie can only find his own resurrection in the sensual religion he previously practiced so fervently, and that can only be found with the completed Madeleine. Curiously, his image requires only visual stimuli, ignoring the aural; the visually intact Madeleine speaks with the unrefined voice of Judy, but that appears not to distress him. Once again, we must no doubt suspend our disbelief. In completing the visual image, Judy, of course, goes one step too far, putting on Carlotta's necklace, and this intrusion of reality provokes the final unravelling and descent.

The parallels with Wagner do not end here. One of the first vivid images of *Tristan*, built by Wagner leitmotivically into the prelude, involves the "look," the meeting of the eyes between Tristan and Isolde and the disarming power of his stare when she had the opportunity to kill him, knowing he had vanquished her own fiancé. Instead of killing him, she used her magical powers to restore his health, all because of his potent look. In *Vertigo*, the fulfillment of eyes meeting becomes a fairly long and drawn-out affair. Opportunities exist at Ernie's restaurant before the opera or in the Mission Dolores graveyard, but she studiously avoids his rapt stare. Not until she bolts up in his bed without a stitch of clothing on do their eyes meet, and this meeting of eyes parallels the erotic realization of the moment. Madeleine, like Isolde, has healing powers for Scottie and only through the recreation of her can he find redemption and the cure for his vertigo. He finds the cure but not the redemption; when she plunges the final time, he loses all, left suspended at the precipice as surely as he was at the beginning, hanging from the eaves trough.

The mysterious Madeleine, the woman with another identity in the past and of another nationality, has a bond with Isolde as well. The foreign Carlotta Valdes remains as inscrutable to Americans as the Irish Isolde does to the English. The further Madeleine descends into that identity, the more powerfully she draws Scottie into her foreign realm. Just as Tristan cannot reverse his attraction to Isolde, despite the possible consequences, Scottie cannot detach himself from the peculiar attractions of Madeleine. Midge, presented as the archetypal American woman, while warm and gentle as well as independent, practical and industrious, cannot compete with the enigmatically distant Madeleine.

To cap these various tacit Wagnerian associations, Herrmann makes them overt with the musical score. In spite of Herrmann's claim that he disliked Wagnerian leitmotifs, he uses them consistently in his film scores, and *Vertigo* is no exception. Herrmann would certainly not be the first composer indebted to Wagner who went out of his way to denigrate the indebtedness; Arnold Schoenberg wrote at length about Brahms no doubt in part to disguise his own musical leanings toward Wagner, something he preferred not to acknowledge.[8] In *Vertigo* not only does Herrmann use leitmotifs, but he actually borrows material almost directly from *Tristan*, in some cases with very striking resemblances.

The most important leitmotif of the film, Madeleine's theme, first emerges when Scottie, along with the audience, catches his first view of Madeleine; we hear the theme in various altered forms following that, but it returns in its full glory when the revived Madeleine steps out of Scottie's bedroom wearing his bathrobe. There are distinct similarities in this theme to the opening of the prelude to *Tristan*. The four-note figure which becomes the melodic cell of the Madeleine theme comes through as a variant of the four-note figures which generate Wagner's theme, and the chordal accompaniment parallels Wagner's accompaniment, including the famous "Tristan chord" and its resolution. In fact, at the beginning of the seventh bar of the Madeleine theme, Herrmann actually uses the Tristan chord, and the chord falls on the same notes (with only one tone altered by a semitone) and in the same position as Wagner's first placement of the chord at the beginning of the prelude.

Herrmann also adopts Wagner's six-eight meter, and uses rhythmic patterns and suspensions that parallel Wagner's. After the initial statement of the motivic material Wagner moves into a distinctive three-note dotted rhythm figure, and at a similar point Herrmann adds the same dotted three-note figure. In Wagner's prelude, the various musical figures have leitmotivic associations, although these defy precise identification. Some possibilities include sorrow, desire, the look, the love potion, longing and death. Virtually all of these are pertinent to *Vertigo*, and Herrmann's appropriation of various ones would seem to imply the same multiplicity of emotions, desires and consequences.

Other moments in the film have a distinctively Wagnerian aura, and Herrmann underlies these occasionally with other characteristic Tristan-esque passages. One stands out especially, this being the climactic moment described by Hitchcock when Judy fixes her hair to complete the final physical transformation to Madeleine. As she emerges from the washroom their eyes meet in ecstasy, before their passionate embrace. The moment can only be defined as operatic, and Herrmann provides an apt operatic accompaniment. Again he borrows from the *Tristan* prelude, this time the grand and explosive figure at bars 16–17, a rising figure leading to Wagner's first bombardment of the listener with the full orchestral palate. In *Tristan* this passage can be variously associated with longing and desire, and Herrmann knew exactly what he was doing using it here.

While cinema may be of a narrative nature, taking the viewer through a progression of events as a plot unfolds, it may also be formal, clearly divided into parts with formal linkages among or between the parts. Some films, such as Otto Preminger's *Laura*, take this to the extreme, with a palindromic form – the center point of the two parts occurring with the return of the live Laura. "As you know," Hitchcock reminded Truffaut about *Vertigo*, "the story is divided into two parts. The first part goes up to Madeleine's death, when she falls from the steeple, and the second part opens with the hero's meeting with Judy, a brunette who looks just like Madeleine."[9] While the design of *Vertigo* may not be as precisely mirrored as that of *Laura*, one still finds a remarkable symmetry in the events closest to the central axis (Madeleine's fall to her death), and other palindromic aspects as well which reach toward the mid-point from the beginning and the end:

Symmetrical Plan for *Vertigo*

1   Scottie left suspended (from eaves trough)
2   Visual image of Madeleine

3   Ernie's restaurant: no eye contact or words
4   Flower shop
5   Art museum: Madeleine looks at Carlotta portrait
6   Scottie follows Madeleine from her building through descending streets
7   Offers drink to revived Madeleine
8   Letter of thanks
9   Passionate kiss
10 Midge's self-portrait ploy (dressed as Carlotta)
11 Madeleine's dream: grave
12 Mission tower: looking up
13 Staircase: up

Mid (1) Madeleine falls (to death): Scottie left suspended

13 Staircase: down
12 Mission tower: looking down
11 Scottie's dream: grave
10 Sanatorium: comfort from Midge
6   Madeleine's building, car, woman who bought it
5   Art museum: woman looks at Carlotta portrait
4   Flower shop
8   Judy writes letter
3   Silent dinner with Judy at Ernie's
2   Recreates visual image of Madeleine
7   Offers drink to Judy
9   Passionate kiss
12 Return to Mission tower
1 (mid) Judy falls (to death): Scottie left suspended

This type of symmetrical form, taking a narrative and placing it in a distinct type of formal, temporal context, may seem unfamiliar to film goers, but that will not be the case for music lovers. Musical forms from the 18th century, such as rounded binary form or in a more extreme way the crab canon, depend on it. Twentieth-century composers intent on recreating certain facets of the 18th century in their music, the so-called neoclassicists such as Sergei Prokofiev and Igor Stravinsky, have integrated these balanced forms into their works. The first movement of Stravinsky's Symphony in C, written in 1939–40, stands as a striking example of this type of symmetry. Similarly, the type of two-part structure used in *Vertigo* can be seen in Ravel's *La Valse*, and here the musical ambiguity of the beginning and the middle parallels the ambiguity in *Vertigo* associated with Scottie's convalescence early in the film and his complete breakdown (the stay at the sanatorium) at the middle, shortly after Madeleine's death. Symmetrical forms can be used in opera as well, and they have been from Mozart's *Così fan tutte* to Alban Berg's *Lulu*; the music from the middle of *Lulu* follows so symmetrical a pattern that it actually forms a precise palindrome – underlying an inserted film, the second half of which Berg wanted to be shown in reverse sequence.

This type of symmetrical form, as music lovers know well, radically alters our perception of time, and the resulting suspended temporal state suits Scottie's situation and illusions in this film exceptionally well. Stravinsky, for one, has tried to verbalize this type of temporal experience, going so far as to say that music itself lacks the power to express anything at all, but instead defines the relationship between humanity and time, capturing the essence of the present instead of submitting to the passage of time from the past to the future.[10] Borrowing terms from his philosophical friend Pierre Souvtchinsky, Stravinsky in *Poetics of Music* identifies "ontological" time as his preferred temporal approach in music, shunning contrast in search of unity, "introducing in the mind of the listener a feeling of euphoria and, so to speak, of 'dynamic calm'."[11] In opera, especially 18th-century *opera seria* which uses *da capo* arias, one finds a vivid illustration of this principle. These arias use an A-B-A symmetrical form, and in effect they take the characters singing them out of the sequence of passing time which one finds in recitative. The arias become contemplative, reflecting on events in a way that allows the character to rise above the action and become suspended in time in his or her ecstasy, agony, elation or sorrow. More often than not the subject matter used in these operas comes from classical mythology or legend, appropriate to the timeless quality generated by the music.

In *Vertigo*, the temporal effect resulting from the symmetrical form beautifully parallels the cinematography. After the titles the film begins with hard action, a cops-and-robbers chase over San Francisco rooftops, but that ends abruptly when Scottie slips and desperately clings for dear life at the edge of the roof. At that point action is suspended as he stares into the dizzying abyss and his suspended state here anticipates the rest of the film. He quits his job and appears to wander aimlessly, no longer inhabiting the real world of real time. During his mental breakdown after Madeleine's death, any sense of time vanishes entirely, as a moment of his blank stare represents an indefinite passage of time where one unbearable moment defies differentiation from the next. Midge attempts to impose time, structuring her time with Scottie around her working schedule, or trying to find a time limit in months for his stay at the sanatorium.

For a dweller in suspended time, Madeleine proves to be the perfect companion, since as an illusion she comes from the same region. The timelessness of the illusion reinforces itself through her absorption into the past, into the being of Carlotta Valdes who lived a century ago – a past so distant it cannot be imagined. At Muir Woods she touches a cross section of a giant sequoia tree with markers representing centuries, uttering "somewhere in here I was born, and there I died. It was only a moment for you – you took no notice." Like Scottie she wanders, and her wanderings cannot be accounted for although the miles travelled show up on the odometer of her car. Increasingly she lives on the edge of a razor separating life and death, and she cannot always tell which side she stands on as she descends through an endless corridor taking her further from reality. Her appearance, actions, dreams and magnetic attraction to the past all draw her further into a repudiation of temporality, to an incorporeal world.

Unlike Madeleine, Judy's existence shuns mystery and illusion. She works for a living, has had a normal past in Kansas, and has been in San Francisco for a definitive amount of time: three years. After her chance encounter with Scottie, she becomes quickly drawn into his world: she skips off work and presumably quits altogether, and the more he transforms her into Madeleine the more tenuously she grasps reality. Scottie, though, hopes to re-enter the normal world through her, to get free of the past, as he tells her before they mount the stairs of the tower near the end. As Judy becomes Madeleine, necklace and all, and Scottie recognizes that Judy and Madeleine are one and the same, she returns to that razor's edge that had haunted Madeleine, and meets the same fate. Scottie may reach the top of tower, but he fails utterly in getting free of the past – or free from his enveloping timescape: just like the beginning and middle, the end leaves him suspended from above, looking down, damned, into an eternal abyss. Narrative could not break through form, and the curtain falls on a tragic opera.

$$\boxed{20}$$

CARMEN COPIES

Few subjects have appeared as consistently and recurrently in the entire history of cinema as the story of Carmen. And, aside from the dozens of films which focus on this sultry and dangerous woman, numerous others include musical excerpts from Georges Bizet's famous opera.[1] Since 1875 no other opera has held the appeal for opera audiences that *Carmen* has, and that alone would seem to make it a natural for cinematic sequels, in spite of an apparent gulf between opera and cinema audiences. The popularity of the opera may help to explain why DeMille made his *Carmen* with the diva Geraldine Farrar in 1915, or why others appeared during the silent era, with Marguerite Snow, Marion Leonard, Theda Bara, Marguerite Sylva, Pola Negri, Raquel Meller and Dolores Del Rio in the starring roles, but that fails to explain the more recent fascination, especially in the early 1980s.

The appeal to the screen of Carmen in the last half century appears not to come from the opera itself or for that matter the music from the opera – and certainly not the singing. Going back to the source of the subject, the novella by Prosper Mérimée written in 1845, does not help much either. As interesting as that work may be, with its fascinating characters, its ambiguity of narrative voices – which remains unclear if we should listen to the moralist historian or the subjective Don José – or its political implications for pan-European attitudes in the face of nationalist xenophobia,[2] it fails to rise to the level of an important piece of literature. It joins the ranks of many pieces cranked out for publication in the large array of serials such as *La Revue des Deux Mondes*, the periodical in which it happened to appear. Had it not been for Bizet's opera of thirty years later, one suspects that it would have lain dormant after the 19th century, resuscitated perhaps from time to time by doctoral students of French or comparative literature in search of new or esoteric material. The opera, of course, takes a very different tack from the novella, and that should not surprise anyone considering the differences between the media; Bizet's opera may already be a sequel to the original, but the explosion of interest in 20th-century cinema owes much more to the opera than the novella — in spite of the treatments of the plot.

The story shocked readers of *La Revue des Deux Mondes* when it first appeared in the middle of the 19th century, so much so that some cancelled their subscriptions to the periodical, and it shocked opera audiences in Paris in 1875 even more. Literary journals appealed to a broad spectrum of society, and one would expect the majority of subscribers to be able to cope with subversive material. Opera, on the other hand, has no such breadth of appeal; an opera which mercilessly taunts certain members of its audience should be expected to boil their anger and frustration to the same level as Don José's. In spite of that, the opera remains the most popular work in the entire repertoire, suggesting that those who should have been offended by it in fact welcomed it. Perhaps we have a vague parallel here to opera in late 18th-century Paris, where no opera could be presented without scenes of ballet, not because of any intrinsic value of dancing but because of the titillation that well-shaped legs in motion would provide. The bad girl Carmen can arouse male viewers in a much less subtle way, and no doubt many will enjoy her seductions while they can (throughout about 95% of the work), quickly reverting to their conventional morality with her destruction at the end.

Carmen does not only stir something in male viewers; her defiance of male authority made her appealing to women fighting for basic rights in the late 19th century, including the vote and in some countries even legal recognition as persons. For those less politically inclined, she also offered an alternative to the conventional role of woman as wife — as a bearer of children, provider of domestic stability, and social ornament. Not only did this appeal to some women but it did to the rising bohemian culture in general, espoused, for example, by the writer Karl Kraus and his numerous supporters at the turn of the century in Vienna. For those interested in politics instead of gender issues, Carmen had much to offer as well, as Carmen the gypsy breaks down national barriers, specifically those of Spain and France, and by implication all of Europe. Borders mean nothing to her: she will work in any country she likes, and will probably master the language very quickly.

If these issues struck home with audiences in the late 19th and early 20th centuries, they did with even greater force in the second half of the 20th century, when feminism and resistance to some very odious forms of nationalism took on an urgency unknown in the past. From the vantage point of the beginning of the 21st century, the moral imperative of her destruction is passé – this concession to male domination and an acceptance of the rightness of misogyny. Some recent feminist writers address this issue,[3] insisting that the final scene of the opera purges the work of its humanity, returning like a perfect cadence to a misogynist stability. Bizet gives no apparent alternative to this, although Mérimée does with his ambiguity about which of the narrative voices we should accept. One of the most powerful appeals of the Carmen story for over a century and a half has been its resistance to submitting to any one interpretation; those who attempt this will be successfully countered by conflicting positions.

Mérimée offers the most enduring modern reading, although its modern possibility arises from a literary approach that does not translate into something cinematic and has not been a major factor in the numerous Carmen films. Certain aspects of plot in these films may in some cases resemble the novella more than the opera, although that does not necessarily draw these films closer to the novella than the opera. Opera, with its parallels to cinematic images, never lurks far beneath the surface, and one will find very few screen versions of Carmen which do not quote the music of Bizet's opera, sometimes only briefly but in other case extensively. Of the dozens of Carmen films that could be considered, I will focus on two by major directors: Otto Preminger and Jean-Luc Godard.

As one might expect of Hollywood, a number of the Carmen films have been little more than vehicles for sultry sex symbols to strengthen their pin-up status. Even DeMille's *Carmen* with Geraldine Farrar, in spite of the role it played in elevating the image of cinema, had much to do with the steamy spectacle of Farrar herself. While DeMille may have had some higher objective here, Raoul Walsh's *Carmen* (1915) made for Fox and released on the same day as DeMille's, starring the vamp Theda Bara, appeared to have no purpose beyond Bara's bumping and grinding. Walsh made another version in 1927, *The Loves of Carmen*, starring Dolores Del Rio, and the appearance of this strikingly beautiful Mexican woman produced a much more successful result. When Charles Vidor tried a Carmen copy using the same title in 1948 with Rita Hayworth in the lead role, it was obvious that the film existed for no other reason than to capitalize on and keep Hayworth, the American pin-up queen of the war years, exposed.

Carmen Jones

The life of Carmen on film took a very different turn in 1954 when Otto Preminger entered the fray with his *Carmen Jones*. Using Oscar Hammerstein's Broadway revue of the same name, Preminger revised the script with his former student Harry Kleiner, making some changes but leaving the original lyrics untouched. As often happens with Preminger, getting a clear picture of how things actually unfold can be difficult, especially when Preminger himself tells it. According to Willi Frischauer, Darryl Zanuck, chief at Twentieth Century-Fox, asked Preminger to make the film, and Preminger, working by this time as an independent director/producer, had his doubts since the all-black film would not resemble any black community in the United States.[4] Preminger himself tells a very different tale: "fascinated by the idea of transposing the story of *Carmen* into present-day American life with an all-black cast," he took the project to his friends Arthur Krim and Robert Benjamin at United Artists, but they would not touch it, in spite of Preminger bringing them their first big hit with *The Moon is Blue*. Preminger happened to be doing some work at the Fox studios, and Zanuck, having heard of the backing problems, summoned him to his office and offered his support.[5] Zanuck had not liked Preminger when Preminger worked for the studio, but changed his mind after the great success of *Laura*, a film Preminger had rescued from certain disaster and transformed into a masterpiece.[6]

The truth probably lies somewhere between the two accounts. Zanuck undoubtedly saw some commercial advantage for this unique extension of the all-black film tradition, and Preminger liked the artistic and social potential of the subject. Preminger, a Jew from Vienna, proclaimed his freedom from prejudice toward blacks, although that did not exempt the film from questions about racial sensitivity. The European

Preminger presumably had a limited knowledge of the black experience in America, and his way of addressing it was through a European story which he found relevant to blacks. He tried to express his lack of prejudice to the cast by the equality with which he would treat them: "I want you to know that I grew up in Europe. For me there is no difference between black and white people. So if you behave badly I will be just as tough with you as I would be with white actors."[7] Notoriously gruff, in fact enjoying making a spectacle of it, Preminger used what he could to show his fairness.

Yet the charges of racism have refused to go away, both at the time he made the picture or closer to the present. Preminger may have found parallels in the story to American life of the time, and could accept the change of the Spanish occupiers of Seville to the U.S. army, the bullfighter to a prize fighter, and the smugglers to those on the boxer's gravy train, but making the cast completely black in fact avoids the tension between different racial communities unlikely to understand each other. Instead of being a white oppressor (the group Don José belongs to in the opera), Joe, who wishes to get ahead in aviation, represents a church-going element of the African American community which not only has high moral standards but aspires to be like whites. Carmen represents a very different part of black culture, one which many whites fear since it strikes them as hovering at the edge of crime, loose morals, and perhaps even primitivism. Anyone sensitive to the plight of African-Americans, as many were in these early civil rights days, would have found this story misdirected as it gives only two apparent alternatives for blacks: be antagonistically separate or be like whites. The latter proves impossible in this case, as Joe loses the battle to seduction and turns violent, reverting to the world of the separate blacks.

This surely was not the message Preminger wished to give, although the plot as it stood left little alternative. He saw it in terms of black dignity, and the all-black cast (including every member of the crowd at the boxing match) made a statement about the capabilities and equality of blacks. Transposing a European story to the African American experience had its risks, and as it stood it did not work. Preminger may have seen himself in the role of promoting civil rights, but in this respect he probably achieved very little. More radical blacks subsequently have very much resented this type of white/European use of blacks, accomplishing nothing of social value and not advancing the cause of blacks in American cinema.

This may have been a step forward from the blackface acting of the 1920s, but one must question even that because of the white-voice dubbing for the arias and ensembles from Bizet's *Carmen* which dominate the film. Preminger claimed that he wished "to make a dramatic film with music rather than a conventional film musical,"[8] and in that he may have succeeded; if nothing else, he made one of the great operas accessible to American film audiences in an ingenious way. Three members of his cast, Dorothy Dandridge (Carmen), Harry Belafonte (Joe), and Diahann Carroll (Myrt), would eventually become top-billed actors, but in 1954 they had not yet reached that level. Dandridge and Belafonte were making strides in Hollywood while also building their careers as nightclub singers, and they did not have voices suitable to their respective roles in Bizet's *Carmen*. Preminger wanted neither opera nor film musical, but instead something between these, so he hired singers who could generate that in-between sound to dub the actors. He believed mistakenly that no black singers existed who could do it, so he hired white singers with the range but without the big *bel canto* voices. One of these, Marilyn Horne, would later become a famous stage Carmen, but as a teenaged voice student in 1954, she sang with a lightness of voice appropriate to the nature of the film. Belafonte would in due course become one of the most familiar voices of the century, but here he lip syncs Le Vern Hutcherson, who occasionally sounds operatic, but mostly croons.

Giving the lyrics to white singers created an enormous problem, and one wonders if Preminger, for whom English was a second language, heard it. His black characters apparently needed to have colloquial accents, and the lyrics leave no room for the singers to miss it: for the "Flower Song" Joe sings "Dere all de same, she jus' a dame," while Carmen's "Seguidilla" runs "Dere's a café on de corner." An aspiring opera singer like Horne, studying with a fine teacher like William Vennard, would be a perfectionist on matters of elocution, and confronted with these lyrics but with no idea of the sound of the vernacular, she reverted to what she knew how to do, which was pronouncing the lyrics exactly as written. The obvious happened: Horne sounds like a white singer doing a hopelessly embarrassing imitation of an idiomatic black way of talking, and so do the other white singers. Only two members of the cast actually sang, and one of these, Brock Peters, did the voice of Rum (Roy Glenn) since his own role of Sgt. Brown had no singing. The other, Pearl Bailey as Frankie, comes as a breath of fresh air, and in spite of being forced into something unnatural for herself, this great African American singer does not disappoint us. A drum intro at Billy Pastor's café leads into her feature number – in fact, Carmen's gypsy song – and even Bailey must contend with the fabricated dialect in the lyrics ("Beat out dat rhythm on a drum"). Susan McClary argues that this scene, with its primitive dancing, proves to be the most contrived and overtly racist,[9] and her position cannot easily be refuted.

If the work fails to say anything meaningful about blacks in America, it nevertheless proved to be a fascinating experiment in opera/cinema. Preminger claimed that he and Kleiner did not use the libretto of the opera but that they went back to the original story by Mérimée. In what way they did this will escape most observers of the various works; this story of a soldier, his home-town sweetheart, a promiscuous parachute maker, and a prize fighter follows Bizet's and librettists H. Meilhac and L. Halévy's from beginning to end, and uses Bizet's music whenever possible for singing numbers and accompaniment. The spirit of Bizet permeates the work, and Dandridge offers a sexy and real flesh and blood Carmen, unlike the strutting and posturing Hayworth. Similarly Belafonte plays his struggle between duty and sensuality with a believably naive intensity, preventing us from asking why he should lapse into this world but accepting that it can happen. Preminger was no stranger to opera, despite his claims to the contrary, directing Lawrence Tibbett in *Under Your Spell* in 1936, and even using some operatic devices in *Laura*. His next work after *Carmen Jones* was another all-African American opera, *Porgy and Bess*, and only a few years later his extravaganza *Exodus* (1960) would be dubbed a "Matzo Opera."[10] Like many outstanding directors, Preminger knew how useful opera could be in forming a cinematic vision, and in the case of *Carmen Jones* the opera shaped the idea so forcefully that it virtually created a new opera/cinema genre.

Prénom Carmen

By all appearances Jean-Luc Godard seemed to be creating an anti-opera with *Prénom Carmen* (1983), shunning spectacle with a type of reductionist chamber cinema, and avoiding the music of Bizet's *Carmen* with the exception of two insignificant characters whistling bits of the "Habañera." Nothing could be further from the truth. Bizet's opera permeates the film from top to bottom, but mainly by implication; since almost everyone knows something about the opera, including the image Carmen projects as well as some of the music – especially in France, Godard could proceed assuming this implied knowledge. Godard himself makes this very clear, emphasizing the endurance of the myth as musical instead of literary: "Carmen is a great feminine myth which exists only through music, and I can well understand that quite a few film directors in this epoch might feel that they want to make a film of it."[11] He knew perfectly well that few had read Mérimée's novella but that almost everyone knew of the opera. With that assumption in mind, he did not have to clutter his film with the familiar musical excerpts.

The issue of the myth immediately arises in the title: *Prénom Carmen* (perhaps more correctly *Prénom: Carmen*). The earthy Carmen (played by the Danish Maruschka Detmers) of this film may seem anti-intellectual (although one should remember that members of the criminal gang she belongs to need a university education to get in), but she does, in a strong French tradition, have some anthropological/linguistic concerns. She asks Joseph (Jacques Bonaffé) at one point what comes before a name, and he simplistically replies a "prénom." That does not satisfy her as she had in mind something that precedes verbalization, and here he cannot help her. This question ties in with another one that she asks twice in the film, once to her shell-shocked asylum inmate uncle Jean (played by a dazed-looking Godard) near the beginning, and also at the end, just before she dies from the gunshot inflicted by Joseph. "What's it called," she asks a Spanish room-service waiter with her last breath, "on one side, the innocent, the guilty on the other?" We do not doubt the importance of this question since she struggles to raise her head, interrupting her death, to ask it – even goading him with "think, stupid." The waiter's answer, "sunrise," may suggest hope, but it may also be a ruse. She seems to be searching for something that precedes a prénom, and Godard had already given it to us at the very beginning with the title: *Prénom Carmen*. One need only invoke the name Carmen, and the mythical duality of innocence and guilt this Carmen hopes to identify immediately comes to mind, not from the novella but from the opera, which places Don José between the innocent Micaela and the seductress Carmen. Carmen should know this since her own name offers the clue, but like the young people described by a perplexed Uncle Jean, she has an excellent memory but cannot remember anything. With the operatic myth assumed, Godard can proceed with his modern version of the myth.

Despite his recognition of the opera, Godard does not ignore the novella. Carmen does not belong to a band of warm and cuddly smugglers, hopelessly sweetened by Bizet's music; this gang of cutthroats in the film, like Mérimée's, has no redeeming qualities, least of all their education, and they do not hesitate to shoot innocent bystanders when they rob banks or attempt kidnapping. In most respects though, the plot parallels the opera's, although instead of a heroic rival – the bullfighter Escamillio, in Godard's budget film Carmen must settle for a lowly foreign guest worker. As for a real model, Godard opts for a familiar one for him from American cinema, and here he uses none other than Preminger's *Carmen Jones*. In one of the quarrels between Carmen and Joseph, she reminds him of the American film, repeating in English that if he loves her that's the end of him. Here of course she quotes Carmen Jones (also calling him Joe instead of Joseph, which he corrects), and she then goes out to work, leaving him to the boredom of the hotel room as Carmen Jones did with Joe in Chicago.

All of Godard's films are autobiographical in one way or another, but in this one he goes much further, literally putting himself in as a character. He can enjoy the self-depreciation of depicting himself as a washed-up director who can only stay in a mental asylum by convincing his keepers daily of his madness, and this also allows him to be outrageous, making, for example, scatological comments to his nurse. When Carmen speaks of her dissipated uncle she refers to herself as being his favorite relative, that he loved her when she was younger, and that he wanted to put her in his films. The viewer immediately assumes incest, and that he perhaps wanted to put her into a pornographic film; later someone whispers "dirty old man" before he makes his entry near the end of the film at the Intercontinental Hotel. This aside belongs to the same category as the whistled excerpts from the "Habañera," and it tells us something about Godard's attraction to the Carmen myth fostered by Bizet; its deep imprint on him and the familiarity of the myth make it seem as though it belongs to his family – something as taboo as to love too much. The personal side of the film takes another interesting twist with the apparent blurring of serious crimes such as armed robbery or kidnapping and filmmaking. The crimes seem to be carried out under the guise of a fictional documentary film, one that Uncle Jean wishes to be involved with, although he never really knows what's going on. Filmmaking itself becomes illicit, and for someone who loves it as much as Godard does, able to spend his life this way instead of working in the French bureaucracy, he allows himself a touch of guilty pleasure.

Much in this film does not differ fundamentally from many of Godard's earlier films, confirming his longstanding preoccupation with the Carmen myth and the role he sees for this type of woman in the confrontation between men and women. The active and in-control female set against the passive or impotent male so evident here differs little from his films of the 1960s with Anna Karina in leading roles, films which in strong ways documented his relationship with her as his lover, wife and ex-wife. In *Pierrot le fou*, for example, a film referred to in various ways in *Prénom Carmen*,[12] after escaping crime and civilization to the Mediterranean shore, Ferdinand (Jean Paul Belmondo) opts for the contemplative life of the writer, while Marianne (Karina) cannot take the boredom of that, needing dancing, adventure and danger. She ends the relationship, leaving him for someone else, and he, like Don José, tracks her down and kills her. In *Prénom Carmen*, the disintegration follows the opera in an especially striking way, as Joseph's impotence vividly parallels his operatic counterpart's. In Act 2, after Don José arrives at Lillas Pastia's tavern and Carmen dances for him privately, expecting lovemaking to follow, he, distracted by the military trumpet call, attempts to prove he loves her with the "Flower song," the flower having been substituted as a pin-up on his jail-cell wall. His passion in fact has little to do with her, but, as McClary correctly points out, it seems to chronicle his own masturbatory practices.[13] The shower scene near the end of *Prénom Carmen* has been described by those who care to notice it as a pathetic attempt by Joseph to get an erection,[14] but it could also be seen as masturbation.

Pierrot le fou also has another important bearing on this film. The active Marianne, who strongly resists the contemplative world of literature, not only loves music but in a sense actually becomes music. For her music and life are synonymous. For Godard, the director who sees

Carmen as "a great myth which exists only through music," this idea takes a fascinating turn in *Prénom Carmen*. Viewers of Godard's films always knew that music held a special place for him, but in this film we discover how crucial a role it actually plays. Earlier chapters explained how D. W. Griffith and Eisenstein had created their cinematic images from a pre-verbal impulse – a type of primordial musical essence; Godard explains exactly the same principle, showing how it operates in his film:

> If you take *Alexander Nevsky* by Eisenstein, for example, the battle scenes, these were first written in the form of a score by Prokofiev and this gave Eisenstein ideas; he had the score changed and then they shot the scenes in accordance with the music they had worked on together. My film has much less ambition but three quarters of the scenes in my film were also made in this way. For example, the attack on the bank came to be after I heard a certain part of the 10th Quartet [by Beethoven] and I understood, since I was planning this film, in which there was to be a crime element, I understood that Carmen could in fact be part of a small gang and so then came the idea that Don José is a policeman and in this way we came back to the real story of Carmen.[15]

He takes this further, noting that "the music has a certain control over the images," and in places where the love scenes may seem vulgar or detached "the music comes and takes over as if it were saying, 'Come on, let's go, let's go on, this is serious'."

Not only does the sound of the music serve this purpose but so does the visual image of music making, and in intercutting from the Carmen action to a string quartet playing Beethoven quartets, he takes the principle used by Eisenstein as far as it will go, making the sight of music making as important as the sound: "And in filming the ones who execute the music, I was striving for a physical feeling of music, especially with the violin, where I really had the feeling of carving [carving the images to be shown next]."[16] Eisenstein did this occasionally, showing for example a youth playing a double pipe during battle, but for the most part the transference between sound and visual image existed between director and composer, allowing these images to fuse in perfect unison. Godard brings the viewer in as well, who must watch a string quartet playing, and grasp that this visual aspect of the play-ing is crucial to the film – even before we see that Claire the violist loves Joseph (making her the operatic Micaela) or that the quartet plays in the hotel lobby during the scene of the bungled kidnapping attempt.

Just after Uncle Jean meets with the gang in a hotel room, some-one asks him about the reason for the quartet, and he quickly inter-jects "I'll tell you later." Unlike his crude joke to his nurse near the beginning of the film, when he tells her that if he stuck his finger in her arse and she counted to thirty-three, he would get a fever, and near the end of film he mumbles that it took her a long time to count to thirty-three, he never does answer the question about the quartet later. He leaves us to our own devices on this one to figure out not only why a quartet but why Beethoven in a film modeled on Bizet's *Carmen*. The answer he gave later in interviews proved to be not very useful – as enigmatic as the film itself. One can imagine the hidden twinkle in his eye as he espoused that "I didn't choose Beethoven, it's Beethoven, in a way, who chose me. I followed the call. When I was 20 myself, which is the age of the characters in my film, I had listened to Beethoven at the seashore, in Brittany, the last quartets, and dis-covered the Quartets there."[17] It may be reassuring to know that he knew the quartets (he claimed he had never seen Bizet's *Carmen*, but somehow absorbed it with the rest of the French population), but that tells us nothing about their connection with this film. Here we have little more than Uncle Jean telling an incredulous listener that three years ago he directed Marlene Dietrich and Beethoven.

The easy way out would be to consider the music as we can with Antoine Duhamel's score for *Pierrot le fou*, a score Duhamel composed with no instructions whatever about the nature of the film, and which Godard then inserted in blips and fragments.[18] Sometimes the tone of the music appeared to correlate with the narrative, but that happened purely by chance, causing the viewer to add emotion where none existed. Similarly Godard would offer long visual takes, as in the Ford Galaxy theft scene, and to that adds fragments of the music, which apparently continues during the silent parts, reversing the customary role of music as the seam through discontinuous editing of the visual shots. In all of this, Godard challenges the way we usually watch films, and in *Prénom Carmen*, with pre-existing music presented disjointedly, we may imagine something similar. The Godard of the early 1980s, though, should not be confused with the one from the mid 1960s, and now he forces us to think about what the Beethoven quartets may be about – or at least what they may mean to him – something few viewers will be equipped to manage.

Since this film concerns an opera, we can learn much about his treatment of opera/cinema by looking at a piece he did just a few years later, his contribution to producer Don Boyd's *Aria* (1987), what Leonard Maltin calls a "godawful collection of short films by a cadre of internationally respected directors, each one supposedly inspired by an operatic aria." To Maltin's horror, "precious few make sense, or even seem to match the music."[19] Maltin would no doubt have been troubled by body builders in Godard's piece who seem unruffled by the naked beauty of two female attendants who remove their uniforms to the fragmented presentation of music from Jean-Baptiste Lully's 17th-century opera *Armide*. Godard's reading actually does make sense, bringing an old and enduring legend up to date. In the opera, Rinaldo remains indifferent to the charms of the sorceress Armida. Rinaldo comes to her under a spell, and she approaches the sleeping Rinaldo with a dagger, but cannot strike. She calls on Hate to remove her love for him, and the tale ends when Rinaldo's fellow knights persuade him to rejoin the crusades.

Like the uninterested Rinaldo, the body builders seem to be eunuchs, unresponsive to look or even touch. One of the women draws a dagger, and both women lip sync the Lully aria. They get rid of the dagger and move in sexually on one of the weight lifters – their Rinaldo – while other men watch as voyeurs. These women of the eighties have no magic spells, and Rinaldo remains oblivious. One attendant laments that "he hasn't found my eyes charming enough," while the other, invoking the mythical Hate, says "oh how I'd love to hate him." They stand naked as all the men file past them en route to the shower, not one so much as looking. One woman screams "non" and the other "oui" as the piece ends. Not only do the modern women lack spells, but the men, who now compete by preening themselves, are completely impotent. The subject of *Armide* gets at the same male/female relations as *Carmen*, and Godard's short piece continues the familiar theme in his own works. The fragmented music may reflect on the gaps in the modern world which prevent the intense emotions of Lully. Fragmentation, though, belongs to Lully's world as well; his operas are filled with scenes that serve no narrative purpose, existing only for visual and audible indulgence.

The music in *Prénom Carmen* proves to be much less straightforward, in part since it does not come from opera at all, but also because Godard uses some of the most devilishly complex works in the entire musical repertoire. Godard does not limit himself to any one of the Beethoven quartets but starts off with one of the middle period "Razumovsky" Quartets (Op. 59, no. 3) and proceeds through Op. 74 to the late quartets later in the film, especially Opp. 131, 132 and 135. The quartet fragments arise as randomly as one might expect from a string quartet in rehearsal; the first passage we hear comes from the second movement of Op. 59, no. 3, an Andante, and with other quartets too we pick up somewhere in the middle of things.

For Beethoven the quartets stand as a very special part of his output, especially the late quartets which not only seem related to each other but reveal personal matters that the composer generally does not allow in other types of works. Personal issues emerge in a number of ways, most certainly in the music itself which often begs extramusical interpretation, but also in the often extended expressive headings to movements which may actually tell us how the movement should be understood. When Beethoven labels a movement "Heiliger Dankgesang eines Genesenen an die Gottheit, in der lydischen Tonart" (Holy song of thanksgiving of one recovered from an illness, in the Lydian mode), as he does with the third movement of Op. 132, and alternates between molto adagio and "Neue Kraft fühlend" (Feeling new strength), there can be little doubt about its significance. Godard uses this movement extensively, and curiously in a way as Beethoven intended it.

Other revealing headings also exist in the excerpts used by Godard. Aside from the ones that Beethoven tells how we should interpret, the music of many other movements suggests extramusical possibilities, and here Godard also plunges in, allowing members of the quartet – especially the violist Claire – to offer personal interpretations. The quartet leader talks about passages as sad, tragic or violent, and while that may be normal musician's parlance, Claire's comments, such as those about fate and torrents of life, are not. Godard himself thought of the Beethoven quartets as representing fundamental music, just as the ocean is a primal image: "I wanted music which had marked the history of music itself, both its practice and theory, and the Beethoven Quartets represent this."[20] Here he returns to Eisenstein's idea of music as a primordial force, a pre-verbal urge which can embrace at a primary level, something that can precede even the stirrings of myth. Like the multi-facetedness of the ocean, which can be a symbol of life and death, or sex and oblivion, the music he has in mind can bring together primary conflicts, conflicts which lie at the base of myths such as the myth of Carmen; the ocean and quartets run throughout as parallel images, both aurally and visually. For Godard, Beethoven does this better than Bizet, and the quartets therefore become an operatic accompaniment in a fundamental way.

The primary conflict reveals itself in the quartets at every turn through musical forces which define opposition. Even in the first two bars of the Andante we hear at the beginning of the film, Beethoven sets a melodic line in the first violin against a pizzicato repeated note in the cello, in musical terms juxtaposing the active and the static. That becomes a major factor at the beginning of Op. 131 (a passage we do not hear), where the fugue subject begins with an active leaping figure which then lapses into something more lyrically passive. That opposition runs throughout this unusual seven-movement quartet, and only resolves in the sonata-form finale, which we hear in the film shortly after seeing Carmen use a male urinal. The gender conflict so dominant in Godard's films seems to have a strong parallel to Beethoven's musical contrast of active and passive passages. As we hear the start of the Op. 131 finale, accompanying the lovemaking of Carmen and Joseph, Godard also shows us the ocean, reflective of the cinematic image of the ocean in relation to sex (one need only recall Hitchcock's use of it in *Vertigo* as Madeleine and Scotty embrace and kiss with ocean breakers crashing behind them, implying what could not be shown). The fusion of opposites in the quartet finale and the ocean offer another answer to Carmen's vital question about the word which brings both innocence and guilt together.

When Carmen tells of her desire to show what a woman does to a man (not what she does with a man), the music shifts to the "Heiliger Dankgesang" of Op. 132. The song of thanksgiving or celebration along with the feeling of new strength belongs decidedly to the woman; Carmen now holds control as she can come and go while he must stay behind, and she too sets the agenda for their lovemaking. Claire also comes into the picture at this point, and she stops playing to write in her score: "And the clouds, will they reveal the torrents of life?" Joseph tells Carmen that he has no friends, male or female, although he knows one girl (Claire, unnamed) but she's too special. He then reveals his docile, withdrawn nature: "loneliness forces me to be my own best friend," as the passive music of the molto adagio sounds. When the andante ("Neue Kraft fühlend") begins, so does confirmation of Carmen as a social creature as well as her being in control of this intimate and sexual situation. While Claire succumbs to fate, recognizing that "we're not our own masters; what has been determined must be," Carmen will have none of predetermination, always ready to feel her own strength.

The fate motive takes a new turn later in the film, as events hurtle irrevocably toward Carmen's death at the hand of Joseph. Yet, this is not the fate which Godard wishes to impress on us; it appears to have more to do with the withdrawn existence of Joseph and Uncle Jean, both of whom try to get involved near the end and both make a horrible botch of it, causing death, arrests, and general chaos. Both should have accepted their fate, which was to accept their isolation. To confirm this, Godard has the quartet accompany the scene with Beethoven's last quartet, Op. 135, a work with an astounding musical message before the finale. Before the grave (very slow) introduction to the finale, Beethoven gives the heading "Der schwer gefasste Entschluss" (the hard-taken decision), and follows this with two three-note motifs, one grave and the other allegro, with a text beneath them. This is a string quartet, not a cantata; should the cellist sing the first one in bass clef and a violinist the second in treble? Of course not – these are meant for the eyes of the performers, not to be performed. The first one asks the question "Muss es sein?" (must it be), and the second, in fast tempo, resolves that "Es muss sein!" These mottos then sound in the introduction to the finale, and Godard presents it with emphasis, allowing the grave "Muss es sein?" to cut in over the lento movement then in progress, just as Claire returns to her seat while the quartet plays in the hotel, and continues the clash for some time.

Here in the last work he composed, Beethoven asks the big question, one which had plagued him throughout his life, as in these lines written to a friend at the age of thirty: "I have often cursed my existence; Plutarch taught me resignation. I shall, if possible, defy Fate, though there will be hours in my life when I shall be the most miserable of God's creatures. Resignation! What a wretched resort; yet it is the only one left for me!"[21] Two and a half decades later he could, in his final musical proclamation, accept it. The struggle subsided as the opposing forces were absorbed into something else; for Godard the same was possible in the urge that precedes the prénom, the myth that can fuse innocence and guilt, or the coming together of dusk and dawn. The message is intimate, as it is for Beethoven who makes his in an intimate musical genre; for Godard the presentation moves from chamber music to chamber opera; his concluding dedication reads: "In memoriam small movies."

21

OPERASTRUCK

After spending a rapturous night with the brother of her fiancé, Loretta (Cher) realizes the next morning what she has done. In this delightful scene from *Moonstruck* Loretta and Ronny (Nicolas Cage) accuse each other of ruining the other one's life, but establish the impossibility of that since their lives were already ruined before they met. Loretta still has her fiancé to contend with, and delivers a sharp slap to Ronny's cheek. As that fails to dislodge his love struck expression, she cranks up the intensity with a whallop to his face, demanding that he should snap out of it. This will not help to reconcile the bad blood between the brothers, and she insists they forget it ever happened; if that proves impossible at least they should take the knowledge of it to their graves without breathing a word to anyone. Ronny, whose existence has been dragged from the bakery furnaces he stokes in the basement below his flat up to a feverish pitch of ecstasy he has not previously known, will not allow the moment to vanish so quickly. In his half delirious stupor he makes the proposal which proves fateful: "I love two things – you and the opera. If I can have the two things I love together for one night, I would give up the rest of my life… come with me tonight to the Met." "Where's the Met?" she asks.

We can all understand his new-found passion for a beautiful woman, and most male viewers of *Moonstruck* have also fallen head over heels for the character played by Cher, but what is this about the opera? It seems fairly safe to say that most North American moviegoers would not have the faintest idea why he places opera with such elevation among the things he loves most. In fact, Loretta seems equally confused by this; not only does she not know how to find the Metropolitan Opera, but when she goes with Ronny to see Puccini's *La Bohème*, while impressed that there is "some turnout" for this kind of thing, she comments during the intermission that she does not get it. By the end of the opera she apparently does get it. During some touching moments of Act 3 she and Ronny instinctively hold hands and a tear comes to her eye. Descending the stairs at the end of the opera she seems somewhat unnerved by the impact of *Bohème*; as a working woman she sees the pathos in the situation, lamenting how awful it was for poor Mimi to be "coughin' her brains out and still have to keep singin'." Perhaps she would put in a call to the management of the Met in the morning about the deplorable working conditions.

To her remark about the turnout, which she may have been comparing to a Mets baseball game, Ronnie proudly proclaims that "it's the biggest thing there is." What should we make of this attitude toward opera coming from such an apparently unlikely working-class devotee, sweating in a dirty undershirt in a bakery oven hell-hole, shoveling coal into one fiery aperture and bread sticks into another, and in fact living with the barest of furnishings in the same crumbling building? Of course most of us cannot understand his passion for opera because we do not come from Italian descent. For centuries opera has been the foremost entertainment for the Italians, so powerful that any other type of theater in Italy had to struggle to be taken seriously. And when notable Italian playwrights have come along, such as Metastasio, Goldoni or Da Ponte, they either succumbed to writing opera librettos or left the country to find employment – especially to Austria during the 18th century where Italian held sway as the language of culture.

Opera emerged during the second half of the sixteenth century in Italy as the extravagant entertainment known as *intermedi* for celebrations of the wealthy or the state. With discoveries about the extraordinary capabilities of the singing voice by Giulio Caccini and others at the same time, the possibility of fusing bel canto singing and lavish shows set the wheels in motion. Jacopo Peri, Claudio Monteverdi and others saw the potential, and the new artform quickly blossomed. From Monteverdi onward, many of the great composers of opera have been Italian – Paisiello, Bellini, Rossini, Donizetti, Verdi and Puccini to mention only a few. Some of the greatest German opera composers, such as Handel, Gluck and Mozart, either perfected their trade in Italy or wrote predominantly Italian operas. Many of the great opera singers have come from Italy, from Farinelli in the 18th century to Caruso in the 20th, and most of the great non-Italian opera singers have had an Italian training or have been taught the Italian manner of singing. Like the English who like to claim that while other countries have writers they have a literature, the Italians can also boast that while other countries have opera composers, they have an opera.

It should be made clear, that in spite of its origins, this has not simply been an entertainment for the high and mighty in Italy. At many major opera houses in the world, such as the Staatsoper in Vienna or the Met in New York, people unable to afford the regular ticket prices can be accommodated with standing-room places, the chance to gain entry for roughly the equivalent of one hour's wage. Other great houses, including Covent Garden in London, will designate some of the worst seats at a similarly low price, although one has little chance of seeing more that about one-tenth of the stage from these seats. Not so in Italy. Here all classes come to the opera. Historically, the gulf between the upper and lower classes could be maintained in the design of theaters, with the aristocracy in the boxes and the commoners on the orchestra floor. One should not imagine for a moment that patrons came to the opera house merely to see and hear operas. During the 18th century tables set up in the boxes could be used for dining or card playing, and more comfortable sofas allowed patrons to carry on lovemaking or tête-a-têtes. Singers often had to make a special effort to be noticed, and that included various types of vocal acrobatics, vocal competitions among singers, or simply singing signature tunes which everyone would associate with a particular singer, regardless of the opera being performed. The rabble on the orchestra floor tended to be more aware of the action on stage, and hawkers made fruit available for expressing displeasure as well as refreshment. The *abbati* kept a close watch on things, these members of the lay clergy who were the real opera critics, shouting "Viva Leo!" or "Viva Pergolesi" as they spotted acts of musical plagiarism.[1]

More staid non-Italians, especially the English, have tended to take a dim view of goings-on in Italian opera houses, in the 20th century as well as the 18th. A keen English observer of Italian life, and an even keener observer of the English in Italy, E. M. Forster, describes a delightful opera scene in Florence in his novel *Where Angels Fear to Tread*. A group of well-bred English people, in Italy to rescue the child of a deceased relative who scandalously married an Italian whom they perceive as coarse, indolent and incapable of raising this child as they see fit, attends this performance of *Lucia di Lammermoor* by Donizetti. The experienced traveler Philip understands what to expect: "However bad the performance is tonight, it will be alive. Italians don't love music silently, like the beastly Germans. The audience takes its share – sometimes more." At the opera Harriet's worst fears about the lack of decorum come true:

> The audience accompanied with tappings and drummings, swaying in the melody like corn in the wind. Harriet, though she did not care for music, knew how to listen to it. She uttered an acid "Shish!"
> "Shut it," whispered her brother.
> "We must make a stand from the beginning. They're talking."
> "It is tiresome," murmured Miss Abbott; "but perhaps it isn't for us to interfere."
> Harriet shook her head and shished again. The people were quiet, not because it is wrong to talk during a chorus, but because it is natural to be civil to a visitor. For a little time she kept the whole house in order, and could smile at her brother complacently.
> Her success annoyed him.

As the theater filled up, Harriet lost her power to control the behavior. Greetings flew from box to box and compliments to the orchestra, chorus and soloists, bringing the response of "Ridiculous babies!" from Harriet. When Lucia sang,

> the theatre murmured like a hive of happy bees. All through the coloratura she was accompanied by sighs, and its top note was drowned in a shout of universal joy... Miss Abbott fell into the spirit of the thing. She, too, chatted and laughed and applauded and encored, and rejoiced in the existence of beauty.

Not only drawing strength from the audience for performance purposes, the singers also engaged in antics with certain individuals in the house, as happened when a small boy threw Lucia a carnation and she darted over to kiss him:

> Now the noise became tremendous.... But the young men in the adjacent box were imploring Lucia to extend her civility to them.

She refused, with a humorous expressive gesture. One of them hurled a bouquet at her. She spurned it with her foot. Then, encouraged by the roars of the audience, she picked it up and tossed it to them. Harriet was always unfortunate. The bouquet struck her full in the chest, and a little *billet-doux* fell out of it into her lap.[2]

Charles Sturridge, in his 1991 film of the novel, nicely captures the pandemonium of this scene. While every night in an Italian opera house may not be quite like this, even today when Italian opera companies perform in London they must be warned in advance that the polite applause of the audience should not be taken as a sign of dissatisfaction.

In Italy, of course, opera stands as much more than an entertainment: it remains a necessity of life. For Italian Americans, Italian traditions die hard, and not the least of these is a passion for opera. The sound of *bel canto* singing, entirely unlike anything conveyed through a microphone, can arouse its listeners to a level of ecstasy, not so much through the projection of vocal power but through the extraordinary delicacy and subtlety possible for a great singer, through the control of the *messe di voce* or the ability of a singer in the highest possible register to take a loud tone and decrescendo to something deliciously *piano*, not giving up one iota of the ability of that tone to project. For those who grew up with these sounds, a finely executed *messe di voce* approaches a goal of perfection and fulfillment, offering a rare or even unique sense of satisfaction. Few composers give as many opportunities for it as Puccini, and few operas allow it as sumptuously as *La Bohème*.

This opera by Puccini, of course, infiltrates Norman Jewison's film at every possible level. We may hear Dean Martin singing "That's Amore" during the titles, but visually Jewison prepares us for the opera. The titles begin with Lincoln Center in the background; we see the Met with its famous fountain in the foreground and the great windows of the Met which reveal Chagall's double panels. But, this not being a movie for opera snobs, the camera takes us around to the back of the house, showing a truck which has been wending its way through adjacent streets, finally entering the loading dock area of the Met. We may not hear any sounds from the opera or even arrangements of tunes from it for another half hour, but when these come we will not be surprised.

Connecting a tear-jerker opera with a comic film may at first make little sense. Puccini offers love and death, not in a profound way as

Russian or Scandinavian writers at the end of the 19th century may have, but in the simplicity of these things merely happening. The story itself, based on Henri Murger's novel *La vie de Bohème*, has surprisingly little potential: a struggling writer who shares a Paris garret room with some bohemian friends meets a girl who lives in the same garret and they fall in love; they break up and she dies of tuberculosis – end of story. Why should we care? Had it not been for Puccini, we probably would not. Few operas play as frequently as *La Bohème*, perhaps second only to *Carmen*, and Ronny's passion for it is no exception. The music, of course, carries the work almost entirely, so much so that it scarcely matters if viewers know the plot; anyone in the audience who cannot figure out from the music itself when Rodolfo and Mimi fall in love, when Musetta behaves flirtatiously or frivolously, when Rodolfo and Mimi break up, or when Mimi dies, should not bother coming to this opera. Of course we know these things, and Puccini's music, tunefully recurrent and emotionally effective, tells us everything we need to know and forces us to be drawn into this little drama, sharing the characters' ecstasy in love and pain in death. Here we have soap opera (or melodrama) at its best, and most audiences cannot help but be operastruck.

We should not, though, confuse this type of melodrama with high tragedy. Mimi's death may be sad, and Puccini has persuaded millions of this, but only in the sadness do we find it tragic. In fact, considering the nature of the work, it would be a let down if she did not die at the end; our emotions have been tampered with and we need to leave the theater with the assurance that something sufficiently moving or serious has happened to justify the emotional tugging. Since the opera starts as a comedy, with manipulation of the landlord and Musetta's deception of the aging but infatuated Alcindoro in Act 2, its shift to the melodramatic in the Act 3 break-up or the Act 4 death becomes all the more effective.

The theme of love and death or the balance of melodrama and comedy also plays out in *Moonstruck*, but the film, of course, most assuredly offers comedy. Whenever anything that may seem serious happens, other forces quickly counterbalance that with something to defuse it. An old woman at the airport curses a plane carrying her sister who admitted not loving the man she stole from the woman placing the curse; the curse will not do much good since the woman who lost her lover does not believe in curses. When Loretta first meets Ronny in his bakery dungeon, he rants on in the language of tragedy about how his brother Johnny ruined his life, left him maimed and without a fiancée. He embellishes it with demands for the big knife so he can end his miserable nether-world existence, escape the heartbreak and the haunting memories. He has an audience for this performance, and one of the viewers, the bakery sales girl with eyes like lemon Danishes and no doubt an addiction to pulp fiction, puts it all into perspective: "He's the most tormented man I know. I'm in love with him."

The audience can laugh at this, and so can Loretta, although she restrains herself: "that's the bad blood between you and Johnny?" His ruin resulted from an accident; he lost his hand in a meat grinder because Johnny, so he claims, distracted him. Loretta cannot believe the lunacy of his logic, and her equally preposterous explanations of what now controls his life – or the fact that he has no life – seem entirely appropriate responses to such excessive melodrama. No one but a person saturated in opera could invent Ronny's view of fate and his place in the general scheme of things; his explanation for the bad blood is nothing short of operatic, where motives or the principles of cause and effect appear extraneous. If Scarpia from *Tosca* behaves with extreme cruelty, he does not need a motive: opera makes him do it. If Rudolfo and Mimi keep falling in and out of love for no apparent reason, that's opera. If Ronny's life lies in ruins because he turned an accident into fate, that's his operatic business.

Views of death lurk never far beneath the surface of this film, but seldom with serious consequences. That belongs to a longstanding tradition in comedy, of getting coffins mixed up, of ashes from urns disappearing into fireplaces, or, in a film by Jewison's countryman, Claude Jutre, *Mon oncle Antoine*, of a coffin falling off the back of a sled driven by a mischievous boy and a drunken old man in the dead of winter. After the titles *Moonstruck* begins in a funeral home, with one of Loretta's clients who cannot keep his books straight but claims to be a genius at making the dead look better than when they lived. From this scene we move on to a number of characters who seem to be among the walking dead: Loretta herself looks older than her thirty-seven years, having given up when a bus hit and killed her first husband; Ronny, who saw the loss of his hand as a fatal blow; Loretta's father, who cannot sleep because it reminds him of death and pretends to be alive by keeping a mistress ("a cheap piece of goods," according to Loretta) and hoarding his money; Johnny's mother, whose flirting with death controls Johnny's life; an aging windbag of a professor (John Mahoney) who feigns life by dating his female students; and the old man with the dogs (Loretta's grandfather) who visits his friends at a graveyard. When Loretta and Ronny embrace wildly, they acknowledge they have been dead, and unaccustomed to being alive, stumble awkwardly into their new-found life.[3] In the end no one dies, not even Johnny's mother, and the lack of death here proves as essential in this comedy as the necessity of it happening in *La Bohème*.

The chance meeting of Loretta and Ronny runs closely in parallel to the chance meeting of Mimi and Rodolfo in Puccini's opera, although the musical cues from the opera are not necessarily the ones the viewer would expect. Each act of the opera has a distinctive tone, Act 1 with the experience of love, Act 2 the flirting and caprices of Musetta, Act 3 the break-up of the lovers, and Act 4 Mimi's death; most of the musical cues from the opera in this film come from Act 3, with Act 2 a close second. As things move upward from the basement ovens to Ronny's flat during his first meeting with Loretta, we hear (and see the LP) a recording from the opera, not, as we might expect, music from Act 1, but an excerpt from Act 3 where Mimi bids Rodolfo "addio," asking him to put her few possessions aside. When Ronny later takes Loretta to the Met, we see precisely this scene from Act 3. If Rodolfo wishes to keep Mimi's pink bonnet, though, he may as a reminder of their love; Ronny lifts the stylus before Rodolfo can ask if it is really over and they should abandon their dreams of love.

Unlike the opera, with its docile and pliable prima donna, Loretta can look after herself, and at this point, just recently engaged, and in a tense and awkward situation with her fiancé's brother, not only does she not expect love but Puccini's music also reduces the possibility. A few minutes later, after raw meat and a nasty confrontation involving her absurd analysis of him and his turning the table on her, they embrace. We may think propriety forces her to draw back and shout "wait a minute," but not so; she now initiates the embrace, regaining her position of the woman on top.[4] As he carries her to his bed, they both acknowledge that they were dead, and she tells him to take his anger at Johnny out on her, leaving nothing but her bones; the Act 1 love duet of Mimi and Rodolfo now swells in the background. At that moment in the opera Rodolfo sees Mimi wrapped in a nimbus of moonlight, and before they sing in ensemble he bursts out with "oh, sweet face bathed in the soft moonlight. I see in you the dream I'd dream forever!" While ecstasy now runs parallel in film and opera, the vivid presence of the moon in the film will come shortly, fusing moonstruck and operastruck.

The moon montage, after the description by Loretta's uncle Raymond of Cosmo's moon, begins with Cosmo (Vincent Gardenia) asleep in bed and his wife Rose (Olympia Dukakis) wishing for something other than sleep; she goes to the window and looks at the moon. It continues with Loretta looking out the window at the moon at Ronny's flat with him embracing her from behind, and quickly shifts to the bedroom of Raymond (Louis Guss) and his wife Rita (Anita Gillette), who become youthful and aroused by the moon (he like Orlando Furioso, he boasts the next morning). The montage ends under the Brooklyn Bridge, the dogs howling at the moon, prompted by Cosmo's old father (Feodor Chaliapin) who howls in laughter with them. A popular non-classical arrangement of music from *La Bohème* accompanies this four-minute montage, this time of Musetta's well-known solo from the Act 2 street scene in which we discover notable aspects of her personality, if we did not already know (Marcello had earlier jokingly given her last name as "Temptation" – a man-eating bird). To this melody, one of the best known in the opera, she describes the pleasure she gets when people (i.e. men) inspect her beauty from head to toe, her enjoyment at the thought of their desires, the looks in their eyes – "that show they understand from my frank behavior my charms that lie concealed." This erotic outpouring embarrasses the old Alcindoro, Musetta's admirer, but the young garret dwellers relish it. Certainly the sexiest aria in the opera, it fits aptly with the two central segments of the montage; it works for the first part as well where Rose wishes her husband would not only look at her but touch her as well. The old man, his wife long dead and himself relegated to the junk heap of family obsolescence, indulges in a kind of unrestrained *joie de vivre* that eludes everyone else in the film.

The film ends with Loretta and the right brother together, Cosmo, having given up his mistress and understanding the importance of family, together again with his wife, uncle and aunt enjoying the scene, Johnny out in the cold (unable to trade a living mother for a wife), and the old man confused but happy that his son, Cosmo, will pay for the wedding to whichever brother Loretta marries. As they break open the champagne and celebrate, Puccini sounds one last time, now an ensemble from near the end of Act 2, shortly before Alcindoro gets duped into paying the entire dinner bill. In this comic scene Puccini gives us intrigue (love between Musetta and Marcello under the nose of Alcindoro), duplicity (Alcindoro must take Musetta's shoe to a shoemaker, during which time he will receive the bill and lose Musetta), and a proclamation from Marcello that "my youth, you're still alive, your memory's not dead... If you came to my door my heart would open it!" This joyous and comical moment sums up the film, and after the camera turns the celebrators into a family portrait and drifts off to portraits of the past, the music of *La Bohème* takes over entirely, transforming the final scene into one not only dominated by opera but specifically the music of the opera. For the end titles Dean Martin may lighten things up again with "That's amore," but merely as a diversion and a connection with the beginning: the final scene made clear that we had been watching and listening to opera.

OUTING OPERA IN PHILADELPHIA

993 proved to be an interesting year for the coming out of homo-sexuality, not only in the mainstream American film industry but elsewhere as well. Jonathan Demme's *Philadelphia* appeared that year, not only breaking a longstanding taboo but doing it with grace as we see the character of Joe Miller (Denzel Washington), transformed from a typical homophobic male to a defender of fundamental human rights. A book appeared in the same year which may not have attracted as much public attention as *Philadelphia* but probably had a stronger impact in its more circumscribed orbit: Wayne Koestenbaum's *The Queen's Throat: Opera, Homosexuality and the Mystery of Desire*. One would not nec-essarily take note of these two releases in the same breath except that they proved to have a strong connection.

In a film which had some difficulty revealing what it was about and stood in constant danger of sinking into a morass of political cor-rectness and niceness, one scene stood out in its treatment of passion, misunderstanding and, for some, embarrassment. The scene in question shows Andrew Beckett (Tom Hanks) in his apartment with Joe, being prepped for a question and answer session in court; Andrew ignores Joe, instead responding to a recording of Maria Callas singing a well-known aria from Umberto Giordano's opera *Andrea Chenier*. Joe, like most people, has no idea how to deal with this display of ardor, and it embarrasses him noticeably; at the same time, he could not help but be touched by it, and the glow of emotion that emanates from Andrew prompts him, with the sounds of Maria Callas still in the background, to embrace his infant daughter and wife with feelings apparently unfamiliar to him. For gay men, this scene awakened all the complex associations that Koestenbaum's book addresses, and perhaps caused some to squirm a little as the film plunged in an exaggerated way into what has become a stereotype of male homosexuality.

At the beginning of this scene Andrew asks Joe, "do you mind this music – do you like opera?" Joe answers, stammering, as most viewers of the film would: "I am not that familiar with opera." Not only unfamiliar with opera, he, like the typical moviegoer, has even less idea what opera may mean to Andrew – why opera can stir Andrew so deeply. Throughout the scene Demme privileges the viewer with two distinctly different vantage points for viewing it, one through the eyes of the character we most likely identify with, Joe, and the other from the position of the camera itself, perched for the most intense scene over the shoulder of Andrew, looking down on him in his dance of death with the movable IV rack. As we look through Joe's eyes, we may initially feel embarrassment and discomfort, but the look gradually changes to wonder and eventually compassion, although probably not understanding. At the end of it he appears shaken, now perhaps more embarrassed by his inability to grasp fully or articulate what has just happened than by Andrew's display. Q and A goes by the boards, certainly out of the question now: "Gee, I better get out of here."

Joe has been touched, though, as has the viewer, and Demme causes that to happen in the way the scene unfolds. As Andrew becomes Maria Callas and his performance aspires to grand opera, Demme takes the plunge, removing him from the real world by imbuing him with the red-hot glow of passion and suffering that only grand opera can realize so instantaneously. Joe, in color-coded contrast, has been shrouded in blue, as also occurred earlier during the birth of his daughter, but now from time to time his face catches some of the flaming glow emanating from Andrew. On departing the room he returns to a deep-freeze of blue in the antechamber, temporarily recovering his cynicism, doubts and cool demeanor. But that will not last; as he re-enters his personal world, so completely remote from Andrew's, the nondiegetic sounds of Callas, in gradual crescendo as he goes into his daughter's room and his bedroom, cut through the bluish hues as warmth engulfs his face and the faces of those he loves.

In the opera scene itself, Andrew tells us everything we need to know, announcing the opera and its singer for viewers like Joe who would not recognize it, and providing a blow by blow account of the libretto:

Ah, this is my favorite aria – it's Maria Callas – it's *Andrea Chenier*, Umberto Giordano; this is Madeleine who's saying now during the French Revolution the mob set fire to her house and her mother died... the place that cradled me is burning. Do you hear the heartache in her voice, can you feel it, Joe? [Joes sort of nods, and shrugs his shoulders.] In come the strings and that changes everything. It fills with a hope – that will change again – listen. Listen. I bring sorrow to those who love me. Ah, that single cello. It was during this sorrow that love came to me (a voice filled with irony). It said live, still. I am life. Heaven is in your eye. [pause, as Callas sings] Everything around you is the blood in the mud. I am divine. I am oblivion. I am the god who comes down from the heavens to the earth and makes the earth a heaven. I am love. I am love.

But this is no "Live from the Met" commentary. Andrew now lives the aria as Madeleine does and as Callas expresses it, taking us through it with his expressions of pain, of ecstasy and envelopment; the emotions of the aria soar above the foundation of death from which it arises. That climaxes when he pauses and lets her sing "fa della terra un ciel! Ah! Io son l'amore" (I bring you heaven on earth! Ah! I am love). The vocal climax arrives on "Ah," a high b held for more than two measures; unlike a Joan Sutherland or a Caballé whose voice would soar on this note, Callas struggles with it, forcing us to hear the pain in her voice, not allowing us to be fooled by a moment of transcendence that arises from the depths of despair. Andrew responds to this fully, his grimace giving the parallel to Callas's voice and the emotion it evokes. Andrew has not been giving mere commentary; he has become Madeleine through Maria Callas, and her voice becomes his voice. We no longer watch cinema here as he leads us toward the climax; cinema, with sound, visuals and emotion, now gives way to opera.[1]

"La mamma morta" may be Andrew's favorite aria, but it and Madeleine's position in the opera apply to Andrew's situation as well. Madeleine's pre-revolution life has been privileged, as she was born into wealth and close to the reigns of power. The French Revolution changes all that: her house burns, her mother dies, and the life she knew before vanishes forever. With little to sustain her but her sense of spirituality, she no longer looks on the preservation of her life as a high priority. The time for her own happiness and survival has forever passed, and if the one person in the world she still loves must die,

Andrea Chenier, she will change places with someone else condemned to share his fate. In the act, she can see her death as worthwhile, and because of her spirituality can realize an epiphany in what arises from her personal tragedy. Like her, Andrew recognizes when he brings forward his suit of wrongful dismissal that there can be little or no personal gain. Now he falls back on his love of the law, those rare moments when one can feel the satisfaction of justice being done, and fights a case, through which he will probably not survive, which will establish a precedent in law for future cases of its kind. When he sings Madeleine's aria, he too sees the futility of his own life but grasps on to the vision of something larger than himself, a victory that can only arise from coming to terms with his own mortality. The aria ends with the words "The angel drew beside me, kissed me; it was the symbol of death. Mine is not a body of the living. Now you may take it. I offer you a corpse." She offers this to Gerard who would take her against her will; Andrew makes the same sacrifice to a society hostile to those who contract AIDS through what some in that society perceive as same-sex promiscuous indulgence.

Philadelphia, though, invokes another even more powerful image, and this one may have left the gay community feeling uneasy about how the rest of the world perceives it. When Andrew asks Joe if he likes opera, proclaims "La mamma morta" as his favorite aria, and takes us into the innermost regions of his soul by way of an aria, we have little doubt that for Andrew few things can rival the importance of opera. In fact, this section of the film invokes the stereotype that all gay men love opera, and the various negative connotations that accompany that assumption. Stereotypes, of course, should not be taken as fact, but in this case a number of prominent gay writers have fueled, if inadvertently, the possibility of truth in the assumption.

Perhaps foremost among these writers stands Terrence McNally, whose play The Lisbon Traviata opened at the Prominade Theater in New York in October 1989. La Traviata, of course, is one of Verdi's most familiar operas, and Lisbon refers to a pirated recording of a performance of that opera with Maria Callas in the leading role which took place in Lisbon. In the play, two middle-aged characters go to great lengths to try to acquire a copy of this recording, a rare treat for anyone familiar with all Callas's other recordings. The older of these characters (Mendy) McNally describes as "appealing, somewhat out of shape. Wears good clothes well. Intelligent. His manner can be excessive and may take some getting used to."[2] The younger one (Stephen) is "good looking. Fair. Is trim. Somewhat closed and guarded in his manner." In the way they discuss opera in Act 1, including their own vast record collections, they reveal themselves as much more than opera aficionados: they know every vocal nuance – for that matter every breath taken – by every singer in these recordings. Their conversation mingles life and opera, going even beyond equating the two with Mendy's declaration that "Opera doesn't reject me. The real world does." The more serious action of Act 2, with two younger characters as well, unfolds in distinctly operatic fashion; a tense moment with scissors near the end of the play might very well have come from *Tosca* (Callas's well-known 1963 London performance of it that remains well known from a video recording).

Not everyone in the play likes opera, but failure to do so implies deficiency. On the phone with the much younger Michael, Mendy snaps, "I'm not surprised you don't like opera. People like you don't like life." On another occasion, in an aside away from the phone, he complains "They're playing *Sweeney Todd* so loud over there I don't know how they can think. I'll never understand what people see in musicals. I mean, why settle for *The Sound of Music* when you can have *Dialogue of the Carmelites?*" Only the initiated familiar with the composer Francis Poulenc would get this reference, and McNally seems to feel confident that his audience will. His characters, though, who do not like opera, in spite of the put-downs, find themselves in good company, in fact among certain writers annoyed by the stereotype. One of these writers, Bruce Bawer, puts the issue in focus in his book *A Place at the Table: The Gay Individual in American Society* with the terse comment "I don't like opera."

The stereotypical view implies that gay men like opera because it allows them to indulge their love of camp in a respectable setting, or because the exaggerated delineation of gender and the absurdly inflated portrayals of love in opera allow them to relish a type of satire on heterosexual love. Bawer expands on this in his jab about not liking opera:

> Certain gay people who love opera like to say that all gay people love opera. They say that we love it because, as people who have been compelled to keep our emotional lives under wraps, we find

the overblown emotion of it liberating. This is doubtless true of many so-called opera queens. Yet one gay opera fan of my acquaintance objected strongly to this whole line of argument about gays and opera. "It demeans opera," he said, "and it demeans those of us who happen to be gay but who also happen to love opera for *itself*, not for some psychological boost it also supposedly gives us as gay people. To be a gay opera fan is not necessarily to be an "opera queen." Opera is art. I don't respond to it as a gay man who iden-tifies with divas or finds the melodrama wonderfully campy or thinks that the whole thing speaks in some special way to me as a homo-sexual; I respond to it as a human being who's capable of appreci-ating beauty."[3]

Noble sentiments these, but in some ways unnecessarily purist or perhaps even academic. An element exists among opera experts, as we discovered in Joseph Kerman's *Opera as Drama* from 1956 and much academic writing since, which insists that the only element of opera of any consequence is the drama, especially that generated by composers themselves – the musical procedures responsible for carrying the essence of the drama. Of course fine composers like Mozart, Verdi, Wagner and Berg can do this, but these composers also recognize the other dimensions of opera. Its success depends on the sensuality of its visual impression, and even more on the sensory effect of the sound, especially of the solo voices. Mozart and Verdi always composed their operas with specific voices in mind, and they wrote in such a way to display those voices to the greatest advantage. Those who focus on the dramatic side of opera tend to look at *opera seria* from the 18th century dominated by the castrati as part of the dark ages; it follows that Puccini or other composers who place their highest value on the voice itself remain similarly unenlightened.

Then Wayne Koestenbaum and *The Queen's Throat* entered the fray. His account may be very personal, but it reminded everyone who enjoys opera, regardless of the necessity of that reminder, that opera moves us in many ways other than through the dramatic devices of high art. Koestenbaum indulges in all the excesses of opera so annoying to some, the enjoyment of camp, the identification with divas, divas' costumes, the bigger-than-life emotions, and visual extravaganza, but at the same time he reveals something much deeper – beyond mere indul-gence, satire and pomp. This other element emerges most vividly in his central chapters "The Callas Cult" and "The Queen's Throat: Or, How to Sing." Singing in opera resembles no other kind of use of the voice, and *bel canto* singing can induce a state of euphoria for those who revel in this type of singing. The voice itself can inadvertently betray that which we may wish to conceal. At the age of puberty the voice changes, usually accompanied at the time by breaking or flipping from a confident low voice to a less secure high sound. At times of intense emotion the voice will often do exactly that, betraying a lack of full control. The voice itself has a natural break, and the techniques of bel canto minimize or entirely disguise that break between lower and upper registers. Some singers though, and Callas in particular, in spite of their training, allowed the break to be audible, and in so doing added an element of emotional engagement or vulnerability to their vocal quality.

For the most part, though, *bel canto* singing represents a type of vocal perfection, a mode of expression the non-singer can only dream about, something which projects the operatic characters into the realm of the unattainable and makes their emotions seem to be elevated beyond all earthly comprehension. The great singer can make this appear to be happening with the greatest of ease, as a voice capable of filling a cavernous space with no amplification devices whatever seems to float out of the body, so mysterious to the untrained ear that it seems like an out-of-body phenomenon. The singer, of course, has paid a price for this ability, not only through many years of rigorous training and apprenticeship, but through sheer hard work in the act of singing itself; in the opera house, sometimes more because of the distance between viewer and singer than anything else, we experience illusion.

The mere act of breathing requires hard work from the singer, as abdominal muscles must press the air out of the lungs while other muscles in the solar plexus area counteract that pressure from below, preventing the air from escaping too quickly. Amateur singers generally think that high notes can only be sung with a tremendous rush of air, but the exact opposite is true. The flow of air can be compared to the pipes of an organ; low-note pipes are long and wide and need much air in order to sound. If one attempts to force the same amount of air through the tiny narrow pipe for a high note, the resulting sound will be overblown and diffused. High notes require a very small amount of highly controlled air, so little that a great tenor can hold a candle in front of his mouth while singing a high a and the flame will not flicker. This cannot be achieved without excruciatingly hard work which the great singer can entirely disguise, offering the audience an illusion of soaring transcendence.

This ruse of operatic performance, so fundamental to the impression and achievement of opera, did not happen, as Koestenbaum so ably describes, with Callas. She does not make singing sound fluid or soaring but forces us to suffer along with the deficiencies in her voice, her gulps for breath, and her projection of the flaws; as Koestenbaum puts it, she "put forth the effect of nature as opposed to the appearance of order, and offered an acceptable, digestible anarchy, a set of sounds on the verge of chaos – but enjoyably so. Here lay the danger, the lure: she was a mess *and* she was a goddess.... Enjoying Callas's muffled voice [sounding, according to record producer Walter Legge, as though she were singing into a bottle], one declared affinity with hidden things." Her upper register wobbled, and "we loved the mistakes because they seemed autobiographical, because without mediation or guile they wrote a naked heart's wound.... The infallible performance does not require an audience.... Callas's unattractive sounds forced her audience to reevaluate the difference between the beautiful and the grotesque... she outstares the ugliness, dares it to ruin her good time."[4] In the end she achieved something apparently contrary to the expectations of opera: "Superficially, Maria Callas took away opera's campiness by making it believable and vivid. And yet by importing truth into opera, an art of the false, she gave the gay fan a dissonance to match his own."[5]

Earlier in *The Queen's Throat*, Koestenbaum describes a scene from *The Lisbon Traviata* which has some bearing on Andrew's opera scene in *Philadelphia*:

A tableau of two throats, Maria Callas's and the opera queen's, ends *The Lisbon Traviata*. While Callas, on record, spins "an elaborate web of coloratura," Stephen, the opera queen, whose lover has just abandoned him, "throws his head back with her as she reaches for a climactic high note, but no sound comes out.... Stephen's mouth is open, his head is back, his eyes are closed. Callas is all we can hear." By lip-synching to Callas, the opera queen is not brought closer to the magical realm of the vocal, the articulate, the expressive, or the open-hearted. In fact, the tableau convinces us that a passion for Callas has closed the queen's throat, has taken away his power to love. While no sound "comes out" of the queen's throat... Callas on record is singing Violetta, the consumptive courtesan. Stephen may regret that he can't follow Callas into her hedonistic coloratura, but the subtext of *Traviata* reminds us that pleasure will kill Violetta as surely as, in homophobic scenarios of AIDS, it has killed gays.[6]

In *Philadelphia*, Andrew moves from commentary to ventriloquism, eventually lip-synching Callas as "La mamma morta" moves into its climax. He too becomes physically engulfed in the aria, pacing, throwing his head back, gesturing and grimacing, showing the full pain of her sustained high b on his face. Like Violetta he must face a painful death, but here the comparison ends. We do not hear the voice of Violetta, the consumptive courtesan; Demme recreates Madeleine, perhaps shell-shocked, but still able to put her death to a worthy cause. From the depths of despair, she rallies all her spiritual energy, enough to convince her that not only does God exist but God will envelop her with love and transport her to where she can be oblivious to her corporeal suffering. Andrew too, finds this state. He, of course, is no opera queen indulging an old obsession; his response to opera here penetrates as far as can be possible, entirely free of camp or extravagance. Maria Callas provides the entry to that state as her voice finds all the pain in his suffering yet transports him to the place of ecstasy that only her uniquely contradictory voice can find.

If Andrew, like Madeleine, discovers love, the viewer will still recognize this as opera, and only in opera (or a film by Demme which imitates opera) could love be found under such circumstances. Contrary to the homophobic society which wishes to discard people such as himself, Andrew finds himself surrounded by a network of friends, family, a companion and physicians who offer him nothing but love and support. The enemy in this case lives in the hearts of bosses, their henchmen and the corporate structure in general. Few viewers of this film will likely be taken in by this state of grace among his circle – especially his family. At least one reviewer, nonplussed by the excessive goodness and tolerance of these people, could not "help wishing the Addams Family would drop in for drinks. Is Demme really suggesting that AIDS sufferers across the nation are sitting around with their siblings and boyfriends, bottle-feeding the youngest generation?"[7] If this is opera (i.e. fantasy), the predetermined conclusion may be even more so; could one imagine the case being lost, or the inevitable death of the protagonist not happening? Of course, we could not leave the cinema with a live Andrew, any more than we could depart the opera house with a living Madeleine; the audience cannot be cheated of the requisite deaths in either case. Demme, like Andrew, appears to ask his audience if they mind this music – if they like opera, and later, if they can feel it. We may shrug our shoulders like Joe, but Demme gives us no chance to answer in the negative – the central emotional effectiveness of the film depends on receptiveness to the possibility. People who normally would scoff at opera and all its trappings, including the most youthful element in the audience, will likely have to confess that this scene moved them and that they could feel its impact spreading throughout the film.

$$\boxed{23}$$

OPERA OBSESSION

Beyond the category of opera lover there exists a much more intense and all-consuming category: opera obsession. This phenomenon is no stranger to the screen, exposing audiences to these bizarre fanatics who need opera as much as they need air to breathe. For them opera is a religion in its most extreme form, offering an intense spiritual and euphoric experience that all but defies description. This state of being can be so intoxicating to those who experience it that they will readily sacrifice respectability and all sense of normalcy. They will happily indulge in the ultimate state of the irrational, and do extraordinary things to sustain it. Not only art lovers but political scientists as well will recognize vestiges of this phenomenon in the works and ideology of one of the central figures of the 19th century: Richard Wagner. Wagner's operas aim for union of spiritual and sexual rapture, a state that conventional wisdom may condemn as subversive but Tannhäuser and others assure us that these can be sanctioned by the highest religious authority. Not only could these operas arouse religious zealotry but they could also awaken political enthusiasm, as Wagnerian irrationality spawned a political force in Austria and Germany at the end of the 19th century. More recent opera obsession may not be as dangerous, but since it remains every bit as potent, we can do little but observe it in amazement.

Jungle opera

Commerce and technology may seem at odds with irrationality and fanaticism, but they can be taken as means to an end which allow visionaries to reach their operatic goals. Wagner understood this principle perfectly, and persuaded Ludwig II of Bavaria to use his wealth in support of high art. We can also see the principle in action in a cinematic representation, in a film which indulges in the most bizarre form of opera obsession imaginable: *Fitzcarraldo*. Werner Herzog's film may be in German for a European audience, but the idea of a Mecca for opera now goes far beyond the remoteness of Wagner's Bayreuth to one of the most unlikely and strange places on the planet for an opera house: the depths of the Amazonian jungle. Fitzcarraldo (Klaus Kinski) dreams of an opera house in the jungle, and he will stop at nothing to raise the money to achieve it. If people of means will mock or not support him, he will defy them, thumbing his nose at their respectability. He recklessly engages in an impossible business venture filled with danger from hostile natives who have no other use for Europeans than as a source for shrunken heads. This venture involves the improbable scheme of dragging a ship over a mountain, which he succeeds in doing with the help of the natives who would have mounted his head too had they not regarded his ship as a potentially sacred vessel. The scheme may actually have succeeded had it not been for the fact that the natives had a vision even more irrationally compelling than his. They held a consuming spiritual aspiration to ride through the Pongo rapids, which no one had previously done and survived (Fitzcarraldo's point in hauling the ship over the mountain was to avoid these rapids); while he and his remaining crew sleep off their drunken celebration after reaching the adjoining river, the natives set the ship on its unstoppable course downstream. They could not have cared less about his dream and helped him only to achieve their own divine joyride.

Fitzcarraldo's superhuman actions to reach his geographic goal parallel his *idée fixe* about opera. The film opens with his arrival in Rio to hear Caruso sing at the opera house; he has rowed hundreds of miles up Amazonian rivers to get there, and shows an incredulous attendant his bloodied hands. Nothing will stop him and his brothel madam companion (Molly, played by Claudia Cardinale) from entering. This may be the last opportunity of his life to hear Caruso, and he refuses to face death without this experience. When Caruso appears to point at him in an on-stage gesture, he takes this as a sign that he has been chosen by divine forces to build his opera house in the jungle. As he returns down the river to his territory, he listens in rapt concentration to a cylinder of Caruso singing the role of Pagliacci.

Fitzcarraldo (Klaus Kinski plays Caruso singing Verdi to calm the natives)

His opera in the jungle dream consumes him completely, and attempts to find backers prove fruitless, in spite of Molly's ability to bring all the wealthy men of the region to one place at the same time. In a moment of madness and desperation, we see him in the belfry of the church frantically ringing the bells; he proclaims that the church will remain closed until he gets his opera. Now the religion of opera directly confronts the religion of God. For him an opera house is a cathedral which would be erected to the highest of all religions, and the religion of churches must surrender. He fares no better with towns-folk than he does with business leaders, and the police throw him into jail as a common drunkard.

He acquires a ship through a backer bemused by his passion (who also hopes to gain information about his competitors in the rubber business), and heads upstream into menacing territory. Most of the crew deserts at the first sound of the headhunters' drums. In a moment of inspiration he plays a phonograph cylinder of his favorite singer performing his favorite composer: Caruso singing Verdi. The drumbeat stops and the natives become friendly, and he deludes himself into thinking that opera achieved it – that these natives now share his oper-atic quest. He has, he may well think, become like Verdi himself, as the *Risorgimento* force who rallied the Italians into rebellion against their Austrian oppressors in the middle of the 19th century. If opera could make Italy into a nation, surely it could tame savage breasts and con-quer the hostile jungle. One of his earlier tormentors had called him a "conquistador of the useless," and he had responded by fingering this naysayer's "world as a caricature of grand opera." The river through the jungle may be full of illusions, but aside from the suspension of disbelief this has little in common with opera. In the end the only opera in the jungle takes place as a floating performance of *I Puritani* aboard the rapids-battered ship which no longer belongs to Fitzcarraldo; enjoying a fine cigar and red chair for that performance will have to suffice for his obsession.

Mixed gender

While opera obsession easily becomes confused with religion, it has an even more peculiar relationship with sex, and this transports us back to the very origins of opera. As one might suspect, just as the notion of opera as a surrogate religion touches on subversion, the connections with sexuality similarly prove somewhat less than wholesome. We may like to think of operas from the 17th and 18th centuries as grand artistic works loved because of their dramatic intelligibility, but certainly at the time no one thought of it in that way. In the balance of singers and composers there was no contest: singers reigned supreme, commanding astronomical salaries, and composers had to take the scraps thrown to them. Castrati and divas singing their signature tunes (arias) in the wrong operas did not bother anyone, and in fact audience members might actually interrupt their other activities to listen at those points. Needless to say, with arias regularly popping up from other opera, integrity of the artistic work did not interest many in the audience or managers; operatic pastiche became the order of the day.[1]

Opera singers of the 17th and 18th centuries shared much in common with pop stars of the present, in more ways than one. Aside from the popularity and the obscenely large amounts of money they could make, they also stood out with their extravagant costumes and (for male stars) their high voices. High voice does not mean tenors or countertenors but castrati, singers who had been castrated before puberty on the outside chance that they might develop into great singers (the odds were considerably less than 1%, and most ended up in chapel choirs or domestic service as eunuchs). Parents caught having this done to their boys faced the penalty of excommunication, and stories abounded of riding accidents and a host of other more bizarre explanations. Charles Burney, the noted 18th-century music historian, tried to discover where the "surgery" took place, and while he suspected Naples, he could not verify it.[2]

For those who did succeed, fame and fortune awaited them, although their lives turned out to be much less glamorous than some have suggested. Casanova, for one, told fantastical tales of castrati who looked like women, playing boudoir games with pursuers fascinated by which sex they would discover. He also told of castrati who had sired children, although he produced very flimsy proof for this impossible achievement.[3] Again cinema has made its comment, with the very popular *Farinelli* (1994), giving us a remarkably insightful picture of what operatic life may have been like in the early 18th century – one suspects a more accurate view than some of the stodgy textbooks on the history of opera deliver. Once we get beyond the fact that this film makes no claim to biographical accuracy in its depiction of Farinelli we can envisage something of the adulation, humiliation, the sexual exploits, costumes, and the spectacle which surrounded castrati and opera at the time.

From the inception of opera, sexual identification has proved delightfully troublesome. The great heroes of antiquity and mythology were represented by peculiar castrated beings with long arms and legs, narrow waists, and sweet high voices;[4] here there had to be suspension of disbelief in the extreme. By the end of the 18th century, the twilight of the castrati had come, but that by no means put an end to the presence of sexual ambiguity in opera. For one of his most famous operas, *The Marriage of Figaro*, Mozart wrote the role of the adolescent boy Cherubino for a woman. In Act 2, we have a woman playing the role of a boy who must get into a woman's disguise – a woman impersonating a woman. If we are unclear who should be attracted to her, that parallels the confusion of the characters in the opera. The Countess indulges Cherubino (even more so than in the Beaumarchais play, and we have every right to question if the Countess prefers the male or female Cherubino). When the Count attempts to land a kiss on Susanna's cheek in the darkened garden of Act 4, it catches Cherubino instead, now in male garb. Over a century later Richard Strauss had exactly this character in mind with his Octavian in *Rosenkavalier*. Even in one of the most serious of operas, Beethoven's *Fidelio*, the plot depends on the cross-dressing Leonore being mistaken as the male Fidelio, prompting confusion in Act 1 which leads to a proposal of marriage from the hapless Jacquino.

In an art form with so much confusion about gender, it should not surprise us that this has spilled over into some of its cinematic representations, and that the peculiar treatment of sexuality in these films should sometimes take on an obsessive quality. One of these films, *M Butterfly*, a reworking of Puccini's *Madam Butterfly* with a gender twist (as the title implies), takes us through a combination of naiveté and obsession which requires so much suspension of disbelief that it could only be an opera. A French diplomat in Beijing hears a Chinese diva sing a famous aria from *Madam Butterfly*, and he becomes hooked, in part because of his embarrassed acceptance of the Western double standard of European (or American) men trifling with Oriental women. His pre-occupation with the diva becomes representative of Western attitudes in general, and unlike Pinkerton, the American naval officer in the opera, he will have to pay dearly. In the opera Cho-Cho-San adores her American admirer too naively; in the film the fascination of René Gallimard (Jeremy Irons) with the diva (John Lone) turns into obsession, so much so that he loses his grasp of reality; in short, it becomes an opera obsession. The audience eventually discovers that the diva is not a woman but a drag queen. Gallimard does not discover this until his trial some years later when the French government charges him with passing state secrets on to his Chinese lover. In the meanwhile, the diva produces a child which he/she claims to be Gallimard's off-spring, and while the mode of sexual intercourse may have been ingenious, an incredulous court (and audience) marvels at his apparent ignorance of basic anatomy – to say nothing of the fact that he has never seen his lover's naked body.

Gender confusion reigns supreme here. Gallimard assures us of his heterosexuality – not by his relationship with his wife but instead by sexual activities with female diplomats. He develops a fetish for a female impersonator, never questioning the ruse. When he finally sees his error and must endure the humiliation of notoriety, he reverses the gender role, becoming Cho-Cho-San in a finale prison performance, playing her music and transforming himself into her with kimono and heavy makeup. For his (now her) finale, he produces a shard of mirror and punctures his throat, making his exit in suicide as Cho-Cho-San does in the opera. Yet the viewer will remain unclear on a couple of points. Does he commit suicide because of humiliation, loss of the object of his obsession, or because of confusion about gender? We may also question why the diva had to be a female impersonator (aside from the fact that a real incident gave rise to this story and when life appears stranger than fiction, it should not be altered). If the object was espionage, presumably that could have been accomplished more successfully by a real woman whose duplicity would then not have to extend beyond politics to gender. Something else appears to be at work in David Cronenberg's film/opera; with the gender confusion he takes the audience not only into the world of opera but also into the bizarre, decadent and sexually ambiguous side of opera as well, an art form built on a castrated foundation in the 17th and 18th centuries. The apparent model may be an opera by Puccini, but the essence reverts back to a much earlier time.

Opera may be something much more than an innocent diversion which appeals to dedicated opera lovers and people in positions of authority: it can be subversive, dangerous and even fatal. Perhaps something lurks beneath the surface, the sort of thing that Oscar Wilde recognized in the Preface to *The Picture of Dorian Gray*: "All art is at once surface and symbol. Those who go beneath the surface do so at their peril." In his own *Salome* Wilde gives us surface and symbol, exposing a world of perversion – the obsession of Herod for Salome's body and the obsession of Salome for Jokanaan's (John the Baptist's) body – but deflecting our attention away from that with ripe, sensual, beautiful images, verbal parallels to the visual images of Aubry Beardsley used to illustrate the first English edition. One can perhaps even picture Sarah Bernhardt in the leading role giving a performance of such beauty so as not to cause revulsion at her kissing the lips of a decapitated head, nor questioning of Herod's final order to have her crushed beneath his attendant's shields. Of course she behaves as a degenerate, and when Richard Strauss transformed the play into an opera, he took us with his music beneath the surface, vocally and symphonically indulging in the most nether and dissolute regions. Now with a blunt object he explodes Wilde's images, and forces us to wallow in Herod's lust with the protracted dance of the seven veils, and Salome's perversity as she musically defiles the great prophet.

Camp

Cinema has strayed into perverse regions as well, although when it does we may be more inclined to think of it as camp than its operatic models such as *Salome*. In fact, at its most campy, cinema aspires to an operatic state thoroughly detached from reality. The ultimate camp film, the *Rocky Horror Picture Show*, can best be described as a rock opera – a fusion of the most popular forms of entertainment from the 19th and 20th centuries. Not only is the film operatic in its treatment of the unreal, the character types, the grand gestures and the nature of the conflict, but the plot itself will be known to some opera enthusiasts. We tend not to associate Franz Schubert – the great composer of songs, chamber music, sonatas and symphonies – with opera but in fact he wrote operas fairly prolifically. One of his first operas, *Des Teufels Lustschloss* (*The Devil's Pleasure Palace*) uses a virtually identical plot to the *Rocky Horror Picture Show*. The opera opens with newlyweds traveling to their new home, and when a wheel on their wagon breaks late in the day they must seek shelter for the night. They end up at a haunted castle, and an endless stream of horrors descends on them. Their tormentors may not be as kinky as a Tim Curry in drag, but they come close with the likes of Amazons. In the end, we discover that the bride's uncle inflicted these tortures because he wished to test the valor of his niece's new husband. Was Schubert indulging in camp here, something that recent discoveries have shown he very much enjoyed?[5]

Associations with *Salome* may lead in a different direction, although attempts to be serious with this type of subject matter in cinema may simply point to another type of camp. None could be stranger that Patrick Conrad's *Mascara* (1987), a film that takes us from the respectability of the Brussels opera house to the depraved underbelly of the city, where pillars of the community play obsessive and dangerous opera games in the bowels of the earth – tunnels constructed during World War II. Not only does Conrad give us the descent to regions beneath the surface, a darkened staircase with an infernal red glow at the end of the passage – and deeper penetration into the earth via a freight elevator, but when we reach the lowest level of this decadent Hades, he treats us to a lip-sync version of Salome's encounter with the head of Jokanaan by a diva impersonator.

Conrad serves up an international array of actors – Charlotte Rampling, Michael Sarrazin and Derek de Lint – in the worst imaginable roles, acted so badly one may be inclined to think of Harrison Ford in *Star Wars*. In this opera within an opera within an opera, it could not be otherwise: normal acting would be self-defeating since it might stifle the illusion of opera. Sarrazin plays the chief of police who not only loves to go to the opera with his sister (Rampling), indulging the great loves of his life (his sister and opera), but belongs to the decadent, underworld club where anything goes – including dangerous liaisons with transsexuals. Even murder has no moral stigma here, committed by the chief of police; in fact, the only moral imperative seems to be the fear of getting caught. The denizens of this club, it appears, include at least half the leaders of the community, men with such a consuming passion for opera that they are not merely satisfied to enjoy it at the opera house but must live it out themselves.

That indulgence takes them into the material of opera which most respectable viewers can ignore, into the depravity of Salome and Lulu, the rage of Elektra, the evil of Scarpio, the seductions of Faust, or the madness of Norma. And most of all, they love spectacle – to be part of it for a few glorious moments; a dazzling gown for Euridice generates the spectacle and forms a link between the high opera of Brussels and the depraved opera of the underworld. Here we have a rare form of camp, a police-chief opera queen as vicious murderer – a creature far too nasty to understand self-parody. What should we make of this? Should parents not let their children attend opera lest they may turn out this way? Can opera be a dangerous fetish comparable to drugs? Did Patrick Conrad simply come up with a very bad idea and execute it dreadfully? If this is where Strauss ultimately takes us when he mucks about beneath the surface, then we should be grateful to Oscar Wilde who has the sense to leave things at the surface and symbol level.

We may wish to dismiss Conrad's film as the bizarre effort of a minor director, but Stanley Kubrick takes us down the same obsessively perverse path with his final film *Eyes Wide Shut* (1999). The obsessive indulgence here, the sexual rite Dr. Bill Harford (Tom Cruise) cannot restrain himself from attending, takes place not only in Venetian carnival masks and costumes, but those wishing to enter must utter the password "Fidelio" – the title of Beethoven's one opera. Kubrick worked with a conception so fundamentally operatic that normal acting would simply interfere. Like the famous quartet near the beginning of *Fidelio*, Kubrick opted for a tempo of *andante sostenuto*, making his leads speak so slowly that the result may be in danger of yielding eyes completely shut in the audience before Nicole Kidman utters her next word. Perhaps we should not regard this as spoken dialogue at all but as something akin to singing, suggesting that Kubrick had an underlying musical idea and through tortured vocal elongation implemented an operatic conception of Arthur Schnitzler's *Traumnovelle* (*Dream novel*).

Pirated voice

The obsession with Euridices's gown in *Mascara* reflects back on a much more successful opera obsession film of a few years earlier, Jean-

Jacques Beineix's *Diva* (1982). Here we have an actual diva in a leading role, Wilhelmenia Wiggins Fernandez in both singing (an aria from Catalani's *La Wally*) and speaking roles, but the film focuses more on her gown and the forbidden electronic reproduction of her voice. A young admirer obsessed with her – a motor bike-riding postal worker – not only steals her gown but also makes a pirate tape of her in recital, a valuable commodity because she refuses to make recordings. Devoted fans of Maria Callas will, of course, understand the scenario; possessing the unique gown allows this inconsequential youth an exclusive entry into her world, and possessing her voice, something that only he has, allows an even bolder invasion of her. But his fascination appears not to be sexual; he genuinely admires her as an opera lover, and when he gets to know her and she adopts him almost as a pet, he returns the gown and the voice. The cassette of her voice becomes confused with a cassette which is incriminating to a prominent but corrupt police inspector, and the post boy must contend not only with her potential wrath but also the need of the inspector and his criminal cronies to eliminate him and the tape. Opera once again proves dangerous, now through the association of an illicit vocal tape and an explosive criminal tape.

The diva in *Diva* has strong views on the issue of recording. She loves to sing, which she cannot do alone, but depends on an audience for energy. She regards a concert as something special, a privileged moment: "don't try to keep it," she remarks in English. Recording has no artistic value for her. She can see recording as nothing more than a commercial venture, and like Fitzcarraldo, she firmly believes that commerce must adapt itself to art – not art to commerce. She finds commercial recording objectionable and pirated performances as something much worse, comparable to rape and robbery.

Before Beineix used Fernandez in *Diva* there had been a long tradition of opera singers in speaking and/or singing roles in films, and this phenomenon was explored in chapter 4; another unusual case will be explored in the next chapter. Unique in this case is the fact that whereas such roles normally went to famous divas or tenors, few people knew of Fernandez before this film, and in fact the film played a major part in launching her career. Her appeal then did not arise from fame, but worked in various other ways. As an African American she brought an element of the foreign and the mysterious to a French film, and she had to be convincing as an actor, in which she succeeded. But most of all, she brought her voice as her greatest asset, a captured voice which the plot makes illicit. Enjoying her voice as an illicit pleasure, as we can with the post boy Jules, adds a wonderful dimension to the film, allowing us to pick the forbidden operatic fruit.

24

SURROGATE VOICE:
MARIA CALLAS AS MEDEA

Cecil B. DeMille knew he had a recipe for success in 1915 when he took the most famous American diva of the time and put her on screen in a role that people already associated her with from an opera. The screen Carmen played by Geraldine Farrar differed from Bizet's *Carmen*, but no one could mistake the connection, considering Farrar's operatic background. In fact, as I argued in chapter 1, Farrar not only dignified the screen with her presence, but DeMille provided a type of surrogate voice in silent cinema, allowing her to "sing" through her facial gestures. The arousal of emotions here depended on something that went beyond the visual images themselves – a transferral to the screen of the emotions the great diva would bring as a singer. We may not actually hear the sound of her voice, in fact an impossibility in 1915, but by association we nevertheless do hear, adding in our mind's ear the sounds that her distinctive voice would bring from Bizet's opera.

Considering the success of *Carmen*, one would expect other film-makers to follow suit, bringing already established stars of opera to the screen. Numerous other opera singers took leading roles in cinema, as chapter 4 makes clear, but almost invariably these films featured the operatic life, placing singers in roles that glamorize the world of opera, and most importantly, allowed them to do what they do best: sing. The idea of a singer in a non-singing role proved to be something of a dead end. One could argue that after Farrar no opera singers came along with the right combination of qualities of dramatic ability, intriguing personality, physical appearance, and general popularity necessary to make the transition from the opera stage to the screen. In most cases, the type of stage presence demanded by opera would have disadvantaged them as film actors; accustomed to exaggerated stage gestures, they often lacked the flexibility to adjust to the requirements of the screen.

It took roughly half a century for another diva to come along who could make the transition and in fact she did it only once. Unlike the numerous opera stars in cinematic singing roles, Maria Callas appeared in the leading role of one film in which she plays a non-singing part; this did not lead to what she hoped might be a new career, and it did not open the door to anyone else from her profession to make the transition. The latter point should not surprise us: Maria Callas was one of a kind, and her invitation from a major director happened because of her unique qualities. When the invitation came in the late 1960s, no other woman anywhere could rival her fame; the world adulated her because of a combination of dramatic talent, striking beauty, intriguing personality, and lifestyle. Not only did she reign supreme in the sphere of opera, but if we use paparazzi as the measure of fame, she had no serious rivals in any other area as well.

If she had made her cinematic debut in Hollywood, her notoriety would have been considered her primary asset, and it would have been exploited to market the film. For Pier Paolo Pasolini, the Italian director who cast her in his *Medea* (1970), a work unlikely to capture the popular imagination, her fame was of little or no consequence. She may have hoped in the late 1960s for a new vehicle to keep her in the public eye without having to use her voice, which suffered all the worst symptoms of neglect after its long fallow period; if she entertained such an aspiration, she based it on ignorance and misunderstanding of Pasolini's type of cinema. It appears that she went into his film expecting Hollywood, but instead she encountered an exceptionally high quality art cinema, which, because of its subject matter and the nature of its images, could not possibly appeal to a mass audience. Unlike Fellini and Antonioni, or even Zeffirelli and Visconti (both of whom Callas knew well), Pasolini's fascination with more esoteric aspects of mythology and indulgence in the realm of taboo kept him out of the mainstream not only in North America but Europe as well.

Pasolini's *Medea* has received a considerable amount of negative press, not only from Callas supporters disappointed that it did not advance her career, but also from some writers on Pasolini, who seemed miffed by his choice of Callas for the leading role and the static nature of the film. The film's producer Franco Rossellini suggested the possibility of using her to Pasolini and considering Pasolini's negative view of opera and its fans, she would not have readily come to mind to him. His own homosexuality did not place him among those who gravitated toward opera, and in fact he spoke sarcastically of it being "queenish to carry on about the opera."[1] In all probability his disdain had more to do with opera's admirers than opera itself, for as his friendship with Callas blossomed, so did his appreciation of a composer such as Verdi, whom he finally recognized as a great talent. As for Callas, eager earlier in her career to develop as a dramatic singer, she had allowed herself to be shaped by Visconti in his stage productions of the operas *La Vestale*, *La Traviata*, and *La Sonnambula*, and Pasolini knew therefore that she could work under intensive direction.[2] Considering what he wanted from her as Medea, her life in the world of opera proved to be her greatest asset.

Pasolini also knew perfectly well – in Italy he could not help but know – that Callas had recreated the operatic role of Medea, reviving the opera of that name by Luigi Cherubini, a work this Italian composer had premiered as a French opera in Paris in 1797. *Medea* has had few modern revivals, but for the dramatically intense Callas, who thrived in roles of women in the grip of madness or obsession, it seemed to be a natural. Instead of the original French version with connecting spoken dialogue, she opted for an Italian translation with added recitatives by the 19th-century German composer Franz Lachner. These accompanied recitatives change the work profoundly from Cherubini's original, and Callas, more interested in drama than authenticity, told *The Sunday Times* in a interview that she considered the recitatives the most important parts of *Medea*. This *Medea* received its premiere at the Florence Festival in 1953 under the direction of Tullio Serafin, and went to La Scala later that year with Leonard Bernstein as conductor and Visconti as stage director (Bernstein insisted on cutting one of her arias, and she, accepting his artistic judgement, did not protest). Callas appeared regularly in the role until 1961 at opera houses throughout the world, including Covent Garden in London and at the Dallas Civic Opera. She recorded it with the La Scala company for Mercury Records under Serafin's direction in 1957.

The opera, as the title clarifies, tells Medea's story and not Jason's. The parts of the myth involving Jason's quest for and retrieval of the

Golden Fleece, the broken promise of Pelias to hand power of Thessaly over to Jason, and Jason's departure for Corinth to court Glauce, daughter of King Creon, have no place here. Cherubini begins with Medea's arrival in Corinth and her angry confrontation with Creon and Jason; Creon banishes her and Medea tries to persuade Jason to return to her, which he refuses. Creon not only banishes her but takes her (and Jason's) children from her as well, but he agrees to postpone her exile for one day. She needs no more than that day to set her plan of revenge into action. She sends gifts of jewelry and a diadem to Glauce, but dips them in poison which will cause death when they contact skin. She completes her vengeance by murdering her own sons in a temple and setting the temple ablaze so the bodies cannot be retrieved. She perishes in the fire, but her own death seems inconsequential to her.

Cherubini, a very astute composer, whom Beethoven regarded as the best living composer next to himself, understood the potential of the subject for opera. Here stood a woman from a primitive culture, living among civilized Greeks whose ways she did not understand, a woman who had the powers of sorcery and a boundless capacity for passion and vengeance. In opera, we do not need explanations for her actions any more than Verdi needs to provide motives for Iago's demonic deeds in *Otello*. Medea stands as a type of operatic precursor to Iago; no amount of Freudian analysis will explain her heinous crimes, especially the infanticide. Opera can take a character such as this from mythology and present her to us as a raw, unadulterated barbarian who does evil because of her evil nature.

The memory of Callas's performance of the role survives in the Mercury recording. Reviewers could not agree, and they never could about her singing, some complaining about the swallowed tone and the distracting strain in the upper register, while others rhapsodized about the compelling drama in the voice itself.[3] As Wayne Koestenbaum so ably recognized (discussed in chapter 22), what some reviewers regretted about her voice proved to be her greatest asset. When her voice makes the listener feel uncomfortable, when we think she may come unstuck because of the tormented sound on a sustained high note or what seems like ventriloquism in the lower register – a voice produced in an unidentifiable foreign object – her piercing edge adds an intensity to the character which could not come through any normal mode of *bel canto* singing.[4] On this recording that painful sound stands in marked contrast to the flowing, glorious tone of the young Renata Scotto as Glauce, convincing the listener that Medea's anguish cannot be compared to that of anyone else. And since that agonized sound of Callas is such a personal one, resulting from her own distinctive vocal insecurity, we can, without knowing anything of the person herself, identify the distress of the role with the woman singing it, not for a moment doubting her complete ability to feel these intense emotions.

There can be little question that Pasolini sensed these things about Callas, since everything about her in his *Medea* not only has an aura of the operatic but suggests the raw anguish of her vocal emotions. In fact, the coming together of Pasolini and Callas proved to be a highly charged event for both of them. Just as she could not play a role without putting herself into it, he too did not make films that lacked personal significance, dealing with painful subjects – even those from classical mythology – that came from deep within himself. In the case of *Medea* that appeared to begin for him as a struggle between the polar forces of rational, enlightened and pragmatic thought on the one hand, and notions of irrationality, superstition and primitive religion on the other; here he wished to indulge his own inclination for the latter and the apparent impossibility of it in a civilized society.[5] As he got to know Callas better, something else happened, although his reading of it may have differed from hers. A strong affection developed between the two of them, and despite her dislike for Marxists and homosexuals, both of which he was, she found in him not only a friend but something stronger – a brother, as she noted after his death.[6] For his part, Pasolini indulged an even deeper affection, verifying it in his own poetry, thinking of her as an illicit lover with whom he cheats not only on his wife but also his gay lover. Callas the woman and Callas the darling of gay opera lovers could inspire both types of sexual fantasy, making his feelings about her all the more illicitly complex. His poetic/sexual fantasy about her went to the point on one occasion of his intuiting a request for love from her, and that request was embodied in her gift of singing.[7] Curiously then, in the making of *Medea*, Pasolini, if not to some extent Callas herself, lived out some aspects of the complex relationship between Medea and Jason.

The feeling that Pasolini had for Callas seemed intimately tied up with her voice, in which he recognized a sensuality he could not resist; regardless of how that played out in personal terms, it formed the basis of the role she would play in the film. He called her "little bird with the powerful voice of an eagle/ a trembling eagle." In response to the request for love he believed she made, he answered with verse:

I pretend to receive;
I thank you, sincerely grateful.
But the weak fleeting smile
is not of timidity;
it is dismay, more terrible, much more terrible
than having a separate body in the realms of being —
whether it is a sin
whether it is only an accident: but in place of the Other
for me there is a void in the cosmos
a void in the cosmos
and from there you sing.

Linking Callas with Medea, she "accompanied him toward the infernal gods of opera and song: bringing with you that odor from beyond the tomb, you sing arias composed by Verdi that have turned blood-red and the experience of it (without a word being uttered) teaches sweetness, true sweetness."[8] Here we have no ordinary director/actor relationship, but instead a highly complex fusion of personal, mythic and poetic elements.

In his *Medea*, Pasolini recasts the myth so that it becomes his personal myth. Primary forces stand in conflict to each other, and the opening of the film introduces us to these forces individually. The centaur represents one side: he is verbal, reasonable and full of advice for the infant and youthful Jason. Like an enlightened teacher he educates Jason, equipping him intellectually for the world he must live in, and part of that education includes the awareness that one day he will discover something fundamentally different from his own rational Greek culture. This centaur talks incessantly, in both his animal and human forms, defining himself with words, syntax and logic, appealing to the intellect, demonstrating the role of language in the definition of a sophisticated society.

The camera suddenly takes us to Colchis, a primitive society inhabiting a primitive landscape, a non-verbal society where communication takes primordial forms of rites and rituals that recognize forces higher than the self, a deification of nature in which nature must be blessed for it to be cooperative. That blessing takes the most extreme possible form, of human sacrifice, and we see a youth ritually slain, dismembered and his body parts and blood rubbed on trees and plants to invoke growth. Along with the primitive people and landscape, Pasolini provides the appropriate sound background, of drones and wailing that induce trance-like states. In the midst of this ritual sacrifice we catch our first glimpse of Medea, daughter of the Colchian king, Aeetes, cloaked in distinctive garb with heavy layers of beads. Medea, we quickly discover, communes better with nature – her atavistic god – than she does with humans; her powers of sorcery which appear as demonic to the Greeks in fact derive from a deep respect for and religious awe of nature, whose power she can summon through unification with it. Completely out of her element in rational Greece, she gradually loses all, including her husband Jason. Only when she reverts to her primitive dress and rituals can she regain any measure of control.

In the clash of cultures represented in the film, Pasolini betrays his own nostalgia for the primitive one; he regrets that in the process of civilizing Europe from antiquity through the Enlightenment to the present, much of value has been lost. The greatest casualty has been religion, not the formalized one with its church hierarchy, but a much less definable one which allows for the irrational, where one respects if not worships nature, where intuitive emotions stand higher than logic and jurisprudence, in short, where humanity can relive the wonders of mythology and discover a poetic essence. The selection of Maria Callas to play the character who represents this irrational dimension in fact was a stroke of brilliance. In Pasolini's own words, "here is a woman, in one sense the most modern of women, but there lives in her an ancient woman – strange, mysterious, magical, with terrible inner conflicts."[9]

While he may have been responding to personal qualities he recognized in her, in part this sense of her could not be entirely separated from the world she inhabited, not the world of glamor, adoring fans, and high-profile lovers, but the world of opera. Opera may have given her fame and prestige, but for Callas the world of opera embodied much more than that as she put her entire being on the line in every role she took on. Not just as a soprano but as a dramatic actress she lived her roles in a way that no one before her imagined possible and in so doing transformed the artifice of opera into something intensely stirring and believable. Emotions that could be worn on the sleeve became deep and disturbing in her performances, and she represented the strongest possible realization of passion, obsession and irrationality that opera signifies. Irrationality links opera to the *ancien régime*, challenging the foundations of enlightened thought – something in purely sensual terms that defies logical description. Maria Callas carried the weight of this representation on her shoulders, radiating it in her appearance, and Pasolini could not have found another person on earth more suited for his Medea than her.

Historically, opera has been a recreation of myth and legend, not only through the subject matter used for plots but also in its mode of presentation. Opera may use words, but never in the manner of normal discourse; the words themselves first become molded poetically, and then go through another transformation to something of a purely sensory nature via the singing voice. The ordinary use of words seems too diminished to capture the essence of myth, but presented as music invoking the highest power of the human voice, the mythic level can be reached. Through its sensual qualities cinema too, can approach the mythic, and one way of doing this is to transform itself into opera, in a sense allowing us to experience the glory of the singing voice without it actually being heard. Here too, Callas proved to be the ultimate vehicle for this type of transposition. Not only could most viewers looking at her on the screen hear her extraordinary singing voice, but many could hear her specifically in the role of Medea, agonizing with vocal pain as she confronts each crisis and reverts to her most primitive essence. Now, her speaking voice and even more her physical appearance become the surrogates of the singing voice, allowing us to hear the looks on her face or the gestures of her body. Conscious that the transformation does not happen by playing the role as in opera, Callas constantly sought the director's advice: "Tell me, is this gesture too grand? Too operatic? I know the rhythm of my own movements, but when the camera is moving as well."[10]

For Pasolini the effect could best be achieved with her face, and for this he needed close-up shots. The camera becomes Pasolini himself, moving in on the face which enchanted him as much as the rest of the world, but now possessing that image as Jason does in the early stages. The passion that he felt for her brought together his sense of her as a modern but ancient woman, her mystery and magic and the engendering of these in looks and voice. He attempted to capture the mysterious power of her voice in his own poetry, as in these lines:

Oh, a terrible fear.
Happiness explodes
against those panes over the darkness.
But this happiness, which makes you sing *in voce*,
is a return from death.[11]

He too felt the distress in her voice. Pasolini thought of acts of writing poetry and making films as similar, and just as he projects her voice metaphorically to find a poetic vitality, he does the same in his film, now needing only her face to activate it.

In the clash of two worlds in *Medea*, an attempt to transform the ancient, primitive woman into a modern, enlightened woman occurs. Medea cannot adjust to the new ways, to disregard the power of nature and endure the absence of religion, but she has been a willing participant in the transfer, as she steals the Golden Fleece for Jason, divesting it of its sacred powers. She even sacrifices her own brother to their escape from Colchis. Having lost everything of value from her past, her only hope now lies in love. In notes made before shooting started which he showed to Callas, Pasolini explained the transformation as follows:

> Medea watches Jason, enchanted, lost in him. It is a true and complete love; in this moment it is Jason's virility that prevails. Medea has lost her dazed manner, like a disoriented animal. Suddenly she finds in love which humanizes her a substitute for her lost religious sense. In the sensual experience she finds the lost rapport, the sacred identification with reality. So the world, the future, her well being, the meaning of things, all take shape again suddenly for her. It is with gratitude, like one who feels reborn, that she lets Jason possess her, she in turn possessing in him the regeneration of life.[12]

Taking this into the film, the embraces of Medea and Jason would need to engender much more than mere sexual attraction.

The sacrifice of Medea's brother takes on another dimension as well, since he too succumbs to Jason's enchantment, and Medea quickly puts an end to the possible realization of homo-erotic desire. When Medea and Jason embrace, we see not only Callas's face but part of her body exposed as well, heightening the operatic image with an erotic touch. When Pasolini speaks of her sensuality as a rebirth or a regeneration

Medea (Maria Callas gives a visual impression of singing)

of life, he gives us the same message as in his poetic musing about her voice prompting the experience of "a return from death." Perhaps if Jason had continued to love her she could have lived as a Greek, but he does not, and she, deprived of her only hope for salvation, returns to what she knows best: revenge and human sacrifice. A world of logic remains inaccessible to her, but she could perhaps have entered the modern world through another type of irrational experience, a much gentler one of love. In both, where passion reigns over reason, she stands on solid operatic territory as does the film of the belated opera lover Pasolini.

$$\boxed{25}$$

ORPHEUS REINCARNATED

The legend of Orpheus has been of special interest to both opera and cinema. One can easily see why that would be true of opera since the mythical Orpheus could sing so beautifully that even trees and rocks could not withstand the charms of his voice. When opera emerged as an art at the end of the Renaissance, composers such as Jacopo Peri, Giulio Caccini and the celebrated Claudio Monteverdi all turned instinctively to this legend as their starting point. Singing had taken a brilliant turn at the end of the 16th century, with singers like Caccini having discovered the art of *bel canto* singing, and placing this new vocal weapon into the mouth of Orpheus proved to be an irresistible combination. Over the centuries numerous composers of opera, including Luigi Rossi, Stefano Landi, Joseph Haydn, Christoph Willibald von Gluck, Jacques Offenbach, Ernst Krenek and Darius Milhaud have kept the subject alive, revealing the legend as one that could stir just about any age or generation. Reasons for the appeal of Orpheus to cinema may be a little less clear, but at the point where Krenek and Milhaud left off, many filmmakers have entered. In some cases the films recreate the legend itself, giving it a distinctive 20th-century setting; in others the myth lurks somewhere in the background, suggesting an Orphic treatment. While opera in the 17th and 18th centuries hesitated to follow through to the tragic conclusion of the myth, cinema has been much more prepared to explore the darker side.

A brief recounting of the myth will be useful. Orpheus, son of Apollo and a consummate musician (instructed in the lyre by his father), has married the beautiful young Eurydice. Not long after the marriage, the shepherd Aristaeus, struck by Eurydice's beauty, pursues her and in her flight she steps on a snake which fatally bites her on the foot. Orpheus sings of his grief to all who will hear, but as no one can help him, he descends into the underworld to try to bring her back. Passing through ghosts in the Stygian realm he reaches the throne of Pluto and Proserpine, and sings to them, accompanying himself on the lyre, of his love and grief. He melts their hardness, making even the Furies weep, and Pluto agrees to let him take Eurydice back, but on the condition that he should not look at her until they reach the upper air. They almost succeed, but nearing the return, in a moment of forgetfulness, Orpheus looks back to see if she still follows, and thus, he loses her to death a second time. He tries to release her again, but this time Caronte, the forbidding ferryman of the river Styx, will not let him pass. Eventually he returns to the upper air, avoids all contact with women and sings unceasingly of his grief. When he relentlessly repulses the Thracian women, they turn violent and try to kill him. His singing and playing tame their stones and spears, but when their shrieks drown out his voice, their missiles penetrate the barrier. These fiends tear his body limb from limb, and throw the pieces into the river Hubrus. The Muses bury the body parts, and Jupiter places his lyre among the stars. In death he again passes into the underworld, and now he and Eurydice can roam the Elysian fields together, looking at each other as much as they like.

For filmmakers much potential lies in this myth, but had it not been for opera's recreation of it, that cinematic potential would have been much more difficult to recognize. In opera, Orpheus's voice provided composers with the ultimate challenge to write songs or arias which should move the emotions (or affects early in the 17th century) in the most persuasive way possible. With the advent of the feature-length film, cinema quickly saw moving the emotions as one of its primary objectives (if not its highest purpose), and in that it too could follow the Orphic lead, although not specifically with the voice. A singer like D. W. Griffith could see how that emotional energy could be transferred to visual cinematic images, and DeMille and others soon arrived at the same point. They also recognized how crucial music was in defining and accentuating emotions and cinematic music has for a century now played the role of the lyre of Orpheus in both silent and sound films.

Aside from the fundamental and central place of emotions in cinema, the legend has suggested other possibilities to filmmakers as well, some relating to matters of plot and others to more complex issues of philosophical stance, tone or even form. The most obvious plot type involves the rescue of the damsel in distress in which the hero must pass through what appear to be infernal regions and tests to succeed. The treatment of death in cinema may also be of an Orphic nature, exploring a fascination with death as a temporary state, with the probing of the apparently fine line that separates life and death (or the living from the dead), death with lots of blood, gore and body parts, or the descent into a type of abyss that may be a type of living death. In fact, certain aspects of the Orpheus legend may have spawned an entire genre of death films in Hollywood – fantasy pieces where dead folks continue to be among us. As a formal device, the mirror has become a persistent image of the gateway between life and death, and various directors not only use mirrors as the passageway but also generate larger mirror images or palindromic shapes to structure an entire film, with the central point of the palindrome as the line which divides life and death or states symbolic of them. In a good number of cases, the connection with the operatic Orpheus will be made explicit through various types of operatic images, the most likely being musical quotations of familiar passages from operas such as Gluck's *Orpheus*.

Reel Orpheus

At least two films follow the Orpheus legend with a high degree of accuracy, and both are cinematic masterpieces. The earlier of the two, Jean Cocteau's *Orpheus* (*Orphée*) of 1950, with music by the noted French composer Georges Auric, gives us a poet instead of singer who seems to love death more than his wife. Only when Eurydice dies does Orpheus (Jean Marais) care much about her, for in that way he can probe death as he never has before. Since a beguiling princess (Maria Casarès) personifies death, Orpheus's affection for death takes on a poetic/erotic aspect. Death may seem to have an abrupt and authoritarian manner, but beneath the surface she ultimately reveals herself as a sentimentalist, as in love with Orpheus as he is with her. She visits him as he sleeps and looks longingly at him, wishing to transpose his temporary rest into a permanent one. She plays an active role in the death of both Orpheus and Eurydice, and when they return from the underworld at the end, they do so in a state of death, Orpheus now symbolically unified with his lover Death. At various significant points Death turns on the radio to the sound of "The Dance of the Blessed Spirits" from Gluck's opera *Orpheus*.

Death for the poet turns out to be a disappointingly prosaic state. As Orpheus searches for Eurydice in the underworld, the landscape looks like a cross between a Paris slum and a wasted 19th-century industrial site. The industrial image persists as the Princess Death and her assistant Heurtebise are disciplined by a tribunal which might be a union grievance committee. Neither life nor death prove to be desirable states to Cocteau but the goal in this film of his Orpheus trilogy appears to be the blending of the two. The industrial tribunal in death has its counterparts in life with officiously incompetent police and critics of poetry that include a women's league, publishers of poetry journals, and a new generation of untalented poets, all of whom, with the ferocity of the Thracian women, contribute to Orpheus's demise.

Cocteau's mirror images may not be original, but they certainly are ingenious. When the Princess takes the young dead poet Cégeste to the underworld, she does so through a floor-length mirror. To create an illusion of a mirror that could be passed through, Cocteau used a vat of mercury which a hand could penetrate.[1] Orpheus cannot follow through the mirror and loses consciousness when he attempts it; he comes to in a desolate region lying face down over a reflecting pool. Here he brushes with death and sees enough of his own reflection to set him on a new poetic course. The mirror, as the gateway between life and death, also stands for the poet as the means to look into his inner self, yielding a reflection which may be shrouded in death. When Eurydice returns Orpheus must "beware of mirrors," and she dies again when he catches a glimpse of her through the rear-view mirror of the Rolls, the radio of which transmits garbled and nonsensical messages from the underworld. At the end, he returns to the upper air through a cinematic palindrome – a mirror image – with the film running in reverse; he re-enters his old world through the mirror, now in reverse. The mirror, then, proves to be an image even more powerful than self-reflection in that it also gives symmetrical shape to poetic/cinematic images. In the pursuit of form one also finds the self, and in the process one discovers the balance between life and death.

While Cocteau's images draw from the verbal and poetic, the other Orpheus film is surely one of the most visually beautiful films ever made, Marcel Camus's *Black Orpheus* (*Orfeo negra*) of 1958. This was not the French director Camus's only film by any means, but none of his other films attracted anything close to the attention this one did. Few words need to be used as Camus achieves his ends with the music, colors, costumes and images of carnival in Rio, with bodies that gyrate to the music, the players showing their exuberance and passion as well as fear and dejection through physical gestures and facial expressions. Orpheus (Breno Melo), a streetcar conductor, does what anyone would do before carnival in Rio: he spends his last money on getting his guitar out of a pawn shop, rents his costume, and helps someone who has no money for a costume. The guitar, Orpheus's lyre, becomes a magical image, capable in the minds of two young boys of making the sun rise when played by Orpheus, and also when accompanying his singing of sealing love between Orpheus and the pure and young Eurydice. The magic of the legend itself takes over, cementing a love that even an old cynic who encounters Orpheus recognizes as special.

While Orpheus's singing avoids anything operatic, the stunning visual beauty transports the film into a type of operatic experience. His voice may be appealing in itself, but it gains power through the visual images – the dazzling pageantry, motion, color and gestures of carnival. Camus handles the play of solo and chorus scenes with brilliance, allowing a solo dance from Orpheus to become a duet with Eurydice, all within the swirling confines of the massive carnival chorus. Conflict unfolds in this balance of soloists and chorus as well, as Orpheus's fiancée Mira attempts to break from the chorus into the space of the soloists, and Death (the harasser of Eurydice from her home village wearing a death mask) also emerges from his place in the chorus to terrify the vulnerable Eurydice. Even as Eurydice arrives in Rio and searches for her cousin before Mardi Gras, we see her wending through crowds of revelers, periodically trapped by death-masked celebrators, portending ominously of her future. In the ecstatic joy of the love of Orpheus and Eurydice, the unbearable torment of their separation, the descent into the voodoo-like underworld, and Orpheus's demise at the hands of Mira and her Thracian friends, voices defer to visual cinema at its best, giving us emotions with an intensity otherwise associated with *bel canto* singing.

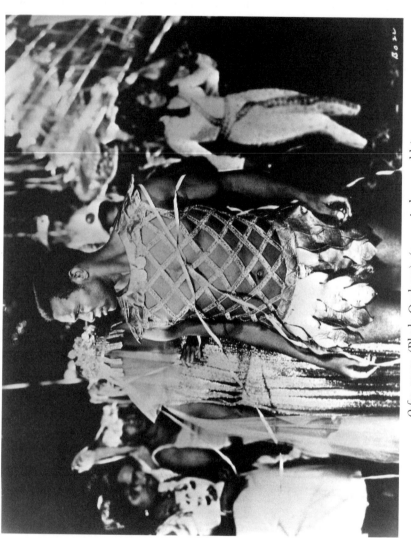

Orfeo negra (Black Orpheus) (a carnival ensemble)

Phantom Orpheus

Other films take various aspects of the Orphic theme, in some cases with strong operatic references, but few with the full exploration of *Orpheus* or *Black Orpheus*. One of the earliest of these, a film already discussed in chapter 3, *Phantom of the Opera* (1925), focuses of course specifically on opera and weaves its plot in an Orphic manner.[2] Here Christine, the budding opera diva, has much in common with Eurydice in that she will be transported to the underworld – a world of death – led by her vocal mentor the Phantom as a figure of death. She enters this realm by passing through her dressing-room mirror, using the means of entry that Cocteau would borrow a quarter of a century later. As they descend deeper into this underworld (the bowels of the Paris Opera House), her grip on consciousness becomes tenuous as the blurred camera shows her eyes glazing over. To get to their final Hades, Christine must be transported over the subterranean lake in a gondola, and the Phantom now becomes the boatman who conducts dead souls across the river Styx, and prevents live ones from going further. When they reach the Phantom's chamber the sense of this as a place of death becomes explicit, as she sees that he sleeps in a vampirish coffin, where sleep reminds him of its more permanent state. She faints, reaching a transitional state of death, and he rushes to her, making an exaggerated operatic gesture of concern as he does.

The role of Orpheus in this case goes to Christine's aristocratic lover Raoul, who must descend into the underworld to rescue her. He does not know how to get through the mirror in her dressing room, but discovers the way from a mysterious police inspector. Raoul, like Orpheus, must cross the river/lake, but not being a singer he lacks the means of going further. A relative of his tries to propel the gondola across, but the Phantom as the unrelenting guard of the underworld prevents that, drowning this unfortunate would-be rescuer in the process. Raoul manages to get to the death chamber by a combination of luck and compromise on Christine's part, but like Orpheus he does not succeed at this point in the rescue attempt.

Outside of his watery, dungeon-like element the Phantom proves much less adept, and poor horsemanship in the realm of the living turns out to be his undoing. His final act, a Mandrake the Magician ruse, pretending to have an explosive substance in his hand, buys precious seconds but nothing more. He meets his demise at the hands of the angry crowd, succumbing to a vicious beating. His maniacal attackers throw his body unceremoniously into the Seine, their actions apparently blessed by the looming figure of Notre Dame Cathedral above them.

Orphic themes

As Cocteau's mirror images suggest, as well as providing the point of entry to the underworld, the mirror can project itself formally as well, as the visual image of a symmetrical or palindromic shape. Otto Preminger takes this possibility to the extreme in his 1944 classic, Laura, and he gives the plot a distinctive Orphic twist. Preminger divides the film into two equal halves, the first acquainting us with Laura (Gene Tierney) whom we presume to be murdered, and the investigating detective MacPherson (Dana Andrews) who develops a crush on her. The second part of the film begins with the return of Laura among the living (someone else, we discover, was murdered in her apartment). As MacPherson probes her personal effects, he in a sense wills her back to life, and he finds her by falling asleep in her apartment, entering a temporary death state to bring her back. Lydecker (Clifton Webb) assumes the role of death, while the duplicitous Carpenter (Vincent Price) plays the role of Aristaeus.

In Laura's apartment MacPherson fantasizes about this beautiful young woman, and as he rummages through her bedroom he looks into mirrors at every turn, as if expecting to see her instead of his own reflection. These mirrors frame the center point of the film – Laura's return to life while MacPherson sleeps – and project a much larger formal mirror as well, the symmetrical shape of the entire film. The film begins with the opening titles over the visual image of Laura's portrait accompanied by David Raksin's famous Laura theme; it ends with the same image and music for the end titles. Moving toward the center, Preminger gives us a symmetrical pattern of Lydecker's voice-over narration, the matching French clocks (one of which hides the murder weapon), and a series of other scenes and use of the Laura melody which take us to her entry as the center point. Lydecker as death comes for Laura as Eurydice near the end, and MacPherson as Orpheus succeeds in thwarting Lydecker's second attempt to murder her. The happy ending here, in deviation from the Orpheus legend, comes closer to the typical operatic treatment of the subject, such as Gluck's, in which the gods allow Eurydice to be rescued a second time. A studio mogul like Darryl Zanuck would have insisted on that type of *deus ex machina*, and thus he plays the hidden role of Apollo.

Numerous other recent films explore various aspects of the Orphic theme, including perhaps even James Cameron's inflated *Titanic* with its persistent quotations from the on-board string quartet of Offenbach's *Orpheus in the Underworld*. Indirectly Kenneth Branagh's *Dead Again* pursues the theme as well, as a young man and woman in modern Los Angeles discover their love through the reincarnation of an opera composer (the singer) and his beloved wife, who has been murdered – not, it turns out, by her husband. Opera stands central to the plot, and a bizarre twist on Orpheus's voice in this case may be the attempt of Branagh to use an American accent.

Roman Polanski's *Frantic* provides an even tighter example, as the wife of a noted American physician (Harrison Ford) is abducted by underworld figures in Paris, and for most of the film we watch Ford as Orpheus traverse the seedy underside of the Paris crime and drug world to rescue his Eurydice. Once again voice becomes an issue as the American physician speaks no French and must get along in Paris by other means. The luxurious hotel suite that husband and wife share offers an excellent view of the *Place de l'Opéra*, with a panoramic view of the Opera House itself. After the rescue occurs, the happy couple get into a taxi and head to the airport to fly to their Elysium fields on the other side of the Atlantic. A more sordid treatment of the subject comes with Patrick Conrad's *Mascara*, which not only explores the Straussian obsession of Salome but also takes us into the Orphic underworld. The film opens with a brother and sister attending a performance of Gluck's *Orpheus*, and the plot fixates on the brother's obsession with Eurydice's gown, taking us into a decadent, deadly and sometimes operatic underworld. The brother turns out to be death and the costume designer Orpheus; this time, focusing on the blood and gore from the legend, the Thracian denizens of the degenerate club kick and beat Orpheus to death, and throw his body into the harbor which substitutes for the river Hubrus.

For one of the greatest of all directors, Alfred Hitchcock, the theme of Orpheus became a persistent image in various of his films, almost suggesting a unifying motif running through his works, and in some instances, opera helps to magnify the connection. A case could perhaps even be made for *Psycho*, in which the psychopathic Norman Bates (Anthony Perkins) plays death as well as Caronte, both taking lives and blocking those in search of his victim Marion Crane (Janet Leigh). In the second half of the film Marion's fiancé (John MacIntire), with the help of Marion's sister (Vera Miles), descends into the twisted and deadly world of Norman, in search of Marion whom no one yet suspects has died. True to the legend, he does not succeed.

While the threads may be tenuous in *Psycho*, a much stronger possibility can be found in one of Hitchcock's early American films, *Notorious*, of 1946. Here a love affair develops between Devlin, an American agent (Cary Grant), and Alicia (Ingrid Bergman), the daughter of a German-American traitor, and while they may have marriage on their minds, that ends when she takes an assignment of spying on Nazi sympathizers in Rio. That takes her into a marriage of convenience with Sebastian, the leader of the group (Claude Rains), and his Nazi world filled with intrigue, villainy and death stands as the underworld. She continues to maintain contact with Devlin, and at a gala reception at the waterfront Nazi house Devlin and Alicia descend to the forbidden nether region of the house – the wine cellar which houses the illicit plutonium stored in wine bottles. A broken bottle proves costly to Alicia since its discovery will result in an attempt by Sebastian's mother to poison her.

Alicia now becomes Eurydice, dying slowly but surely from poison put in her coffee by the nefarious mother, a snake if ever there was one. Devlin as Orpheus suspects that Alicia's ruse of hangovers does not ring true, and he drives to the house to find her, winding down a dark, waterfront road to get there. At the house he must get by the doorman and Sebastian, who finds himself in a delicate situation since knowledge that Alicia works for the U.S. government could incriminate him in front of his German colleagues – who do not hesitate to execute traitors. During a lull Devlin searches for Alicia's room, and discovering her near death, he gets her up and supports her down the stairs. Sebastian now becomes Caronte who should block their passage, but Devlin plays his trump – willingness to reveal to Sebastian's colleagues Alicia's identity as an American agent. His silent song, as it were, proves profoundly persuasive, and Sebastian helps them to the waiting car as his skeptical colleagues look on. Devlin slams the car door on Sebastian, abandoning him to his likely fate, and escapes the underworld with Alicia. Prescott, the CIA coordinator in Rio, plays Jupiter, granting Orpheus the happiness of love fulfilled.

For Hitchcock's most stunning recreation of the myth, we return to the first film examined in this section: *Vertigo*; others of course have recognized this connection, including Royal S. Brown.[3] Descent into Madeleine's underworld receives not only visual reinforcement with cars going down San Francisco's hills, Madeleine plunging into the bay, vertiginous images from stepladders to building roofs, and vortex swirls that may very well lead to hell, but also Bernard Herrmann's music with it falling sequences and modulations at strategic points. Here Hitchcock remains true to the legend, as Scottie's second attempt to bring Madeleine back results in failure. While Scottie may not use an Orphic singing voice, both Hitchcock and Herrmann provide it for him, as chapter 19 described, by creating a film with opera deeply enmeshed into its essence, and by bolstering that with a musical score in which the operatic references cannot be mistaken.

PART SIX

OPERA RETURNS AS CINEMA

FINALE: DIRECTORS' OPERAS

With so many major directors throughout the 20th century envisaging cinema as opera, it should not surprise us to see the reverse as well: notable directors presenting opera as cinema – not only in the early years of cinema but recently as well. In a sense it brings us back to the starting point; if opera at one time provided a service in bringing respectability to the movies, cinema has returned the favor, attempting to endow opera with the same level of popularity as cinema. By presenting opera in the movie house instead of the opera house, a massive new audience could be reached, although the producers bringing us these film/operas have taken a risk in gambling that there would be an audience. The successes have been moderate, enough generally to justify the undertaking, but not always sufficient to inspire future projects.

In creating films of operas, directors such as Francesco Rosi, Joseph Losey, Ingmar Bergman or Franco Zeffirelli have been motivated by much more than simply making opera more accessible. The endeavor bears no resemblance to the phenomenon of putting opera on television, widespread throughout Europe and North America, in which producers record a staged performance of an opera and broadcast it to an audience of opera enthusiasts. These proceed from the assumption that audiences really want to be at the opera house, but for various reasons they cannot, and the television broadcast becomes a surrogate for the live performance. Directors of film/operas have something very different in mind, an actual piece of cinema with all that entails concerning visual images; usually a stage will not be in evidence, although some directors such as Bergman or Peter Sellars may wish for aesthetic reasons to show a stage or perhaps even an audience, as happens in Bergman's *The Magic Flute*. In many cases, one finds a reverse process to the notion of an opera (or aspects of an opera) inspiring a film; now cinema inspires the opera, and the idea of music at the heart of the experience gives way to something fundamentally cinematic, and in some cases the music may even be marginalized.

Opera has drawn around itself a cadre of experts and buffs who may very well be offended by the very idea of turning opera into cinema. Their objections may include a number of factors, such as the loss of sound quality in something electronically reproduced, the loss of the electricity of the live performance, or the distortions that will usually be inflicted on the opera itself – the cutting, arranging, rewriting, adding or other types of meddling with the original score that directors will insist on to make the opera in question their own work. The issue of sound quality need not trouble us too much. Recordings of operas have been around as long as recording technology has been possible, and singers such as the diva in *Diva*, who consider recording sacrilegious, have proved rare in the extreme. Surely a recording will be even better if it also includes visual images, and the possibility for high sound quality improves in films and videos all the time.

A more troublesome matter concerns musicologists or music critics who believe that one right way exists for an opera to be performed, and that the sky will fall if a director alters the text or the music. In actual practice, virtually no opera since the beginning of the medium has ever remained unchanged when performed in different cities or even for different productions in the same city, and the composers, while they lived (or live), participated in these alterations. They readily made these changes in response to different tastes, the singers involved, the resources available, and whatever other variables came into play. Composers such as Mozart and Haydn would add new arias or more interesting orchestral parts to other composers' operas, again for the reasons given above. Opera has refused to encumber itself with a single way of doing things, and in fact, the least authentic approach to opera is the one that insists on one correct reading. If the composers themselves refused this, we should not be distressed by the changes made by directors who turn them into films. We may still find the changes objectionable, but that will be in relation to the overall aesthetic, dramatic or cinematic approach of the director, not the permissibility of changes.

Cinema, of course, offers directors options which the stage does not, such as the use of close-up on faces, the focus of the camera on specific objects, and a vast array of other visual images; the result may be something very different from a traditional opera. A brief look at four very different directors' operas will follow: Zeffirelli's *Otello*, Losey's *Don Giovanni*, Sellars's *Cosí fan tutte*, and Rosi's *Carmen*.

Zeffirelli's *Otello*

Shakespeare's *Othello* has a special quality that allowed the play to appeal to a composer like Giuseppe Verdi, in spite of the views of critics such as Eduard Hanslick who found the story unsuitable for musical setting,[1] and that lies in the fact that it already has music built in. Plays, stories or legends with that feature can have a powerful bearing on a medium such as opera, as proved true for the earliest composers of opera and their fascination with the legend of Orpheus – the singer of mythology who could move not only hard-hearted listeners but even inanimate objects with the beauty and persuasiveness of his songs. The composer in this case need not manufacture the opportunity for such a musical number, one which would stand at the heart of a work, since the legend itself provided it, and all the composer had to do was create what he could do best: a glorious song or aria which, as the musical idea underlying the aesthetic direction of the work, would carry the rest of the work with it. Shakespeare provides a similar possibility in *Othello*, in spite of the fact that he does not make Desdemona the central character of his play, and that lies in her "Willow song" in the fourth act. His focus may be on the tragedy of Othello, but one cannot grasp how profoundly Othello errs without the revelation of Desdemona's complete innocence – something which can be revealed much more deeply in music than with words. Shakespeare knew this and so did Verdi, who tipped the scale away from Othello's tragedy to the pathos of Desdemona; Verdi progressively makes the opera her opera, especially the final act, which she claims most strikingly with her wistfully beautiful "Willow song." Verdi adds an "Ave Maria" for good measure, but musically it seems almost trivial compared to the "Willow song." Here he reveals what he wanted the work to be. Without the "Willow song" the opera would be a mere shadow, pointless in its drive toward the final act since it would have neither tragedy nor pathos; the work would lack musical essence and hence a spiritual and emotional foundation, reverting to the sensationalism of an ugly murder story of a psychopathic killer.

Zeffirelli's *Otello* (1986) omits the "Willow song." This was no oversight or removal because Zeffirelli may have found the number boring; anyone who prefers Verdi's "Ave Maria" to the "Willow song" either has no ear for music or does not wish music to be a significant factor in his opera/film. To give Zeffirelli the benefit of the doubt, a director with a long association with opera, including working with Maria Callas, it appears he followed the latter track in this film. Unlike directors such as Griffith, Eisenstein, Pasolini or Godard who would start with a fundamental musical notion and allow the visual images to emerge from that, Zeffirelli takes an opera and strips it of its music, opting for visual leitmotifs which push the music into the background, making what he and musical director Lorin Maazel leave of the music a mere soundtrack, simply there to add emotional touches at localized points.[2] Even the recording quality of the music seems intentionally poor, further reducing Verdi in favor of the screen.

In the spirit of operatic transformation, Zeffirelli had every right to make this his work, even if he prefers it to be a story about a crazed killer. Of course, he hoped it would reach as large an audience as possible, and what better way to achieve that than to make it sensational, a story familiar to television or horror film viewers, of a madman who attempts (Michael Douglas in *Falling Down*) or actually succeeds (*Kill Her Gently*, among others) in killing his wife. Add to that another deranged killer (Iago: Justino Diaz), the type who goes into his workplace and starts shooting (or even worse, discovers how to make someone else do the killing) after he has been passed over for promotion, and he has the perfect recipe for a riveting, pot-boiling box-office winner.

Zeffirelli considered *Otello* to be the high point of his career, comparing it to a great Hollywood epic,[3] but it appears that its strongest affinity to Hollywood lies in the relative position of the producer(s) to the director. In this case the film was produced by Menahem Golan and his cousin Yoram Globus, founders of the low-budget Golan-Globus Productions; after 1979 they became directors of the New York-based Cannon Films, a company famous for its aggressive promotion and exploitative products. One need only look at their films from immediately before *Otello* to see where their interests lay: *The Delta Force, America 3000, Cobra, Invaders From Mars,* and *The Texas Chainsaw Massacre Part 2,* all from 1986. They then rounded out 1986 with *52 Pick-Up,* and launched into 1987 with *Over the Top, Street Smart, Beauty and the Beast,* and *Superman IV.* All of these aim for the most popular audience possible, and we have no reason to imagine that they had anything else in mind with *Otello*; perhaps the one that tells us most about where they were heading is the film they produced immediately prior to *Otello*: *The Texas Chainsaw Massacre Part 2.* With Zeffirelli's *Otello* we appear to have *The Cyprus Wife Strangler Part 3: Descent into the Heart of Darkness.* Should we assume that the sensitive opera- and Shakespeare-loving Zeffirelli would object to this direction, the director who brought us *The Taming of the Shrew* (1967) with Elizabeth Taylor and Richard Burton, and in 1990 a *Hamlet* with Mel Gibson? This Italian/American production would earn some revenue in Italy, but not much in a country where people go to live opera; its commercial viability depended on its success with the massive American movie-going public, a public much more accustomed to horror films than opera.

One could imagine that the director with a fascination for Shakespeare might wish to steer his *Otello* toward *Othello* by marginalizing Desdemona (Katie Ricciarelli) in the final act, but nothing could be further from the truth. To do that he would need to make his film a tragedy, and that he refuses to do. Instead of being a hero who self-destructs, Otello succumbs to a lurking already-present madness, and simply slips further down the slope of his incipient insanity until he writhes on the ground in a crazed seizure, and fully embraces his psychopathic status by reverting to a savage. Interpretations that suggest a polarity between Roman Catholicism and some sort of African primitivism[4] are probably too generous; instead of anything fundamentally religious, the images follow well-known ones from the horror genre, and other familiar filmic images as well, that the American public would recognize. Zeffirelli also plays the race card, but not at all like Shakespeare, who makes Brabantio, Desdemona's father, a racist; a white actor/singer (Placido Domingo) plays Otello in blackface, starting as an Al Jolson nice guy who reverts to a nefarious *Birth of a Nation* Silas Lynch, an evil black played by a white. The blackface, obvious to everyone, now makes him more menacing than Moor, a mad killer all the more to be feared by the pure of heart. He has much in common

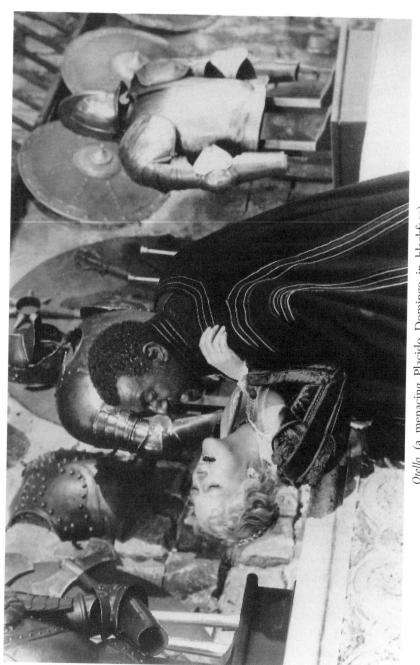

Otello (a menacing Placido Domingo in blackface)

with General Kurtz as we see him at the end of *Apocalypse Now*, less a genuine primitive than a maniac run amok.

Dropping his cross necklace into the flaming cauldron, Otello makes his final plunge into complete madness. We see him approaching that going down staircases and darkened tunnel-like passages, always descending en route to the heart of darkness. Before going to Desdemona's bedchamber he indulges in a satanic ritual, a familiar image from horror films, something which makes him all the more frightening as his irrationality becomes complete, blustering senselessly on his murderous course. Desdemona can now be seen as nothing but a victim, and she lies on her bed in the pure whiteness of her wedding dress, waiting for the inevitable as a bride of Frankenstein, or, if we like, any one of a number of possible other cinematic images. Perhaps she can be thought of as the chaste Nina waiting for Nosferatu, and Otello obliges at the end by kissing her on the neck. Immediately after Otello stabs himself with a dagger, an apparently disembodied hand appears on the steps nears Desdemona's face, and the hand contorts in frightful gestures before the camera reveals Otello as its owner. Now we have Oliver Stone's *The Hand* (1981), in which the severed hand of a cartoonist returns on a nightmarish murder spree; since Otello has completely lost his mind, he cannot really be held responsible for the murder, but the hand – perhaps guided by the devil or an alien force – signifies the evil force. The force indeed: Otello heads for Desdemona's room wearing a hooded cloak recalling the master of the force – the emperor in *Star Wars*. The body count rises quickly at the end as Otello strangles Desdemona, Iago stabs Emilia, Otello skewers Iago (the two latter killings do not happen in Verdi), and Otello finishes himself off in a Cyprus saber massacre.

We may hear the fractured strains of Verdi's music, but any resemblance to the opera is strictly illusionary; in fact, Zeffirelli gives us little more than a phantom of the opera, a blackface Otello who wears his face paint like Lon Chaney wears a mask. The *Otello* of Golan-Globus-Zeffirelli owes little to Shakespeare as it takes irrationality to a new depth, and presumably needed singing instead of spoken dialogue to create the right effect. In that respect it comes closer to Verdi, but it veers sharply from the opera in its search for a new cinematic genre which combines opera, horror movie and television psychopathic murder story. Adding to the genres of soap opera, horse opera and space opera, the producers and director appeared to come up with a new one: kiss and kill opera.

Losey's *Don Giovanni*

In spearheading the idea for a film of *Don Giovanni* in 1978, Rolf Liebermann, chief administrator of the Théâtre Nationale Opéra de Paris, hoped to bring this already popular opera to the masses, making it accessible to people who would avoid opera houses. In that he and Daniel Toscan du Plantier, president of Gaumont Films in France, succeeded brilliantly; according to one set of statistics, more people have seen Losey's film than all attendees of *Don Giovanni* at theaters since the first production in Prague in 1787.[5] In France alone the film grossed over $6,000,000, and it did well elsewhere, including England, Italy and the United States (where it received its premiere), but made at a cost of over $20 million, the revenues neither brought in a profit nor allowed it to break even.[6] No one was more surprised by the choice of Joseph Losey to direct it than Losey himself, since he had no interest in opera and in fact had never even seen *Don Giovanni* on the stage. Losey's ignorance, though, fit into Liebermann's scheme, since who better to present opera to an ignorant public than a director completely unburdened by operatic ideas – and with no ear for music or languages.[7] The result irked many critics and musicians, including Carlo Maria Giulini, who complained that "the film was wrong. No one has the right to do a thing like this to the libretto and to the music. It is not allowed!"[8] Not allowed by whom? Mozart himself wrote different versions for Prague and Vienna, and the recent surfacing of Mozart's own parts for different productions of *The Marriage of Figaro* reveals that each production differed significantly from the next,[9] and that would have been true of *Don Giovanni*.

The film differs strikingly from traditional productions of the opera on stage, not only making changes to the score and libretto but abandoning the kind of propriety of the opera house which prevents the underlying sexuality implied in the work from coming to the fore. To achieve this, Losey hit on an ingenious approach, one which actually forces a major rethinking of this highly provocative and much discussed work. Losey picked up on an idea that Mozart himself makes possible: when Donna Anna, Don Ottavio and Donna Elvira come to Don

Giovanni's palace in Act 1 seeking retribution for Don Giovanni's attempted rape of Donna Anna and murder of her father, they do so as maskers, suggesting the festivity at the palace is a carnival ball. The producers use Vicenza, Venice and other surrounding areas for the setting, and Venice loves carnival, celebrating it over a period of days with distinctive Venetian carnival masks and costumes. During carnival time anything goes; the usual world turns upside-down, promiscuity grips almost everyone, cross-dressing and cross-social notions take hold, and any type of insult goes. Not only did Venice adore carnival, but so did Mozart, whose scatological letters and even much of his revolt against parental and social authority come out of a carnival spirit.[10] If the serious maskers come to a carnival ball, why not place the entire opera in a carnival setting; it makes perfect sense to do this and it helps to make sense of otherwise troubling aspects of the work. Already during the playing of the overture, Losey shows us characters in carnival costumes and masks.

Our sensibilities over two centuries after Mozart and librettist Lorenzo da Ponte wrote *Don Giovanni* seem rightly offended by the opening scene, in which Don Giovanni appears nothing short of a rapist and a murderer. At the end of the scene Leporello quips to the Don, "Bravo! Pretty good for one evening. To rape the daughter and then skewer the father!" To make matters worse, during the scene of high tension between Giovanni and Donna Anna and the fatal crossing of swords with her father the Commendatore, Leporello gives his own absurd running commentary on the action, integrated comically by Mozart into the ensemble. The events and their consequences could not be more serious, yet Mozart seems to laugh at them and make the audience laugh at actions that should be no laughing matter.

We could, as Losey seems to, look at the opening scene as a little carnival play, giving us the upside-down world of that season instead of brutal crimes. In search of some carnival amusement, Giovanni enters Anna's bedroom, and she at first takes it in the spirit of the season. When he becomes physically aggressive, she, no doubt having been warned about the dangers of masquerades and carnival nocturnal visits, fends him off and even goes after him, intent on exposing the intruder. Her alarm rouses the household, including her father, a solid moralist who has no use for the tomfoolery of carnival. Giovanni does not want to cross swords with the old man, but given no choice he hurls the insult "Misero! Attendi. Se vuoi morir" ("miserable wretch, prepare yourself, if you want to die"). He finishes him off, symbolically invoking the insult directed by youths to their fathers or anyone in authority, made famous to the rest of the world by Goethe in his description of carnival in Rome: "Sia ammazzato il Signore Padre!" ("death to you" or "to hell with you..."). In Goethe's description, "the old man scolds him for this outrageous behaviour; the boy claims the freedom of the evening and curses his father all the more vehemently."[11] In Losey's film, Giovanni goes through this entire scene concealing his face as anyone would during carnival.

After the opening carnival scene with its costumes, attempted seduction, violence, and disrespect for elders, other facets of carnival spring up at a fairly rapid pace. Leporello presumes to offer his master advice on his way of life, shrinking the social distance between servant and master. Giovanni does not take it kindly at this early stage in the work, but that does not prevent an episode of social cross-dressing in Act 2 as Giovanni needs Leporello's cloak and mask to seduce Donna Elvira's maid, and Leporello will need to "become" his master to engage Donna Elvira. In that scene in the film, Elvira wears a Colombine-like costume, making her a character in a *commedia dell'arte* or carnival farce. The three women of the opera stand in very different positions as they respond to the seductive conventions of carnival: Anna refuses to participate at all, invoking her moral upbringing and sense of propriety. The peasant Zerlina, who understands the convention better than anyone, plays along with it as far as it will go, her only fear being that of getting caught by her groom Masetto. In the duet "La ci darem la manno," she musically crosses the line of virtue; Theresa Berganza may look a little too old for the role, but she plays it with body language of the sexual receptiveness that Mozart's music suggests, finally pulling Giovanni to the bed and allowing his face to sink into her ample breasts. Her scream in the finale of Act 1, as Losey sets up the scenario, has more to do with the anticipation of discovery by Masetto than an objection to the advances of the Don.

As Don Giovanni sings the champagne aria, Losey invokes in the whirling background the most famous of the carnival paintings, *The Battle between Carnival and Lent* of 1559 by Pieter Bruegel the Elder. Don Giovanni stands in the foreground as the king of carnival, leading all those around him in excessive eating, drinking and lovemaking, like his counterpart in the painting who leads the festivities as he rides a massive wine barrel. The Bruegel image comes again during the famous dance scene in which Mozart brilliantly choreographs three simultaneous dances (minuet, deutscher and contradanse) representing the three fronts of action on stage and allowing the social mixing that would be normal during carnival, although Losey does little with this scene. Sprinkled throughout the film Losey places naked women, bathing in the open or lying on a bed between Giovanni and Leporello as they plan their next caper. Their naked presence does not seem out of place during carnival time, when displays of nudity occur with frequency. When the Commendatore's statue nods and speaks in the graveyard, this could be the distorted vision of two carousers who have had too much to drink. When the statue comes to Giovanni's carnival dinner, he could be a reveler wearing a very ingenious costume. The dinner itself, a sumptuous spread, has all the carnival features of excessive indulgence in food, wine and even bodies strewn about in embrace. An attractive young person walks by the Don and gives him a desiring look; we cannot tell if this is a girl or a beautiful boy. The episode with the statue, in which the Don insults the highest possible authority – God – unfolds as an unsuccessful end-of-carnival morality play. For the concluding vaudeville, carnival has passed and Ash Wednesday has arrived; the promises made in the spirit of lent will surely be broken as the next carnival season approaches.

Despite his ignorance of opera in general and *Don Giovanni* in particular, Losey has offered an appealing reading. The balance shifts in this work of cinema from music to visual images, although Losey should not be blamed for the poorly recorded, high-reverberation music, the soundtrack of which he received in advance and had to accommodate. In fact, he seemed unusually responsive to Mozart, recognizing the sensuality in numbers like "La ci darem la mano" or the diffusion of seriousness in Leporello's buffoonish running commentaries on serious events. By recognizing the carnival potential implicit in the libretto and also evident in the music, he brought a striking interpretation to *Don Giovanni*, removing the offensive criminal aspects and finding an approach that both the 18th and 20th centuries can share. Morality still takes a beating in this reading, crudely with the drubbing Masetto gets from Giovanni and more subtly with Giovanni's defiance of moral authority both earthly and heavenly.

Curiously, though, despite the apparent carnival setting, Losey does not invoke the *joie de vivre* of carnival time. Not only do his characters, with the possible exception of Zerlina, not indulge in unrestrained pleasure seeking, but they seem to be a little bored or even worse – going through the motions of a tedious ritual.[12] Here other interpretations open up as well, especially the infusion of Losey's Marxist inclinations which prevents the upper classes from enjoying themselves too much.[13] Carnival may be a social equalizer, but that remains temporary to the season, and Losey's Don Giovanni must be punished not for his crimes against women, God or a fellow aristocrat, but instead for his offences against the lower class. Whereas Mozart's music of the concluding vaudeville and chorus subtly mocks the moralizers, Losey's watery final scene diverts us from Mozart and Marxism, offering neither irony nor progress. In the end, we seem to revert back to the epigram by Antonio Gramsci which set the tone at the beginning: "il vecchio muore, e il nuovo non puo nascere: e in questo interregno si verificano I fenomeni morbosi più svariati" ("the old is dying and the new cannot be born: in this interregnum, a great variety of morbid symptoms appears").[14]

Sellars's *Cosí fan tutte*

In North America opera will probably fare better on television than in movie houses, and while that usually means "Live from the Met" tapings of staged productions, occasionally we can tune into something more unusual. Such a production of Mozart's *Cosí fan tutte* aired on PBS in 1991; with the overture accompanying seaside and street scenes in Westchester County, unsuspecting viewers may have checked their TV guide to see why the opera had been replaced by a New York State travelogue. After the overture we move to a seaside diner run by Despina, the on-again, off-again girlfriend of Don Alfonso, a shell-shocked Vietnam vet. Typical beach riff-raff like Guglielmo, Ferrando, Dorabella and Fiordiligi frequent their diner. They all more or less sing the music as Mozart wrote it (with some exceptions), but the slangy text given in subtitles hardly strikes one as a faithful translation of Da Ponte's libretto. Similarly, their gestures seem light years removed from the opera house.

The youthful, American director Peter Sellars (born in 1958), who describes himself as "incredibly obnoxious," staged Mozart's three *Da*

Ponte operas at the PepsiCo Summerfare in Purchase, New York, in the late 1980s, and filmed these in Vienna for broadcast in 1991. His productions with his selected troupe work best for film or television because of the acting and facial gestures required of the singers, subtleties which would be lost in a large opera house. Sellars does not simply modernize his settings for shock value (although he enjoys shocking his viewers) or to attract the age 18 to 25 movie audience. He goes much further, apparently changing an opera such as *Così* to a work which could belong to the 1980s, recognizing a relevance of Mozart to his time. In so doing he sacrifices the traditional idea of a Mozart opera, what some may consider the authentic 18th-century idea, and needless to say has annoyed critics and musicologists in the process.[15]

Oblivious to the embarrassment many critics have felt about this work, a mistake, as Edward J. Dent believed, or unworthy of Mozart, according to Joseph Kerman,[16] Sellars looks at it as a complex study of sexual politics in the 1980s. The work ceases to be a comedy in his hands as coloratura and ornamentation become signs of madness. Instead of Despina making the audience laugh by satirizing Mesmer with a magnetic resuscitation of the Albanian suitors when they attempt suicide, she hooks jumper cables from a huge "Die-Hard" battery to their crotches, and gets a very different kind of rise. In fact, the 18th-century images, which scholars go to great lengths to discover, he readily sacrifices to a modern set of images in the production: we chuckle at the recognition of the Albanians as the two klutzy Czech swingers (the "wild and crazy guys") created by Steve Martin and Dan Aykroyd on TV's *Saturday Night Live*,[17] at Guglielmo's Phil Donahue impersonation, thrusting a mike into the faces of audience members during his aria "Donne mie," or at Despina's *LA Law* legal disguise and computer-printout marriage contract.

Così fan tutte refuses to be, as Dent would have it, "simplicity itself,"[18] and neither does it have a libretto-music gap, which Kerman insists on.[19] As with *The Magic Flute*, the audience must reconsider the first act after it has heard the second, to realize Mozart and Da Ponte have consciously misled us. In this case the water-tight, symmetrical, marionette-like comedy of Act 1 breaks down in Act 2, most of all with Fiordiligi's accompanied recitative "Ei parte...senti" and rondo "Per pieta, ben mio, perdona," and also the three arias that follow, which reveal character and force dissymmetry. With "Per pieta" the comedy gives way to seriousness, not a parody of the *opera seria* style as Fiordiligi's "Come scolgio" in Act 1 had been, but now in a genuine recognition of moral dilemma and distress.

Sellars takes "Per pieta" very seriously, actually as the lightning rod for the ultimate collapse of everything later in the work, and shows us a dark reading of the text and music. In the rondo Fiordiligi wishes to be forgiven, hidden, and to be rid of her illicit passion. But, as we learn in the recitative, she has already given in to the flames of forbidden desire; any thought of erasing this, of passing herself off as innocent, would be self-deception, and Mozart too clarifies this musically. The enormous leaps in the vocal line, used by Mozart to reinforce hyperbole in "Come scoglio," now return in more troubling ways, mocking her presumed strength as they land on diminished seventh chords or fall on offbeats. Sellars rejects any possibility of innocence, recognizing the exposure of human frailty inherent in the music. Toward the end of the rondo Fiordiligi begins to strip off her clothes, not in a sexually provocative way, but instead as an exposure which leaves her vulnerable, lacking the defence of personal dignity and social identity. In this vulnerable state she must play the next scenes, including the encounter with Dorabella and Despina as well as the submission duet with Ferrando.

Conventional wisdom has it, as does Edward Dent, that, "needless to say, all ends happily."[20] This happens in most productions, but decidedly not for Sellars. If we view Fiordiligi's submission to Ferrando as a genuine moral failure, then how can the work end happily? These two couples face a lifetime of recriminations. According to Sellars, Mozart offers no enlightened lesson, begging tolerance for indiscretions. Instead, he sounds the death-knell for the Enlightenment itself, recognizing that dark and evil thoughts and actions permeate every level of social and personal interaction. We know that things are amiss in this production when wedding guests arrive in their pajamas and the two brides look like escapees from television's *Hee Haw*. The mirth in the wedding scene drips with irony, but Sellars does not allow the couples to treat it that way, forcing it beyond irony. To words like "Sing to happy days before us/ And a life of new delight!" or "Happy, happy end of sorrow,/ Bright new promise of joy hereafter!/ Glowing hope for life tomorrow,/ Filled with tender love and laughter," Sellars's troupe plays the scene with the most hang-dog, lugubrious faces imaginable.

Matters get worse in the final scene. After the identities of the suitors have been revealed, the libretto indicates a happy ending. Don Alfonso says "Laugh about what's past and over/ And I'll laugh along with you," and the final chorus ends with "He will answer with knowing laughter./ He has learned that life's adversities/ Turn to joy another day." All of this, of course, prods ironically, as do the sisters' words, "Oh, my sweetheart, I hope to show you/ All the loving faith I owe you!/I will prove my worth to you." Mozart, as in the conclusion of *Don Giovanni* with the vaudeville and mock liturgical style of the moral, builds irony into the music. But irony we do not get from Sellars. The issue of the right lovers getting back together proves moot, as the swirling motion prevents any sense of pairing. The swirling becomes a *La Valse*-like apotheosis, with complete disintegration. In the end Fiordiligi has become a raving madwoman, subject for a future "Diary of a Mad Housewife."

Sellars has broken with stodgy tradition, giving us an unusual reading, but one which in many respects squares with the libretto and music. Does it give us anything better than stodgy tradition? Mozart, as we know from some of his letters or the riddles he wrote for the carnival of 1786, loved to play with double or multiple meanings. If one solves the riddle or understands the deception, that should not hinder enjoyment of other levels of meaning. While we may find sexually explicit references in the riddles or his letters to his female cousin "the Bäsle," such interpretations become most satisfying set against a background of more innocent possibilities.

Similar options of multiple meaning lie in Mozart's music as well, or in the interactions of librettos and music. Irony proves a major factor in these settings, but we lose irony if a director hits us over the head with a reading that insists on menace if not barbarism, however valid it may be. While one cannot resist commending Sellars for recognizing the darker side of this work, so utterly absent from most productions, he has, nevertheless, missed the point. He indulges an obsession, as one who solves a riddle, of a single correct answer, a trait as regrettable for directors as for critics, and fails to recognize that the essence of Mozart lies in the process of dissimulation, in the enjoyment of the multiple meanings. Sellars has given the audience the answer (his answer) instead of the riddle, and therefore has unfairly inflicted his obnoxious side on us, making the director a biased informer instead of a wily accomplice.

Rosi's *Carmen*

The idea of filming Bizet's *Carmen* in 1983 may not have been Francesco Rosi's, but in a most striking way he has left an indelible mark on the notion that opera and cinema have much in common. In his hands *Carmen* appears as though Bizet designed it for the screen,[21] giving a new dimension to the possibility of opera returning as cinema. Daniel Toscan du Plantier of Gaumont Films lost money (although not much) on Losey's *Don Giovanni*, but he seems to have regarded the project as a brilliant failure, begging for another attempt to bring opera to the masses through film. The choice of *Carmen*, the most popular opera in the repertoire, augured well, but the selection of Rosi as the director seemed odd, considering his record as a director of political films. With a budget about one-third of *Don Giovanni's*, Toscan now discovered he could not only reach the audience he hoped to reach but an opera/film could make a profit as well; first screened in March 1984, it played to almost half a million viewers in and around Paris in its first eleven weeks,[22] and it continued to do well internationally.

Toscan seemed to have an uncanny knack for choosing directors, finding Losey's ignorance of opera to be an asset for *Don Giovanni*, and with Rosi he also recognized what he needed, despite Rosi's directorial track record. The mixture of North and South so predominant in *Carmen* paralleled the Italian Rosi's own life; born in Naples in 1922, he was the child of a father whose family came from Calabria, "in the deep-south region of forests and mountains, cut off from the world around, where the peasants are proud, honest, hardworking, austere, with a great will," as Michel Ciment describes it. His mother, in contrast, grew up in a well-to-do Neapolitan family, inclined in Rosi's words toward "grandeur and confusion, generosity, braggadocio, carelessness, and nonchalance."[23] Rosi remains preoccupied with the South of Italy, "this '*Mezzogiorno*' that the Italians themselves have called their Africa, stereotyped for its backwardness, poverty, violence, and mysticism," symbolic for him of something much larger. Straddling these two cultures, he fuses an ability to be cerebral with a fascination for the emotional, sensuous and superstitious; in Rosi's words, "what involves me is the passage from the passionate to the rational and vice versa."[24] Aside from his dual temperament he also speaks fluent Spanish.

Rosi's *Carmen* (Julia Migenes-Johnson performs the "Habanera")

Much has been said about the way Rosi's *Carmen* deals with social dominance by males, the struggles of women to free themselves from this, and even the use of the images of the matador and bull to focus on this conflict.[25] As fascinating as these discussions may be, I will allow them to continue simmering and focus on the issue of the fusion of opera and cinema. *Carmen* certainly concerns the clashing of two cultures – the two that make up Rosi's own background – and much in the film explores the ways these cultures look at themselves and each other. As the film begins, various types of separations appear to be in place. Two cultures coexist uneasily but they do not meet: we have on the one hand the world of the South, with its bullfights, religious pageantry, gypsies and exoticism – in short, the realm of violence, disorder, sensuousness, superstition and the irrational. On the other side stand the occupying soldiers from the North, neatly but plainly dressed, superimposing order and control, bringing rational principles and calm. Their worlds do not mix: when a soldier attempts to dance with Carmen, his superior officer, Don José, pulls him away.

The audience for this film will likely identify with the soldiers as cultural imperialists, as outside onlookers peering at an unfamiliar world. We will probably look in the same mystified way that the soldiers do at what surrounds them, at townsfolk with an easy-going attitude who themselves look with acceptance at gypsy women dancing and beckoning. The soldiers, like the audience a step removed, do not understand the culture they witness, where men can quip with Carmen about her next love and she can display herself both emotionally and physically in her "Habanera" answer. Since they cannot grasp it, they can only fantasize about it, in their own minds turning raw sensuality into pornography, asking each other if they are aroused by these southern women, and leering at them with binoculars from their bird's-eye-view vantage points. They look on as mere voyeurs, peering from a distance at an alien, unruly, irrational world.

Too much of these allurements can turn one's rational world upside down, arousing passion and obsession. When Carmen directs the full force of her sensuality at Don José (the "Seguidilla"), he cannot resist, but because of his upbringing in the North, he does not understand what she offers. Instead of diversion, he sees her as the image of an object to be possessed, something which must be wholly his. As he falls – not for her but for an illusion – he attempts to cross over in a strange and impossible way, not embracing her culture or even trying to bring the two cultures together; by attempting to take her out of hers, he reduces her from a person to a sexual object. It seems to matter little to him if he has the woman herself (he certainly cannot give her a sensuous kiss) or some facsimile of her as the flower represents – something he can treat like a pin-up and indulge pornographically. He may be drawn into her world, but not willingly as his own irrational need for possession forces him into a smuggler's role. His obsession drives out his last shred of rational control, and disaster looms as he tries to possess the unpossessible. To the end he cannot cope with the illusion nor understand her or her culture, and his possessive kiss is the kiss of death. As an imperialist he tries to take the spoils, but with his touch he destroys the beauty he cannot comprehend.

The message may be a political one, and here Rosi would be on firm ground considering his background as a director, but the imperialism in question may be as much cultural as political. In this return of opera as cinema we also have an invasion of opera by cinema. Early in the century DeMille had tried to bring cinema up to a new level with *Carmen*, something he saw as essential to the survival of cinema, and now Rosi, returning the compliment, seemed to be trying to bring opera back to the level of cinema, something he (or his producer Toscan) perhaps saw as essential to its survival. Rosi accentuates the culture clash in *Carmen* at the beginning of Act 2 with the sophisticated court dance and the rough gypsy dance. Almost immediately the two worlds intersect as Escamillo in an elegant carriage passes through the gypsy camp and offers his love to Carmen; later Carmen enters his world as his honored guest and lover at the bullfight. Yet the two worlds remain suspicious of each other as the soldiers enforce an arbitrary division, like dispassionate viewers at an opera watching through opera glasses from up in the gods. What they see – the exotic, sensuous and irrational world of the South – resembles opera with its irrationality, sensuous singing and music.

Don José seems to stand as an object lesson on how not to bring two forces together. At other more subtle levels the fusion does occur, perhaps in the meeting of cultures which remains free of the destructive Don José and his uniformed cohorts, but most strongly for Rosi in the fusion of the forces of opera and cinema. The film begins as pure cinema, with visual images and a noise track that includes sounds of the bullring and music unrelated to Bizet's. Rosi leaves no doubt here that we have come to see cinema, not a recreation of an opera house, and when the opera begins, it does so as an addition of a soundtrack to a noise track, an overture as introductory music accompanying the titles after visual images have been secured.[26] The visual images as the work proceeds continue to offer cinema, based sometimes on the art illustrations of Gustave Doré for Théophile Gautier's romantic travelogue of Spain *Voyage en Espagne: Tra los montes* (1843),[27] but also occasionally derived from familiar cinematic images. H. Marshall Leicester, Jr. has noted some of these, including the José/Zuniga duel as the swashbuckling Errol Flynn crossing swords on the castle stairs with Basil Rathbone in *The Adventures of Robin Hood*, the mountain smuggler scenes or the Gypsy on a horse interrupting the José/Micaela duet from *The Good, the Bad, and the Ugly*, Escamillo's Gene Autry wave of the hat as he rides off into the sunset, or the good Micaela dwarfed against a mountainous background like Maria against the Alps in *The Sound of Music*.[28] Others could be added, such as the fight between José and Escamillo as the fight between Marlon Brando and Lee J. Cobb from *On the Waterfront*, a film by one of Rosi's favorite directors, Elia Kazan.

Carmen has been a leitmotif throughout this book, from the opening chapter on DeMille's foray into feature films, through Chaplin's burlesque leading off section 3, to the focus in chapter 20 on Preminger's and Godard's contributions to this familiar cinematic subject. It seems only fitting then to conclude with Carmen, not to kill her off as a fated *femme fatale*, but to celebrate her as an operatic essence that breathed life into early cinema and has continued to fan the cinematic flame. Unlike those directors who assumed that the opera could only live on in a drastically altered form, Francesco Rosi recognized that the fire in Bizet continues to burn, and that the opera itself still has much to say to cinema. In the way that Rosi stands as the model for how North and South can come together, in his film he conceives the medium in a manner that allows the ultimate fusion of cinema and opera. From DeMille to Rosi this fusion has worked, and cinema since Rosi's *Carmen* shows no signs of giving up on the possibility.

Notes

INTRODUCTION

1. Quoted in Ken Wlaschin, *Opera on Screen* (Los Angeles: Beachwood Press, 1997), 153.
2. Quoted in Jeremy Tambling, *Opera, Ideology and Film* (Manchester: University of Manchester Press, 1987), 42.
3. Alfred Hitchcock, "On Music in Films: An Interview with Stephen Watts," reproduced in *Hitchcock on Hitchcock*, edited by Sidney Gottlieb (Berkeley, Los Angeles and London: University of California Press, 1995), 244.
4. Stanley Cavell, *A Pitch of Philosophy* (Cambridge, MA: Harvard University Press, 1994), 136.
5. Ibid., 137.
6. It seems surprising that only three years later Citron would use the identical title.
7. I speak of directors as guiding forces but that does not necessarily mean I see them as *auteurs*. They stand at the center of a larger collaborative process, and for this study that focuses especially on their exchanges with composers.
8. Of the numerous studies on film music, some of the most useful ones include Royal S. Brown, *Overtones and Undertones: Reading Film Music* (Berkeley, Los Angeles and London: University of California Press, 1994); Claudia Gorbman, *Unheard Melodies: Narrative Film Music* (Bloomington: Indiana University Press, 1987); Kathryn Kalinak, *Settling the Score: Music and the Classical Hollywood Film* (Madison: University of Wisconsin Press, 1992); George Burt, *The Art of Film Music* (Boston: Northeastern University Press, 1994); Christopher Palmer, *The Composer in Hollywood* (London and New York: Marion Boyars, 1990); Caryl Flinn, *Strains of Utopia: Gender, Nostalgia, and Hollywood Film Music* (Princeton: Princeton University Press, 1992); *Music and Cinema*, edited by James Buhler, Caryl Flinn and David Neumeyer (Hanover, NH and London: University Press of New England, 2000); Roy M. Prendergast, *Film Music: A Neglected Art*, 2nd ed. (New York: W. W. Norton, 1992); and Tony Thomas, *Film Score: The Art and Craft of Movie Music* (Burbank: Riverwood Press, 1991).

Chapter 1 – Silent opera: DeMille's *Carmen*

1. For further reading on early cinema, see Charles Musser, *The Emergence of Cinema: The American Screen to 1907* (Berkeley, Los Angeles and London: University of California Press, 1994); Eileen Bowser, *The Transformation of Cinema, 1907–1915* (Berkeley, Los Angeles and London: University of California Press, 1990); and David Robinson, *From Peep Show to Palace: The Birth of American Film* (New York: Columbia University Press, 1996).
2. See Sumiko Higashi, *Cecil B. DeMille and American Culture: The Silent Era* (Berkeley, Los Angeles and London: University of California Press, 1994), 20.
3. John Dizikes, *Opera in America: A Cultural History* (New Haven and London: Yale University Press, 1993), 402.
4. Charles Higham, *Cecil B. DeMille* (New York: Charles Scribner's Sons, 1973), 52–3.
5. Gabe Essoe and Raymond Lee, *DeMille: The Man and His Pictures* (New York: Castle Books, 1970), 36.
6. See the list of Carmen films in Ken Wlaschin, *Opera on Screen* (Los Angeles: Beachwood Press, 1997), 85–6.
7. Wlaschin, *Opera on Screen*, 173.
8. *The Autobiography of Cecil B. DeMille*, edited by Donald Hayne (Englewood Cliffs, NJ: Prentice-Hall, 1959), 139.
9. Quoted in ibid., 139.
10. *The Autobiography of Cecil B. DeMille*, 141.
11. Ibid., 143.

Chapter 2 – D. W. Griffith as a Wagnerian

1. *D. W. Griffith: Father of Film*, Episode 1, written and produced by Kevin Brownlow and David Gill, 1993.
2. Quoted in Richard Schickel, *D. W. Griffith: An American Life* (New York: Simon and Schuster, 1984), 497.
3. Schickel, *D. W. Griffith*, 42.
4. Quoted in Martin Miller Marks, *Music and the Silent Film* (New York: Oxford University Press, 1997), 103.
5. Marks, *Music and the Silent Film*, 105.
6. Quoted in ibid., 141.
7. Lillian Gish with Ann Pinchot, *Lillian Gish: The Movies, Mr. Griffith, and Me* (Englewood Cliffs, NJ: Prentice-Hall, 1969), 152.
8. Ibid., 152.
9. Quoted in Marks, 137.
10. Ibid., 138.
11. Quoted in Schickel, 291.
12. Ibid., 467.

13. Barry Millington, *Wagner*, rev. ed. (Princeton: Princeton University Press, 1992), 87.
14. See Joachim Köhler, *Wagner's Hitler: The Prophet and His Disciple*, translated by Ronald Taylor (Cambridge: Polity Press, 2000).
15. John Hope Franklin, "*Birth of a Nation* – Propaganda as History," *The Massachusetts Review* 20 (Autumn 1979): 431.
16. Quoted in ibid., 425.
17. Ibid., 430.

Chapter 3 – Stage fright: *Phantom of the Opera*

1. More recently, opera in Paris has moved to the Opéra Bastille.
2. Peter Haining, Forward to Gaston Leroux's *Phantom of the Opera* (New York: Barnes and Noble, 1985), 7.
3. Ibid., 8.
4. Ibid., 8–9.
5. For a detailed analysis of the connection between the film and the opera it features, see Michal Grover-Friedlander, "'The Phantom of the Opera': The Lost Voice of Opera in Silent Film," *Cambridge Opera Journal* 11 (1999): 179–92.
6. Grover-Friedlander also makes the association with *Caligari* in ibid., 188.

Chapter 4 – A life at the opera

1. For details on the films and roles, see Roi A. Uselton, "Opera Singers on the Screen," *Films in Review* 4 (1967): 193–206, 284–97 and 345–59.
2. See Ken Wlaschin, *Opera on Screen* (Los Angeles: Beachwood Press, 1997), 209.
3. Ibid., 283.
4. See Enid Rhodes Peschel and Richard E. Peschel, "Medicine and Music: The Castrati in Opera," *The Opera Quarterly* 4 (1986–7): 30–6.
5. See the review of *Farinelli* by Marylis Sevilla-Gonzaga in *Opera News* 60 (4 March 1995): 47.

Chapter 5 – Synesthesia: *Alexander Nevsky* as opera

1. In *Film Form*, edited and translated by Jay Leyda (New York and London: Harcourt, Brace and World, 1949), 195–255.
2. "Dickens, Griffith, and the Film Today," 211.
3. Ibid., 249.
4. Ibid., 254.
5. "Methods of Montage," in *Film Form*, 75. For a more extended explanation of these principles, see David Bordwell, *The Cinema of Eisenstein* (Cambridge, MA: Harvard University Press, 1993), 184–90.

6. See Bordwell, *The Cinema of Eisenstein*, 185.

7. Eisenstein, *The Film Sense* (San Diego, New York and London: Harcourt Brace Javanovich, 1974), 74.

8. "The Structure of Film," in *Film Form*, 152.

9. Glass made these comments in a lecture at the Scotia Festival of Music, Halifax, Canada, 27 May 1999.

10. "The Structure of Film," 178.

11. Published as the Introduction to Israel V. Nestyev's *Sergei Prokofiev: His Musical Life*, translated by Rose Prokofieva (New York: Alfred A. Knopf, 1946), ix–xix.

12. "P-R-K-F-V," xiii.

13. Ibid., xiii.

14. *The Film Sense*, 158.

15. Ibid., 158–9.

16. Ibid., 159.

17. Theodor Adorno and Hanns Eisler, *Composing for the Films* (London and Atlantic Highlands: Athlone, 1994), 152–7; Roy M. Prendergast, *Film Music: A Neglected Art* (New York: W. W. Norton, 1977), 223–6; Royal S. Brown, *Overtones and Undertones: Reading Film Music* (Berkeley, Los Angeles and London: University of California Press, 1994), 138; Bordwell, 188.

18. *The Film Sense*, 189 and 216.

19. "The Incarnation of Myth," in S. M. Eisenstein, *Selected Works*, Vol. 3: *Writings, 1934–47*, edited by Richard Taylor, translated by William Powell (London: BFI, 1996), 165.

20. Ibid., 168–9.

21. "The Stucture of Film," 152.

22. "The Incarnation of Myth," 168.

23. "Dickens, Giffith, and the Film Today," 234.

CHAPTER 6 – The leitmotif

1. See François Thomas, "Musical Keys to *Kane*," in *Perspectives on Citizen Kane*, edited by Ronald Gottesman (New York: G. K. Hall & Co., 1996), 180. For the full instrumentation of the opening, see Robert C. Carringer, *The Making of Citizen Kane* (Berkeley, Los Angeles and London: University of California Press, 1985), 106.

2. A number of studies ably describe the function of leitmotif in film music, including Claudia Gorbman, *Unheard Melodies: Narrative Film Music* (Bloomington and Indianapolis: Indiana University Press, 1987; Royal S. Brown, *Overtones and Undertones: Reading Film Music* (Berkeley, Los Angeles and London: University of California Press, 98–9; and Justin London, "Leitmotifs and Musical Reference in the Classical Film Score," in *Music and Cinema*, edited by James Buhler, Caryl Flinn, and David Neumeyer (Hanover, NH and London: University Press of New England, 2000), 85–96.

3. See Sabine M. Feisst, "Arnold Schoenberg and the Cinematic Art," *Musical Quarterly* 83 (1999): 93. Feisst argues that Schoenberg's demand may not have been unreasonable.

4. Quoted in Christopher Palmer, *The Hollywood Composer* (London and New York, 1990), 28.

5. Ibid., 29.

6. See Royal S. Brown's graphic of this in *Overtones and Undertones: Reading Film Music* (Berkeley, Los Angeles and London: University of California Press, 1994), 108–9.

7. See Roy M. Prendergast, *Film Music: A Neglected Art* (New York: W. W. Norton, 1991), 91–2.

8. See William Darby and Jack DuBois, *American Film Music: Major Composers, Techniques, Trends, 1915–1990* (Jefferson, NC: McFarland & Co., 1990), 395.

9. Various writers, including Carringer, *The Making of Citizen Kane*, 108 and Thomas, "Musical Keys to *Kane*," 179, note the *Dies Irae* connection.

CHAPTER 7 – Titles music as operatic overture

1. See Bellamy Hosler, *Changing Aesthetic Views of Instrumental Music in 18th-Century Germany* (Ann Arbor: UMI Research Press, 1981), 5–11.

2. See Angus Heriot, *The Castrati in Opera* (New York: Da Capo Press, 1975), 64–83.

3. See my *Mozart in Revolt: Strategies of Resistance, Mischief and Deception* (New Haven and London: Yale University Press, 1999), 170–1.

4. Ibid., 41–2.

5. Actually three overtures, as *Leonore* no. 3 is a revision of *Leonore* no. 2. See Maynard Solomon, *Beethoven* (New York: Schirmer, 1977), 200.

6. Ernest Newman, *Wagner as Man and Artist* (New York: Vintage, 1952), 203–6.

7. See Gary Schmidgall, *Literature as Opera* (Oxford: Oxford University Press, 1977), 202.

8. Alexander Pushkin, *Eugene Onegin*, translated by Charles Johnston (Harmondsworth, UK: Penguin, 1981), 232.

9. See Schmidgall, *Literature as Opera*, 239–43.

10. For descriptions of the music provided for silent films, see Martin Miller Marks, *Music and the Silent Film: Contexts and Case Studies, 1895–1924* (New York and Oxford: Oxford University Press, 1997).

11. For a fuller discussion of the music, see Kathryn Kalinak, *Settling the Score: Music and the Classical Hollywood Film* (Madison: University of Wisconsin Press, 1992), 113–16.

12. Umberto Eco, "*Casablanca*: Cult Movies and Intertextual Collage," in *Casablanca: Script and Legend* (Woodstock and New York: The Overlook Press, 1992), 258–63.

13. For discussions on the view of women in *Mildred Pierce*, see Pamela

Robertson, "Structural Irony in *Mildred Pierce*, or How Mildred Lost her Tongue," *Cinema Journal* 30 (1990): 42–54, and Pam Cook, "Duplicity in *Mildred Pierce*," in *Women in Film Noir*, edited by Ann Kaplan (London: BFI, 1978), 68–82.

14. See Royal S. Brown, *Overtones and Undertones: Reading Film Music* (Berkeley, Los Angeles and London: University of California Press, 1994), 99–100.

15. Victor Seroff, *Sergei Prokofiev: A Soviet Tragedy* (New York: Taplinger, 1979), 219.

16. Brown describes this well in ibid., 200–11.

17. See Roy M. Prendergast, *Film Music: A Neglected Art*, 2nd ed. (New York: W. W. Norton, 1991), 58–9.

CHAPTER 8 – Casting opera in our teeth: Chaplin's *Carmen*

1. Charles Chaplin, *My Autobiography* (New York: Simon and Schuster, 1964), 174.

2. See Susan McClary, *Georges Bizet: Carmen* (Cambridge: Cambridge University Press, 1992), 145.

CHAPTER 9 – Attack of the anarchists: *A Night at the Opera*

1. See the longer description of carnival in chapter 28. Lawrence Kramer also emphasizes carnival in his "The Singing Salami: Unsystematic Reflections on the Marx Brothers' *A Night at the Opera*," in *A Night in at the Opera*, edited by Jeremy Tambling (London: John Libbey, 1994), 261–4, although he steers his reading much more heavily toward the phallic.

2. See Tom Cheesman, "Gluttony Artists: Carnival, Enlightenment and Consumerism in Germany on the Threshold of Modernity," *Deutsche Vierteljahrsschrift für Literaturwissenschaft und Geistgeschichte* 66 (1992): 643.

3. Kramer also makes this observation in "The Singing Salami," 265.

CHAPTER 10 – Deflated and flat: opera in *Citizen Kane*

1. Andrew Sarris, *The American Cinema: Directors and Directions, 1929–1968* (New York: E.P. Dutton, 1968), 78.

2. See Robert L. Carringer, *The Making of Citizen Kane* (Berkeley, Los Angeles and London: University of California Press, 1985), 115.

3. Simon Callow, *Orson Welles: The Road to Xanadu* (London: Jonathan Cape, 1995), 555.

4. *The Citizen Kane Book* (London: Secker and Warburg, 1971), 82.

5. Quoted in ibid., 82.

6. Callow, *Orson Welles*, 505.

7. Forrest McDonald, *Insull* (Chicago: University of Chicago Press, 1962), 242–3.

8. Ronald L. Davis, *Opera in Chicago* (New York: Appleton-Century, 1966), 186.
9. Quoted in ibid., 160.
10. Quoted in ibid., 160.
11. Pauline Kael, "Raising Kane," in *The Citizen Kane Book*, 11.
12. Callow, 23.
13. Carringer, *The Making of Citizen Kane*, 108.
14. Quoted in Steven C. Smith, *A Heart at Fire's Center: The Life and Music of Bernard Herrmann* (Berkeley, Los Angeles and London: University of California Press, 1991), 79.
15. Quoted in ibid., 80.
16. Quoted in ibid., 80.
17. Smith, *A Heart at Fire's Center*, 80.

CHAPTER 11 – Bursting out into opera: Fellini's *E la nave va*

1. See Paula Willoquet-Maricondi, "Federico Fellini's *E la nave va* and the Postmodern Shipwreck," *RLA: Romance Languages Annual* 6 (1994): 383.
2. See Claudio G. Fava and Aldo Viganó, *The Films of Federico Fellini*, translated by Shula Curto (Secaucus, NJ: Citadel Press, 1985), 185 and Luisetta Elia Chomel, "Ambiguity as the Theme of Fellini's Last Film: *And the Ship Sails On*," in *National Traditions in Motion Pictures*, edited by Douglas Radcliffe-Umstead (Kent: Kent State University Press, 1985), 56.
3. See Claudia Gorbman, "Music as Salvation: Notes on Fellini and Rota," *Film Quarterly* 28, no. 2 (Winter 1974–5): 17–25. Peter Bondanella also refers to the music as a metaphor of salvation and calls the three films the "salvation trilogy" in *The Cinema of Federico Fellini* (Princeton: Princeton University Press, 1992), 129.
4. Quoted in John Baxter's *Fellini* (New York: St. Martin's Press, 1993), 336.
5. John Tasker Howard, *The World's Great Operas* (New York: The Modern Library, 1959), 131.
6. Debussy, *43 Songs*, edited by Sergius Kagen (New York: International, n.d.), vii.

CHAPTER 12 – The charming opera snob in *Hannah and Her Sisters*

1. All quotations from the film are taken from Woody Allen, *Hannah and Her Sisters* (New York: Vintage, 1987).
2. See Leonard Quart, "Woody Allen's New York," *Cineaste* 19, nos. 2–3 (1992–3): 17.

CHAPTER 13 – Misreading Wagner: the politics of Lang's *Siegfried*

1. Quoted in Patrick McGilligan, *Fritz Lang: The Nature of the Beast* (New York: St. Martin's Press, 1997), 104.

2. Quoted in David J. Levin, *Richard Wagner, Fritz Lang and the Nibelungen: The Dramaturgy of Disavowal* (Princeton: Princeton University Press, 1998), 97.

3. Quoted in ibid., 96.

4. See McGilligan, *Fritz Lang*, 103.

5. Levin develops this in chapter 1, "Representation's Bad Object: the Nibelungen, Aggression and Aesthetics," *Richard Wagner, Fritz Lang and the Nibelungen*, 3–29.

6. Theodor Adorno, *In Search of Wagner*, translated by Rodney Livingstone (London: NLB, 1981), 23.

7. These include Jacob Katz, *The Darker Side of Genius: Richard Wagner's Anti-Semitism* (Hanover, NH: University Press of New England, 1986); Barry Millington, "Nuremberg Trial: Is there Anti-Semitism in *Die Meistersinger?*" *Cambridge Opera Journal* 3 (1991): 247–60; L. J. Rather, *The Dream of Self-Destruction: Wagner's Ring and the Modern World* (Baton Rouge and London: Louisiana State University Press, 1979); Leon Stein, *The Racial Thinking of Richard Wagner* (New York: Philosophical Library, 1950); and Marc A. Weiner, *Richard Wagner and the Anti-Semitic Imagination* (Lincoln: University of Nebraska Press, 1995).

8. Lotte H. Eisner, *Fritz Lang* (New York: Oxford University Press, 1977), 79.

9. Siegfried Kracauer, *From Caligari to Hitler: A Psychological History of the German Film* (Princeton: Princeton University Press, 1947), 94.

10. Eisner, *Fritz Lang*, 79.

11. Ibid.

12. McGilligan, *Fritz Lang*, 169.

13. Ibid., 176.

14. Ibid., 24.

15. Quoted in Eisner, *Fritz Lang*, 76.

16. William M. Johnston, *The Austrian Mind: An Intellectual and Social History, 1848–1938* (Berkeley, Los Angeles and London: University of California Press, 1972), 101.

17. Steven Beller, *Vienna and the Jews, 1867–1938: A Cultural History* (Cambridge: Cambridge University Press, 1989), 157.

18. Ibid., 158.

19. Quoted in Levin, 131.

20. Edward Timms, *Karl Kraus, Apocalyptic Satirist: Culture and Catastrophe in Habsburg Vienna* (New Haven and London: Yale University Press, 1986), 67.

21. Kracauer, *From Caligari to Hitler*, 92.

22. For comparisons of variations of these images, see Eisner, *The Haunted Screen* (Berkeley and Los Angeles: University of California Press, 1973), 150–67.

23. See Sabine Hake, "Architectural Hi/stories: Fritz Lang and *The Nibelungs*," *Wide Angle* 12, no. 3 (1990): 44.

CHAPTER 14 – Cinema as grand opera: politics, religion and DeMille

1. See Jane Fulcher, *The Nation's Image: French Grand Opera as Politics and Politicized Art* (Cambridge: Cambridge University Press, 1987), 6–11.
2. See George Martin, "Verdi and the Risorgimento," in *The Verdi Companion*, edited by William Weaver and Martin Chusid (New York: W. W. Norton, 1979), 13–41.
3. Ibid., 21.
4. Ibid., 22–3.
5. See Barry Millington, "Nuremberg Trial: Is there Anti-Semitism in *Die Meistersinger?*" *Cambridge Opera Journal* 3 (1991): 248.
6. Quoted in Sumiko Higashi, *Cecil B. DeMille and American Culture: The Silent Era* (Berkeley, Los Angeles and London: University of California Press, 1994), 134.
7. See Robin Blaetz, "Cecil B. DeMille's *Joan the Woman*," *Studies in Medievalism* 6 (1994): 109–22.
8. Thomas H. Pauly, "The Way to Salvation: The Hollywood Blockbuster of the 1950s," *Prospects: An Annual Journal of American Culture Studies* 5 (1980): 269.
9. Charles Higham, *Cecil B. DeMille* (New York: Charles Scribner's Sons, 1973), 278.
10. See Alan Nadel, "God's Law and the Wide Screen: *The Ten Commandments* as Cold War 'Epic'," *Proceedings of the Modern Languages Association* 108 (1993): 425.
11. Ibid., 423.
12. Ibid., 427.

CHAPTER 15 – Bombarding the senses: *Apocalypse Now*

1. Adolf Hitler, *Mein Kampf*, translated by Martin Manheim (London: Pimlico, 1992), 16. See also Joachim Köhler, *Wagner's Hitler: The Prophet and His Disciple*, translated by Ronald Taylor (Cambridge: Polity, 2000).
2. See the list of sources given in note 7, chapter 13.
3. Barry Millington, "Nuremberg Trial: Is there anti-semitism in *Die Meistersinger?*," *Cambridge Opera Journal* 3 (1991): 249.
4. Quoted in ibid., 250–1.
5. Millington, 249. Millington develops the visual and musical aspects at some length.
6. Quoted in Nancy Uscher, "Wagner, Strauss, and Israel," *The American Music Teacher*, 33, no. 6 (June/July 1984): 8.
7. A concert conducted by Daniel Barenboim with the Berlin Staatskapelle orchestra in Jerusalem on 7 July 2001 was similarly disrupted when Barenboim asked the audience if he could perform Wagner's Prelude to

Tristan und Isolde as an encore. See Canada's *National Post*, 9 July 2001, A1 and 9.

CHAPTER 16 – Wagnerian images from sound to sex

1. Ken Wlaschin, *Opera on Screen* (Los Angeles: Beachwood Press, 1997).
2. Quoted in J. Francisco Aranda, "Out of Innocence," in *The World of Luis Buñuel*, edited by Joan Mellen (New York: Oxford University Press, 1978), 38–9.
3. Quoted in Francisco Aranda, *Luis Buñuel: A Critical Biography*, edited and translated by David Robinson (London: Secker & Warburg, 1975), 91.
4. Raymond Durgnat, *Luis Buñuel* (Berkeley, Los Angeles and London: University of California Press, 1977), 40.
5. Henry Miller, "The Golden Age," in *The World of Luis Buñuel*, 174–5.
6. Quoted in Carlos Fuentes, "The Discreet Charm of Luis Buñuel," in *The World of Luis Buñuel*, 66.
7. Quoted in Aranda, *Luis Buñuel*, 91.
8. Ibid., 163.
9. Quoted in Ernest Newman, *Stories of the Great Operas* (Garden City, NY: Garden City Publishing, 1948), 59.
10. Jo Leslie Collier, *From Wagner to Murnau: The Transposition of Romanticism from Stage to Screen* (Ann Arbor and London: UMI Research Press, 1988).
11. Ibid., 106, 113–16.

CHAPTER 17 – Wagner's *Ring* cycle of adolescents: *Star Wars*

1. Kael's review in *The New Yorker* (30 May 1983), 89.
2. Angell's review in *The New Yorker* (26 May 1980), 123.
3. *The New Yorker* (30 May 1983), 88.
4. For an expansion on this, see G. Thomas Goodnight, "Ronald Reagan's Re-formulation of the Rhetoric of War: Analysis of the 'Zero Option,' 'Evil Empire,' and 'Star Wars' Address," *Quarterly Journal of Speech* 72 (1986): 390–414, and Janice Hocker Rushing, "Ronald Reagan's 'Star Wars' Address: Mythic Containment of Technical Reasoning," *Quarterly Journal of Speech* 72 (1986): 415–33.
5. Jonathan Rosenbaum, "The Solitary Pleasures of *Star Wars*," *Sight and Sound* 46 (1976–7): 207.
6. See Kathryn Kalinak, *Settling the Score: Music and the Classical Hollywood Film* (Madison: University of Wisconsin Press, 1992), 198–9, and Greg Oatis, "John Williams Strikes Back, Unfortunately," *Cinemafantastique* 10, no. 2 (Fall 1980): 8.
7. See James Buhler, "Star Wars, Music, and Myth," in *Music and Cinema*, edited by James Buhler, Caryl Flinn and David Neumeyer (Hanover, NH and London: University Press of New England, 2000), 44.

8. Royal S. Brown makes this connection in *Overtones and Undertones: Reading Film Music* (Berkeley, Los Angeles and London: University of California Press, 1994), 100.

CHAPTER 18 – What's opera, Doc?

1. Hugh Kenner, *Chuck Jones: A Flurry of Drawings* (Berkeley, Los Angeles and London: University of California Press, 1994), 95.
2. Leonard Maltin, *Of Mice and Magic: A History of American Animated Cartoons* (New York: McGraw-Hill, 1980), 264.
3. See Kenner, *Chuck Jones*, 59.
4. Ibid., 94.
5. I could not resist the title of an essay by Robert W. McEachern: "Gender Twouble: Bugs Bunny, Cross-Dressing and Patriarchy," *The Mid Atlantic Almanac* 3 (1994): 1–12.

CHAPTER 19 – Dizzying illusion: *Vertigo*

1. Geoffrey O'Brien, "*Vertigo*: a film by Alfred Hitchcock, restored by Robert A. Harris and James C. Katz [review]," in *The New York Review of Books* (December 19, 1996), 56.
2. Donald Spoto, *The Art of Alfred Hitchcock* (London: Fourth Estate, 1992), 275.
3. Quoted in François Truffaut (with the collaboration of Helen G. Scott), *Hitchcock* (New York: Simon and Schuster, 1967), 188.
4. Truffaut, *Hitchcock*, 188.
5. See *Hitchcock and Art: Fatal Coincidences* (Milan: Mazzotta, 2000), 235. This is the catalogue of the exhibition at The Montreal Museum of Fine Arts, 16 November 2000 to 18 March 2001.
6. Quoted in Truffaut, *Hitchcock*, 186.
7. Quoted in ibid., 186.
8. See Richard Taruskin's "Revising Revision," a review of Kevin Korsyn's "Towards a New Poetics of Musical Influence" and Joseph N. Straus's *Remaking the Past: Musical Modernism and the Influence of the Tonal Tradition*, in *Journal of the American Musicological Society* 46 (1993): 137.
9. Quoted in Truffaut, *Hitchcock*, 184.
10. Igor Stravinsky, *An Autobiography* (New York: W. W. Norton, 1962), 53.
11. Igor Stravinsky, *Poetics of Music*, translated by Arthur Knodel and Ingolf Dahl (Cambridge, MA: Harvard University Press, 1942), 31.

CHAPTER 20 – Carmen copies

1. Phil Powrie lists 39 in an appendix to his "Francesco Rosi's *Carmen* and the Fantasy of Realism," *Word & Image* 9, no. 1 (1993): 28, and Ken

Wlaschin adds more in *Opera on Screen* (Los Angeles: Beachwood Press, 1997), 85–90.

2. For a full study of the novella see Evlyn Gould's *The Fate of Carmen* (Baltimore and London: The Johns Hopkins University Press, 1996).

3. For example Catherine Clément in *Opera, or the Undoing of Women*, translated by Betsy Wing (Minneapolis: University of Minnesota Press, 1988), 48–53 and Susan McClary in *Feminine Endings: Music, Gender and Sexuality* (Minneapolis: University of Minnesota Press, 1991), 56–67.

4. Will Frischauer, *Behind the Scenes of Otto Preminger* (New York: William Morrow & Company, 1974), 134–5.

5. Otto Preminger, *An Autobiography* (Garden City, NY: Doubleday & Company, 1977), 133–4.

6. See Gerald Pratley, *The Cinema of Otto Preminger* (London: A. Zwemmer, 1971), 60–1.

7. Preminger, *An Autobiography*, 137.

8. Ibid., 133.

9. McClary, *Georges Bizet: Carmen* (Cambridge: Cambridge University Press, 1992), 134.

10. Frischauer, *Behind the Scenes of Otto Preminger*, 196.

11. Gideon Bachmann, "The Carrots Are Cooked: A Conversation with Jean-Luc Godard," *Film Quarterly* 37, no. 3 (Spring 1984): 14.

12. Verena Andermatt Conley hints at the connection with *Pierrot le fou* in "A Fraying of Voices: Jean-Luc Godard's *Prénom Carmen*," *L'Esprit Créateur* 30, no. 2 (Summer 1990): 75.

13. McClary, *Feminine Endings*, 59.

14. Phil Powrie views it this way in "Godard's *Prénom: Carmen* (1984), Masochism, and the Male Gaze," *Forum for Modern Language Studies* 31, no. 1 (1995): 69.

15. Bachmann, "The Carrots Are Cooked," 16.

16. Ibid., 17.

17. Ibid., 14.

18. See Royal S. Brown's description of Godard's manipulation of Duhamel's music in *Overtones and Undertones: Reading Film Music* (Berkeley, Los Angeles and London: University of California Press, 1994), 201–19.

19. Leonard Maltin, *1997 Movie & Video Guide* (New York: Signet, 1996), 56. For a serious look at Godard's contribution to *Aria*, see Edward D. Latham, "Physical Motifs and Concentric Amplification in Godard/Lully's *Armide*," *Indiana Theory Review* 19 (Spring/Fall 1998): 55–85.

20. Bachmann, "The Carrots Are Cooked," 15.

21. *Beethoven: The Man and the Artist, as Revealed in His Own Words*, edited by Friedrich Kerst and Henry E. Krehbiel (New York: Dover, 1964), 85. The mottos also have a possible lighter interpretation, relating to a comic canon Beethoven wrote to the words "Es muss sein! Ja ja ja ja! Heraus mit dem Beutel!" Beethoven intended this as a message to a friend who

owed him money. See Joseph Kerman, *The Beethoven Quartets* (London: Oxford University Press, 1967), 362.

CHAPTER 21 – Operastruck

1. For some very vivid descriptions, see Angus Heriot, *The Castrati in Opera* (New York: Da Capo, 1975), 65–83.
2. E. M. Forster, *Where Angels Fear to Tread* (Harmondworth, UK: Penguin, 1976), 105–10.
3. Kathleen Rowe develops the image of death in *Moonstruck* in *The Unruly Woman: Gender and the Genres of Laughter* (Austin: University of Texas Press, 1995), 202–5.
4. See ibid., 209.

CHAPTER 22 – Outing opera in *Philadelphia*

1. See Anthony Lane's description of the scene in his review of *Philadelphia* in *The New Yorker* (27 December 1993), 150.
2. All quotations from the play are taken from *Three Plays by Terrence McNally* (New York: Penguin, 1990).
3. Bruce Bawer, *A Place at the Table: The Gay Individual in American Society* (New York: Poseidon, 1993), 167.
4. Wayne Koestenbaum, *The Queen's Throat: Opera, Homosexuality and the Mystery of Desire* (New York: Poseidon, 1993), 136–7.
5. Ibid., 145.
6. Ibid., 45.
7. Lane's review, *The New Yorker* (27 December 1993), 149.

CHAPTER 23 – Opera obsession

1. See Angus Heriot, *The Castrati in Opera* (New York: Da Capo, 1975), 64–83.
2. Charles Burney, quoted in ibid., 42.
3. Jacques Casanova, *The Memoirs of Jacques Casanova de Seingalt*, translated by Arthur Machen, vol. 3 (New York: Dover Publications, 1961), 1737.
4. See Enid Rhodes Peschel and Richard E. Peschel, "Medicine and Music: The Castrati in Opera," *The Opera Quarterly* 4, no. 4 (1986–7): 27–9.
5. Rita Steblin documents his membership in a nonsense society in "Schubert Through the Kaleidoscope: The "Unsinnsgesellschaft" and its Illustrious Members," *Österreichische Musikzeitschrift* 52 (1997): 52–61, as well as *Die Unsinnsgesellschaft: Franz Schubert, Leopold Kupelwieser und ihr Freundeskreis* (Vienna, Cologne and Weimar: Böhlau, 1998).

CHAPTER 24 – Surrogate voice: Maria Callas as Medea

1. Enzo Siciliano, *Pasolini: A Biography*, translated by John Shepley (New York: Random House, 1982), 332.
2. Ibid., 333–4.
3. See the review of the recording of *Medea* by H. C. Robbins Landon in *The Music Review* 22 (1961): 341.
4. Wayne Koestenbaum, *The Queen's Throat: Opera, Homosexuality and the Mystery of Desire* (New York: Poseidon, 1993), 136–7.
5. See Maurizio Viano, *A Certain Realism: Making Use of Pasolini's Film Theory and Practice* (Berkeley, Los Angeles and London: University of California Press, 1993), 238–9.
6. Arianna Stassinopoulos, *Maria Callas: The Woman Behind the Legend* (New York: Simon and Schuster, 1981), 298.
7. Siciliano, *Pasolini*, 334–5
8. Quoted in ibid., 333–5.
9. Quoted in Stassinopoulos, *Maria Callas*, 297.
10. Quoted in ibid., 300.
11. Quoted in Siciliano, 334.
12. Quoted in Stassinopoulos, 297.

CHAPTER 25 – Orpheus reincarnated

1. For a description of Cocteau's visual illusion, see Arthur B. Evans, *Jean Cocteau and His Films of Orphic Identity* (Cranbury, NJ and London: Associated University Presses, 1977), 106–7.
2. See Michal Grover-Friedlander's discussion of the Orpheus connection in "'The Phantom of the Opera': The Lost Voice of Opera in Silent Film," *Cambridge Opera Journal* 11 (1999): 190–1.
3. Royal S. Brown, *Overtones and Undertones: Reading Film Music* (Berkeley, Los Angeles and London: University of California Press, 1994), 161.

CHAPTER 26 – Finale: directors' operas

1. See Marcia J. Citron, *Opera on Screen* (New Haven and London: Yale University Press, 2000), 90.
2. See Marcia J. Citron, "A Night at the Cinema: Zeffirelli's *Otello* and the Genre of Film-Opera," *The Musical Quarterly* 78 (1994): 710–20.
3. See Citron, *Opera on Screen*, 72.
4. Citron puts this forward in ibid., 715–10, and *Opera on Screen*, 90–6.
5. Jeremy Tambling, *Opera, Ideology and Film* (Manchester: Manchester University Press, 1987), 159.
6. Edith de Rham, *Joseph Losey* (London: Andre Deutsch, 1991), 270.
7. Ibid., 260.

8. Ibid., 269.
9. Dexter Edge addressed this in his paper "The Original Performance Parts and Score for Mozart's *Le nozze di Figaro*," American Musicological Society, New York, 4 November 1995.
10. I develop this premise in my book, *Mozart in Revolt: Strategies of Resistance, Mischief and Deception* (New Haven and London: Yale University Press, 1999).
11. J. W. Goethe, *Italian Journey* [1786–1788], translated by W. H. Auden and Elizabeth Mayer (London: Penguin, 1970), 468.
12. Citron, in *Opera on Screen*, 168–70, finds it a pessimistic production.
13. See Tambling, *Opera, Ideology and Film*, 167–8, and Citron, ibid., 173–6.
14. Quoted in Tambling, 167.
15. The most negative view came from Donal Henahan in "When *Auteur* Meets Opera, Opera Loses," *The New York Times* 19 December 1990, H23. Jeremy Tambling deemed it an interesting failure in "Revisions and Re-vampings: Wagner, Marshner and Mozart on Television and Video," in *A Night in at the Opera*, edited by Jeremy Tambling (London: John Libbey, 1994), 70–3.
16. Edward J. Dent, *Mozart's Operas* (Oxford: Oxford University Press, 1947), 192 and 206 and Joseph Kerman, *Opera as Drama* (New York: Alfred A. Knopf, 1956), 113.
17. David Littlejohn, "Reflections on Peter Sellars's Mozart," *The Opera Quarterly* 7, no. 2 (1990): 18.
18. Dent, *Mozart's Operas*, 189.
19. Kerman, *Opera as Drama*, 106–16.
20. Dent, *Mozart's Operas*, 190.
21. Michel Ciment, "Rosi in a New Key," *American Film* 9, no. 10 (Sept. 1984): 39.
22. Phil Powrie, "Francesco Rosi's *Carmen* and the fantasy of realism," *Word & Image* 9, no. 1 (Jan-Mar 1993): 19.
23. Ciment, "Rosi in a New Key," 40.
24. Ibid., 41–2.
25. See Tambling, *Opera, Ideology and Film*, 35–6; Susan McClary, *Georges Bizet: Carmen* (Cambridge: Cambridge University Press, 1992), 141–5; and David Wills, "Carmen: Sound/Effect," *Cinema Journal* 25, no. 4 (Summer 1986): 36.
26. H. Marshall Leicester, Jr. comments about this scene that "Bizet's music kicks in when people get excited, in "Discourse and Film Text: Four Readings of *Carmen*," *Cambridge Opera Journal* 6 (1995): 268.
27. See Powrie, "Francesco Rosi's *Carmen*," 19–27.
28. H. Marshall Leicester, Jr., "Discourse and Film Text," 273–6.

Index

Walthall, Henry B. 34
Walton, William 83
Warner Brothers 91
Washington, D.C. 168
Washington, Denzel 274
Waterston, Sam 142
Watts, Stephen 3
Webb, Clifton 314
Webber, Andrew Lloyd 41
Weber, Carl Maria von 30
  Der Freischütz 43, 44, 87
Wedekind, Frank 164
Weininger, Otto 157, 160, 164
Weissmuller, Johnny 112
Welles, Orson 1, 7, 74, 116–26
  Citizen Kane 44, 73–5, 83, 93, 116–26
Werfel, Franz 157
West, Norma 131
What's Opera, Doc? 214, 223–8
What's Up Tiger Lily? 78
Wiene, Robert 224
Wiest, Diane 141
Wiggins Fernandez, Wilhelmenia 294
Wilde, Oscar 293

Salome 18, 164, 291
  The Picture of Dorian Gray 291
Williams, John 8, 78, 83, 213, 220–1
Wilson, Woodrow 33
Wlaschin, Ken
  Opera on Screen 5, 197
Women's suffrage 175–6
World War I 152–3
World War II 37, 180
Wray, Fay 79
Wurlitzer organ 14, 89
Wyler, William
  The Heiress 80–1

xenophobia 247

Yes, Giorgio 55
Young, Victor 184

Zanuck, Darryl 250, 315
Zeffirelli, Franco 10, 224, 297, 321, 324–7
  Otello 323–7
Zito, Pasquale 131
Zola, Émile 164